Sandra Knauer, LCSW

Recovering from Sexual Abuse, Addictions, and Compulsive Behaviors
"Numb" Survivors

*Pre-publication
REVIEWS,
COMMENTARIES,
EVALUATIONS . . .*

"With so little significant and helpful material regarding dual diagnosis available to the clinical community, this book is a welcome resource. Rather than providing a step-by-step recipe for treating clients with dual diagnosis, the author most effectively shows the process of healing and recovery. She addresses the extremely complex subject in simple, understandable language, richly supplemented with illustrations appropriate for professional therapists, students, and survivors.

What becomes abundantly clear throughout the book is the function the addictive and compulsive behaviors play in protecting the client from constantly living with extreme emotional pain. By not treating the underlying causes, which happens so often in treatment, and removing the only protections the client has, we (therapists) leave him or her vulnerable to relapse.

Recovering from Sexual Abuse, Addictions, and Compulsive Behaviors: 'Numb' Survivors, is a book based on Knauer's success with both her own personal treatment and in treating others. The real strength of the material she presents is the love and respect she clearly has for her clients (survivors), as well as herself, as a survivor.

This book will be a useful supplement in teaching a variety of courses. It would also be a good book to refer to survivors or to use as a springboard for discussion with groups of survivors. It may provide them with some relief and the courage to address both the behaviors and the underlying causes."

Leta Cooper, LCSW
*Field Instruction
Liaison/Lecturer,
Delaware State University,
Georgetown*

More pre-publication
REVIEWS, COMMENTARIES, EVALUATIONS . . .

"**B**ecoming a psychotherapist is part choice, part fate, and partly a compulsion to venture into certain aspects of humanity that most people would rather avoid. Those therapists who are well into their practice must then venture into Sandra Knauer's new book, *Recovering from Sexual Abuse, Addictions, and Compulsive Behaviors: 'Numb' Survivors.* Knauer courageously peels away the layers of denial surrounding the difficult subject of interpersonal abuse and its developmental connection to other disorders such as addictions and other compulsive behaviors. She aptly conceptualizes sexual abuse as an assault on the human spirit. Without indulging in the pornography of grief, Knauer shares the horrible truths about abuse in all its incarnations, taking the reader to a deep understanding of the long roots and longer consequences for the victim and the societal context. By bringing us close to actual survivors, by sharing the personal letters of her 'experts' (survivors she has treated in the clinic), she puts a human face on the most inhumane acts imaginable while developing practical concepts for assessment and a durable model for positive growth."

Richard Brousell, MFT, MAC, LPCMH
Marriage and Family Therapist
in Private Practice,
Wilmington, Delaware

"**R**ecovering from Sexual Abuse, Addiction, and Compulsive Behaviors: 'Numb' Survivors stands out among the many books currently available on healing from sexual abuse; specifically, in its focus on the connection between childhood sexual abuse and the child/adult's predisposition toward addictive and compulsive behaviors.

Sandy Knauer is a seasoned clinician whose sensitivity in her sharing of clients' experiences effectively illustrates the theory she presents. This results in a thoughtful melding of theory and practice. The section on the healing process is very clear and helpful, particularly the chapter on boundary setting, which should be required reading for any client in this process. Knauer's discussion about how the use of trance as an early coping mechanism creates a vulnerability for later addictive behaviors has intriguing implications for both a new understanding about the dynamics of the addictive process as well as very concrete recommendations for what changes are needed.

This book will be a fine resource for survivors looking for a validating and helpful guide to their healing process. It will also be a supportive resource for clinicians as we join our clients in their healing."

Kathryn Harris, LCSW, BCD
Newark, Delaware

THSWPP

The Haworth Social Work Practice Press
An Imprint of The Haworth Press, Inc.
New York • London • Oxford

Recovering from Sexual Abuse, Addictions, and Compulsive Behaviors

"Numb" Survivors

Recovering from Sexual Abuse, Addictions, and Compulsive Behaviors
"Numb" Survivors

Sandra Knauer, LCSW

The Haworth Social Work Practice Press
An Imprint of The Haworth Press, Inc.
New York • London • Oxford

Published by

The Haworth Social Work Practice Press, an imprint of The Haworth Press, Inc., 10 Alice Street, Binghamton, NY 13904-1580

Cover design by Marylouise Doyle.

Library of Congress Cataloging-in-Publication Data

Knauer, Sandy.
  Recovering from sexual abuse, addictions, and compulsive behaviors : "numb" survivors / Sandra Knauer.
    p. cm.
  Includes bibliographical references and index.
  ISBN 0-7890-1457-2 (alk. paper)—ISBN 0-7890-1458-0 (pbk. : alk. paper)
    1. Compulsive behavior. 2. Adult child sexual abuse victims—Rehabilitation. 3. Substance abuse—Treatment. 4. Self-esteem. I. Title.

RC533 .K58 2001
616.85'8369—dc21

2001017010

This book is dedicated to all of the adolescent group members who struggle every day to deal with their memories and fears without addictive or compulsive behaviors. These adolescents are the bravest people that I know. Courage can take many forms. In the adolescent groups, courage is personified by young people dealing with the worst abuse possible in the most honest and open ways imaginable. I thank them for allowing me to share their journeys. These are the aliases that the group members chose so that I could personally acknowledge their courage and faith: Angel, Annie, Big "D", Captain, Catalina, Cookie, Cougar, D~Lay, Dimples, Edward, Half-Pint, Harley, Heart, Jay, J.R., MacDaddy, Marie, Matthew, Mickey, Natalie, Ness, Peaches, Pebbles, Pooh Bear, Reba, Renee, Rozanda, Shady, Shorty, Soni, Spice, Teapot, the Tifster, and all the other group members who have moved on. They are my inspiration.

ABOUT THE AUTHOR

Sandra Knauer, MSW, is a Licensed Clinical Social Worker who specializes in treating sexual abuse on a multigenerational basis. She has worked with Delaware Guidance Services since 1992, specializing in the treatment of sexual abuse. She has facilitated sexual abuse survivors' groups—both adolescent and adult—in Dover, Newark, and Wilmington, Delaware.

She has also completed an internship with Delaware Child Protective Services in its Sexual Abuse Unit, and with the Delaware Attorney General's Rape Unit. Since 1987, she has been a Court Appointed Special Advocate (CASA) for abused, neglected, or dependent children.

She is the author of *No Ordinary Life: Parenting the Sexually Abused Child and Adolescent,* and is a member of the National Association for Social Workers and the National Association for Sexual Abuse Professionals.

With her co-therapists, Knauer has begun the process of establishing a treatment center that will specialize in treating and empowering survivors of sexual abuse. They hope to treat a continuum of survivors from the most fragile to those who have healed enough to go out into the world and give hope to those who don't believe that it is possible to recover from sexual abuse. This center will be a testimony to the ability of the human spirit to triumph over abuse and adversity.

CONTENTS

In memory of

Dea,
age 18 years,
passed away February 14, 2000

We give thee
but thy own,
Whate'er the
gift may be;
All that we have
is thine alone,
A trust,
O Lord,
from thee

William Walsham How

AUTHOR'S NOTE

Although all of the case histories mentioned in this book are based on actual clients with whom I have worked, the cases have all been combined or changed so that client confidentiality can be maintained. Client confidentiality is of the greatest importance.

Although I do not have a CAC or a CADC to treat drug or alcohol addiction, I do have access to and receive guidance from therapists who do specialize in treating drug or alcohol addiction.

Foreword

Working in the adolescent sexual abuse survivors' groups was a very powerful experience. All other concerns were secondary to an open and honest examination of survival of sexual abuse. The groups drew adult volunteers and as many as twenty-two members per meeting, most of them brought by van from downstate locations an hour or more away. An adult group was started for parents and the groups began to interact with each other. Never, in the over three years that the open-ended groups ran, did anyone betray a confidence, especially among the boyfriends who joined the groups to support their girlfriends. There was no trauma too intense, no emotional weight too great, no victim too isolated for the group to deal with. As the male cotherapist and the nonsurvivor therapist, I was often overwhelmed by the emotional burdens that emerged in the groups, but I learned about the hope that always springs from honesty and compassion.

After all that, we began to realize that there was a countertherapeutic force affecting some of the older group members, which was potentially stronger than the groups and certainly beyond our clinical reach. This force was drug abuse. This book is about facing up to that challenge and bringing the power of survivorship to the wilderness of addiction. We cannot allow the differing specializations of mental health treatment versus substance abuse treatment to segregate themselves any longer. Both problems must be met with a dual priority. The true measure of our professionalism and our creativity is required to bring together all of our resources for this population of clients and families. By joining together, we can relinquish our illusions about the nature of sexual and substance abuse and see a real connection to the large number of children, adolescents, and families who are enduring these problems and know firsthand how interrelated these problems are. Working in this manner may be overwhelming, but it is truly the most hopeful direction to take. To do less would rigidify us into repeating our cycles of limited effectiveness in counseling both client groups.

Please consider this book in light of these considerations and let us know what you think.

Bob Davis, LCSW

Preface

In the years that I have specialized in treating survivors of sexual abuse, I have been consistently surprised by how survivors will turn to almost every conceivable substance or behavior in an attempt to "numb" the emotional pain resulting from their sexual abuse. Time and time again I have seen survivors from very young children to those in their seventies looking outside of themselves in an attempt to try to find the one "thing" that will take away the emptiness that these survivors feel inside. Invariably, the survivors' quest to find solace for their emotional pain is doomed to fail, because what the survivors are seeking has been within themselves the entire time: the ability to love and value themselves is what survivors unknowingly seek. Often early in survivors' childhoods, at the time of their sexual abuse, survivors are taught that they must not or are not allowed to express their true feelings or their "true selves." If survivors being abused do not express how they feel about their abuse, they wonder how horrible it would be to express their true feelings and be abandoned by all of the people they value. Imagine the self-sacrifice survivors make in an attempt to keep whomever or whatever it is that they cherish.

I want to encourage those who would see individuals who may be sexually promiscuous, have weight issues, eating disorders, addictions, or compulsive behaviors as being "weak" or "flawed" to take a second look. Perhaps underlying issues may be driving that person's behaviors. In the case of sexual abuse, it is the message that the survivor doesn't "matter," that he or she "asked" for the sexual abuse, that the survivor "deserved" the abuse. Imagine what such a message does to the victim's self-esteem. Is it any wonder that survivors may not value themselves?

This book is about courage and the ability to forgive. I have such admiration and affection for the survivors with whom I work. If the observer has the courage to look beyond the exterior of the addicted survivor or the survivor with compulsive behaviors, he or she will find that often it is the addiction or the compulsion that has enabled the survivor to survive. Once survivors refrain from their addictions or compulsive behaviors, all of the emotions they have fought so hard to deny must be faced. It has been my experience that survivors are the bravest people that I have ever met. My hope is that, after reading this book, you too will also feel the same respect and affection that I feel for these very special people—the "numb" survivors.

Sandra Knauer

Acknowledgments

I would first like to thank my youngest daughter, Megan, for her suggestion that I write a book about my life. Working with survivors is my life. Of all of the hats that I wear, the hat of survivor is the one that has shaped my life the most. Megan, you are going to be the best therapist ever! I look forward to sharing what I know to be the most wonderful profession in the world with you: being a therapist. You have the heart, courage, and the understanding to reach generations of clients. They will be lucky to have known you. I know that I wouldn't have missed knowing you for anything! I love you, Meg!

Thank you to my eldest daughter, Samantha. Sam, no case study could have ever taught me all the wonderful things that you have. Every day I marvel at your ability to survive and to thrive. You have taught me the meaning of courage. You are so very special. I love you more than you could ever know.

Cameron, you are the best son that a mother could ever want. Without your help with the computer I would have never been able to write this book. Thank you for all the long nights that you worked with me and kept me company. You will never know how much you have helped me to look forward to brighter tomorrows. You have the sensitivity necessary to see what struggles survivors face. This survivor loves you with all of her heart.

Chrissy, you liven up our lives in your own special way. Our lives would not be the same without you. You can count on my love. After all, that's what moms are for.

I would like to thank my husband Carl Knauer for understanding how important my work is to me. For over thirty years you have watched me struggle and finally resolve my own issues through my work. Thank you for understanding, loving, and believing in me.

Thank you to John Knauer. John, you more than anyone understand the price that someone pays when he or she is abused in childhood. Working on your own issues and helping others is the best way to grow. Thank you for all of the interest that you show in my work.

xvi   *Sandra Knauer*

Sandra Dyer deserves a big thank you for her suggestion of *"Numb Survivors,"* the subtitle for this book. Sandra, you have been the sounding board for countless ideas that I have had over the years. You will never know how much your friendship has meant to me. Joanne Hinds, you also deserve a thank-you for putting up with all of my typing while on our trip to Cape Cod. Both you and Sandra are special to me.

I would like to thank Brenda Belizzone for all of her help (and patience!) in preparing the final manuscript. Hopefully, this will be the beginning of a long and productive collaboration.

I want to thank Penny McGuckin for all of her moral support. Penny, you more than anyone understand my heart. Thank you for being there when I needed you. Things will work out the way that God means them to work out. I have faith.

Tamu Boyd, thank you for listening and preparing the difficult intakes involving sexual abuse. I know how difficult it is to hear the details, but because of you I'm able to work with the most wonderful clients of all—the survivors.

Mary Schreiber, PhD, thank you for all of your hard work involving my dream of a treatment center devoted specifically to treating sexual abuse survivors. You are an inspiration to other women who have not yet realized their worth or potential. Without being aware of it, you will have made better the lives of countless people by the work that you did on the proposal. God sent you just when I needed you.

Thanks to Ben Fileti, LCSW, and Ernestine Thigpen, LCSW (yes, Teenie, that's you), for supervising my training through AASECT (the American Association of Sex Educators, Counselors, and Therapists). Ben and Teenie, you have given me the guidance that will someday enable me to help multitudes of other survivors regain their sexuality. By the training that you and AASECT have provided, I will be able to help guide survivors from the sexual abuse they have experienced all the way back to healthy sexuality. I have developed the greatest respect for AASECT and all of the professionals involved with this wonderful organization.

Thank you, Carl Chenkin, PhD, for the supervision that you provide. The supervision does make a difference. Although I may sometimes struggle with boundary issues (after all, I am a survivor!), you understand that my intentions are pure and that I am working on my issues. Thank you for not giving up on me! Thank you, Barry Moore,

LCSW, for your guidance with the downstate group. I think that you understand how much the group members mean to me. Both the downstate group and I have developed a genuine fondness for you and what you add to the group. Thank you also for having patience with me. Thank you, Jon Baylin, PhD, for all of your support and guidance in developing the Best Practices Sexual Abuse Clinical Pathway. Jon, I really value your input. You understand how important the multigenerational piece is to the survivor's recovery. That means more to me than you will ever know.

Thank you also to Christina Eilers, MSW. Christina, I really appreciate how you facilitated the downstate adult survivors' group while I was away. You share my respect and affection for survivors. The adult group members were as fond of you as I am.

To my best friends, Christina Hallon and Sally Heinz, you have been the light at the end of the tunnel that has enabled me to "hang in there." I still think that our friendship would make a wonderful story that demonstrates the power of positive thinking and love.

Bob Davis, LCSW, thank you once again for being there when I needed you. If guardian angels exist, you surely must be one. *Now* do you believe that God talks to me? You are not only dedicated to working with survivors but you help lift my spirits. I can't count how many times we have laughed together. No matter where I go you will always be a part of my heart.

To Scott Barnthouse: Scott, thank you for being my partner in private practice. Your support has made all of the difference. Despite the difficult subjects with which we both deal, we somehow manage to laugh. No matter how outlandish my ideas are concerning work, you always listen patiently and get back to me with your suggestions. I hope you have enjoyed our collaboration as much as I have.

Finally, to my sister, Annette McClain: This book is proof that love and forgiveness always triumph over abuse and adversity. Annette's Haven will be a testament to that very fact. You share so many things with me—especially the ability to make something so very good from something so very sad.

Introduction

As I looked around the room where the adolescent survivors met for their weekly group, it was obvious that addiction could take many forms. Some of the survivors had been using drugs or alcohol for years of their young lives. Other survivors had eating disorders. Some of the group members were either sexually addicted and talked frequently of prostituting, while other group members suffered from sexual anorexia. Almost all of the group's survivors engaged in risky behaviors that at some point were self-abusive. Survivors of childhood sexual abuse will use any number of substances or behaviors to help them deal with the pain of their abuse.

I had just distributed an article titled "Traumatic Child Sexual Abuse, Psychological Death, and the Reduction of the Belief in the Power of God," written by Lee Hardiman (http://lee_hardiman.tripod.com/trauma-god.html). The previous group's meeting had centered on a question: If there was a God, why hadn't He answered the young survivors' prayers when they had cried out to him to stop their abuse? The adolescent survivors' groups range in age from about twelve to eighteen years. The groups are open-ended with participants entering the groups at various times.

As the group members began to read the article by Hardiman, many became enraged and threw down their handouts. Most of them never bothered to finish the article. They automatically assumed that the article was in defense of the idea that there was indeed a God in the conventional sense of most organized religions. Several of the group's members left the group meeting in disgust. Even the group's members who remained to discuss the article left their handouts on the floor when the meeting was over. Not one group member took the handout with them when they left the group meeting.

These young survivors could not integrate the idea that God, as most organized religions portray Him, could really exist if He had let young children be used as sexual objects. One survivor recounted how she had prayed to God to stop her father from raping her. She was furious that "God" had *caused* her abuse to happen and to continue all throughout her childhood and most of her adolescence.

Another teenage survivor asked: If God had so much power and knew everything that was going to happen, why had He allowed her uncle to brutally rape her time and time again? Why hadn't God answered her prayers and made the abuse stop or made her parents stop drinking and using drugs long enough to have them see the abuse that was happening right in front of them?

A seventeen-year-old male survivor in the group attempted to convince the other members that there was indeed a God. This survivor's godparent had been one of the few people in his life who had bothered to try to help the survivor deal with the horror of having been molested. This survivor had never told his parents or anyone else that it was his uncle who had raped him. This uncle was the only immediate family in his young life to whom he had felt any emotional connection. For several months after the rape, he had not said a word about it, because he didn't want to risk losing the only emotional attachment to his family that he had. The pressure to keep the rape a secret became enormous. It was during his attempts to convince the group that there was truly a God that this young man had finally disclosed that it was his uncle who had raped him. Once he had made the disclosure to the group and therapists, the abuse had to be reported. He wanted to know why God hadn't stopped him from disclosing the abuse and probably losing the only remaining family he had.

In the article that I had given as a handout, the author, Lee Hardiman, discusses how survivors of childhood sexual abuse lose their belief in God through a sort of psychological death: "It seems that some children a) are taught that there is a God who loves and protects children, b) are repeatedly abused, c) ask God for help and receive none, d) experience a form of psychological death, and e) stop believing that God will save them." Hardiman cites numerous studies by researchers of sexual abuse, such as Finkelhor and Browne (1986), Allender (1992), Summit (1983), and Terr (1990), who talk about how childhood sexual abuse can alter or distort the child's cognitive and emotional orientation to the world, and make the child feel helpless, powerless, and trapped. Haugaard and Reppucci (1988), Herman (1992), Johnson (1989), Briere (1992), Meek (1990), and Waites (1993) are reported to indicate in their research that the trauma of this sort of abuse can lead to psychic numbing or dissociation.

Hardiman quotes Dr. Judith Herman (1992) as stating that "traumatized people lose their trust in themselves, in other people, and in God." Herman states that when in situations of terror, people cry out for their mothers and for God. When this cry is not answered, the sense of basic trust is shattered. Hardiman continues that incest survivors interviewed about their belief in a God who could protect them confirm this type of loss.

Despite my pleas to listen to the difference in meaning between religion and spirituality, the young survivors in the group refused to even try to understand what I was attempting to explain. They were angry at God for what had happened to them and nothing was going to change their minds.

According to many specialists who treat addictions, a big difference exists between belief in organized religion's concept of God and the concept of spirituality. Spirituality is defined as a sense of belonging to something bigger than oneself, a connection to the world and to the others in a way that has meaning. The person who has a sense of spirituality has a feeling of belonging to others and a sense of his or her own values. The addictive process begins when survivors attempt to control what is happening in their environment by their own *willpower.* According to twelve-step programs, people who are in the addiction process have become spiritually isolated and withdrawn. Survivors begin to believe that to obtain relief from the emotional pain of their abuse, they must reach for something to quell the turmoil and the anger that they often subconsciously feel. In reality, when survivors are using a behavior or a substance to the extreme, they are in fact continuing the abuse that their abusers began.

My two cotherapists in the groups were surprised by the amount of anger that the article by Hardiman had generated. Because I am an incest survivor, I am aware of how much survivors want to desperately believe in God despite their unanswered cries for the abuse to stop. It was our task to help these young survivors regain their sense of spirituality and connection if they were ever going to be able to live a life without serious addiction. To help these young survivors heal, we would first have to ask them to refrain from using whatever substance or behavior was "numbing" their pain. In essence, to heal, one can't go around the pain. To heal, one must first *go through the pain and feel the pain.* To assist these young survivors in healing from their sexual abuse, we would need all the help that a Higher Power could provide. The following chapters will document what it was like to try to ask people who had experienced the worst kind of abuse imaginable to stop using the very substances and behaviors that had made their survival possible. It would take a lot of trust, love, and understanding to accomplish our task. I never doubted that the healing would take place. I have faith not only in a Higher Power, but in the love and connection that exists between all of the survivors and the therapists involved in the adolescent groups.

If you are a survivor who has not had an addiction to food, drugs, alcohol, excess spending or shopping, gambling, working, or any sort of behavior or substance that has caused pain either to you or others in your life, count yourself blessed. We hope that this book will help you develop compassion for your fellow survivors who *do* have addictions or compulsive behaviors. Perhaps after reading this book, you might identify a behavior that you had never previously considered as being abusive or addictive as having the potential to indeed be so.

If you are not a survivor, you may be shocked and saddened at the lengths to which survivors will go to try to deal with the pain of their abuse. My fellow therapists and I hope that by reading this book you will look beyond the negative behaviors that survivors demonstrate and will be able to see the courage and heart that survivors have inside of themselves that enable them simply to have survived their abuse. I love and respect the survivors in my caseload and in this book. I feel sure that you will also develop the same feelings for them as you read their stories. Try to imagine the courage that it takes to stop using whatever behavior or substance that enables you to "function" and know that by doing so you will have to relive your worst nightmares. These young people exemplify the very essence of what it means to be a survivor.

PART I:
THE DEVELOPMENT OF ADDICTIVE AND COMPULSIVE BEHAVIORS

Chapter 1

The Need for Anesthesia

When written in Chinese, the word "crisis" is composed of two characters. One represents danger, and the other represents opportunity.

William James

Addiction: To be seen as an addict is to be seen as being inferior or defective. If you are like most people, the image that comes to mind when thinking of addiction is of a drug addict or an alcoholic. Usually the addicted person is considered "weak" or "lazy."

All forms of abuse are harmful. The sense of shame that surrounds sexual abuse continues to make it very difficult to talk about, although it seems that in recent years our society is finally able to discuss sexual abuse a little more openly than in the past. By and large, however, sexual abuse is often still kept hidden. This is especially true of incest. Incest continues to be the "family's business" unless it is too obvious to ignore.

Some survivors of sexual abuse are in so much pain that they cannot deal with their abuse in an open way. Some survivors are not *allowed* by their families to disclose the sexual abuse. How could someone not be allowed to disclose their abuse? Family systems theory states that families are intricately balanced. If one member of the family changes something, everyone else in the family is affected by that change. Families that are fragile and barely able to function in the best of times cannot afford to make changes that might benefit one family member at the expense of all of the other family members' welfare.

Disclosing sexual abuse and forcing the family to deal with the abuse is a stressor that some families just cannot handle. The cost of keeping the sexual abuse a secret is enormous. Usually, it is the victim of the sexual abuse who must pay the price to keep the family intact.

This price can be paid in several ways. Sometimes the survivor will disclose to only one or two family members. Very quickly the survivor learns that to be part of the family he or she must make peace with the abuse and keep quiet about his or her feelings. Other survivors feel that they simply *must* disclose the abuse. After telling others outside of the family system about the sexual abuse, the survivor may find that some family members may have joined forces against the survivor. The survivor is then ostracized from the family. Readmission into the family circle requires that the survivor recant their allegations of the sexual abuse. Nothing polarizes a family as much as allegations of sexual abuse.

Anesthesia is the term I use to describe the means by which the survivor of sexual abuse is able to deal with the emotional and sometimes physical pain of the abuse and still function on a day-to-day basis. It takes an enormous amount of energy to withhold the feelings of rage and helplessness that result from sexual abuse. Anesthesia can take many forms. Different survivors resort to different behaviors to relieve the pain of the abuse. All forms of anesthesia have one aspect in common: whenever the survivor is engaging in the behavior, he or she is so enthralled by the anesthesia that he or she is in a state quite similar to the trance state that is induced during hypnosis.

The purpose of the anesthesia is to take the focus off the pain of the abuse. The messages that the survivor receives from sexual abuse are complex and hurtful. Sexual abuse is a complete violation of a person's boundaries. Nothing is more sacred than our bodies. To be sexually abused sends the survivor the message that one's body is not one's own, that sexual services are all that are of value in the victim, and that the victim's feelings do not matter at all to the perpetrator. No wonder survivors need to resort to compulsive behaviors and addictions to numb their emotional pain. Sexual abuse grooms the victim for later adult dysfunction.

To survive the pain of sexual abuse, some survivors become experts at dissociation. Dissociation is the ability to compartmentalize experiences in such a way that survivors may not consciously be aware of specific memories and events that they have experienced. Dissociation is the ability to function in the here and now while not having to deal with past traumatic and painful experiences. At some level, a part of the survivor knows and remembers the abuse. The part of the survivor that must function in the present is spared from having to integrate the trauma of the abuse into present day-to-day functioning.

Not all survivors have the fortune, or perhaps the misfortune, of being able to dissociate. For most survivors, dissociation is not an option. These survivors must find another way to take the focus off their pain.

The cost of being able to dissociate can be quite high. Dissociation at its most extreme form leads to dissociative identity disorder (DID), formerly called multiple personality disorder (MPD). DID clients report losing large amounts of time and memories that can cause confusion and difficulty maintaining relationships. These survivors report having difficulty maintaining any semblance of organization or structure in either their personal or professional lives.

Most adults are able at some point in their lives to integrate their earlier experiences, whether the experiences were positive or negative. DID clients do not have this ability. Earlier memories and experiences are held only by certain parts of the person. The core personality often has no conscious remembrance of experiences or lessons learned in the earlier parts of life. DID clients may be doomed to repeat the same mistakes over and over again; they may never be able to benefit from their mistakes.

The ability to dissociate may have helped the DID client survive the original abuse, but what happens when the client no longer needs to use this survival tactic to function? The problems that are caused by dissociation can continue when the trauma is over and the ability to dissociate is no longer necessary. The survivor has difficulty not resorting to dissociation whenever *any* problem occurs in his or her life. The DID client must learn a new way of dealing with stress and trauma or risk living a life of confusion and chaos.

The ways that survivors are able to numb the pain of their abuse are as numerous as the ways that they may have been abused. One common way that survivors numb themselves involves what is known as the trance state. By definition, the trance state involves the "looping" of thoughts so that persons are so totally involved in whatever is causing the trance state that they are unaware of other things that may be happening around them.

The need for anesthesia seems to be especially linked to survivors of sexual abuse. The anesthesia can take many forms. Perhaps the best known form of anesthesia is alcohol, although alcohol is not the only form of anesthesia that is currently widely used.

Drugs are very popular in the adolescent groups that I facilitate. Marijuana, crack cocaine, and heroin are the most commonly abused drugs at the present time in these groups. Eating disorders are also closely tied to sexual abuse. Younger adolescent survivors seem to have a higher proportion of anorexia nervosa or bulimia. Older survivors seem to suffer most often from binge eating disorder or compulsive overeating. Survivors are at very high risk of developing addictions whenever they begin to abuse a substance. When the survivor's substance abuse begins it may well be the very first time that he or she has been able to block out the emotional pain of sexual abuse.

Survivors may not only abuse substances. They may also develop compulsive behaviors that may deaden the emotional pain of the sexual abuse. The most commonly used compulsive behaviors include compulsive gambling, compulsive spending, compulsive television watching or video-game playing, compulsive overeating, and countless other possible compulsive behaviors.

Whatever addiction or compulsive behavior the survivor employs, the intention is always the same: to deaden the emotional pain of sexual abuse. Are survivors consciously aware that they are attempting to deaden the pain of the abuse? I believe that most of the attempts to deaden the pain occur on an unconscious level. The survivor is only aware that it feels good not to think about the abuse for just a little while. The more successful the survivor is in using a certain tactic to deaden the pain, the more apt the survivor is to develop an addiction to that tactic. The following chapter addresses the process of developing an addiction or a compulsive behavior.

Chapter 2

The Nature of Addiction, Compulsion, and the Trance State: An Addict's Limited Range of Dysfunctional Choices

Medicine is a healing art. It must deal with individuals, their fears, their hopes, and their sorrows. It must reach back further than a disease that the patient may have to those physical and emotional environmental factors which condition the individual for the reception of disease.

Dr. Walter Martin

We do not remember days, we remember moments.

Cesare Pavese

Although survivors may be different in the ways that they act out compulsively or addictively, they seem to have certain feelings that are seen across the board that act as triggers for the acting-out episodes. Survivors seem to share a feeling of impending doom. Whenever things are going well, the survivor cannot stop looking for what will go wrong next. When things are going wrong, the survivor believes that things will get worse. This feeling of dread and gloom becomes generalized to every life circumstance that the addicted or compulsive survivor experiences. Along with this generalized feeling of dread and gloom comes a feeling that the survivor is walking a tightrope. The slightest misstep could mean that everything will fall apart. Imagine the stress of maintaining a daily existence with that kind of constant pressure!

The fear of abandonment is a constant fear. When survivors feel that they are about to lose someone without whom they simply "can't exist," they are much more apt to engage in whatever addiction or compulsion might provide the comfort that they so desperately need. Getting close to others and risking vulnerability is another feeling that is apt to set off an episode of addictive or compulsive behavior. Although survivors could point to fear of abandonment, generalized anxiety, and the feeling of living life in a constant state of tension, the real problem is the way in which they have taken the feelings from their original abuse and made it such a part of their personalities that they are no longer even aware that these feelings from the long ago abuse are the driving force behind the current addictive or compulsive behaviors.

Sherry is a good example of a survivor molested all through childhood and young adolescence who does not seem to make the connection between her abusive history and her current self-abusive behaviors, such as drug addiction and constant codependent relationships.

> Sherry will do anything to keep from losing the people to whom she has become close. The slightest fear that someone will be leaving her is enough to set off a drinking or drug-abusing episode. Reassurances mean little to Sherry because she learned long ago that people do not really mean it when they tell you that you can trust what they say. Almost everyone that Sherry has ever trusted enough to let close to her has managed to either let Sherry down or to betray her.

Researchers Strober (1984), Cattanach and Rodin (1988), Mynors-Wallis (1992), and Terr (1991) have all found that people who have had stressful life events (such as sexual abuse) use eating as a major way of dealing with the tension that results from the stress. Dr. Sarah Leibowitz of Rockefeller University (Marano, 1993a, p. 131) has spoken about the relationship between tension and brain chemistry. It appears that tension makes us crave carbohydrates. These same changes in brain chemistry cause our bodies to retain the new body fat that we obtain through the overeating, which, in turn, reduces the tension that we feel. What a vicious cycle for the food-addicted survivor!

Oppenheimer and colleagues (1985) feel that because of intense feelings of inferiority resulting from abuse, food-addicted survivors may isolate themselves and comfort themselves with food. We all need to be social creatures, at least to some extent. When survivors feel such shame and disgust at themselves that they withdraw from others and overeat to comfort themselves, they have begun the cycle that may ultimately lead to morbid obesity and even greater social withdrawal.

By its very nature, addiction causes survivors to become withdrawn and isolated. In the addiction process, survivors will turn more and more often toward whatever behavior or substance they are abusing. In turning toward the abused substance or behavior, the survivor is in fact turning inward. The more involved the survivor becomes with the behavior or substance, the less likely the survivor is to get the support that will enable him or her to break free of self-abusive behaviors.

Jane was sexually abused by her father when she was four years old and by her maternal grandfather all throughout her childhood and adolescence. The family in which Jane grew up was very dysfunctional. Jane's mother was an active alcoholic. Jane's father offered the only real nurturance that Jane received during her childhood. Unfortunately, Jane's father was also an alcoholic—an angry alcoholic. When her father was drinking, Jane quickly learned to stay out of his way. Her father would snap at the slightest thing and hit whoever happened to be closest to him.

Jane's mother was often the recipient of her father's rage. Jane would see her father slap or punch her mother whenever he became drunk. Jane's mother was very fragile and petite. Jane would resort to desperate acts to divert her father's attention away from her mother. In an attempt to try to protect her mother, she would deliberately harm herself.

Harming herself did divert her father's rage from her mother. Unfortunately, harming herself also became a pattern in Jane's life. Harming herself seemed to become the established behavior that Jane would use whenever she felt that something had happened that she simply couldn't deal with. In reality, Jane was using her self-abusive behaviors as a way of expressing the overwhelming emotions she felt that she could not verbally express.

Suicide attempts became another pattern in Jane's life. Time after time Jane would make suicide attempts that brought her to the very brink of death. Whenever Jane was not attempting suicide, she would

engage in such risky behaviors that she was slowly committing suicide through them. Jane would drink and drive, take large amounts of
prescription medications with alcohol, or use illegal drugs to try to
stop her emotional pain.

Contributing to Jane's emotional distress was Jane's inability to
tell her mother about the sexual abuse that she had experienced. Jane
felt that her mother could not handle all of the day-to-day stressors
that came along with raising a family. Jane believed that her mother
would never be able to handle the stress of knowing that someone in
the family had sexually abused her child.

I believe that Jane also felt that her mother would not do anything
about the abuse because Jane's father was the family breadwinner.
Jane's mother had also been sexually abused by Jane's grandfather.
She had not been able to defend herself against her own father's sexual abuse. Jane felt that her mother probably could not protect Jane
against his abuse either.

Jane's substance abuse and compulsive self-abusive behaviors became the anesthesia that enabled Jane to endure her emotional distress. Jane would have been much better off if she had been able to express her emotional pain. As time went by, Jane became more and
more deeply entrenched in using drugs and suicide attempts as a way
to cope with her life. Her wrists are marked by countless scars from
trying to kill herself with razor blades. Jane has been through numerous rehabs in an attempt to deal with her drug use. She has used everything from marijuana to heroin in an attempt "to not feel." It is the
"not feeling" that has caused Jane to need to self-mutilate in an attempt to feel "alive" again. Jane fluctuates between needing to feel
alive and needing to numb the emotional pain. There is real truth to
the saying, "That which is suppressed is expressed." Until Jane finds
the ability to verbalize her feelings and to connect emotionally with
some sort of higher power, Jane will most likely repeat her behaviors
in an attempt to try to find peace. All too many survivors find their
peace in death.

All addiction involves a progression that is predictable and fore-
seeable if the behavior is used in lieu of dealing with underlying pain
and feelings. According to Craig Nakken in *The Addictive Personality* (1996), all addictions share the following characteristics.

1. *Addiction involves acting-out behaviors.* These behaviors can include such behaviors as buying large quantities of food that the food addict plans to eat while alone. Since the activity involves eating large quantities of food and will cause the addict shame, the activity must be done while alone and isolated. As the addict progresses in the seriousness of his or her addiction, the shame will continue to increase until the addict must be isolated more and more often. As the addict isolates himself or herself more frequently, the chances of someone else being able to recognize what is happening becomes more remote. There will be fewer people to help stop the progression of the addiction.

Addictions that include acting-out behaviors include making large purchases that the addict cannot pay for, going to casinos to gamble when the addict cannot afford to do so, eating disorders, or any sort of addictive behavior that originally causes the addict to feel pleasurable feelings such as fulfillment, relaxation, or excitement. As the addiction becomes more serious, there will be fewer pleasurable feelings and more negative feelings attached to the addictive behaviors. Finally, the addict will reach a point where he or she will feel shame or disgust at his or her own behaviors.

2. *Addiction involves nurturing through avoidance.* Whenever a person employs an addictive behavior, it is an attempt to take the focus off a problem that the addict would rather not face. When a person has been sexually abused, the last thing that he or she wants to do is deal with the powerful and negative feelings that the abuse causes.

To nurture themselves, survivors will go to extreme lengths to feel cared for and comforted. Nakken says that when the addict loses control of the substance or the behavior that they are using to avoid dealing with whatever is causing them pain it is an "emotional evading of life" (p. 7). Sometimes the addict will use food, alcohol, or drugs in an attempt not to "feel" the pain or face the memories. When a relationship breaks up, don't we often have the image of the wounded person "drowning sorrows" in alcohol in a bar? This is what Nakken means when he refers to the emotional evasion of life. When addicts lose control of whatever they are abusing, they then must deal not only with the pain of the original abuse but also the pain caused by the loss of the addictive substance or behavior.

3. *The addict employs what Nakken refers to as emotional logic.*
Nakken states that the addict builds an emotional defense system to protect the addictive belief system. Obviously, addicts
know intellectually that a food, drug, or an addictive behavior
cannot bring them what they seek emotionally. Addicts try to
meet their emotional needs for closeness through their relationship with the abused behavior or substance. Because intimacy
can never be experienced with a behavior or substance, addicts
are doomed to fail in their search for closeness and nurturing.
Not only is the addict trying to obtain nurturing, but he or she is
also trying to stop the emotional pain that he or she feels. Addicts want immediate relief. An addictive behavior or substance
will give immediate relief, but only for a short time and never in
a way that truly addresses the addict's core issues. When the addict's pain is removed, even if only for a very brief moment, the
addict believes that he or she has found an answer to the problem. Nothing could be farther from the truth. Because being
close to others requires reaching out and addiction involves
turning inward, the addict will only make his or her situation
worse.

One of the stereotypical images of addicts is of manipulation. Addicts are portrayed as doing whatever it takes to obtain whatever substance or behavior they are abusing. This stereotype holds truth. Addicts
will not only manipulate substances; they soon learn to manipulate
people to reach their desired goals. As Nakken states, not many people will stand being manipulated and soon the addict is left alone,
feeling even more isolated. Since codependents have such a high tolerance for inappropriate behaviors, the codependent is a perfect "fit"
for the addict. The cycle begins to deepen and widen until finally addicts either are ruined by the addictive behavior or feel so much pain
that they must finally face the issues that caused the addiction in the
first place.

The more socially acceptable and readily available a substance or
behavior, the greater the number of people who will have problems
with it. For example, our country has a real problem with obesity.
What substance is more readily available and socially acceptable
than food? The problem that those who compulsively overeat must
face becomes apparent when their weight begins to balloon outside
the social norm. At this point, the compulsive overeater faces societal
scorn when eating in public and soon learns to indulge in overeating

in private. Isolation only causes the overeater to eat more hurriedly and compulsively. No wonder our nation struggles with its weight! Whenever survivors turn to food to nurture themselves, they must then deal with the consequences of overeating: social isolation and criticism.

Addictions can change over time. Survivors often shift addictions. For example, some women will shift from an eating disorder to codependency when they meet someone to whom they are attracted enough to lose weight. To the observer, it may appear that the survivor has conquered his or her food addiction. In reality, the survivor has simply substituted codependency for overeating. In order to deal with both the issues of codependency and overeating, the survivor must be aware that neither another person nor a substance can ever replace the nurturing that the survivor missed when the sexual abuse occurred. This is a bitter pill for the survivor to swallow but a necessary one if the survivor is to heal.

Whenever survivors employ either an addiction or a compulsive behavior in order to cope with their life circumstances, there is always a predictable pattern in their behavior. Survivors will first find that they have begun to exhibit a behavior that is out of control. They will then attempt to control the behavior. When their internal emotions become stirred up enough, they will begin the release phase of the addiction or compulsion where they will return to the compulsive or addictive behavior to help deal with their emotions. This cycle of release and control will go on until they find an intervention that will finally work and end the need to repeat the cycle.

Simone is a survivor who was molested by her grandfather when she was in her early teens. All of her life Simone has felt that she was not as pretty or as smart as her older sister. When the grandfather molested her, it served only to reinforce the image that Simone had of how she was "less than" her sister or any of the other girls that she knew. When Simone began to eat snack cakes when she was feeling lonely, it seemed like an innocent way to "treat" herself for all of the unpleasant things with which she had to deal. The more that Simone ate, the heavier she became. The heavier that she became, the more Simone isolated herself and turned to food for comfort. The cycle had begun that would eventually cause Simone to weigh over 350 pounds.

When a person becomes this heavy, it is difficult to find any sense of hope or encouragement to lose this great amount of weight. People

with addictive or compulsive behaviors are used to expecting immediate gratification from the substances or the behaviors that they
abuse. To Simone, the idea of having to lose a pound or so of weight a
week seemed like it would take forever. It was only when Simone's
husband left her alone with their two small children to care for that
Simone knew that she had to go back into the workplace to support
the children and herself. Desperation caused Simone to finally look at
her weight and what it was costing her. She did not care what happened to her, but she loved her children dearly and did not want them
to have the same kind of life that she had had.

Simone came into therapy and began to try to honestly address the
issues in her life that had caused her need to resort to compulsive behaviors. Many times during treatment Simone felt that treatment was
making things worse than they had been when she was compulsively
overeating.

One of the most interesting things about survivors who are adults
and are in treatment is the sense of emptiness and feeling alone that
they complain about once they cease their addictive or compulsive
behaviors. Simone was no different. After she had lost about sixty
pounds, she began to complain of feeling lost. Her sense of being
alone would alternate with her rage and hostility toward all of the
people in her life who had let her down—especially her husband.
Even though Simone had not been happy with her husband for a long
time, she still felt that he had betrayed her by leaving the marriage.
Survivors are terrified of being alone. A survivor's fear of abandonment is a constant source of pain. The untreated survivor would rather
settle for the most unsatisfactory of relationships than attempt to find
someone with whom he or she could be happy. The idea of taking the
risk of being alone is simply too painful. Simone had no choice; her
husband was already gone, so she began to address her fears and buried hurts while in treatment.

As Simone continued to abstain from overeating, she began to realize that she could deal with her issues successfully without turning
to overeating. She was able to experience her feelings and deal with
them without her feelings overpowering her. She allowed herself the
time to grieve her hurts and losses. As the weight came off, Simone
began to realize how alone she had been her entire life. When her
grandfather had molested her, Simone had not felt that she could turn
to her parents or any other adults for help. At some level, Simone

knew that if she were to disclose the abuse, the family would not defend her. Simone knew instinctively that the cost of disclosure would be censure from the family. Simone had begun to overeat as an unconscious attempt to "stuff" her feelings and bury her anger. Once Simone felt free enough in treatment to allow herself to express her rage, she was well on her way to recovery from overeating.

Although Simone's story sounds like it has a happy ending, Simone is still not out of the woods. Unless she is able to learn new ways of coping with situations in which she is taken advantage of or becomes angry she will be destined to repeat either her compulsive overeating or perhaps to even go on to another compulsive or addictive behavior.

Reaching the core issues that survivors have is only part of the treatment. Teaching survivors to learn how to set boundaries and value themselves is the other crucial part of treatment. Learning new coping behaviors is perhaps the most difficult task for survivors. Many survivors feel that if they cannot provide the services that people in their lives value them for, then no one will care for them at all. So many survivors would rather be taken advantage of than risk not being noticed at all. The saddest part of this is that our children watch how we, as adults, behave. If we don't demonstrate boundaries that show that we value ourselves, our children are likely to follow our example.

Addiction is a very subtle sort of "dis-ease" in that it has far-reaching implications concerning the way that we really feel about ourselves. The way that we care for our bodies truly reflects the way that we feel about ourselves. I see these dynamics played out time and again with the survivors that I work with in the groups and in individual treatment. Often survivors who have been sexually abused will not take proper care of their body. It is not unusual to see survivors totally ignore health issues despite serious consequences that may be apparent to everyone but the survivors.

Alice is an example of a survivor who doesn't seem to realize the seriousness of her health issues.

> Alice is only nineteen years old and weighs 375 pounds. Not only does Alice have a considerable amount of weight to lose, but she also is a chain smoker. Alice also engages in very risky sexual behaviors. It is not unusual for Alice to have sex with someone who she has just recently met without practicing safe

sex. Alice is sexually promiscuous; she will have sex with any number of different partners with whom she is only vaguely acquainted. Alice has no idea with whom her partners have slept. Whenever she catches a cold or feels very ill Alice refuses to see a doctor because she is afraid that the doctor will be angry with her because of her weight or that he or she will tell Alice that she has a serious illness, such as AIDS, as a result of her sexual promiscuity. The doctor has requested on numerous occasions that Alice lose at least one hundred pounds. Alice promises the doctor that she will lose the weight but only returns to the doctor's office the next time even heavier than the time before.

It is not unusual to see even younger survivors engaging in care for themselves that leaves much to be desired.

Sue is a twelve-year-old female survivor who was sexually abused by her paternal grandfather. Sue's family doesn't have much money, but they do have Medicaid for health care. The family can also use a dental clinic for dental care. Despite the fact that Sue has many teeth with serious cavities, Sue's family will allow her to eat large amounts of candy, even though her teeth are often aching from it.

Such lack of self-care is really a reenactment of the survivor's prior abuse. If significant others in our earlier lives don't value us, then chances are we won't value ourselves either. Survivor after survivor in my office will engage in behaviors that are clearly demonstrating the fact that they don't care about themselves.

This lack of self-care appears to me to be representative of inner feelings that the survivors hold about their own value and self-image. Ailments that contain a psychological component are often expressed by survivors who are not able to express their feelings. Illnesses with a psychological basis include migraines, stomach problems, ulcers, asthma, chronic fatigue syndrome, and colitis. Illnesses such as AIDS also are sometimes more apparent and may be triggered by some sort of psychological stressor in the body's immune system. Both shingles and herpes can also be triggered by psychological stressors. This is not to say that psychological causes are solely at the root of all of these ailments, but that they certainly can contribute to the development of these ailments.

It is often the case that the only time that survivors will begin to care for their bodies is when they have begun recovery from addictive or compulsive behaviors. When beginning this recovery, survivors begin to realize for the first time that they can "feel." Once survivors begin to feel, they realize how much pain the compulsion or the addiction has been covering and what it has cost them, not only in terms of self-esteem but in actual physical costs to their bodies. It is at this point that survivors begin to realize that only they can care for themselves in a way which values their bodies and their emotions.

Once survivors begin to value themselves physically and emotionally, they realize the cost of the shame and alienation that the addiction or compulsion has caused. In reality, the foundation of addiction is the isolation and sense of being alone that is at the root of trying to employ a behavior or substance to excess without anyone knowing how much or how often the survivors are employing this behavior or substance. By its very nature addiction occurs in relative isolation. The emptiness that survivors feel is what causes the addictive or compulsive behavior in the first place. The use of the compulsive or addictive behavior further isolates survivors so that they can use in private. The cycle of addiction and compulsive behaviors is an ever-widening and repeating cycle; eventually the survivors have nothing left in their lives except the addiction or compulsion.

In their frantic attempts "not to feel," many survivors believe that they have found the secret to having control over their lives.

> Sharon is a sixteen-year-old survivor who was molested by her biological father while she was very young. Her father has not been a part of Sharon's life since she was two years old. Her biological mother has an anxiety disorder that causes her to be constantly on edge and to become panicked at the slightest problem. Sharon has had to parent her mother ever since she was a very young child. Because of all of the anger that Sharon has had to repress toward her mother for not being the parent that she needed, Sharon has developed a problem with alcohol. Whenever her mother makes Sharon angry, Sharon will begin to look for the first opportunity to drink. After she has had enough to drink, Sharon will become sleepy and be able to control the rage that she has had building up inside her toward her mother's dependence on Sharon. Lately, it has taken so much alcohol to

keep down her rage that Sharon has been taken to the hospital for alcohol poisoning.

Aaron's way to "not feel" is to use anger and threats of violence as a way to keep others at a distance from him. Aaron's family has a multigenerational history of being both physically abused and physically abusing others. As long as Aaron can threaten and intimidate others, Aaron is safe from the possibility that someone else can threaten and intimidate him. Aaron's fear of others has increased proportionately to his use of fear to control those around him.

John Bradshaw (1986b) states that addiction is an attempt for the addict to be able to be out of control when the addict doesn't know how to be spontaneous. In other words, the addict fluctuates within a very narrow range of behaviors that consists of two discrete poles: (1) total and rigid control and (2) being completely and totally out of control. For the addict, no middle ground exists. It must be one extreme or the other.

Bradshaw's (1986a) description of the cycle of addictive or compulsive behaviors goes as follows:

1. The cycle begins when the emotional pressure builds up inside the person. The addict begins to think of the addiction or of the compulsion.
2. Something occurs that triggers the addictive or compulsive behavior. Sharon's rage at her mother being the trigger for Sharon's need to drink is a good example.
3. The internal pressure within the person becomes so great that the addict can't stand it and reaches for the substance or the behavior that will help quell the feelings. At the root of all addictive or compulsive behaviors is a sense of emptiness.
4. The end part of this phase is when the addict has indulged in the substance or in the behavior and now begins to feel the guilt, low self-esteem, sense of shame, and fear from using. This is the part of the cycle where alcoholics might say that they are so ashamed of their behavior that they will never drink again. The compulsive behavior will cause such intense remorse that the addict will beg to have the negative behavior forgiven and will make promises never to indulge in the behavior again.

5. At this point there is the possibility that an intervention may occur. When addicts begin finally to realize that all of the food, drugs, alcohol, gambling, shopping, or whatever substance or behavior that they are using to quiet their feelings is *not* going to be the solution to their problems, they may begin to realize that they need to find another solution to their situation. Some addicts reach this point in a relatively short amount of time. Other addicts take a lifetime to reach this point. Some addicts never reach this point at all and die from their addiction or compulsion.

The reality of the situation is that whenever we indulge in addictive or compulsive behavior we are out of touch with what is real because the addictive or compulsive behavior harms us even further and won't fix or fill the emptiness inside of us. Addicts must ask themselves what it is that they are *really* feeling and face those feelings head on. Usually the feeling that lies at the root of the need for compulsive or addictive behaviors will involve shame, anxiety, fear, guilt, anger, or loneliness.

> Anthony, a twenty-six-year-old survivor, feels a terrible sense of shame due to the atrocities that he committed while he was involved in gang-related activities in his neighborhood home in New York City. The feelings of shame are so overwhelming at times that Anthony thinks that he can't bear to feel them. Anthony is as much a victim of the violence in his neighborhood as are the people that Anthony victimized. In Anthony's neighborhood, the motto was "Either eat or be eaten." Violence is a way of life there. Anthony has adapted a compulsion toward rage as a way of keeping himself safe. As long as others are afraid of Anthony's rage, they won't get close enough to see how vulnerable Anthony really is. They won't see the shame that Anthony feels at what happened while he was in the gang. They also won't be able to give Anthony the love and caring that all of us need as we journey along life's paths.

The seeds of dysfunction that give root to addictions and compulsions are found in our childhoods. The only way that we can gain access to these foundations of our addictive or compulsive behaviors is to refrain from using whatever it is that we use to kill our emotions. Because alcohol is the substance used by the greatest number of people to numb their feelings, when treating alcoholism we should realize that alcoholics are people who probably have a long history of emptiness and isolation, which has resulted in them placing alcohol as a sort of higher power in their lives. Emotional dissociation is the result of using substances or behaviors to keep us separated from our feelings. This sense of emotional dissociation also explains why some addicts can commit the most awful acts or atrocities while under the influence and feel no remorse. In essence, the addict's feelings are separated from his or her emotional being.

One of the most interesting dynamics that I have ever witnessed occurred when the adolescent group members I facilitate in our downstate clinic began to "feel" as if they were one person. On the night that the group started back up again after a brief summer hiatus, the group members were particularly rowdy and boisterous. Now, if you have ever been in a room with nine or ten adolescents you will understand that being noisy and loud is simply part of the nature of adolescence. When I attempted to explain to the group that if clinicians from the "outside," who were not survivors or were not familiar with adolescents' behaviors, observed the group's behaviors they might interpret the group's behaviors as being chaotic and non-productive. The group taught me a lesson that I will never forget.

Kristie, a fifteen-year-old survivor, summed up what this book is intended to be all about. Kristie looked me in the eye and said,

> Sometimes we get loud and laugh because we are tired of feeling depressed and sad. For just a little while we want to forget and laugh. If we act different or talk about stuff that seems as if we don't care about what has happened to us it's only because we want or need to get our minds off of what has happened. It's like just for a little while you can focus on something else or do something else that makes us *not feel what has happened to us and how much it has hurt us.*

Such wisdom from people who are so young!

What was totally amazing was that the entire group immediately understood exactly what Kristie's remark meant. It was as if they were one person who had understood the same thoughts and feelings. The newest group member, Helen, who had come for the very first time that same evening agreed and understood what the established group members meant.

Over the years, my cotherapists and I have noticed that the groups have been running the dynamics about which Kristie commented. When the group begins to "feel" too much pain immediately there comes a shift in the group's mood. Individuals will act up or draw attention to themselves. The group member who had previously been talking or disclosing intense feelings will have the group's attention drawn away from him or her. Not only does this shift in the group's attention allow the group member who was speaking to regain their composure but it also allows the group to regain its composure. The group acts as if it were one single entity and attempts to change the speaker's mood. This need to change the mood is what addictive and compulsive behaviors are all about. This is what the need for anesthesia is all about. Thank you, Kristie, for explaining what I have been attempting to conceptualize for a long time. In one brief evening, Kristie was able to explain so simply what clinicians for so long have attempted to understand: addictive and compulsive behaviors. The irony of the situation, as with so many other things in life, is that to heal from the sexual abuse you need to stop running from the pain and instead embrace the pain and grieve your losses. Inch by painful inch that is exactly what the groups have done as members return time after time to laugh, act up, and for very intense moments deal with the painfulness of their abuse and their lives. The group has managed to take away the mystery of addictions and compulsions by explaining it in terms that all of us, whether clinician or layperson, can understand. When we hurt, we will do whatever it takes to keep from feeling the pain until we are ultimately able to endure and deal with what has hurt us.

The real basis of addictive or compulsive behaviors is our alienation from our innermost feelings and thoughts. If we are shame based and feel that we are "worth less" than others, we may engage in addictive or compulsive behaviors as a way to decrease the amount of discomfort that we feel. As we use more of the abused substance or compulsive behavior we feel greater shame, which leads to increased use; so the cycle continues.

In families in which there has been sexual abuse, the interweave between the adult partners in the child's family of origin is interesting. Almost always one of the adult partners will be an addict of some sort and the other partner will be a codependent. The partner who is an addict may be addicted to work, sex, drugs, food, alcohol, gambling, religion, rage, power, spending, or any number of substances or behaviors. The partner who is the codependent will attempt to shift his or her own focus toward distractions such as work, the children, PTA meetings, dieting, religion, or feelings of sadness or anger, all in an attempt to deny the significance of the behaviors of the addicted partner.

Children caught between these two partners will be forced into a set of rigid roles in an attempt to provide some sort of balance for the family system. Being forced to live one's life from a rigid role does not allow for the expression of genuine feelings or being in touch with one's inner self. For the abuse victim to be able to express anger at his or her abuse and abuser is paramount to being asked to relinquish his or her place in the family system. If abuse victims go against what the family system needs them to be in order to maintain denial in the family, the family cannot tolerate such disloyalty. Many survivors in my caseload were abandoned when they refused to recant their allegations of sexual abuse by someone who the family needed to believe was not capable of sexual abuse.

The irony of addiction or compulsion is that when involved in a rigid role, survivors are totally out of touch with their true feelings. It is only when acting out compulsive behaviors or addictions that survivors are acting "out" their need to lessen this rigid sense of control. Compulsion is the pathological relationship that one has to a person, an event, or a substance that leads to harmful and negative life events or consequences. In other words, addictive or compulsive behaviors tell others that survivors don't feel comfortable with the emotional "lid" that they must keep on their true feelings. Acting-out behavior is their way of releasing the tension of holding in their true feelings.

I have seen countless survivors deny the harmfulness of their sexual abuse. Whenever these survivors meet with the nonoffending parent who did not protect them when the sexual abuse was happening, the survivors will most often take on a parental type of role. It is almost as if survivors sense that the nonoffending parent is too fragile to handle any criticism that they might offer toward the nonoffending parent's ability to parent. The survivor's reaction when the nonoffending parent leaves the room is important. Almost invariably, the survivor will act out in whatever manner he or she has used in the past to numb his or her feelings. Survivors have told me that on the way home after a session such as this they stopped at the donut shop or liquor store to indulge in their food or alcohol addiction. The cost of denying their feelings of anger (that often are also mixed with love and compassion for the nonoffending parent) is so high that survivors need to find something quickly that will help keep their true feelings under cover. If the perpetrator is a parent, the child may demonstrate very mixed emotions.

Many attempts have been made to develop a profile of the typical sexual abuse perpetrator. Although these attempts have not been fully successful, they have identified some traits or characteristics that perpetrators have in common. Perpetrators lack a sense of empathy for their victims. They usually come from a family of origin in which they were deprived of the basic needs of mothering that all children require. Perpetrators are shame based. Their families are isolated from others who might be able to identify the abuse and to intervene. Perpetrators make demands that require the victims to take care of them. The repressed rage that perpetrators carry with them acts as a catalyst that causes them to recreate their own abuse situation with their child victims. Because perpetrators have little sense of empathy, they tend to see children as being their "property." Perpetrators are often also sex addicts, or they come from families where there is a rigid sense of religion. Some perpetrators may show signs of psychosis. Perpetrators who are psychotic often cannot even feel their own emotions, let alone appreciate the emotions of their victims.

In incest families, the boundaries that should surround each individual family member are almost nonexistent. An enmeshment confluence exists in which each individual member of the family has little of his or her own reality. No boundaries exist in the family. The family is patriarchal and closed to the outside world. Nothing comes into the family and nothing goes out. An interesting statistic indicates that over 80 percent of those who have addictions were sexually abused. This high correlation between addictions and sexual abuse indicates the degree of harmfulness of sexual abuse and incest and the lengths that these victims will go to try to deaden the pain of their abuse. Dr. Carlton E. Munson of the University of Maryland at Baltimore has developed a diagram that describes the Repetition Compulsion Process (see Figure 2.1), in which the person who has experienced a traumatic event will keep repeating the compulsive behavior in an unconscious attempt to bring resolution to the traumatic event

FIGURE 2.1. The Repetition Compulsion Process

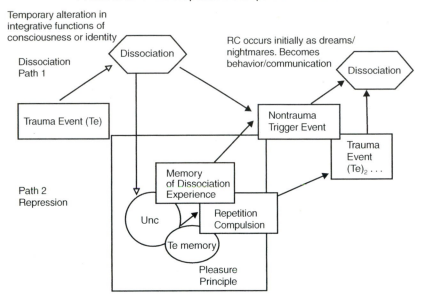

Source: Reprinted with permission of Dr. Carlton Munson and The Haworth Press. Copyright 2000. From *Diagnosis and Treatment of Childhood Trauma* (in press).

and be able to return to the natural state. Many researchers feel that childhood trauma can be so disruptive that the trauma interferes with the child's developmental tasks from the point at which the trauma occurs forward.

Munson describes two possible pathways that may be taken by the person who has experienced what he terms a Traumatic event (Te). Path 1 consists of the use of dissociation as the main defense the person might use in attempting to deal with the trauma.

Let us suppose that the original Te which the person might experience is childhood sexual abuse. To function on a day-to-day basis, the survivor might be able to dissociate from the trauma of the abuse. Whenever a nontraumatic trigger event happens (e.g., someone criticizes the survivor and makes the survivor feel insignificant or inadequate), memories of the feelings of the original Te threaten to bubble to the surface. In an attempt to deal with these feelings, the survivor repeats whatever compulsive behavior originally enabled him or her to dissociate from the feelings of the original trauma. This ability to dissociate from the original trauma means that until the past traumatic event is dealt with, the survivor will keep repeating the compulsive behavior in the present. It is as if the compulsive behavior in the present is representative of the original trauma of the past. Although the survivor is able to dissociate from the original trauma, he or she cannot successfully put the trauma in the unconscious or repress it. In other words, since the survivor has dissociated from the trauma, he or she has no means to resolve the feelings that have resulted from the trauma.

Munson's Path 2 deals with repression. Once the original trauma (sexual abuse as in the first instance) has occurred, the survivor represses the feelings and memories of the abuse into his or her unconscious. Whenever these feelings or memories are triggered by a non-traumatic trigger event, the survivor will repeat whatever compulsive behavior soothed him or her originally. Although repression allows the survivor to put the original traumatic event in the past, according to Munson's model the original traumatic event still drives the survivor's behaviors. Behind all of the dynamics of Munson's model of the Repetition Compulsion Process is the idea of the Pleasure Principle. People will try to avoid pain, including emotional pain, in any way that they can. Whatever method of relief (the Pleasure Principle) helped to deal with the original trauma will be returned to repeatedly in an attempt to avoid the painful memories and feelings of the original trauma.

As Munson has mentioned in his theory, the therapist must offer the trauma survivor another model for dealing with the trauma. This is where I have found twelve-step groups offer their greatest promise. Twelve-step programs give survivors, whatever the compulsion or addictive behavior might be, a different way of looking at what they have been doing to kill their pain. Twelve-step programs ask survivors to refrain from the compulsive behavior long enough to feel the full effects of the original traumatic event and deal with those feelings without the anesthesia of whatever addictive/compulsive behavior the survivors may have employed in the past. This time, however, the survivors will not have to deal with the memories and feelings all alone. The survivors will have the support of the other members of the twelve-step group. All of the group's support and knowledge dealing with similar situations will be at the disposal of survivors who are fighting their addictive behaviors.

Munsons's model gives weight to the adage, "Those who forget the past are doomed to repeat it." How sad it is that survivors pay over and over again for their original sexual abuse experiences when all they are attempting to do is numb the pain. Survivors have told me about the addiction process in terms that make it appear as though two sides to the survivor actually exist.

> Chantal is a thirty-year-old survivor who talks about her bout with smoking crack cocaine as being the greatest battle that she has ever had with herself. Chantal actually refers to the addictive part of her as another person who fights her for control of her behaviors.

The addictive part of the person aligns with the negative behavior at the expense of the addict's self-esteem and sense of self. In other words, the potential to reach personal heights of accomplishment or development is sacrificed to the addiction. The true self (the part of the person who abhors the addiction process) sees what is happening with the addictive process but cannot gather the strength to stop the process. Imagine what it is like being held hostage to your own behaviors.

Nakken (1996) describes the addiction process in stages. Stage I occurs when the survivors surrender to the power of the addiction. They try to deal with their problems, but more often find themselves withdrawing from others and using lies and denial as tools with which to deal with their emotional pain. Each time they use the addictive substance or compulsive behavior they feel "less than," so they will feel justified in using again. The negative label that survivors receive for their negative behaviors gives them more leeway in their acting-out behaviors. The best description of this behavior can be summed up as, "If I have the name, I might as well have the game."

Nakken's Stage II involves the increased usage of the addict's delusional and defense systems. The addict becomes more skilled at manipulation and suffers an increased sense of isolation, withdrawal, and shame. This stage is when the idea of "willfulness" becomes very apparent. Addicts feel that they can refrain from the addiction or compulsion through simple willpower, without ever addressing the underlying causes for the behaviors. Because the addicts have developed an increased tolerance for the substance by this stage, their use will increase proportionately to the amount of anger, pain, and shame that they experience. At this stage, addicted survivors will act out more frequently and more intensely. This is the stage in which the addicted survivor begins to feel more different and separate from others. The survivors' own sense of values may have been compromised by their own behaviors or compulsive need to abuse.

Nakken's Stage III involves the phase of the addictive or compulsive process in which the survivors no longer find pleasure in their abusive behaviors. At this point, the survivors begin to realize that all of the drugs, alcohol, food, etc. in the world isn't going to fill the void that they feel inside because the emptiness is a *spiritual* emptiness. The survivors' behavior may become so labile that it is almost impossible to predict from moment to moment how they will act. Nakken refers to paranoia, free-floating anxiety, and a greater number of unresolved feelings occurring at this point. Because survivors feel that others can tell simply by looking at them the negative actions that the survivors have taken, the survivors isolate themselves even further. At this point, addicted survivors will use whatever means necessary to get others to comply with their desires. Although their negative behaviors may push others away from them at the same time, addicted survivors cling desperately to those closest to them. Suicidal ideation is not uncommon at this point. The emotional pain that survivors feel is so great that they may attempt to kill themselves simply to end the pain. The original momentary relief that the addictive or compulsive behavior provided is not seen for what it really is—only an empty promise.

Nakken states that addicts will remain in Stage III unless there is an intervention of some sort. Intervention occurs when addicts face something so threatening that they hit bottom. At least the *lucky* ones hit bottom; some survivors never live long enough to reach this point. All along this process are signs that the addicted survivors may relapse. Because the addicted survivors want immediate relief from the emotional pain, one of the first signs of relapse might be their sense of impatience. Everything takes too long because the addicted survivors want relief *now*. At this point, meetings for the addiction are not a priority. Addicted survivors cannot get over their sense of guilt and shame, which further perpetuates the addiction process. Addicted survivors push their own feelings and thoughts onto those closest to them and accuse others of doing what they themselves have considered doing or have already done. They are very sensitive to what they perceive others are saying, thinking, or doing. In reality, addicted survivors themselves have no real perception of what *anyone,* including themselves, is truly saying, thinking, or doing. The addiction or compulsion process is confusing; it interferes with survivors' perceptions so much that reality is only a hazy perception.

Ellen is a nineteen-year-old survivor who was raped by several neighborhood boys when she was eleven years old. Ellen never told anyone of the gang rape because the boys had threatened to kill her if she told. When Ellen was fourteen, she was already using drugs and alcohol to kill the painfulness of the memories of the gang rape. By the time she was seventeen, Ellen had such a bad drug and alcohol addiction that she had begun to prostitute herself in order to provide for her addictions. At nineteen, Ellen cannot stand the thought of trying to make it through the day without using. She begins the day with a couple of drinks and a marijuana joint. By noon, Ellen is so high that she barely can remember what day it is. Ellen's behaviors became so severe that she was brought into the local emergency room. She had been so badly beaten by a "john" that she had a broken nose and several cracked ribs. It became apparent that Ellen was not going to live much longer if something was not done about her addictions. Ellen was given the opportunity to go to the local rehab. The idea of going for help for her addictions really appealed to Ellen until the drugs and alcohol began to disappear from her system. The moment that Ellen began to feel the emotional pain resulting from a lifetime of abuse she demanded to be released from the rehab. It isn't that Ellen doesn't want to get clean and sober. It's just that addicts don't have much tolerance for pain—especially if it is pain that they are used to killing with substances and behaviors. If we add to this emotional pain all of the shame that addicts have for the behaviors that they have exhibited while they were under the influence, the result is that their first impulse is to get relief by using whatever substance or behavior they have used before to numb themselves. Ellen had no patience to try to delay her gratification from the drugs and alcohol and actually feel the pain of her feelings and memories. Until Ellen is able to hold off using her anesthesia and face her feelings, she is at constant risk for relapse.

Not all survivors are searching for the same things when they develop an addiction or a compulsion. Sometimes they will be searching for a way to control their environment. In this instance, survivors will see power as a form of security and control. The more power and control survivors have, the better they will feel about themselves and the more self-confidence they will have. For survivors who exhibit this sort of addiction, the trance state is a place of security and predictability. Usually these are the survivors who may have an underlying anxiety disorder. Perhaps they may have a genetic predisposition toward being obsessive-compulsive or bipolar. There usually appears to be some sort of correlation between the need for control and having been brought up in a chaotic background in this type of survivor. These survivors must always be right when they have a disagreement with someone; being wrong means being out of control. Being out of control means being vulnerable. Being vulnerable is so anxiety provoking that these survivors can't bear it. Power-seeking survivors are more apt to become predators putting their own feelings of inadequacy and anger onto others who then in turn become the power-seeking survivor's victims. Power-seeking survivors can be very difficult people to deal with. They cannot tolerate being wrong, tend to take control over any given situation, and can be very manipulative. The one characteristic that has a tendency to redeem this type of survivor is that they can be very productive in the workplace. Of course, the cost of this productivity is the pain that those under the power-seeking survivor's influence feel. According to Nakken (1996), this sort of addiction always leads to blaming others for the power-seeking survivor's mistakes. To accept the blame for their own choices or actions would again place the survivors in a position of vulnerability. This vulnerability would be too much for the power-seeking survivor's ego to tolerate. This type of personality very much resembles the dynamics that lead to one becoming a perpetrator. These survivors have anger resulting from their own abuse, which they in turn pass on to their own victims. The thought of being vulnerable again is the fear that drives these survivors' own abusive behaviors toward others.

Some survivors do not seek power as much as they look for pleasure. In fact, these survivors become addicted to the idea of pleasure. These survivors are more apt to lean toward active addictions. Their way of dealing with their abusive histories is to turn their heads to what has happened and deny the depth of pain that they have experienced. These are addicts in the true sense, in that they make their higher power an object outside of themselves. The result of this sort of search for power is always pain and sorrow, according to Nakken, because no one and nothing can fill the void inside of each one of us. We must fill the void ourselves by loving and valuing ourselves despite what those who were abusive to us might have told us.

> Lance is a twenty-eight-year-old survivor who seems to be fine after experiencing years of sexual abuse at the hands of his older brother. If asked about his abuse experiences, Lance will minimize the extent and harmfulness of the abuse. Lance has little family and desperately wants to keep the remaining family that he does have. He also has an eating disorder. At twenty-eight years old, Lance weighs almost 400 pounds. Although people often remark about what a nice person he is, Lance doesn't feel like anyone really knows or understands him. He is sure that if they knew the "real" Lance no one would want to be around him. Lance's perception of his own self-worth is based on the abuse that he suffered at his brother's hands. Lance simply does not want to take a chance on losing his brother's love, so he buries all of his feelings under a mountain of food. Lance has given all of his power over to his brother by making his relationship with his brother his "higher power."

Nakken (1996) talks about recovery from addictions and compulsions in terms of having faith in one's principles, powers of resurrection, rejuvenation, and resilience. Our sense of faith enables us to work toward an unknown ending still knowing that we will be able to handle whatever comes our way. Faith enables us not to run away from change like small children but to actively embrace change and to grow and evolve from it. Perhaps the hardest part of recovery for any addict is learning to live in the present moment. Because survivors come from such painful backgrounds, they are always looking for ways to avoid pain in their futures while at the same time trying to run from the pain in their pasts. It is only through the belief in a higher power that we can develop the necessary skills to accept what has happened in the past, know that we will be able to deal with whatever happens in the future, and be thankful for what we have in the present. I agree with Nakken (1996) when he says that we must constantly perform self-examination and self-inventory. This process will allow us to grow and learn from both the mistakes of others as well as the mistakes that we ourselves make. This is also the process of twelve-step recovery programs.

The main difference between addiction and compulsion is that compulsion is any sort of behavior that is reenacted in the same way repeatedly in an attempt to change the person's mood. The compulsive behavior is a reaction to something that is perceived as being very threatening to the person involved with the compulsive behavior, although what is really happening does not have to be threatening at all. It is the abusive or painful history of the person that is the driving force behind the compulsive behavior. In an attempt to survive the current situation and not to feel the trigger that the current pain is of the painful past, survivors will resort to compulsive behavior in an attempt to not focus on or to feel their pain. The compulsive behavior brings a sense of power, control, or security, which is really an illusion. Once the compulsion has served its purpose, the survivors are left wondering why they had to resort to the compulsive behavior. They will not see the painfulness of past emotions and events as the root of their current behaviors. In this way, compulsions and addictions are very similar.

According to Sandra Simpson LeSourd (1990) in *The Compulsive Woman,* survivors feel shame about themselves. Shame turns survivors away from others. Those who are shameful cannot talk about their shame, so they look for relief outside of themselves in the form of addictions or compulsions as a temporary way to alter their moods.

Since shame appears to be at the root of all addictions, and probably nothing is more shaming than sexual abuse, it is a wonder that all survivors don't have an addiction of some sort. Perhaps this is because some survivors have compulsive behaviors that are not as easily identified as being based in shame. Compulsive behaviors may be functional most of the time. LeSourd lists the following ways to identify compulsive behaviors:

- Is the behavior ritualized? In other words, must the behavior be done a certain way each time or the survivor becomes upset?
- Is time distorted while the activity is going on? Time distortion is a sign of trance. Trance indicates that the person is sort of on

"automatic pilot" and has no real conscious knowledge of what he or she is doing minute to minute.

- Does the survivor set rigid rules then go on to violate the rules? Most survivors who are addicted to drugs swear that they will never use again. It is easy to see that they mean what they are saying. Yet without going through treatment they are bound to use again.
- Does the survivor go to extremes such as overdoing or underdoing?

Ginger is a fourteen-year-old survivor who continually goes to extremes whenever she is complimented on something. If she gives her foster mother a gift and her foster mom tells Ginger how much she liked the gift, the next week she may give her foster mom ten more of the same gift.

Despite negative consequences, the survivor will continue with the compulsion. This example is easy to spot in anyone who has an addiction to drugs or to alcohol. Addicts know that the compulsive behavior is harming them, yet despite their most serious and sincere attempts to stop using, they can't seem to stop. Do triggers cause relapse into the compulsive behavior? Relapse is a sure sign that the behavior is a compulsion. It also indicates that the behavior is serving a purpose greater than what the behavior is intended to serve. Many times compulsive behavior will result in such guilt that the survivor will use an additional compulsive behavior to help deal with the guilt from the first compulsive behavior.

Kay is a forty-five-year-old incest survivor who has a problem with compulsive overeating. Over the years, Kay has attempted diet after diet in an attempt to lose the extra 100-plus pounds that she carries on her five-foot-two-inch frame. Each time that Kay attempts to lose weight, she will manage to refrain from overeating for about a week and then will relapse, unless she begins to smoke when she begins to diet. Recently, Kay has begun to wonder which addiction is worse—smoking or overeating. Both addictions are scorned by society. Kay believes that the results of overeating may be more detrimental, since others can see when she is overweight but they can't see the results from her smoking. As long as Kay is careful not to smoke when she is around others, chances are that she will be able to keep her

weight down with smoking for a long time before the negative
health effects of the smoking become apparent to others.

What a sad commentary on how addicts view their self-worth! Rather
than face the criticism of society, addicts would prefer to risk their
health and safety to conform to society's standards of beauty!

LeSourd (1990) estimates that about 70 percent of women at treatment centers for substance abuse are survivors of sexual abuse.
LeSourd estimates that 45,000 to 500,000 incidents of sexual abuse
take place each year and that 50 percent of survivors are sexually
abused by their own families. The high number of women at treatment centers who have been sexually abused is not surprising. We
may never get an accurate count of the number of people who have
been sexually abused because our society places such a stigma on
sexual abuse. Victims of sexual abuse are afraid to talk about the
abuse first because they have experienced the sexual abuse itself, then
they fear that they will be ostracized and blamed if they tell of their
abuse. Many times the survivor is blamed for the abuse and singled
out as being "different."

In their book, *Surviving the Secret,* psychologists Pamela
Vredevelt and Kathryn Rodriguez (1992) list the traits of survivors of
sexual abuse. Survivors will maximize the abilities of others and minimize their own abilities. Survivors will take responsibility for others'
behaviors. Survivors have difficulty being intimate with others and
think that they will gain perfection if they please others. Survivors
worry constantly about problems and sabotage their own efforts to
change.

There is even a difference in the way that one describes the sense of
urgency between the words compulsion and addiction. When describing their addiction to a substance, addicts use phrases such as "I
almost always use when I" or "I usually use this way." In other words,
addiction usually involves a pattern of usage over a period of time. If
addicts will do whatever is necessary to break the addiction initially,
they will not need to have a knowledge of the underlying dynamics of
the cause of the addiction.

Compulsive behaviors involve a reduction in tension that is in *itself*
a reward for the compulsive behavior. The reduction in the tension resulting from uncomfortable feelings is also what will reinforce the
compulsion. Usually the person exhibiting the compulsive behavior
will set up a ritualized manner in which the compulsion is done each

time. It is much more difficult to try to stop compulsive behaviors because they become such an ingrained part of the survivors' behaviors.

Cathy and Susan are two survivors who demonstrate both addictive and compulsive behaviors.

Cathy was sexually abused when she was five years old by her maternal uncle. As Cathy grew older, she tried to tell her mother and father about the abuse, but her parents were so involved with their own addictions to alcohol and drugs that they paid no attention to Cathy. When Cathy was younger, she swore that she would never use drugs or alcohol, but by the time she was fifteen, Cathy was drinking on a regular basis. At sixteen, Cathy was smoking marijuana every morning before school. Whenever I would attempt to get Cathy to face her addictions, she would tell me that she always smoked pot before school because pot helped her to concentrate. If Cathy would attempt to work on the sexual abuse issues, she would usually drink that same night to help deal with the memories and feelings associated with the abuse.

Susan was molested by her older brother from when she was four years old until she was nine. Susan once attempted to tell her mother about the abuse, but her brother caught her before she was able to finish telling her story. Later on, Susan became so fearful of her brother that she recanted the little that she had told and never attempted to tell the story again. Her mother believed that Susan had simply attempted to get her older brother in trouble because he had baby-sat Susan and not allowed her to stay up as late as she had wanted. Susan's method of dealing with the unpleasant memories and emotions surrounding her abuse issues was to constantly "check" things. At first, Susan couldn't leave for school until all of her belongings in her room were "placed the right way." Making sure that things were the "right way" could take an hour or so initially. Later on, Susan would spend several hours making sure that all of her hairbrushes and combs were perfectly lined up and all of the light switches were off. Susan exhibited obsessive-compulsive disorder that appeared to be aggravated by the abuse issues. The compulsive behaviors took the focus off of Susan's real underlying issues, which she found too difficult to deal with.

Addiction may vary according to whatever behavior or substance is abused, but the underlying dynamics and progression of the addiction are almost always the same. Once the addict's attention is drawn toward the addicted substance or behavior, very little will detract the addict until he or she has followed through with the addicted or compulsive behavior. Once the addiction progresses and the trance state has ended, the addict must again return to thoughts of his or her original pain plus the additional shame resulting from the addicted or compulsive behaviors.

Nicole is a good example of an addict who has most of the characteristics seen in addicted persons.

> Nicole was sexually abused by her father and her oldest brother all through her childhood and early adolescence. Nicole's role in the family was to be the "little mother." Nicole was never allowed to express her feelings about the abuse or the role that she was expected to play as parent to her own mother. The anger boiled under the surface for all of the years that Nicole was sexually abused. When Nicole turned sixteen, she began to hang around with a rough crowd who drank and used drugs on a regular basis. Before long, Nicole was using drugs and drinking with the rest of her friends. When Nicole got older, she met a man who seemed nice enough but was really much like her father and brother. Nicole didn't realize it, but she had picked a partner who was going to help her work through her childhood issues.
>
> Although Nicole swore to herself that she wouldn't drink when she became pregnant, she continued to drink along with all of her friends. The guilt and shame that Nicole would feel after each drinking bout served only to increase her need to drink because the feelings of shame and guilt would trigger Nicole's underlying core beliefs that she was somehow defective or inadequate. Nicole would attempt to minimize how serious her drinking had become. She would rationalize her behavior by telling herself that she had had a rough day and deserved a little fun. It didn't take long until Nicole was drunk more often than she was sober. Nicole's attempts to try to change her behaviors didn't work because she needed the security and structure that the behaviors provided. Without these behaviors, Nicole would have to address the emptiness and pain that she felt from never having been loved or nurtured as a child. It was only when Nicole's baby was born with fetal alcohol syndrome that Nicole

was forced to address her addiction and the events that had caused her to reach this point in her addiction.

One of the key factors of addiction or compulsion is the trance state. Whenever most people think of being in a trance state, the first thing that comes to their minds is the stage hypnotist with his subject who will enter into a very deep trance and will do whatever the hypnotist asks. In reality, most people go about their normal everyday lives and engage in a trance state on a fairly regular basis. If you have ever been so engaged in a book or a television program that you weren't aware that someone was calling your name, you have been in a trance state. A trance state is nothing more than a shift in one's focus. The shift in focus is so intense that it blocks out surrounding stimuli that would make the subjects aware of their immediate surroundings.

Iris is a fifteen-year-old member of the adolescent sexual abuse survivors' group. Iris has had an ongoing battle with explosive behaviors and eating disorders for at least the past five years. Iris has recently lost about fifty pounds. As Iris tells the group about the benefits of her recent weight loss, it becomes apparent how totally involved Iris is with her efforts to control her weight.

Iris's facial expression becomes one of intense concentration as she details for the group the various types of diets that she has used in an attempt to lose weight. As Iris details the benefits of her decreased weight, one can see the state of "bliss" that Iris has achieved. Iris is not aware of how quiet the group has become or how concerned they appear to be about her rapid and dramatic weight loss. Iris is so involved with her "addiction" to controlling her weight that she is not able to process outside stimuli. All of Iris's mental processes are fixated internally. Iris is not able to interact with the other group members at this point in any other way than to focus on telling her tales of food intake and weight loss.

Iris's addiction has shifted several times since she has been in group. Initially when Iris came into treatment she was exhibiting such uncontrolled anger and physical rage that she could not attend a regular classroom at her school. Iris had to be placed in an intensive learning center where she would receive constant one-to-one supervision and behavior modification. Iris's addiction to aggression and rage cost her in her relationships with her family and peers and also in her academic life.

Once Iris was able to get her anger and aggression under control, she quickly began to gain weight. Adolescent girls fear one thing more than almost any other thing in their lives: being called "fat." Iris was no exception. Soon, Iris was dieting in earnest. Iris would count the calories in every morsel that passed through her lips. A daily log was begun of everything that Iris ate. Every calorie and fat gram was recorded. Iris refused to talk or think about anything that did not pertain to food or dieting. As the weight quickly began to drop, so did Iris's grades. Although Iris was too closely involved to notice the strangeness of her behaviors, the group was sitting and watching the behaviors and worrying what would become of Iris. Iris has managed to acknowledge that she does indeed have an eating disorder but so far has not been able to successfully stop her compulsion to diet. The best that we can hope for at this point is to keep Iris's weight within a safe range so that her body can function properly. Even attempting to do this much is going to be an uphill fight. Although Iris says that she wants to get well, she will still do her very best to sabotage our attempts at maintaining her weight at a safe level.

Trance state occurs quite often in our everyday lives. I travel through a small town every day on my way to work. I have traveled so many times through this small town that I now have no conscious daily memory of having gone through the town, although I know that I *had* to go through the town to arrive at work. I have driven through this town so often that I can shift my focus of attention somewhere else, yet still safely drive through the town. It is as if I am on "automatic pilot" and don't need my conscious attention to be able to drive.

Hypnosis has the reputation of being mysterious and strange, yet in reality numerous times throughout the day we experience the state of hypnosis. Various levels of hypnosis exist, just as various levels of concentration and focus exist. The lightest state of hypnosis might be experienced when we get engrossed in a television show. The more intense our involvement in an event or activity, the greater our shift of focus and attention. The greater the focus, the more intense our ability to be hypnotized.

Self-hypnosis occurs when a person is able to focus intently in a self-directed manner on whatever it is they want to work. People in a trance state may look and act as if they are perfectly normal, but their attention is focused on something other than that upon which they appear to be focused. Trance state is not a form of sleep but a form of intense concentration with a very defined focus of attention.

> Wanda is an adult survivor who was raped by her two older brothers when she was in her early teens. Wanda weighs over 200 pounds and is only five feet tall. If you were to ask Wanda how she deals with her sexual abuse, she would say that the abuse is all behind her. Watching intently while talking to Wanda about her abuse, what one would notice is how as Wanda is questioned more intently about her abuse she begins to snack on all of the food that she has in her home. Wanda consumes vast amounts of food without even realizing it. Any time that something becomes too frightening for her, she immediately reaches for something to eat. It doesn't matter so much what she eats, as Wanda will eat almost anything. Food is Wanda's defense against the unwelcome feelings that talking about her abusive past brings. By focusing on eating, Wanda is able to place her attention elsewhere.

Why is the trance state a comfort? When survivors are in a trance state, they are more relaxed because they are focusing on the things with which they *are* comfortable dealing. They are able to maximize their energy level because they do not feel drained by uncomfortable emotions. Because survivors have a lack of self-esteem, they have difficulty dealing with their core issues. Survivors have fears and negative feelings surrounding their abuse histories as well as their own sense of self-perceptions. It is no wonder that any behavior that offers even the briefest of respite is welcome. In the trance state, survivors are able to disregard the outside stimuli that may be uncomfortable. Trance is a very common phenomenon. When we read a book, we can turn paper and print into a three-dimensional world that at least for that moment appears to be real. When we are daydreaming, we can turn our thoughts and fantasies into what can become as real as our everyday surroundings. When we think back, our memories feel as if they are presently occurring. All of these are examples of trance state.

I am always interested in which activity survivors will select to help them deal with their abusive pasts. It is usually apparent if the survivors are compulsive overeaters or binge eaters simply by their weight. The younger survivors are also sometimes more apt to openly display the sexual behaviors they employ to use seduction as a way to focus their attention away from their more painful issues.

> Dollie is an eighteen-year-old incest survivor who is constantly focused on her appearance. Dollie will wear the shortest of skirts and the tightest of blouses. All of Dollie's shoes are the highest of high heels. Dollie's walk is "poetry in motion" with her hips swaying rhythmically. Hours are spent grooming and applying makeup, all in an attempt to draw attention to her sexual attributes. Ask Dollie if she ever thinks of her incest history and chances are that she will tell you that she's already dealt with that experience. Take away Dollie's focus on her appearance and Dollie will quickly begin to look for another way to shift her focus of attention away from any reminder of her abusive past.

I believe that trance state can sometimes also be a healing mechanism for survivors. Trance state allows survivors to deal with their conscious memories of the abuse while they are developing the survival skills necessary to deal with the memories that they may have repressed because they were too traumatic to deal with initially. Trance state allows survivors to delve more deeply into that place where their genuine feelings and memories are stored. Survivors are masters at repressing their genuine feelings so that they will be accepted into the situation where the abuse has occurred. As time passes, survivors become so good at repressing their true feelings that soon they no longer are aware what their true feelings are. When survivors are engaged in an addictive or compulsive behavior and are engaged in the trance state, deeper more authentic feelings begin to emerge which allow them to recover pieces of memories and feelings that in their entirety may be too threatening to deal with. If survivors were to go one step farther and engage in hypnotherapy, they could use the process of hypnosis not only to recover and deal with their most painful feelings and memories, but also to insert positive and more healthy coping skills for future situations.

Within each person's life are an unlimited number of responses that he or she may have to whatever choices are presented. Whenever the person begins to return to the same set of responses over and over again, despite the other variety of available choices, this is called "looping." Whenever looping involves a response choice that is pathological with a negative quality-of-life choice response, the person has become addicted or has developed compulsive behaviors. When in the trance state of addiction, the person will choose among a consistently more constricted and narrow band of available choices.

As time progresses and the person becomes more fixated in the narrow band of choices, the trance state becomes stronger and stronger. Society often reinforces the addictions that first appear as simply being "choices." Watching television is a very good example of the trance state. As time spent viewing television becomes more and more lengthy, it has not been unusual to see the average American spend five to six hours per day in front of the television. No one stops to think that turning on the television whenever someone is bored, lonely, or depressed is an addiction. We simply think of this as being a choice. But if every time individuals are bored, lonely, or depressed they turn on the television, is that not really a looping behavior that could be defined as an addiction? Viewing television for extended periods of time can be innocuous when compared to other more dangerous addictions. Whenever one tries to undo this sort of looping behavior, one must face the painful consequences of confusion and facing the original pain of why one used the looping behavior to begin with (remember the original example of being lonely, bored, or depressed). How many of us are willing to venture into such painful consequences willingly? That is why addictions are often faced only when they become so costly and painful that we *must* acknowledge them and deal with changing the addictive and compulsive behaviors. Since addictive or compulsive behaviors usually give immediate gratification, it is even more difficult to withstand the necessary delay of gratification that breaking the addiction or compulsion requires. For someone who is under severe emotional stress, the structure and familiarity of choosing the same response each time a similar problem arises provides a sense of comfort and predictability. As we continue to choose the same response over and over again, we are making the response our "higher power." The response begins to take on a significance much larger than what it can actually provide in real life. To addicts the narrowed response *is* the answer for which they have been looking.

The switching of addictions can initially be seen as the answer to addiction. If one ceases to be addicted to cigarettes and begins to eat hard candy in an attempt to stop smoking, this would be seen as an improvement. What is not so obvious is that the addict is simply switching among a spectrum of choices and is choosing another addictive behavior in place of the tobacco.

Many of the adolescent survivors' group members smoke cigarettes. It is not unusual to see these young group members become very agitated whenever the group discusses intense and painful issues relating to their abuse. Without fail, one group member after another will say that he or she needs a cigarette. In their minds, the time spent outside of the group smoking with their peers has become a time to try to recover from their painful issues and relax with a cigarette. Smoking has become paired with releasing anxiety. Smoking helps these survivors take the focus off their underlying abuse-related issues. Although I desperately want them to quit smoking, I realize that the reality of the situation is that most of them will continue to smoke well into adulthood. Because most of the survivors come from families where both parents smoke (the parents probably began to smoke for many of the same reasons that these young survivors also began smoking), cigarettes were readily available at the time that these young survivors were most vulnerable.

Until the underlying issues of the survivors' addiction(s) are fully addressed, it is likely that survivors may switch from addiction to addiction without ever truly realizing the reason for their addictive behaviors. Given the possibility that one addiction may appear to be more socially acceptable than another, it is possible that addicts could continue to switch among an entire array of addictions and believe that they are healing from their past addictions when they have simply moved on to a new and more socially acceptable addiction. Sarah is an example of such a survivor.

> Sarah is a forty-year-old survivor who was molested by her biological father from the time that she was old enough to remember until she was in her early teens. Sarah developed an eating disorder while in her early teens—compulsive overeating. All of her adult life, Sarah had been grossly overweight. When she was thirty-nine years old, Sarah was able to employ the use of a new weight reduction medication that really did make it easier for Sarah to stick to her weight-loss regimen. At the same time that Sarah had begun to seriously commit to the weight-loss program, Sarah met a new man at her place of employment. As her relationship with the man progressed, Sarah's weight dropped

in direct proportion to her involvement with the man. When her weight had dropped almost to the point of being her ideal weight, the relationship ended with the man. Immediately, Sarah began to regain weight. Sarah had used the addiction to the man, codependency, in place of excess food to take the focus off of her own issues. It is only when Sarah is able to directly confront her issues and keep them in the forefront that Sarah will be able to deal with her feelings without using addictions as a way to deal with her feelings.

How does one know what a truly "nonaddicted" person looks like? Is there really such a thing as *not* having any addiction at all? Can one become addicted to the idea or concept of *not* having an addiction? All of these questions are difficult to answer because it is not known if such a thing as a nonaddictive personality exists.

Deep focus in certain situations (trance state) is often rewarded in our society. For instance, suppose that a survivor is a workaholic. Workaholics will receive all sorts of kudos from their employers for going above and beyond the call of duty. Yet there is a price to pay for such skewed behaviors. Usually, survivors' personal relationships will suffer. Although their place of employment will reap the rewards of their "dedication" (which is really addiction), the survivors will suffer. It is in the employer's best interests to encourage such sort of overzealousness with rewards such as praise or financial reimbursement. Seldom does the employer worry about the employees' welfare.

When we are in a trance state, we are not usually aware that a trance is the dynamic that lies beneath our behavior, especially if the trance is pathological. It is being unaware of what lies beneath our pathological behaviors that is far more insidious than the behaviors that may be negative of which we *are* aware. At least if we are consciously aware of our negative behaviors we have some sort of choice over whether we will continue with them.

How does one reverse the process of a trance state? For example, suppose that a survivor has an eating disorder. Whenever the survivor begins to feel sad or lonely, he or she begins to reach for the candy that is always kept beside a favorite chair in the living room. By simply removing the candy dish from the living room, the survivor has made at least one small difference in the "looping" process. Once one small change has been made, the survivor might make additional changes to reinforce the benefits of the first change. For example, the survivor might begin to identify what it "feels like" to be depressed. The survivor might begin by identifying what the physical signs of depression involve, such as wanting to cry, wanting to be alone, and a sense of emptiness in the stomach. When the survivor begins to notice these feelings, he or she might deliberately choose to remain with supportive others and make an attempt to act "as if" he or she were happy instead of feeling sad. By changing this loop in the trance pattern, the survivor may have taken the necessary steps to stop the addictive behavior(s).

People can be in a trance state and not even be aware that they are in a trance. If we view trance as the movies would have us view it, we would look so bizarre and act so unlike ourselves that it would immediately be noticeable that we are under some "spell." In reality, trance is very subtle and can go unnoticed by both the observer and the one who is in the trance. Many therapists believe that a trance state is much like what happens when a person dissociates. Simply from working with many clients who are able to dissociate I have observed that the most common symptoms of trance include fixed attention, a change in body awareness, the inability to accurately recall what has happened or how much time has passed, an increased focus and attention on what is occurring inside of the survivor, and a slowing down of the survivor's willingness to comply with requests made of him or her. To the parents of many survivors it appears that the child is being disobedient when they first begin to dissociate. The parent will tell the child to do something and the child will either be very slow to comply with the parent's request or will not comply at all. The child may hear what the parent is saying, but the child's attention is so fixed somewhere else that the effort is simply too great for the child to gather enough energy to comply with the parent's requests. Sometimes the child does not even hear the parent make the request. During dissociation, the survivor's sense of reality is very disrupted. The survivor may have problems distinguishing between what is real and what is not real. Sometimes the survivor will suffer from visual or auditory hallucinations. Ellen is one such survivor.

Ellen was molested by her father for most of her childhood. The sexual abuse was so traumatic that Ellen learned how to dissociate by age eight. There was a painting on Ellen's bedroom wall of a beautiful horse in a woods with a pond nearby. Whenever

Ellen could not endure the sexual abuse any longer, she would be able to "go into" the painting and join the horse. Ellen could feel the cool water in the pond. She could smell the pine trees and feel the horse's coarse coat beneath her skin. Ellen's sense of reality was so disturbed that she was not even able to feel or remember her father's assaults. As Ellen grew older, she had less and less need to dissociate because she was able to defend herself against her father's abuse. The dissociation became an unwelcome intrusion in Ellen's life, yet she was not able to do away with it completely. Whenever anything reminded Ellen in the slightest of father's abusive behaviors, Ellen would immediately begin to shift her focus of attention and begin to dissociate.

Being in a trance state allows us to conserve our energy for situations that require our complete attention. It would be impossible to learn complex new skills unless we were very attentive and aware of what we were doing. If every task that we undertook required that much attention and energy, we would have nothing left over for those more simple tasks such as driving the car or watching television.

Although many survivors do not know that they are in a trance state, they are often aware that something "different" is about to happen to them. Survivors will find that they begin to do things that they may not set out to do but for some reason they can't refrain from doing. The survivor may become more and more internally aware and focused. The survivor may have difficulty making a decision or thinking of other options. Survivors may find themselves daydreaming or not paying attention to what is going on around them. Repeated thoughts or words may go round and round in the survivor's head. Sometimes survivors will keep seeing the same experience over and over again. Pat is one such survivor.

Although Pat's sexual abuse happened over twenty years ago, she still needs to dissociate whenever she smells the odor of Old Spice cologne for men. Pat's father wore Old Spice cologne when he molested Pat when she was only five years old. Although Pat's father has been dead for six years, Pat still thinks that she can hear his voice calling her upstairs to his bedroom. Whenever Pat thinks that she hears his voice she will begin to turn inward. Her movements will become much slower and cumbersome. Although it is clear to others that Pat is not herself, it is not so strange or noticeable that others would think that she was in need of medical care. At times like these Pat just seems a little "preoccupied." The major part of Pat's attention is focused on what is going on inside of her. Pat can function and pay attention to what she absolutely must do, but she is much slower and deliberate with her physical movements. Facial expressions and Pat's affect appear to be flat and blunted. Time becomes distorted. What is actually hours may seem like minutes to Pat.

Trance state has an additional seduction in that the trance state itself often offers a sort of reward. When one reinforces certain behaviors, it doesn't take long before one begins to associate a certain response teamed with a certain behavior. For example, if every time that you feel nervous you immediately smoke a cigarette, it won't be long until you begin to associate cigarette smoking with relaxation. If we think of addiction as a sort of behavior in which the person engaging in the addiction has chosen the addiction from a list of what he or she considers limited options, we can better begin to understand the dynamics of addiction. To first understand the dynamics that underlie addiction and pathological trance, we must first suspend character judgment and labeling.

Kendra is a fifteen-year-old survivor who was molested by her biological father and several of her older brother's friends. For most of her adolescence, Kendra has been in foster care. In order to deal with such intense emotional pain, Kendra has thought of only two possible options. She can become so depressed that she attempts suicide, or she can become so angry that she becomes homicidal. Whenever she feels the stress begin to build, Kendra knows that she will either harm herself or attempt to harm someone else. Kendra has become addicted to violence as a way of dealing with her internal feelings. Kendra has chosen violence as a way to deal with her feelings instead of addressing her feelings and realizing that just because she has been hurt that does not mean that hurting herself or hurting others will rectify the situation. Kendra has unlimited options as a way of addressing her issues. She could learn from what she has experienced and choose to work against violence. She could address her innermost feelings and use her experiences to help others. The list of options is limitless, but because Kendra sees only violence as the answer she has become fixated on violence either toward herself or toward others. The reward at the end of the addictive behavior is the distancing that Kendra feels from her most painful feelings and memories.

How does one go about changing pathological trance and addiction? Focusing solely on the negative addictive behavior or making character judgments is not the answer. The answer is in adding to the possible choices from which the addict may choose. The more choices that addicts begin to see in the behaviors from which they may chose, the greater the likelihood that the addicts may chose another behavior that is more healthy or productive.

If addicts focus solely on the addictive behavior, they are not able to *see* the other options that they have. This is why diets do not work. By focusing only on the behaviors of not eating certain foods and restricting what are considered unacceptable foods, compulsive overeaters immediately want what they are not allowed to have. By allowing overeaters to have anything that they want *in moderation,* the addicts are then allowed to choose between many options. Most likely overeaters will quickly tire of those foods that are unhealthy and will begin to establish balance in their eating habits.

If drug or alcohol addicts are made aware of the many choices that they have available, they may then begin to address their addictions. The choices could include continuing to abuse whatever substance they are abusing and suffer the consequences; to begin to address their issues and to feel the emotional pain that the addiction has numbed; to deny that they even have a problem while their lives are falling apart; to shift the addiction to another addictive behavior; or to substitute another behavior that is more healthy or rewarding than the negative addictive behavior. The list of choices could go on and on. At a more concrete level, addicts could make choices right at the moment that they begin to use whatever it is that they abuse. The addicts might decide simply to wait ten minutes to see if they still want to use. They could call their sponsor instead of using. They could exercise or go visit someone instead of using. In other words, they could interrupt the addiction cycle and trance state if only just momentarily. Interrupting the trance state, even if only briefly, reinforces not abusing whatever substance or behavior the addict abuses. Trance state has much to do with the lack of balance in people's lives. A workaholic is an example of someone who is using the trance state to facilitate what may be difficult and tedious work to escape from unpleasant and painful inner feelings. Without the use of the trance state, the worka-holic might find the work unpleasant and unrewarding. When the work addiction is used to take the focus off of something else that is even more unpleasant or difficult to deal with, the addict may not find the work unpleasant or difficult at all. While working the addict will not apply full attention to work. The addict is better able to dream about pleasant things when not focusing on more painful issues. The secondary gain from promotions and financial rewards only serves to reinforce the work addiction. The dynamics of workaholism apply just as much to all of the other forms of addiction. All one needs to do to understand a particular addiction is to substitute whatever the par-ticular addiction is for the word *workaholism*.

Trance state is clearly evident in codependent-like behaviors. The codependent often does not remember the extent of the emotional pain suffered while involved in the codependent relationship. The survivor will only ruminate about the good qualities of the relation-ship and the feelings of intense euphoria whenever the codependent relationship is threatened.

Trance state can also serve a very beneficial purpose, such as in ex-amples of sexual abuse. While a child is being sexually abused, in-tense trauma is involved. Trance state allows the child to endure the abuse without losing the ability to still function in the everyday world. Although the victims may remember the abuse, they are some-what able to distance themselves from the full emotional impact of the abuse because of the trance-like state they enter while the abuse is taking place.

The following chapter considers the impact that the survivor's family of origin has on the survivor and the survivor's predisposition toward addictive or compulsive behaviors.

Chapter 3

Family-of-Origin Issues: How the Stage Is Set for Addictions and Compulsions

Science has established two facts meaningful for human welfare: first the foundation of the structure of human personality is laid down in early childhood: and second the chief engineer in charge of this construction is the family.

Meyer Francis Nimkoff

One of the most interesting things that almost all of the survivors I have worked with have in common is the similarity of their family-of-origin issues. In almost every instance, the survivors' family of origin had some sort of dysfunction besides the sexual abuse.

In many of the families in my caseload, substance abuse of some sort exists. The most common type of substance abuse involves alcohol, although other drugs, particularly cocaine, are becoming almost as frequently used as alcohol. In the families in which this type of addiction occurs, the most obvious result is the strained relationship between the marital partners. A more silent victim, though, is the child raised in such a family who develops low self-esteem. The child sees few options in life, and feels that the dysfunctional situation in which the family finds itself is the situation in which the child is also destined to become involved. The child learns that part of life involves taking care of others at one's own expense. Oftentimes the child will see the adults in his or her life deny the obvious. For example, if the child's father is passed out and intoxicated behind the wheel of the family car in the driveway, the child's mother will say, "Daddy is just too tired from working for us." Children are very intuitive; they know when someone is drunk. The enabling parent is urging the child to

deny the child's own sense of reality. This kind of denial and minimization will follow the child into adulthood and help to perpetuate
the cycle of dysfunction.

> When Cheri was five years old, her father tried to molest her.
> Immediately Cheri tried to tell her mother what had happened.
> Her father had had a problem with drugs and alcohol for all of
> Cheri's young life. The long-suffering mother would clean up
> the father's messes and make excuses for all of his abusive
> ways. Her mother told Cheri, "Your daddy was only trying to
> show you how much he loves you. How can you make it seem
> like something so dirty?" Cheri learned very quickly that her
> mother would not tolerate anything that would force her to deal
> with their home situation in a more realistic manner. Cheri
> learned to try to avoid her father's attempts to touch Cheri inap-
> propriately. Cheri also learned to keep negative things to herself.
> In Cheri's family, everything appears to be normal and happy to
> those outside of the family. Cheri fears that if she tells others
> what is really happening she will be cut off from the rest of the
> family. The worst part of this situation is that although Cheri
> says she hates her father and his abusive ways, at fifteen she is
> dating a much older man who is very much like her father. An
> entire new generation of children may suffer because Cheri will
> be so accustomed to abuse that she will be drawn to the familiar-
> ity of abusiveness.

Sometimes the children in families where addictions or compulsions are happening face denial on so many fronts that the children
are eventually "worn down" from trying to decide what is their own
sense of reality and what is the family's version of reality. Many
times in families such as this the children will align with the abusive
parent, often in an unconscious attempt to restore some of the children's own sense of power. Brenda is a good example of a teenager
who has simply decided that if you can't change things, maybe it is
better just to join in with what is happening because it is inevitable.

> Brenda is seventeen. She was molested by her father from the
> time that she was five years old until she was thirteen. At thir-
> teen, Brenda told her father that if he ever touched her again she
> would kill him. Although her father was high most of the time
> from using cocaine or heroin, he had enough sense to realize

that Brenda meant what she said. At sixteen, Brenda had a baby fathered by her boyfriend. She thought that the baby would be someone to love her and someone who she could love. It did not take long for Brenda to realize that babies do not give much love back when they are young—instead, babies take and take. When Brenda's boyfriend heard Brenda's demands that he get a job and help take care of her and the baby, he quickly left. Brenda was faced with the abusive life that she had always known, only now she had an infant for whom she had to provide. While her friends were out dating and having fun, Brenda was changing diapers and trying to ward off memories of her father's abusiveness. At seventeen, Brenda began to join her father in getting high. Brenda has given up hope. Because of her low self-esteem and the family's sense of denial, Brenda has become extremely loyal to her family of origin. This loyalty is an attempt to have someone who at least will love Brenda and care for her. What a cost she is paying for what she mistakenly perceives as love. What kind of example is Brenda's family giving to Brenda's child?

Sometimes the fear of change is so great for survivors that, in an attempt to provide predictability and stability, some survivors will limit their own opportunities and chances to experience the richness that life has to offer.

Dee is a forty-year-old survivor who has become so restricted by her fear of revictimization that she refuses to venture out of the small backwater town in which she was born and raised. Although Dee is very intelligent and has unlimited potential, she is too afraid of leaving her hometown to pursue her ability to draw and sculpt. Dee has become addicted to rigid structure and safety in her life. Rather than try to spread her wings and grow, Dee would rather feed her addiction for familiarity and predictability.

Dee's addiction to familiarity is rewarded by her family, who sees the self-sacrificing behaviors as Dee being "a woman who puts her family first." No one acknowledges how Dee's inability to leave her hometown is costing her lost potential. The family rewards Dee for never marrying or having children. Dee is the only one who will care for her parents in their old age and illness. Dee enjoys the compliments that she receives for being available to care for her aging relatives. Neither Dee nor her relatives acknowledge that Dee's present behaviors will cost Dee dearly when she grows older. Acknowledging the cost of Dee's present choices would possibly upset the status quo from which Dee's other family members are benefiting. What is ironic is that when Dee was molested by her older brother when she was a child, no one did anything about it. They all accused Dee of "making up" the story. Dee quickly learned that in her family the squeaking wheel did not get the grease. Dee's family values compliance above all else. The family is so enmeshed that trying to stand up for oneself would be viewed as being disloyal.

Family-of-origin issues can become patterns and can be traced back generations in families in which sexual abuse or incest has taken place. In families in which abuse has occurred (not only sexual abuse), certain shared characteristics are evident. The family will almost always have a lowered sense of self-esteem.

Connie's family had seen at least three generations of physical, verbal, and emotional abuse when Connie came into treatment for incest committed by her biological father. Not only was Connie ashamed of the incest and the resulting breakup of her family, but she was also ashamed of the fact that her family wasn't as organized and functional as the families of her peers. The family members' needs were not being met in a consistent and meaningful way. Connie's family did not have the economic resources of those of her friends' families. She always felt that she and her family were "less than" others. The more Connie observed that her family was different from others, the more intense the need Connie felt to deny her observation. Connie's denial was a form of both self-protection and protection for her family.

In families in which sexual abuse has occurred, especially incest, the family will usually have fewer options and choices than in other families. Part of what causes this stems from the dysfunction and chaos within the family. Families that are not functioning well cannot offer optimal support and guidance to the family's children. The adolescent group itself has demonstrated this scenario quite frequently. When discussing what career choices they have available, the group members always limit themselves to employment such as exotic dancing, stripping, or prostitution. Because of the lowered self-esteem, family-of-origin issues often lead to survivors not taking proper care of themselves or not protecting themselves. Barbara is a good example of a survivor who has low self-esteem resulting from the abuse she suffered when she was raped at thirteen. She does not even bother to use condoms when she has sex with men who she only vaguely knows. Barbara's rape was so brutal and she felt such a sense of shame afterward that she never told anyone about the incident. Barbara's family did not know about the rape, but they did notice her use of drugs and alcohol and later on her prostitution.

Many survivors suffer from clinical depression. This is a direct result of belonging to a family that already possesses the dynamics which will lead to incest or other abuse.

> LeeAnn came from a family with a history of role reversal as a way of life. Generation after generation of parents in LeeAnn's family did not get the nurturing or guidance that they needed as children. Because their own needs were not met, the parents could not meet the needs of their children. The parents would then in turn "feed" upon their children. The children never had the opportunity to have a childhood. What is the cost of such dependency? One result is children become clinically depressed and may stay depressed for most of their lives. LeeAnn was such a child. Because LeeAnn could not get the nurturing she needed so much from her parents, she began to turn to food as a way to nurture herself. As LeeAnn entered adolescence, she had the makings of a severe weight problem. Instead of trying to understand the underlying causes of LeeAnn's weight gain, her family would constantly find fault with LeeAnn. LeeAnn never confronted her family with the fact that her father had been sexually abusing her since she was a young child. LeeAnn was trying so hard to placate her family that she was sacrificing her own welfare. In order to keep her family safe from the knowledge of the incest, LeeAnn consumed huge amounts of food. The food was much like a drug would be to a drug addict. Whenever LeeAnn was full from overeating, she would shift her mood from one of melancholy to one in which she would be satiated and sleepy. Heroin users will often demonstrate this sleepiness after they have just had a fix.

Extreme codependency finds its roots in family-of-origin issues that require the survivors to put the family's needs before their own. To be born into such a family means that survivors never have an authentic identity of their own. They must spend their lives being what the family needs to maintain homeostasis. What is the cost of such a denial of identity? Loss of self and the potential of what the survivors could have been is the result of such a deep-seated need to please in order to avoid abandonment. This is what codependency is all about: the loss of self in order to prevent abandonment.

Bill is a seventeen-year-old survivor who will do almost anything that someone requests of him. Bill is kind beyond belief. The only person that Bill will not take care of is himself. He has managed to be so out of touch with his own feelings that he doesn't even sense when he needs something or when something causes feelings to arise in him. Any sort of intense emotion is uncomfortable for Bill. The shame of the situation is that others now value Bill only for his self-sacrificing behaviors. No one bothers to consider Bill's feelings or needs. Bill resents the lack of concern that others show him, yet he continues to try to please those who care so little about him. Bill must look at his own behaviors and realize the part his behaviors play in his problems. Will Bill be able to trace his current behaviors to his past abuse? Probably not.

Nancy is a fifteen-year-old survivor who is always the first to comfort others when they have been hurt or when they are in emotional pain. Nancy is so out of touch with her own feelings about her own family of origin that she has no sense of her own anger toward her mother. Whenever her mother imposes on any of Nancy's boundaries, such as Nancy's need for time with her own friends or her need simply to be a teenager without the responsibility of caring for her mother much as a parent would care for a child, Nancy does not display the anger that most teenagers would display. It is only when Nancy's anger has been repressed for a very long time and cannot be held down any longer that Nancy explodes in rage. Most times, the rage is directed toward people who don't have an important role in Nancy's life. The anger would never be directed toward Nancy's mother. Telling her mother of her anger would be seen by Nancy as being too risky. First, Nancy fears that her mother will not be able to deal with the anger. Nancy fears that her mother might attempt to harm herself. Nancy realizes how difficult a life her mother has had. She does not want to contribute to her mother's pain. Nancy also realizes that she will be the one who will have to deal with her mother's pain and anger at what the mother unconsciously considers to be Nancy's duty to care for her. Nancy has had to deal with her mother's anger whenever Nancy did attempt to tell her mother of her feelings. Nancy's mother's anger can be intense and long term. Nancy does not want risk losing the few privileges that she now has if her mother becomes too angry.

Nancy chooses to allow her anger to "leak" out in a violent way. Numerous times Nancy has carved people's names into the flesh of her own legs. Whenever Nancy cuts her arms or carves her legs she feels a sense of intense relief. If blood is also present when she cuts or carves herself, Nancy feels even more relief. Does Nancy realize that her anger is self-directed? Does Nancy realize that if she were to tell mother and all the other people in her life that she was angry that she would no longer need to harm herself? Nancy has not been able to make the connection between her self-abusive behaviors and her repressed anger. Even when the group tells her that a connection exists between her anger and her self-abuse, Nancy does not believe them. On the occasions that Nancy expresses her rage toward someone outside of herself, the recipient is almost always someone who is insignificant in Nancy's life. The recipient of Nancy's rage and violence seldom realizes why Nancy is so intensely angry. Nancy herself is not able to explain the anger. All Nancy knows is that the rage she feels seems to well up from out of nowhere and is so intense that she can't possibly control it. Rather than risk losing control of what she considers an uncontrollable rage, Nancy denies anger totally.

Family-of-origin issues can cause the survivor to be a victim for life. This seems like a broad generalization. The truth is that if the family of origin does not adequately protect or teach their children to protect themselves and to value themselves, they can develop the life-long pattern of codependent behaviors.

Jerry is a sixteen-year-old survivor who can't take care of herself. Jerry is excellent at taking care of others, however. Jerry

has been molested by six different perpetrators. Her mother
found out about Jerry's abuse after the fact each time the abuse
occurred. Jerry's mother was molested as a child. Her mother
was so fragile that Jerry didn't have the courage to tell her
mother how angry she was toward her mother for not protecting
her. Again, like Nancy, Jerry was afraid that her mother would
harm herself. Once her mother became stronger as a mother and
addressed her own issues, Jerry had great difficulty accepting
her in the role of mother. Still, Jerry continued to deny her anger
toward her mother. Whenever her mother would attempt to discipline Jerry, invariably Jerry would tell her mother that she had
no right to do so. Despite all of her angry behaviors, Jerry continued to deny that she had any anger toward her mother. It took
a long time for Jerry to realize the connection between her anger
toward her mother for not being able to protect her and the behaviors that Jerry exhibited toward her mother.

In a family of origin in which suicide has been a solution to life's
difficult problems, it is not unusual to see survivors make many attempts at suicide with each new attempt being more serious than the
last.

John is a seventeen-year-old survivor who has scars that criss-
cross his forearms in many places. John has attempted to kill
himself with drugs, gang fights, and risky sexual behaviors.
John does not see the risky sexual behaviors as being suicidal
behaviors. John's family has not taught John how to have a
sense of hope about the future. John has decided that if things
are going to stay the same in the future as they are now, he would
prefer to get the pain over with. The most effective thing that
John's family could do to help him would be to teach him how to
"survive" until things improve. By modeling suicidal behaviors,
John's family is helping him see suicide as a viable option for
when things get tough in life.

Other survivors have family-of-origin issues that involve drugs or
alcohol. Survivors might listen to what the parent or adult caregiver is
saying to them, but the message that will be absorbed is the *behavior*
that the adults model. Many times during the adolescent groups the
group's members have laughed about what their caregivers say versus

what the caregivers do. The adolescent group members seem to find this especially true when discussing drugs or alcohol.

Recent research (Finklehor and Browne, 1986) has stressed the importance that the role of peer relationships play in the development of characteristics and behaviors in our children. Although I am not attempting to minimize the importance of peer relationships, I believe that the family-of-origin issues have just as much, if not perhaps more, influence on the development of addictive or compulsive behaviors in the survivors with whom I work.

If the family of origin has a drug or alcohol problem that they employ in an attempt to deal with their problems or issues, then I feel that survivors in that family are much more likely to employ the same means to address their own pain or issues.

One of the most interesting situations, yet perhaps also one of the most painful, occurs when the family members cling to the abuser in the family in denial of the pain that the abuser has caused or is still causing. This sense of denial comes not only from the abusers themselves but also from the victim and other family members in an attempt to hold on to whatever semblance of family structure or unity remains. Usually, survivors believe that this is the best chance they have for having a family or that they must have caused or deserve this situation.

This situation is never more sad than in families in which the perpetrator is someone who is important to the family's financial well-being. Many times the family will sacrifice the victim and protect the perpetrator, usually the father or other male partner, in an attempt to keep the family intact. Most often this situation occurs because the mother does not have the job skills to care financially for the family. The patterns of behavior that are established by this denial of the harmfulness of the abuse are pervasive and almost always set the victim up for further victimization. Prostitutes almost always are incest survivors. What message do we convey to the young survivors in our families when we turn our backs on the sexual abuse that is occurring, all in an attempt to retain financial support? Is it any wonder that these survivors later go on to use sexual behaviors as a way of drawing attention to themselves or for holding on to what they perceive as love?

The family of origin sets the child up in so many ways for later development of compulsive or addictive behaviors. Most of what the child learns early in life is either personally experienced or is modeled by the parents and the relationship that the parents share. To the child, the parents are the authorities on everything in the world. If parents say that something is true, then to the child it *must* be true.

Some of the following situations can establish a lifetime of psychological issues and possible addictive or compulsive behaviors for a child.

1. The child feels an intense need for love or to be cared for that is unmet during childhood.
2. Either of the child's parents have drug, alcohol, or any other sort of addictive or compulsive behaviors. The child may model the parents' behaviors (AMA, 1992).
3. The parents or caregivers also came from an alcoholic or drug-abusing family. Some clinicians who specialize in treating addictions believe that it takes three generations without someone in the family using drugs or alcohol before the family can be said to be free from the effects of substance abuse.
4. One of the parents has low self-esteem or a codependent personality. Either one of these characteristics means that the partner who has this characteristic is very likely to fear abandonment and will have a very high tolerance for inappropriate behaviors from his or her partner. The child may perceive that in order to avoid abandonment one must tolerate the most awful behaviors from others.
5. If the family is isolated, the child is at risk for addictive or compulsive behaviors. Isolation prevents the social contacts that would inform the abused partner that he or she does not have to accept the abuse. Isolation prevents the abused partner from making the contacts that would allow him or her to develop a support system to leave the abusive situation. In isolation, no one from the outside is allowed to see how the addictive or compulsive behavior is progressing. The abused partner is not going to develop the necessary coping skills if he or she is kept isolated from the sources which might teach these skills.

Many people ask why everyone does not have the ability to develop addictions or compulsive behaviors. The truth is that, given the correct circumstances, almost anyone can develop addictive or compulsive behaviors. The previous family-of-origin issues simply increase the *likelihood* of developing addictive or compulsive behaviors. Given a stressful situation or life circumstances, the person who has been raised in a family of origin similar to those just described is more likely to develop addictive or compulsive behaviors.

What is the difference between what we might call "healthy" families versus "unhealthy" families? First, let me say that I know of no family that is without some sort of dysfunction . . . my own family included. Because we bring so much to our union when we decide to choose a partner, it is virtually impossible not to bring our own baggage along from our family of origin. Some parents bring baggage from their family of origin yet they are somehow able to balance their own needs in a healthy constructive manner without imposing on the boundaries of those in the nuclear family. Perhaps these are the families in which the parents have better conflict resolution and communication skills.

When one puts aside the most obviously unhealthy characteristic of sexual contact between a parent or authority figure and a child, no one characteristic is more striking than that of role reversal between mother and child. Over and over again, I see daughters giving their own mothers the nurturance and emotional support that the mother herself did not receive as a child. Although this characteristic might not be glaringly abusive, it is very damaging when one begins to calculate the cost over an extended period.

> Norma is a sixteen-year-old incest survivor who has been her "mother's mother" for as long as Norma can remember. Norma's mother is a longtime incest survivor herself who never felt, after her disclosure, that her own abuse experiences were validated. To remain a part of her own family of origin, Norma's mother had to ignore the cost of her own incest. Imagine feeling that the worst possible betrayal of trust that one can experience has happened yet no one acknowledges or validates the harmfulness or the painfulness of the experience. Instinctively, Norma could feel her mother's emotional pain. Norma would do anything in her power to prevent her mother from ever being harmed again.

How do children protect themselves against such huge demands being placed upon on them, even though the demands are never actually verbalized by the parent? These children simply comply with the parent's requests and give up their own identity to become the person that the parent will value most.

In a healthy family, the child does not have to "parent the parent." Parents realize the uniqueness of each child without trying to bend the child to meet their expectations. In healthy families, the parents are complete within themselves. In unhealthy families, the relationship between the parents is in discord. Many times, the child will be drawn into the parents' relationship as a buffer or as a confidant to either or both parents. This is called *triangulation* in family systems therapy. Triangulation almost always costs the child his or her relationship with one of the parents. The child literally is forced to side with one parent or the other.

In unhealthy families, the parents are not complete within themselves. They are looking for happiness outside of themselves in either addictions or compulsions. These are the very families that are breeding grounds for future generations of other dysfunctional families. The children in this sort of family will carry the issues that their families of origins are unable to resolve into their own adult relationships in an unconscious attempt to resolve them. These are also the families in which everyone is trying to take from instead of give to one another. A constant struggle for power and control exists. The children in such families will see these behaviors as being what relationships between adult partners are expected to be and will carry these dynamics into their own families. Thus an entire new generations of dysfunction begins.

One of the most interesting facts that I have learned through my work with sexual abuse is that most incest families were dysfunctional on a basic level *before* the incest ever occurred; the responsiveness to the child's needs was not there on other levels *before* the abuse occurred. Let me give an example to make this clear.

> Rory is a sixteen-year-old survivor who just recently gave birth to her first child. Rory's incest began at the age of seven when her uncle began to sexually abuse her. What is important in Rory's family is that Rory, like so many other incest survivors, is not the first generation of abuse victims in her family of origin. Rory's father experienced not only sexual abuse as a child, but also verbal, emotional, and physical abuse. Rory's mother is also an incest survivor. Because Rory's parents had never had the nurturing and attention that they needed as children, they could not enter a relationship without expecting their partner to

meet their needs. Neither one of Rory's parents had enough of what they needed as children to be able to meet their own needs or the needs of their partner. Since neither parent was complete in himself or herself or in the relationship with each other, how could they be there to meet Rory's needs? On many occasions, Rory was the one who would meet her parents' needs. When Rory's incest took place, somehow she instinctively knew that her parents would not be able to deal with the situation in a way that would make her feel validated or secure. Rather than risk placing her parents in such a dilemma, Rory simply kept the abuse to herself.

Family-of-origin issues are always difficult to deal with because they evoke such strong emotional feelings. Incest especially is diffi- cult to deal with because it is such a boundary violation, whether the incest is overt in the form of actual sexual contact or covert in the form of emotional incest. For the child who has been sexually abused, intimacy begins to equal sexuality. Childhood sexual abuse victims quickly adapt to the abuse by implementing one of two methods to distinguish to whom they can give their trust: either they trust no one or they trust everyone. Either way, the child has a problem in develop- ing the necessary skills to learn to trust his or her own judgments when determining whom to trust.

Incest survivors have a special problem because they tend to be- come the victims of other sex crimes later in their lives.

Jennifer is an incest survivor who was sexually abused by her older brother when she was between four and ten years old. Jennifer never told anyone of the abuse because her brother had threatened to kill her if she told. When Jennifer was eighteen, she was a victim of date rape. Again, Jennifer told no one of the abuse. At twenty, Jennifer married a man who would later force himself on her sexually when she left him after discovering that he was involved in a homosexual relationship with his best friend. Many of Jennifer's problems could be traced back to the initial feelings of helplessness that stemmed from being the lit- tle girl who was terrified of her much bigger and stronger brother. Jennifer felt helpless and insignificant in comparison to her older brother.

Survivors such as Jennifer are damaged at the most basic level. It is as if the age at which survivors are abused becomes the point at which they stop their developing in some areas.

> Sally is a fifty-year-old incest survivor who was sexually abused by her biological father. For most of Sally's adult life, she has been intimidated by sex. Sally can perform sexually with her husband, but she has never found the joy in sex that she might have if it had not been for the sexual abuse. Sally's sexuality stopped at the point where her father's abuse began.

It is not unusual to see survivors experiencing problems with certain behaviors that might have been in development at the time of the abuse. Table 3.1 illustrates which childhood developmental tasks might be disrupted by sexual abuse at various ages.

Table 3.1. Childhood Developmental Tasks That Might Be Disrupted by Sexual Abuse

Child's Developmental Task	Age of Abuse	Possible Effect of Sexual Abuse
Memory development	0 to 2 Years	Child may have no conscious memory of abuse but may later demonstrate behaviors resulting from the abuse.
Beginning to develop language	0 to 2 Years	Child may show regression in language already learned; may stop learning new words.
Learning to trust others	0 to 2 Years	Inability to trust others; may cry when having diaper changed or when bathed.
		May refuse to allow others to help child become potty trained.
		Fearful of being wiped after using potty.
Learning to explore that which can be seen, felt, or touched	0 to 2 Years	Inhibited or age-inappropriate exploration.
		Child may refuse to leave caregivers.
		Child may insert small objects in vagina or rectum.
		Child begins to masturbate despite being reprimanded.
		If previously bottle weaned, child may regress.

Child's Developmental Task	Age of Abuse	Possible Effect of Sexual Abuse
Basis for secure attachment; primary caregiver "mirrors" child to demonstrate love for child	0 to 2 Years	Insecure attachment; child becomes fearful, timid, or aggressive.
		Fragile ego development.
		Child learns that he or she cannot depend on others to come to his or her aid or to meet his or her needs.
Thinks in terms of self	2 to 4 Years	Overly concerned with welfare of others as he or she wishes had been done for him or her.
		Possible beginning of codependent behaviors or lack of empathy for others (start of narcissistic personality disorder?).
Sense of autonomy/ self-confidence	2 to 4 Years	Shame develops.
		Self-doubt begins to develop.
Learning independence	2 to 4 Years	Child constantly looks to others to learn what to do in any situation.
Child begins to develop self-will	2 to 4 Years	Child begins to realize own sense of will or desire is not respected by abuser or by others.
		Child begins to develop "false persona" in order to adapt and be valued.
		Child may demonstrate anger at having self-will frustrated by smearing feces.
		Child may openly masturbate despite punishments.
		May complain of nightmares.
		May replicate parts of abuse experience in an attempt to master understanding of sexual abuse experiences.
Child develops sense of initiative and self-motivation	4 to 7 Years	Child's sense of guilt or discomfort inhibits enthusiasm or motivation to grow or develop.
		Sense of shame or inferiority increases.
Learning to make judgments	4 to 7 Years	Cannot trust own judgments or perceptions due to nonvalidation of abuse by others.
		Introduces other children to sexual abuse as a way of trying to resolve own abuse experience.
		Open masturbation increases.
		Sex play with animals or increased insertion of objects into vagina or rectum.

TABLE 3.1 *(continued)*

Child's Developmental Task	Age of Abuse	Possible Effect of Sexual Abuse
Learns to begin problem solving	4 to 7 Years	Becomes "perfect" child with little sense of adventure as means of adaptation.
		Becomes oppositional or defiant as a means of dealing with abuse.
		Isolates, withdraws, creates fantasy world.
		If trauma is great enough, child may become proficient at dissociation.
		May express suicidal ideation clearly or actually make suicide attempt.
		Eating disorders may become visible.
Needs support to explore outside of parents	4 to 7 Years	Peers taking on additional importance, sometimes more importance than parents.
Sense of independence	7 to 12 Years	Child lacks sense of competence and mastery.
		Child overvalues others' opinions and perceptions.
		Child undervalues own opinions and self-perceptions.
Development of skills to deal with anxiety	7 to 12 Years	Child's ability to deal with anxiety is maladaptive and often regressive.
		Eating disorders may become apparent as a manner of dealing with anxiety and repressed anger.
		Threats and attempts at self-harm and harm to others may begin.
Learns to have faith in own judgments	7 to 12 Years	Little faith in own judgments due to lack of validation of child's perception or experience of abuse.
Learns to develop ideals	7 to 12 Years	Disillusionment and loss of hope.
		Child may become withdrawn and a "loner."
		Child may become an exhibitionist or promiscuous as a reaction to abuse.
Ability to hypothesize and reason	7 to 12 Years	No pattern or predictability to use as template for future reasoning.
		Chaotic existence.
Peers' opinions very important	12 to 18 Years	Overvalues involvement with peers due to loss of value of adult's attachment to child.

Child's Developmental Task	Age of Abuse	Possible Effect of Sexual Abuse
Cause-and-effect thinking	12 to 18 Years	Much more frequent risky behavior with no care for own mortality or welfare.
		Increased usage of alcohol, drugs, eating disorders in an unconscious attempt to soothe inner emotional pain.
		Repressed anger leading to behaviors such as exhibitionism, promiscuity, or prostitution in an attempt to have some sense of control over the abuse.
		Little thought of negative consequences.
		Self-esteem so low child makes poor choices. Codependent behaviors become very developed.
Sense of identity established	12 to 18 Years	Poor sense of core identity or sense of self; only outward appearance matters.

It is so important to realize that the earlier the sexual abuse occurs, the more damaging the abuse will be. The effects of the abuse will interfere not only with that developmental stage in which the abuse occurred but in all future developmental stages in the same area. The degree of intrusiveness of the sexual abuse will also help to determine the degree of the damage of the abuse. In other words, if the abuse involved intercourse, it might be perceived as being more damaging than fondling. The truth of the matter is that the sensitivity of the child has a great deal to do with the damage done by the abuse. The more emotionally sensitive the child is, the greater the potential for damage. Again, we are presented with the notion that it is not what happens to us that matters so much as what we *think* about what happens to us. The severity, intrusiveness, and duration of the abuse, access by the offender to the victim, sensitivity of the victim, and availability of a support system to the victim all combine to determine how damaged the victim will be by the abuse.

In incest families, long before the incest has occurred, the family usually has not met the child's needs in many ways.

Rania is an adult survivor who, when looking back on her family of origin, finds that the time that the incest began was not the first time that she felt alone in her family. For all of the earliest years of her childhood, Rania's mother competed with her for Rania's father's attention. Rania's mother would become quite angry at any attention Rania's father would pay to her. Her mother had had a dysfunctional childhood, as her father was a very abusive alcoholic who seemed to target her for the worst of the abuse that he handed out. When Rania's parents got married, her mother looked to her husband to provide all of the nurturing and affection that she had never gotten as a child. When Rania was born, there was another person with whom to compete for her husband's time and affection. Was Rania's mother consciously aware of her competition with her daughter? Probably not, but the results were the same: Rania suffered from not getting what she needed in childhood to become a complete and fully individuated human being. Rania learned early in life that to have others love her, she had to become whatever the other person needed her to be. This is the perfect recipe for co-dependency.

When we consider family-of-origin characteristics, it becomes clear that certain characteristics separate healthy from unhealthy families. In healthy family systems, family members have a sense of predictability and safety. Family members in healthy families know that their emotional, physical, and mental safety is a real consideration for other family members. Family members have a sense of being valued for who they are. Members of the family do not need to pretend to be someone other than who they really were meant to be. In an unhealthy family, the family members have no sense of predictability. Chaos is the one constant theme in these families. In unhealthy families, not only is the parent unavailable for the child emotionally and sometimes physically, but the parent oftentimes expects the child to satisfy the parent's emotional needs. The parent may neglect the child and fail to protect the child physically, mentally, and emotionally. Often the parent has a substance-abuse issue, other addiction, or compulsive behavior, which adds to the parent's unavailability to the child.

In healthy families, the family members can talk freely about their thoughts and feelings. No attempt must be made to hide what is happening in the family. Unhealthy family systems are more concerned about how the family appears to those outside of the family than they are about what is really happening inside the family. Appearance is everything to the unhealthy family system because, at some basic level, the family is aware of its fragility.

In healthy family systems, family members encourage one another to grow and to take care of themselves. No one is expected to sacrifice his or her own development, growth, or safety for someone else's benefit. Unhealthy family systems are just the opposite. Family members are not allowed to individuate and develop self-care. Punishment occurs for individuating in unhealthy family systems: family members will no longer claim members who attempt to individuate themselves as family. One is allowed to be only as healthy as the sickest member of the family. In unhealthy family systems, family members are not even aware if the family will exist tomorrow, so family members will do whatever it takes to try to hold the family together. Sometimes holding the family together means that no one in the family is allowed to have an identity of one's own or any sense of privacy. Keeping secrets is the only thing that manages to hold the unhealthy family together. In healthy families, no secret alignments exist between family members because no unhealthy secrets must be maintained. In healthy families, boundaries respect family members as being separate and special in their own right. Unhealthy families, such as incest families, allow the parents to take whatever they need at the child's expense.

The following chapter discusses the cost to the victim of living in an unhealthy family system in which the victim often is expected to "parent the parents" and maintain the family's structure by failing to acknowledge the harmfulness of the sexual abuse.

Chapter 4

Feeling "Less Than"

Loneliness *and the feeling of being unwanted is the most terrible poverty.*

Mother Theresa

Feeling "less than" means that survivors feel such a sense of shame from being abused that they believe others can somehow see how they are damaged or flawed. Some survivors speak of feeling "dirty." It is not unusual to hear of survivors taking baths in scalding water and scrubbing themselves almost raw to try to rid themselves of the dirty feeling. Addictions and compulsions are all forms of defenses to ward off feelings of shame. Other defenses that ward off shame include withdrawal, rage, perfectionism, exhibitionism, and arrogance.

I have found that many of the male survivors with whom I have worked choose to use the defense of rage. It is not unusual to hear male survivors in the coed group brag about how angry they are and how they would attempt to "fuck someone up" if given the opportunity. Female survivors often pick defenses such as exhibitionism. I have observed female survivors who dress so provocatively that most of their feminine attributes are observable. It is almost as if they are "advertising" their femininity. Some male survivors will also dress scantily, wearing sleeveless muscle shirts that are designed to show off all of their masculine physical charms.

Arrogance is often a defense used by survivors who fear that they have issues in common with other survivors who they see as being "beneath" them. By being arrogant, they feel able to separate themselves from survivors who they believe are "less than" they are. These survivors might also include the survivors who appear to be "perfect." Both arrogance and perfectionism have a tendency to make others feel inferior and to keep others at a distance.

Some survivors choose withdrawal from social situations as a defense against shame. These survivors are often so reserved that one hardly knows that they are present. It is almost as if they are trying to fade into the background. These survivors do not usually want to attend group meetings and will attend only if they are able to make friends with at least one other group member. Usually these other group members will have the same sort of personality. They also will cling to the survivor who uses control as a means of dealing with the shame.

Whenever I work with a survivor who has an impulse-control problem, I am on the lookout for shame-based issues. Impulsive behaviors are often shame based. When the survivor seems to react to something that is either said or done in an impulsive manner, I am alerted that one of his or her shameful issues may have been touched upon.

Doug is a fifteen-year-old survivor who is an excellent example of a survivor who uses rage as a way to avoid shame-based issues.

> Doug was raped by his older brother from age five to age twelve. Doug never told anyone of the rapes because of the sense of shame he felt at what he perceived as "being gay." Like many male survivors, Doug did not realize that being sexually abused by another male did not make him gay. Doug finally was able to disclose the rapes while he was an inpatient for drug and alcohol abuse. When Doug disclosed the abuse, he was in the midst of an episode of extreme rage and physical violence. In reality, the rage and physical violence was the way that Doug was able to work himself up so that he could disclose the abuse. Remember that Doug felt shame from what he perceived as his participation in homosexual acts. After disclosing the rapes to the male therapist, Doug began to feel an overwhelming sense of shame and could no longer face the therapist. Doug began a tirade of such verbally and physically abusive behaviors toward the male therapist that it became obvious that another therapist would have to be brought in to work with Doug. Doug insisted on a female therapist. At this point, Doug had managed to project his shame onto the male therapist and no longer wanted to associate himself with that therapist. By choosing a female therapist, Doug was able to distance himself from his own shame—much like biblical examples of projecting the shame onto sacrificial animals.

Lee is an example of a female survivor in group who has used withdrawal as a means of dealing with her shame-based feelings.

When Lee was only four years old, she was molested by her biological mother. Mother-daughter incest is much less frequently reported than father-daughter incest. Mother-daughter incest seldom being reported seems only to add to the sense of shame that victims involved in this type of incest feel. Lee had witnessed her father and mother in such physical fights that she feared for both of their lives. The neighbors would call the police to break up these fights. Lee, even as a young child, knew that her father's behaviors were a source of shame for her. Both her mother and father were alcohol and drug abusers, so they did not feel the shame of their behaviors in the same way that Lee felt it. On the rare occasions that Lee's parents were sober long enough to feel their shame, they would immediately begin to abuse substances in an attempt to quiet their intense discomfort.

Lee was not as lucky as her parents. Lee had no way to medicate her pain and sense of shame because she was so young. Lee wanted simply to "disappear." In a way, Lee *was* able to disappear. She became so quiet and withdrawn that she could be in a room and no one would even notice that she was there. Even when Lee was seven years old and five adolescent boys raped her, she managed to keep the pain and the shock inside. It was only when another survivor managed to befriend Lee that she was able to open up a little at a time. Slowly, by degrees, Lee was able to disclose the horror that she had experienced. It was the fact that the survivor to whom Lee disclosed understood and was not repulsed by Lee's experiences that enabled Lee to share what had happened to her. At any time if the survivor to whom Lee disclosed had acted shocked or repulsed by Lee's disclosure, Lee would have immediately withdrawn back into her shell. As Lee became more and more trusting, she was able to extend this feeling of trust to her fellow survivors in group. Lee is now working on being able to expand her trust to selected people outside of the group. I have no doubts that at some point Lee will have a number of people in her life that she trusts.

Shame is one of our earliest emotions. Usually, shame is evident in young children before the age of two years. The sense of shame is apparent when children cover their faces with their hands, avert their gaze, or blush. All of these symptoms signal that the emotions these children are experiencing are too intense.

Shame can occur in childhood with or without overtly abusive behaviors by those in the child's early environment. Overt abuse that may lead the child to experience a sense of shame may include physical abuse, sexual abuse, or emotional and verbal abuse. It is not uncommon to see survivors who have experienced *all* of these forms of abuse at the hands of their caregivers.

Sexual abuse by itself can cause a form of "soul murder" in which the survivor is never able to become the person that a higher power would have given the individual the ability to become.

> Shyanne is a fifty-year-old survivor who was molested by her biological father. When she was young, Shyanne had the desire to sing. In fact, Shyanne did possess a beautiful singing voice. The abuse that Shyanne suffered at her father's hands was so traumatic that as Shyanne became older she felt too ashamed to draw attention to herself by singing. Although Shyanne intellectually knew that others couldn't actually see her shame, she still felt that somehow they would *sense* her shame. She simply could not relax enough to sing. When a much-younger Shyanne sang she was able to share her soul with those who listened. Shyanne has managed to find other ways to share her innermost being with others, but never will singing be one of those ways.

> Cassie was sexually abused by her biological father for seven years beginning when she was eight years old. Her father used drugs and alcohol to anesthetize Cassie enough to rape her. Her father then persuaded Cassie that she had willingly participated in "their lovemaking." Cassie became so convinced by her father of this willingness that she turned away from all forms of physical affection. Cassie could not even hug a friend without feeling that she was somehow trying to be sexual with them. Cassie's sense of shame has prevented her from becoming close to people who are important in her life. Her sense of shame is so pervasive that she cannot even share the pain that she feels by disclosing the abuse to those people to whom she wants to be closest. Only her mother, maternal grandmother, and therapist understand the reason behind Cassie's aloofness.

Even more insidious is shame-based behavior that comes from covert forms of abuse. What do I mean by "covert forms of abuse"? Covert abuse occurs when the people in the survivor's life to whom the survivor should be able to turn use emotional incest, are so demanding that the child can never live up to the caregiver's demands, or are so critical of the child that the child can never hope to meet the caregiver's expectations. Sometimes shame can become a self-fulfilling prophecy in which survivors *prove* to themselves that they are not worthy of love or of kindness. By believing that they are not worthy of love or kindness, the survivors create circumstances in which they either do not allow others to love them or they act so aloof or angry that others do not have the opportunity to love them. In any case, the survivor's feelings and actions are the result of shame-based emotions that come from feeling "worth less" or "less than."

Shame separates us from others. It isolates us and causes us to withdraw from the very people who might well offer us the support and nurturance that we need to sustain us. Survivors feel a sense of shame early in their lives. Many times even before the actual sexual abuse has taken place the survivor has a family of origin with a lengthy history of shame-based feelings.

Shame is a painful emotion, yet because of the very nature of it we seldom share this emotion with anyone. Shame is partly innate, meaning that we are born with a sense of the uncomfortableness of the intensity that the emotion of shame arouses in us. From a very early age, infants will break eye contact with someone when the eye contact is too intense.

A strong sense of shame can also find its origins in a childhood where the parents are too demanding or too critical of the child. In incest families, role reversal takes place between the mother and the incest victim. Sometimes long before the actual incest takes place the child has been placed in a position of having to assume adult responsibilities that the nonoffending parent (usually the child's mother) is not able or willing to assume. What does role reversal do to the incest victim?

Incest victims are often expected to assume responsibilities that they simply are too young or too inexperienced to perform.

> Carey was molested by her biological father when she was five years old. Carey never told of the ongoing abuse because her father had threatened to kill her if she told anyone of the abuse.

When Carey was only seven years old, she was expected to do almost all of the family's cooking and cleaning. Carey had three younger brothers. Carey's father was an alcoholic who also had serious emotional problems. Carey's mother was a very loving young woman who had also experienced a childhood filled with horrible abuse. Simply because of her tender age and her inability to assume adult responsibilities, Carey was filled with a sense of inadequacy at an early age. Carey was not aware that the problem did not lie in her failure to be able to fulfill the adult demands placed upon her young shoulders. Carey instinctively knew that her family was not like the families of her classmates. The saddest part of all is that Carey thought that the differences between her family and her classmates' families were her fault. Instead of seeing the cause of her failure as being the way that Carey's family was functioning, Carey believed the problem was that Carey *herself* was flawed.

To get through the feelings of being different and shameful, Carey began to smoke marijuana with her family at age eleven. At age thirteen, Carey's father introduced her to hard drugs, such as heroin and cocaine. It was only because the other children in the family began to act out and came to the attention of the school and Family Services that Carey was removed from the family home and the incest. Despite being in a safe setting and eventually disclosing the incest, Carey still would resort to drugs and alcohol on occasion to dull the pain of the shame of the incest.

Although shame is very often tied to sexual abuse, shame can result from any type of abuse.

I have learned much about the harmfulness of shame. Shame means that the person who feels the shame is somehow "flawed" and therefore cannot be cured. Although shame and guilt are often confused, a big difference exists between the two. Guilt is a healthy response to a situation in which we acknowledge that we have done something to harm ourselves or someone else. Shame serves no purpose but to make us feel worthless.

John Bradshaw (1986c) is quite clear in his definition of shame. He says that shame tells us that we are "worth-less." Bradshaw gives examples of early childhood experiences in which a child is given the message by an abusive, absent, or neglectful parent that the child is "worth-less" than the parent's alcoholism, workaholism, rage response, or any other compulsive behavior that the parent may have.

The real meaning behind shame is that we are somehow fatally flawed and we fear the exposure of our shame. We fear that if we let others into our core self they would know us and reject us. Shame causes isolation and withdrawal. I understand shame probably better than many people because of my early experiences with sexual abuse. When I was five years old, I was caught playing doctor with the little boy next door. In reality, I was only reenacting the sexual abuse that I was experiencing. Both the little boy's parents and my own parents created a scene and shamed both the little boy and me. That shame has stayed with me all of my life. In fact, the shaming from that one experience of playing doctor was as shameful as the original sexual abuse. Even when people are bright and caring, shame can still ruin their own self-perceptions. Those who are shamed will simply discount their own accomplishments and focus only on their perceived faults and flaws.

In my mind, nothing is better able to cause a sense of shame than sexual abuse. The most sacred boundary that we as humans have is control of our bodies. When someone discounts the importance of this boundary and sexually abuses a child, no stronger message can be given to the child that the child does not matter or is "worth-less." It is no wonder that many sexually abused children grow up to be adults who have issues with true intimacy. Intimacy requires that individuals have a true sense of being themselves. Individuals cannot just be playing the role that they have adopted in order to survive in this world. People who have been sexually abused often learn at a very early age to suppress their true feelings and true selves in order to adapt and survive the abuse experience. No wonder so many survivors become trapped in rigid roles in which they can never be truly intimate with anyone else. These rigid roles are survivors' attempts to obtain some sort of control in a situation where as a child they had absolutely no control at all. Many times, survivors will go on to become rage addicted. What better way to keep others at a distance where they cannot sense or see the shame than through the use of rage? What a pity that survivors should be abused then go on to abuse others and isolate themselves all in an unconscious attempt to keep others from seeing the shame.

How does one heal from shame? One of the best ways that I know to heal is to join a group setting. In the group experience, survivors can share their shame-based experiences with others in the group. By sharing their experiences, survivors are able to get a sense of what has happened to them being more normalized. There is also increased self-esteem in helping others to deal with their problems.

Shame in childhood can occur without overt abuse. If the parents are overcritical—so that the children feel that they can never measure up to the parents' expectations—the children will develop a sense of shame without ever being directly told that they are shameful. If the parents are too demanding, so that the children feel that they can never please the parents, the same thing will happen. Some researchers believe that a biological component exists in some families that makes them more prone to feelings of shame. Poverty and feeling different from others also can cause a person early on to develop a sense of shame. Perhaps nothing more than sexual abuse can cause a person shame that can be carried for generations without the shame ever being spoken about.

> Kathy's family had always appeared to be "different" from others in her small midwestern town. Although Kathy did not know why she felt different from others, the sense of shame was there nonetheless. What Kathy did not know was that her father and her grandfather were really one and the same person. Kathy was the product of incest.

Wherever a family secret exists shame-based behavior is bound to occur. It is only when we allow the secret to be seen in the light of day that the secret loses its power.

Shame also has it own subculture. It is a "them-versus-us" sort of mentality. For example, in the adolescent survivors' group, the survivors will allow nonmembers to visit the group from time to time as a guest of another group member. Whenever some crucial problem occurs in the group, the visitors will be asked if they are survivors. If they are, the group will listen to what the visitors have to say. If the guests are not survivors, the group members will be polite, but they will let the visitors know that this a discussion for "survivors only."

It takes an enormous amount of courage to deal with shame. It is not unusual to see the survivors' group members together on the steps before the group meeting smoking cigarettes in an attempt to bolster their courage enough to deal with the issues they must discuss in group. When the group gets too intense, it is not unusual for the group members to take another break to meet in small subgroups of two or three survivors each before they rejoin the group and deal with their most painful issues.

Bragging about sexual exploits is another way that the group's members try to bolster their courage when they begin to address their most painful issues. By bragging about their sexual exploits, or about drug and alcohol abuse, the group's members are able to take the focus off more relevant and painful issues. Only those members of the group who understand what sexual abuse "feels like" are considered *real* group members. Although those who are group advisors but not sexual abuse survivors are welcomed, they are not able to become a core part of the group. Total acceptance into the group depends on one criterion alone: being a survivor. I have been accused of thinking that only a survivor can *really* work as a therapist with other survivors. Nothing could be farther from the truth. However, I do believe that not allowing clients to be the expert on their own abuse experience is a tragic mistake whether or not the therapist is a survivor. The survivors in group have commented time and again that they hate it when a therapist tells them, "I know just how you feel." As a therapist, being a survivor allows me the advantage of personally understanding what sexual abuse can do to someone. There are disadvantages to being a survivor who is also a therapist. Sometimes, if an issue is too close to one of my own, I may not be able to see it as clearly as a therapist who is not a survivor could. Boundary issues are a constant struggle. The compassion that I feel for other survivors can make being objective difficult at times. Because of the complex transference and countertransference issues, I am always involved in my own treatment and constant ongoing supervision.

Although not all adolescent survivors in the groups have substance abuse behaviors, certain behaviors such as drug and alcohol abuse seem to run parallel to sexual abuse. These include such behaviors as sexual activity that at times borders on being self-abusive. Adolescent survivors seem to engage in risky behaviors on a much greater scale than do other adolescent non-survivors. Boys who are sexually active are four times more likely to smoke and ten times more likely to use marijuana. Adolescents who have had three or more sexual partners in one year are much more likely to use illegal drugs. The surgeon general has said that tobacco use in adolescents is associated with a range of health-damaging behaviors, including fighting with weapons, drug and alcohol use, and sexual acting-out behaviors. According to Boyer and Fine (1992), trauma and risky behaviors are all part of the abuse that goes on to perpetrate later abuse; it is an ever-widening cycle. It is sad to see an adolescent group member become pregnant, especially because she has not had a chance at a life without the shadow of poverty or abuse hovering over her head.

Shame-based people share certain characteristics, such as sensitivity to any sort of criticism, whether the criticism is meant or simply perceived as criticism; feeling very self-conscious and uncomfortable if given any sort of praise or attention; feeling that they are of little or no value to others; feeling that they are "less than" others and have very low self-esteem; feeling that in relationships they will always come out hurt or seen as being flawed; and, in truth, are much more critical of themselves than others could ever be of them.

When a survivor is shame based, it will not always be apparent. Survivors, like other people who experience shame, use survival skills to hide their feelings of shame in such a way that it appears that the survivor thinks that they are "above" others. Some survivors who feel a sense of shame will appear to be so perfect that they will manage to keep others at a distance so that others cannot see their shame-based flaws. Some shame-based survivors will simply withdraw from others. This type of survivor will find any type of contact with others to be painful and emotionally risky. Although the survivor may be physically present, emotionally, the survivor is never available for those closest to him or her. Some shame-based survivors, especially male survivors, will act so violent and angry that they manage to keep others at an emotional distance because of the fear that the survivors instill in others. When these survivors attack others verbally or emotionally, the attacks may be so sudden and vicious that they will take others completely by surprise. The anger that these survivors feel toward themselves and those who have shamed them is displaced onto those who are seen as being "safe" targets for their anger. The amount of rage that is projected usually is proportionate to the amount of anxiety and degree of closeness that the survivor experiences with those upon whom the anger is directed.

One of the most common forms of defense against shame that I have observed in the adolescent groups that I facilitate is exhibitionism. It is almost as if the survivors beat others to the punch and flaunt whatever has been exploited by their abuse. This type of survivor makes it readily apparent what he or she would really like to hide from the world. These are the survivors that walk down the street in the tightest clothing with the lowest necklines and shortest skirts. The attempts at getting attention are really attempts at trying to gain some sense of control over their own lives and what is happening to them. This behavior is typical of survivors of sexual abuse, particularly incest survivors. It is almost as if the greater the sense of shame, the more attention these survivors will attempt to draw toward themselves. The only thing that happens for these survivors is that their behaviors separate them more and more from the very people that they are attempting to draw closer.

A sense of sexuality and being shame based are closely connected. Survivors are very vulnerable to feelings of sexual shame simply because they have experienced a form of abuse that by its very nature is sexual and secretive. Sometimes survivors will begin to act out sexually in a compulsive manner in an attempt to lower the degree of shame feelings that they feel about themselves. Sheba is such a survivor.

> Sheba is a seventeen-year-old survivor who wears such short skirts that at times when she sits down her underpants can be seen. Sheba always has the heaviest makeup and the tightest clothing. Sheba is a magnet for men who want sex, yet she does not seem to understand that it is her own behaviors that attract this type of men, who only want what they can get from her sexually. It is ironic that Sheba thinks that by engaging in such sexual behaviors she is taking control of the situation and making or gaining something positive out of her abuse experience. Sheba has no idea that in reality she is simply inviting more abuse.

Survivors who are shame based have no real sense of identity. Often these survivors are so afraid they will be abandoned that they will do anything or be anything that others want them to be. By the self-neglect that these survivors demonstrate, they feel such a sense of self-hatred that they sabotage their own lives. Often these survivors will engage in self-abusive behaviors in such a way that over time the survivors harm themselves as much as if someone else had attacked them. Often survivors will engage in drug, alcohol, or food addiction until their health is so poor that what they have done is akin to a form of slow suicide. When questioned about the lack of self-care, these survivors will not have a clue about their own self-abusiveness. It is survivors who are keenly aware of their shame who are at the greatest risk of engaging in the most harmful behaviors. These survivors feel that something is inherently wrong with themselves. The abuse that they have experienced is only an outward sign to the survivors of how much they themselves are flawed. This survivors' sense of shame is so great that they are almost totally isolated from others. The isolation only tends to make the survivors' sense of shame greater.

Survivors who experience shame-based feelings are easy to identify. They are the people most concerned about their appearance: if only the survivors can manage to "look right" then they will then "be right." They are constantly monitoring the opinions of others, looking for the slightest sign of criticism. Constantly fearing that they will experience humiliation before others, survivors would rather live in exile, away from those who would care for them. Feeling that they could never be as good as others, survivors can never risk expressing their innermost feelings for fear that they will be laughed at or humiliated. As time passes, the survivors' sense of shame grows greater until finally they feel that nothing is worthwhile about themselves.

For most survivors, the roots of their shame stem from their childhoods. Shame often has a biological basis, as it is believed that some people are more prone to shame than others, especially those people who are depressed. Parents who give too little or too much attention risk increasing the amount of shame their children feel. I do not mean an occasional lapse in judgment that a parent may have, which may cause momentary decreases in parental attention, or an occasional attempt to make up for a perceived misjudgment by extra attention; I am talking about a significant lack of or too much attention on a consistent basis or over a prolonged period of time.

For survivors, it is difficult to determine which came first: the sexual abuse, the shame-based family, or depression from knowing that if the survivor was valued the abuse would not have occurred in the first place. Signs of biologically based shame include weight gain and weight loss, irregular sleeping patterns, such as sleeping too little or too much, suicidal thoughts and attempts, an inability to focus or concentrate because of feeling down or sad, feeling like everything is an effort, so much that survivors simply lose interest in things or quit enjoying things that they may have previously enjoyed, and finally, simply withdrawing from life in general.

Survivors who come from alcoholic shame-based families may often experience what is known as "scapegoating." By choosing one member of the alcoholic family—usually the most vulnerable member—the family is able to put all of the family's shame onto one person. The way that the members of the family interact with one another simply reinforces their sense of shame, as each member sees his or her own shame reflected in the other members' behaviors. The messages that these family members convey and receive include devaluing messages such as "You aren't good enough," "You don't belong because you are too different" (this is especially true if the child has a physical difference such as hair or skin color), "We never wanted you anyway" (the survivor may simply attempt suicide as a way of satisfying the family's feelings), and, finally, if the survivor discloses the abuse, "It's all your fault. How could you put us through this?"

Anytime survivors attempt to force reluctant family members to face the truth of sexual abuse allegations, the dynamics that indicated the abuse may have occurred were in place long before the actual abuse occurred. Parental behaviors such as valuing a child so little that the child is neglected or abandoned, having so little interest in the child that the child feels "less than" everyone else, and rejecting the child because he or she has made family members face problems that cause the family to regroup or to change their structure are all based in and cause shame.

Shame-based families are especially difficult for survivors because by their very nature shame-based families fear any outside exposure. "Looking good" is valued at all costs. The pressure that the parents place on their children to conform and use whatever means to meet the community's standards forces family members to assume false personas and maintain rigid roles. If the survivor causes a break in the family's denial system by forcing the family to address their real issues, it is the survivor who may be rejected from the family, not the perpetrator. To remain in the incest family, too many times victims must sacrifice themselves by keeping the incest a secret. The cost of this secret is immense for the survivor in terms of lost potential and lost creativity.

The second type of survivors are those who become so good at "numbing" themselves because of their inability to tolerate their own

pain that they begin to identify with those who abused them. These
are the survivors who are at greater risk for becoming perpetrators. If
you were to ask these survivors if they still had deep feelings about
their own abuse experiences, chances are they would say that they
have dealt with their own abuse issues. The survivor simply may be repressing their own strong feelings by putting them on another victim.

> Richard is a sixteen-year-old survivor. When Richard was eight
> years old, he was sodomized by a much older boy. For years,
> Richard never told anyone of the abuse. Richard was also ver-
> bally, emotionally, and physically abused by his family of ori-
> gin. Despite all of the abuse that he experienced, Richard is one
> of the nicest and most polite young men that anyone could ever
> want to meet. It was a big surprise to everyone when Richard
> was arrested for molesting two little girls in his foster home.
> What was not so apparent was that Richard had simply buried
> his feelings about his own abuse because he could not deal with
> the pain that he was feeling anymore.

Feelings don't just go away. Unless we acknowledge and express our
feelings, they will be stored in our minds and our bodies. Richard is
no exception. His anger at the way he was treated became so great
that eventually he could not contain it any longer. When Richard sexually abused the two little girls, he did not think of them as being human or having feelings. At that moment, Richard was only aware that
he was not feeling pain. Richard's own boundaries had been so badly
violated that he thought little of the consequences of seriously invading someone else's boundaries. Richard's family had so little regard
for others' boundaries that Richard barely knew that boundaries were
meant to be respected and used to protect us either from being too
vulnerable to others violating our own space or from having so little
respect for others' boundaries that we become abusive toward others.

Without boundaries, no separation exists among people. It is not
clear where one person ends and another begins. How can we share
with others if we are not complete within ourselves? By not having
boundaries, we do not really share. We simply appear to be sharing
when we are really taking from the other person and not exposing the
most vulnerable parts of ourselves. Some survivors are so terrified of
abandonment because of their fears of being "flawed" or "less than"
that they will so closely identify with a partner that they no longer

have any identity of their own. Other survivors build walls around themselves so that they do not ever have to live a life filled with emotional pain.

The following chapter focuses on how depression often intensifies a survivor's sense of shame and isolation.

Chapter 5

Life Through Gray-Colored Lenses

He who laughs . . . lasts!

Mary Pettibone Poole

It is probably obvious to the reader that depression and sexual abuse go hand in hand. What most people do not understand is the extent to which sexual abuse affects the survivor's life. The best way that I can describe the feeling that a large percentage of survivors carry inside of them is to compare it to the way one young client whom I was working with using EMDR (eye movement desensitization reprocessing) used to describe her feelings of depression. She said, "I feel like I have a big hole in my stomach. It's so empty that nothing ever fills it up. I feel so empty inside." This insightful young woman had been in treatment for years with repeated stays in numerous psychiatric hospitals. Depression had alternated with rage as a constant mental state in her young life. Although this young woman did not use drugs or alcohol, she realized the importance of the role that depression had played in her life. To her, depression felt like a hole in her stomach. This client had used compulsive overeating as a way to take the focus away from her abuse issues, only to realize eventually that there is no way around the emotional pain of sexual abuse. One must ultimately feel the pain of the abuse and deal with it if one is to heal from emotional wounds.

Depression is really one of the most interesting and painful of all emotions. I believe that survivors often experience a high rate of depression because of the unexpressed anger that they feel toward their perpetrators and the significant others in their lives who did not protect them. Unexpressed anger contains much pent-up energy. This energy, which the survivor does not feel safe enough to express, is often turned inward in the form of depression. Because the survivor most often experiences sexual abuse at important developmental stages in their lives, such as childhood or adolescence, the anger is often stored and will be expressed in ways that are appropriate to those developmental stages. This may sound confusing, but the following case history will illustrate this situation quite well.

Sandy is a fifteen-year-old survivor, who has been sexually abused by her cousin, her brothers, and her father. Sandy has clear memories of the sexual abuse by her cousin, but as she tries to remember the details of the abuse by more closely related family members, the details become more and more difficult to remember. In order to deal with the fear of losing her brothers and father if she discloses the abuse, Sandy simply had to "forget" that the abuse had ever happened.

Our minds can be wonderful when we need to protect ourselves. As long as Sandy was in a situation where her father or brothers had access to her and could further harm her, she "forgot" the abuse. The cost of forgetting the abuse was very high, however. Sandy was not allowed to acknowledge that something horrible had happened to her. To keep from acknowledging what had happened to her, Sandy began to withdraw more often into her bedroom and spent time alone. She began to become more depressed, with lengthy periods of tearfulness for what she felt was no reason. To acknowledge even to herself what was happening in her family was just too risky.

When Sandy was thirteen, she went to live with her mother. Sandy's mother was very loving and had no knowledge of the sexual, physical, and emotional abuse that her daughter had experienced. When Sandy began to feel more safe and realized that her mother was not going to treat her as her other family members had treated her, Sandy began to feel even more depressed. The memories and feelings of depression began to manifest themselves as explosive episodes of rage and violence. After each episode of out-of-control anger and violence, Sandy would promise her mother that this time was the last time that she would act so horribly; Sandy honestly did have intentions of controlling her behaviors. When Sandy was not angry, she had become so depressed that even the most simple activity such as going outside in the world became too difficult for her. Staying in bed sleeping, eating, or watching television became the primary activities of Sandy's day. As Sandy began to feel more safe, she began to have more memories of her past abuse. As the memories of the abuse increased, the depression began to express itself more often as rage.

Sandy would express the rage in ways that were much more in keeping with a young child. Sandy's abuse had begun when she was about three or four years old, so Sandy's anger was expressed much in the way that a three- or four-year-old child would express anger: with temper tantrums, fits of throwing things, and saying hateful things to her mother. As Sandy began to express her anger more freely, she also began to lose weight and become more adventuresome in exploring the world outside of her mother's home. As Sandy's weight loss continued and she relied less and less on food as a way of keeping a lid on her memories and feelings in regard to her past abuse, her depression lessened and her anger grew.

The day that Sandy was finally able to tell her father that she did not want to see him anymore because of his past abusiveness was a real turning point for her. Although she was not able to confront him in detail about the various things that he had done to abuse her, Sandy was able to confront him enough to be able to begin the process of having some sense of mastery and control in her life. For Sandy, the healing process had finally begun.

I believe that depression related to unexpressed feelings of harmful events such as sexual abuse is often stored in the body of the survivor. Trying to suppress such intense emotions takes a toll on the survivor's storehouse of available developmental energy. It is only when these survivors feel safe enough that they are able to begin to express their pain. This need to grieve deeply must be expressed in ways that will release this energy, but oftentimes survivors are not even allowed to acknowledge that anything harmful has happened to them. It is only when we are able to acknowledge the pain that we have felt in our lives that we are able to experience the joy and the love that we also have available to us. Young survivors must be able to express their anger and rage at the injustice of the abuse. To have to deny constantly to oneself that the abuse even occurred requires the presence of something as mood altering as depression. Depression keeps the focus off what the survivor is really experiencing. Without even realizing it, Sandy was doing the very thing that she needed to be doing to begin to heal. Sandy was honoring the experience that she had suffered at her father's and brothers' hands in the way we would all honor such a painful experience: she was furious at the injustice of it all and expressed it with rage. It is only when we own and honor the child who we were and the experiences that that child had can we learn to love the person that we have become. The way to honor that child is to own that child's experiences, memories, feelings, and express the grief that the child has held inside. Unless the grief and the anger are acknowledged, the survivor will never be able to be truly intimate and genuine with another human being. All the attempts at avoiding the pain and the grief that the survivor may employ will never really work. This is the point at which doing work on the inner child is necessary. At the very heart of the inner child work lies intensive grief work. If as adults we cannot own our childhood experiences (by *own* I mean genuinely recognize that the feelings we have had are true and accurate) then we cannot forgive ourselves for our own past behaviors and learn to love and care for ourselves in the future. Being angry about not having had our needs met is healthy. Suppressing such powerful negative emotions leads to an adulthood where we do not have the ability to set healthy boundaries with others. This inability to set healthy boundaries with others is especially true in relationships with the significant others in our lives.

Grief work involves energy. This energy is stored in the survivor's body and involves physical reactions. When people begin to experience deep grief after such prolonged periods—as do survivors who may have suppressed their true feelings for so long—the survivor will experience physical symptoms when the suppressed emotions begin to emerge. Some survivors will find that when they begin to express such pent-up emotions, their voices will become shaky. Survivors may feel as if their throat is closing up. Sometimes this is because they have had literally to "choke back" their anger for years. Sometimes survivors will become so upset at the prospect of expressing strong emotions after such a long time that they will literally stop breathing when they feel as if they might say something about their abuse. As humans, we all have the tendency to hold our breath whenever we become afraid or experience intense emotions, especially grief. It is important to tell survivors when they finally begin to feel long pent-up feelings that they must breathe slowly and deeply to center and calm themselves.

It is not unusual for survivors who are depressed to complain of vague aches and pains. These various ailments may be psychosomatic symptoms. In other words, the survivors have not expressed their true feelings verbally so their bodies are speaking for them by manifesting various symptoms. I have found that many times survivors will experience psychosomatic symptoms in the area where the anger is stored in their body. To heal, they must release this negative energy that has been stored in the survivors' bodies.

> Michelle is a seventeen-year-old survivor who is in excellent health, yet she constantly complains of stomach pain. Numerous tests have never been able to confirm any organic cause for Michelle's stomach pains. In reality, Michelle is experiencing this pain because of the anxiety she feels in having to deal with a father who has been physically, emotionally, and verbally abusive to her. Although her father is not the perpetrator who sexually abused Michelle, he was not supportive when Michelle disclosed the sexual abuse. In fact, he became enraged at Michelle and accused her of lying about the allegations of abuse.

There are three main types of depression, each with its own characteristics and criteria. *Major depression* has three discrete and identifiable stages: beginning, middle, and end. Major depression can return and is more resistant to treatment each time another episode occurs. The longer the survivor waits to seek treatment, the more difficult the treatment will be.

Chronic depression is the second type of depression. With chronic depression, the survivor will experience what I consider to be similar to a constant low-grade fever. The survivor will see life through gray-colored lenses. Usually chronic depression involves depression of long-standing duration. A large percentage of survivors would fit into this category simply because they have had to deal with such painful abuse and the effects of the abuse. I have worked with survivors who are so used to being depressed that they do not even realize that other people do not feel depressed all the time as the survivor does. Since the survivor knows little of joy or happiness and often does not remember a time that he or she ever was happy, the survivor does not even realize that another way of life exists. These are the survivors that I feel are more likely to use drugs, alcohol, or compulsive behaviors to deal with their depression.

The third category of depression involves survivors who are *bipolar.* Bipolar disorder formerly was called *manic depression.* I treat many adolescent and adult survivors who enter therapy having already been diagnosed as bipolar. Although I know of no real research that demonstrates a connection between sexual abuse and bipolar disorder, I suspect that a very real connection exists. I believe that survivors may have a genetic predisposition to being bipolar but they may have never developed full-blown bipolar disorder until they experienced something as traumatic as sexual abuse. These types of survivors are also at high risk for substance abuse and compulsive behaviors. They also come from families of origin in which there are parents who are bipolar (bipolar can be inherited, as I previously mentioned). Trying to navigate in an environment in which someone has bipolar disorder, particulary someone you must rely upon as much as your parent, can be very stressful.

Depression is the number one public health problem in the United States today. Two times as many women as men are diagnosed as being depressed, probably because women are more verbal about disclosing their feelings. Men are more apt to focus on activities or use alcohol to dull their pain. People over age sixty-five are four times more likely to be depressed. One in twenty Americans is seriously depressed enough that mental health treatment should be recommended. One in every five Americans will experience depression during his or her lifetime. The symptoms include stress, anxiety, vague aches and pains that have no real pattern or consistency, fatigue, and a general sense of weariness that is not relieved by a good night's sleep or additional rest. Additional signs of depression include loss of interest in things that the survivor previously enjoyed, sleep problems, loss of energy, an inability to concentrate or focus, changes in eating patterns, complaining of a persistently sad or empty feeling, tearfulness, irritability (more often seen in men probably because anger is more socially acceptable in men), drug or alcohol abuse (probably an unconscious attempt to self-medicate), missing time from school, work, or other activities, and talking of suicide (perhaps seen as an attempt to receive attention).

The most serious consequence of depression is attempted suicide. Sexual abuse is so traumatic that survivors often believe suicide is a viable solution to their problems. Whenever individuals are suicidal, they have developed an inability to see the options available to them. The only solution that they see is to end their life. Many times certain periods in our lives or circumstances are likely to cause thoughts of suicide. Such circumstances include:

- Times of stress, such as holidays or family celebrations. (These are times when people expect to be happy and lighthearted, but survivors may be estranged from those who should be closest to them emotionally.)
- When survivors are around people who give them a "hard time." (e.g., questioning by the police, testifying in court)
- Starting treatment with a therapist and realizing how emotionally painful and time-consuming the treatment may appear to be.
- Having a crisis while in treatment and seeing the crisis as an indication that treatment is not going to work.
- Trying to stop abuse of substances or compulsive behaviors and being unsuccessful.
- Thinking that suicide will hurt those who have abused or abandoned the survivor.
- Believing that situations will always be as negative as they currently are.

Depression is rampant among survivors, especially incest survivors. Depression that is not acknowledged or is left untreated can lead to serious consequences. In fact, it is not unusual for depression to cause the survivor to be unable to fulfill the potential that he or she was born with. Many survivors live wasted lives because they are so apt to minimize the damage or the amount of pain they have experienced due to the abuse. In reality, this failure to acknowledge the pain and the tragic results of such unacknowledged abuse is a form of self-inflicted abuse. Many survivors will attempt to hide their sense of shame and feelings of inadequacy by using drugs, alcohol, or compulsive behaviors to dull their senses and keep them from acknowledging the effect of the abuse on their lives.

Terry is a twenty-two-year-old survivor who was raped by several different male perpetrators when he was a young child. All throughout his childhood Terry hid the abuse from everyone. Terry's sense of shame and pain over his abuse was so great that Terry even hid the pain of his abuse from himself. As Terry grew older, the numbers on his bathroom scale also went higher. At the age of fifteen, Terry was a compulsive overeater. Terry had no idea that his overeating was an unconscious attempt to take the focus off his sexual abuse. Terry felt so "different" from the other boys his age. While his friends were thinking about girls and beginning to explore their relationships with the opposite sex, Terry was trying to understand why he felt so attracted to other males. Although the rapes had been committed in a forceful manner, the perpetrators had been very skilled sexually. Since Terry's body couldn't distinguish between good touch and bad touch and had responded sexually, Terry thought that he had been a willing participant in his own sexual abuse. Terry assumed that simply because his body had responded to the sexual abuse that he was homosexual. The other boys in Terry's high school made jokes about what they called "faggots" and "queers." Terry was not about to confide in anyone and take the chance of being labeled even more so than he was already labeled because of his weight problem.

As a way of dealing with his confusion about his sexual identity and his weight issues, Terry began to consume ever-increasing amounts of food and began to purge. Terry was not able to track the pattern of these behaviors and see that the overeating always seemed to correspond to times when his peers would ignore him or, even worse, when they would laugh and make jokes about his weight. Terry would turn to food as a way to keep a lid on his anger and sadness at his peers' rejection. Afterward, Terry would be consumed with anger for being so "weak" and overeating, and he would force himself to vomit in an attempt to remedy his overconsumption of food.

For awhile, Terry thought that he had finally found the way literally to have his cake and eat it, too. The depression continued, but Terry was stoic in his attempts so simply "will" himself to handle the situation. Our bodies never lie. As Terry's bulimia progressed, his body became more and more damaged. Eventually, Terry's health brought him into treatment. It was only when Terry was able to acknowledge the abuse that he had experienced and the pain that this abuse had caused him that he was able to begin the healing process.

The core issue in situations such as Terry's is that the child victim of sexual abuse instinctively knows that what has happened to him or her is abusive. When victims do not receive the validation from those closest to them that they have indeed been victimized and feelings of anger and pain are appropriate, the process that leads to addictive and compulsive behaviors has been established.

When survivors attempt to ignore feelings resulting from their abuse, whatever those feelings might be, depression is the result. It is only when victims acknowledge the feelings that they have kept inside themselves that the true healing process can take place. This is not to say that once victims acknowledge the harmfulness of their abuse that they will not have feelings of deep sadness. But by acknowledging the harmfulness of their abuse, the victims allow themselves to begin the natural grieving process, which then leads to healing.

Depression can be seen as occurring along a continuum of emotions ranging from feelings of emptiness, which is called *empty, depleted depression,* to several other depressive states. Survivors who have become codependent are most likely to develop empty, depleted depression. These survivors are the ones who will give to others until almost nothing is left over for themselves. In reality, these types of survivors are simply doing for others what they wish someone had done for them. The most tragic part of this situation is that these survivors will never meet anyone who will give back what they need. Usually survivors will not *allow* someone to truly give back to them because, first of all, the other person will not know what it was that the survivors want. Even if the other person could read their minds and attempt to give back to them, the survivors will not be attracted to someone who could truly give back to them. If someone could give back to the codependent survivor, why would the other person find the survivor useful? Codependent survivors cannot fathom the idea that they could be valued simply because they *are.* If someone did not *need* the codependent survivor to be the caregiver, then the survivor would have no value (at least in the codependent survivor's unconscious mind).

Agitated depression is characterized by symptoms of being very anxious, acting out in an irritable manner, or being upset. These survivors are unconsciously attempting to protect their vulnerability and feelings of inadequacy by acting in a manner that keeps others from getting too close and discovering what survivors see as their own inadequacy. The survivor acts in a manner that I refer to as "whistling in the dark." The survivor is terrified of being found inadequate or a failure. These are the survivors who I characterize as being on the offensive. They will attack others before they feel that others will inevitably attack them. This type of behavior occurrs consistently in the adolescent groups that I have facilitated. Male survivors will talk about killing perpetrators if they ever attempted to sexually abuse them. The same survivors will always be on the offensive, looking for ways to demonstrate their physical strength and ability to defend themselves in whatever manner necessary. In reality, these survivors have behaviors that would clinically be described as being narcissistically depleted. I tend to imagine this type of behavior as being similar to popping a balloon that is full of hot air and watching it deflate.

Cases of depression are rooted in the failure of significant others in the survivor's childhood to provide the validation and mirroring that the child survivor needed to develop a healthy self-concept. We all need authority figures during childhood to validate our subjective experiences. When this does not happen, the child victim has to try to make some sort of sense out of what he or she knows has truly happened while the people that the child looks to for guidance and nurturance act as if it has not happened. No wonder so many sexual abuse victims simply push the knowledge of the abuse down and use whatever means necessary to keep a lid on their feelings in regard to the abuse. We form our sense of reality and our experiences by those who are most important to us. When we do not find our sense of reality validated, confusion and depression are bound to result. Child survivors will almost always think that *their* own perceptions must be wrong rather than the perception of the adults in their lives. To think that the adults in their lives were sometimes willing to allow the child to be victimized or that they were unable to protect the children and not support the children's disclosure is simply too painful for them.

While working with clients who have been sexually abused and have held their feelings about the abuse in for such a long time that it has resulted in deep depression, I always wonder if it is better to be depressed and express the anger toward oneself or to be angry and direct the anger outside of oneself and lose those one values the most. Some clients switch back and forth between these two extremes. The survivors who have not learned to effectively moderate their anger see only these two extremes as their choices for expressing anger.

Sometimes healing from sexual abuse and depression requires a leap of faith for the client. Many times therapists will sense this reluctance on the part of the client. The therapist will think of it as "resistance." In truth, the client is afraid of letting go of what are familiar and customary behaviors. Even though depression is uncomfortable, it is still preferable to feeling fear.

Allowing oneself the time and right to grieve one's losses is a painful and difficult process. Survivors have so much to grieve, yet the thought of feeling such deep and intense feelings is so frightening that many survivors never allow themselves to venture into their grief.

Many times those who are close to survivors may attempt to encourage them to skip stages in their grieving process simply because those observing them are not able to deal with the painfulness of the survivors' emotions themselves, or they are so inconvenienced by the survivors' grieving that they want to "hurry up" the grieving process. These are the people who will tell the survivor that the abuse happened a long time ago and that the survivor should be "over it" by now.

If survivors neglect to feel the emotions that come to the surface when they grieve, they are setting themselves up for an addiction or compulsion. If those closest to the survivors are not able to support them in their attempts at grieving their losses, chances are that the survivors will attempt simply to skip the grieving process. Following is an example of the futility of such behaviors.

> Lisa is a forty-three-year-old survivor. For over ten years during her adolescence, Lisa was forced to have intercourse with her father. What was especially painful for Lisa was the way that her father abused her. Her father was very skilled at sex and was able to cause Lisa's body to respond to his attempts at sex. Because Lisa was not aware how our bodies will respond to sexual touch even if the touch is abusive, Lisa blamed herself for the abuse. She felt that if the sex had truly been abusive, she would not have responded physically. When Lisa was in her thirties she finally disclosed the abuse to her mother. Lisa was so damaged by the lack of emotional support she received from her mother that when her mother encouraged Lisa to simply put the past in the past, Lisa attempted to do just as her mother had suggested. Despite Lisa saying that she forgave her father for the sexual abuse, Lisa was not allowed to experience fully one step of the healing process: she skipped the stage of being angry about what she had lost (her right to experience sex in a healthy, appropriate manner) and acknowledging her grief and went right to forgiveness. How can one forgive another if one does not first acknowledge that one has been wronged and grieve one's losses? Lisa was not truly able to heal because she was never allowed to grieve fully.

As time went by and Lisa's father became incapacitated due to his ill health, Lisa had even more reasons to grieve. She needed to grieve the parent that she had never had as well as the parent who was dying. As her father's death approached, Lisa began to realize how much her father's abusiveness had cost her. Never again would Lisa have the opportunity to have the kind of parent who would nurture and value her. Lisa was faced with the reality of not only the death of her father but the death of a dream as well. By those closest to Lisa not acknowledging her losses or her need to grieve her losses, Lisa was cheated yet one more time. Lisa will only heal when she is allowed to grieve.

The symptoms of grieving can be confused with other symptoms, but just because the symptoms are not always clearly expressed it does not mean that the need to grieve is not present. Physical symptoms of grieving include feelings of emptiness in the stomach region, a tightness in the throat, and feelings of weight or heaviness in the chest. Those who are grieving will often fluctuate between feelings of grief and feelings of intense anger. Inablity to sleep or concentrate are also signs of grief. Feeling as if one is "at loose ends" is also another common feeling. Being angry at all of the lost opportunities and what might have been are common feelings associated with grieving. Mood swings alternating between anger and intense sorrow are common. Crying at the slightest thing is also common.

It is imperative that we do not allow others to diminish the significance of the abuse and its negative impact upon our lives. As survivors, we need to be able to take the time to acknowledge our losses and the things that will never be because of the abuse. As survivors, we must refrain from running from our abusive histories and allow ourselves to experience the feelings resulting from the abuse and the consequences of the abuse. "Numbing" ourselves with addictions or compulsions simply delays the process of grieving and recovery. Reaching out to others to share our feelings in regard to our grief and abuse is very important. When those we expect to receive support from do not support us, we should reach out to others until we do find someone who can and will support our right to grieve our losses and feel all of our feelings—even when the intensity of our feelings may be uncomfortable for those closest to us.

We need to listen to our bodies when we are grieving. As survivors, we need to learn to care for ourselves in all ways—physically, emotionally, and spiritually. We need to take care of our health, not to anesthetize ourselves because the feelings are painful or inconvenient for others. We need to look for the support of others who will be there for us as we acknowledge the pain of our pasts and as we grieve all of the lost opportunities that we will never be able to regain.

How will we know when we are completing the grieving process? We will be able to concentrate on the tasks at hand, to feel a genuine interest in others and the things that are happening around us. We will be able to enjoy the close relationships in our present life. We will begin to realize that no one has a perfect childhood, and we will be able to have some sort of perspective on our childhood that will allow us to move forward with our life while still acknowledging the pain of our past.

Healing from depression can involve keeping a journal, listening to your favorite music, reading, and enjoying favorite activities. The problem occurs when survivors are so depressed that they cannot participate in any of their favorite activities. Sometimes initial treatment of survivors involves medication such as an antidepressant. Many survivors will be reluctant to take medication. The survivor and the family must be educated to realize that the longer a depressive episode is left untreated, the more difficult the depression is to treat. The greater the number of episodes of depression that the survivor has had, the more difficult the depression will be to treat. Medication literally can make the difference between life and death in situations in which survivors have made past suicide attempts. Once the survivor's depression has lifted enough to enjoy some hope for the future, the survivor can resume activities in a way to lessen the chance of future severe episodes of depression. Some of these ways include: not socially isolating themselves even when they are very depressed; understanding the notion that drinking alcohol is more harmful than helpful in healing from depression; finally, educating themselves that keeping doctor appointments and taking care of themselves in general ways (e.g., eating regular meals, exercising, getting adequate rest) are the surest ways to prevent future severe bouts of depression.

The next chapter addresses what happens to survivors who live with the constant threat of abuse without the promise of any relief. These survivors manage to cope with the constant threat of abuse in a surprising way.

Chapter 6

Fear As a Catalyst
for Addictive Behaviors

*They conquer who believe they can. He has not learned the first
lesson of life who does not every day surmount a fear.*

Ralph Waldo Emerson

The fear that results from severe trauma such as sexual abuse can
be a force that impacts the survivor's entire life. Research has shown
that once a young child has been exposed to severe trauma and fear,
biologically that child is never the same. Neurological pathways that
are established early in that child's development can forever be
changed when the child experiences such trauma.

An article in *U.S. News and World Report* by Shannon Brownlee
(1996) reports that Dr. Martin Teicher, a psychiatrist, has done research at McLean Hospital in Belmont, Massachusetts, which has indicated that children who have been abused tend to have fewer nerve
cell connections between areas in the left hemisphere of the brain
than children who have not been abused. These same children are the
ones who also seem to display more self-destructive and aggressive
behaviors. The left hemisphere of the brain is the area of the brain in
which language and logical thought are processed. This theory of
thought also fits with what Dr. Bruce Perry (Brownlee, 1996), a child
psychiatrist at Children's Hospital and at Baylor College of Medicine, finds: that trauma, neglect, and physical and sexual abuse can
have lasting effects on the child's developing brain. It makes sense
that children who have experienced trauma due to abuse would find it
difficult to process and recover from fear and trauma. These same
children are also the ones we would be likely to see acting out because they do not have the ability to verbalize or process their feel-

ings properly due to neurological problems resulting from such early abuse. Hope exists that later life experiences which are not traumatic or negative might help reverse some of these tendencies toward fear and trauma resulting in substance abuse, compulsive behaviors, self-abusive behaviors, and risky sexual behavior.

Dr. Carlton Munson (in press) from the University of Maryland School of Social Work believes that these are the children who learn to respond to life situations more from the emotional angle than the logical and rational angle. Perry also states in the Brownlee (1996) article from *U.S. News and World Report* that children who are aroused from fear cannot absorb cognitive emotion due to their constant need to be sensitive to threats in their world. The child's attention has been attuned to the emotional and physical responses from others in his or her environment in an attempt simply to survive. Perry goes on to state that such children may have difficulty developing problem solving and language skills. Perry's findings indicate that the cortex (the thinking part of the brain) is 20 percent smaller on average in abused children than in children in a control group.

Severe trauma such as early sexual abuse may lead to *reactive attachment disorder.* In reactive attachment disorder, the child is not able to bond to most early caregivers due to separation from the caregivers in early childhood or due to some other situation that causes the inability to develop a bond between the child and his or her earliest caregivers. The child does not develop the sense of empathy toward others that keeps him or her from objectifying and victimizing or harming others. These are the children who seem to have no conscience and who are always "looking out for number one." The occurrence of early neglect and trauma may be the catalyst that sets in motion the cycle of neglect and trauma for the next generation of children. Early neglect, abuse, and fear resulting from trauma may be the underlying causes of the development of perpetrators of sexual abuse. If many of the perpetrators of sexual abuse were themselves victims of sexual abuse as children, it is not too large a leap to suspect that many of these offenders may have developed reactive attachment disorder due to fear, neglect, and trauma in their own childhoods. Because these offenders demonstrate lack of empathy for their victims as evidenced by the very abuse that they inflict upon them, perhaps we are reaping the seeds that were sown by earlier abuse in the perpetrator's childhood.

One of the most difficult situations with which to deal when working with a survivors' group occurs when a survivor in the group admits that he or she also has been a perpetrator.

Kerry is a twelve-year-old survivor who could pass for a much younger child. Kerry was raped repeatedly both vaginally and rectally by her paternal uncle over a period of eight years, beginning when she was less than eighteen months old. Kerry's mother had a drug and alcohol problem and was also a survivor of childhood sexual abuse. Kerry's mother had been molested by her own father for most of her childhood and supported her substance abuse through prostitution. Kerry has witnessed her mother prostituting herself to finance her drug habit. Little bonding occurred between Kerry and her mother. Kerry's mother was emotionally and physically unavailable for Kerry, thus Kerry had no caregiver to reinforce that she was loved and valued. Kerry learned at a very early age to look out for herself. She also learned that she had to "protect" herself from caring about others, because caring hurt too much.

Kerry demonstrated most of the characteristics of reactive attachment disorder: poor peer relationships, a preoccupation with fire and gore, poor impulse control, stealing and lying, wanting control over everything, destruction of personal and others' property, a lack of consequence in thinking, being indiscriminately affectionate to strangers and people that she didn't know well at all, and being superficially engaging, charming, and manipulative. Because Kerry could be so engaging, it took quite awhile for the group to process the knowledge that Kerry had been placed in a long-term residential treatment center for molesting a younger child in her foster home. Kerry had sexually abused this child during the time frame that Kerry had begun attending the weekly survivors' group for her own sexual abuse issues. No one in the group, including the therapists, had any knowledge that Kerry had become a perpetrator. The group was torn between sympathy and compassion for Kerry's own victimization and fury that Kerry could go on to inflict the same trauma on another innocent child.

The age at which survivors experience the fear and trauma of their own abuse has a lot to do with determining how much damage will be done to them and how they will process the damage. Generally, the younger the victim is when the abuse happens and the developmental stage the victim is in will determine the results of the abuse. If the victim is a little older and has successfully bonded with at least one other caregiver in younger life and has developed some ego strengths, then this victim has a much better reference point to use as a basis to return to when stressed or in times of crisis. The survivor who has not had the opportunity to develop these attachments and reference points is most at risk of replicating the cycle of abuse.

Since traumatic memories allow the child to access only the right side of the brain, and the left side of the brain is responsible for organizing and making sense of information, children who have been abused or neglected very early in childhood may have flashbacks, depersonalization- and derealization-like experiences, and a sense of alienation and isolation and have no way to express such intense internal experiences. Most often the child will exhibit extreme rage or aggressive behaviors.

> Rebecca was raped by her natural father when she was less than two years old. Rebecca's parents had divorced. Although her mother had been given primary custody of Rebecca, her father had kidnapped Rebecca when she was only eighteen months old. Rebecca's father told her that if she ever told about the ongoing abuse, he would kill her mother and go to the nearest playground and do the same thing to the children there that he was doing to her. Rebecca felt such divided loyalties. She wanted to end the abuse by telling, but telling of the abuse (at least in Rebecca's mind) would result in causing other people to be killed or be abused just like she was being abused. Children usually will believe that the perpetrator has the ability to perform all of the acts that he or she claims to be able to do. In a child's mind, the perpetrator has "superhuman" abilities. The intensity of the conflicting emotions in Rebecca's situation caused such emotional stress that Rebecca began to have tempter tantrums that would last for hours. The tantrums would end only when Rebecca could no longer physically continue to scream, hit and bite others, or throw things. Despite the fact that Rebecca was only four years old and quite petite for her age, she was able to inflict a lot of harm on the people who happened to be in her path when she was angry. It took two adults to restrain Rebecca when she finally became conflicted enough to disclose her father's abuse. For a period of at least a month after the abuse was

disclosed, any mention of the abuse was enough to send Rebecca into another fit of rage.

Will Rebecca ever recover sufficiently to prevent her from such acting-out behaviors or to prevent her from going on to harm others in much the same way that Rebecca herself was harmed? I believe that she stands a much better chance of a promising life because of at least one positive part in Rebecca's life: Rebecca has a mother who loves her very much, and Rebecca has bonded with her. The very fact that Rebecca was able to develop empathy for her mother's welfare and the welfare of the other children on the playground demonstrates that although Rebecca may have been abused at a tender age, she still has the ability to care about others. In Rebecca's situation, the fear that she felt due to her own abuse and the possible abuse of other people caused her to use acting out and rage as the means to shift the focus of attention away from what was happening to her and to offer her the anesthesia that these behaviors offered as a means of surviving her terrible abuse. Was Rebecca able to shift her focus of attention away from her abuse by using these behaviors in a conscious manner? I doubt if a child that young could have the cognitive ability to choose such a shift in behaviors in order to process abuse. Could we perhaps surmise that Rebecca's situation demonstrates that the anesthesia and shift in focus she experienced, which allowed her to endure whatever she had to endure in order to survive, is an innate trait? More and more I believe that humans are gifted with the ability to emotionally survive the most devastating abuse by the use of what I would call self-hypnosis: shifting our focus of attention away from those things with which we cannot deal toward those things with which we can deal.

Being a survivor can be frightening for many reasons. Jason is a good example of a survivor who has turned to acting out and using drugs in an attempt to quell the fear that he feels every day.

Jason witnessed his uncle kill a man in a drug deal that went wrong. Jason's uncle also had molested Jason since Jason was only seven years old. How do survivors deal not only with their own sexual abuse but also with witnessing the violence that their perpetrators are ultimately capable of inflicting? In Jason's case, the only way that he could deal with both his own abuse and the murder he had witnessed was by not saying anything to anyone about what had happened. Jason believed that if he told about what had occurred, he would most likely be the next one to be killed. The only way that Jason could deal with the atrocities was to keep them buried deep within himself.

Human beings are not meant to deal with such horrors alone. In order to keep his pain a secret, Jason needed something to numb the pain. When running away and cutting himself didn't work anymore, Jason began to drink and take drugs. Acting out sexually also became a common occurrence. All of the people witnessing Jason's behaviors had no idea what was causing him to act out. They simply felt that Jason was a "bad seed." He was blamed for his negative behaviors and branded a "punk." No one took the time or the trouble to look beyond Jason's behaviors to see what had caused them.

Jason himself believed that he was a bad person. As a consequence of all of the trauma that he had experienced, Jason did not have the mental or the developmental energy left over with which to master his academics. When Jason failed in school, it became just one more sign that he was a waste.

Jason entered an ever-widening cycle in which negative happenings reinforced negative behaviors. The cycle continued until Jason could not stand it anymore and he consequently made a series of suicide attempts. It was only when Jason absolutely could not deal with life anymore and really wanted to die that he finally disclosed what he had witnessed and experienced.

The normal response when most people hear that someone has been murdered is to think that those sorts of things don't happen to everyday people. Jason met with skepticism and disbelief when he disclosed the murder. If we look at the problem from another angle, it becomes apparent that whether Jason was telling lies or not, a problem still exists. If Jason was telling the truth, obviously someone was killed and the murderer needs to be brought to justice. If someone was *not* killed, then Jason obviously has a problem with telling the truth and needs to be dealt with accordingly.

What is not so obvious is that if Jason is telling lies, he obviously still fears the alleged killer because he has gone to great lengths to indulge in behaviors that will quiet all of the feelings that he has about what he *perceives* as having happened. We need to deal with the reality of where the survivors are, not where we believe they might actually be.

In Jason's case, we need to assume that *something* has happened that Jason feels he can't deal with. We must give Jason the support and undestanding that will enable him to feel safe and secure enough to begin to address these issues—whether the issues exist as we see them or not.

Another issue Jason couldn't deal with was that to keep himself safe Jason had asked the perpetrator to have sex with him after the abuse had begun. In Jason's mind, the sexual abuse wasn't abuse at all, because Jason felt that he had asked for the abuse to continue. The perpetrator was very cunning; he knew that if Jason felt responsible for the abuse, then Jason would not report what had happened. Of all the issues that Jason will have to deal with for the rest of his life, the idea that he colluded with the perpetrator in his own victimization will be the most difficult with which to deal.

How do you convince someone that her or she is the *victim* and not a consensual sexual partner? Despite countless hours of therapy and the support of the group, Jason floundered with the issue of seeing himself as an active participant in his own abuse. It is only when Jason is able to let go of the idea that he had any control in the abuse that he will be able to realize that it was really abuse and not consensual. In many survivors' minds, the idea that they caused the abuse is really an attempt to try to feel some sense of control over what has happened to them. Because Jason saw himself as agreeing with the abuse, he couldn't see the reality of what had actually happened. To see that he is a victim will be very frightening for Jason, because it will also mean that he had *no control* over what happened. If he had no control once, then the same thing could happen to him again. For Jason, this was a terrifying concept. In reality, the idea of having very little control over the things that happen to us is a fact with which we all must deal.

Survivors often must deal with issues in their lives that extend beyond the sexual abuse that they have suffered.

> Justin was raped by his stepfather when he was eight years old. Shortly before his stepfather raped him, Justin witnessed his stepfather participating in a robbery. Justin was the only witness to the robbery and subsequent murder. Justin's stepfather knew there was no better way of ensuring Justin's silence than having Justin witness the murder.

What is it like for survivors to have to keep such a frightening secret to themselves? The cost to the survivor is enormous. First, the survivor must stifle all of the normal emotions that a person who has witnessed severe trauma normally would feel. Survivors cannot afford to acknowledge what they have witnessed or experienced; to do so would most surely lead to the most serious of consequences. The cost of containing such explosive and powerful emotions can involve all sorts of compulsive behaviors and addictions.

> Justin used cocaine on a daily basis just to help him make it through the day. He also acted out in a defiant and angry way. Although Justin was not consciously aware of it, most of his acting-out behaviors were an attempt to keep his awareness focused on things other than the abuse that he had experienced or the trauma that he had witnessed. This tactic worked for several years until Justin's acting-out behaviors became as much of a problem as the underlying issues he was avoiding.

The saddest part of Justin's story is that when he finally disclosed that he witnessed a murder, very few people believed him. People like to think that murder doesn't happen very often. If one thinks about it though, why would a man who had brutally raped his own stepson hesitate to kill? One must consider the past behaviors of a person before we conclude that the allegations made against them are false.

Sexual abuse often occurs along with other crimes that are bizarre and distasteful. Many of the cases that I have worked with have involved the occult. Many times survivors will turn to the occult in an attempt to regain some power or to punish the perpetrator. When the perpetrator is involved with the occult, the perpetrator will often use ritual or satanic ceremonies initially to intimidate the victim. Later on in the abuse, the perpetrator will often involve the victim in participating in the abuse itself. Once the victim has been forced to participate in the abuse of another person, the victim is very reluctant to disclose his or her own abuse. The perpetrator counts on the victim to see himself or herself as being involved in the perpetration of the abuse as the best form of insurance to keep the victim silent about his or her own abuse.

Once the survivor has made a disclosure that involves something traumatic and frightening, the anxiety level of the survivor greatly increases. Whereas the survivor initially may feel a sense of relief at sharing the burden of the disclosure with another person, later on the survivor will realize that now he or she does not have sole control over whether the secret remains a secret. Someone else has access to the information that could harm the survivor. At this point, the anxiety level of the survivor goes even higher. This is the time when survivors are most at risk for harming themselves. If the person or people to whom the survivors have disclosed the abuse are not supportive, then the survivors are even more apt to harm themselves in an attempt simply to get the inevitable over with—the ultimate punishment with which the perpetrators have threatened the survivors. The survivors feel that no matter what they do, they are going to be at the mercy of the perpetrator. We must realize that even if what the survivors believe the perpetrator will do to harm them seems unbelievable, this is still what the survivors *perceive* as being the truth. Therefore, the survivors' emotional responses will be tied to what they feel is the truth whether it is indeed the truth or not.

What are the costs to the survivors who have experienced the kind of events that instill such horrible fear? If we address the costs in a physical manner, we would see such symptoms as headaches, vague complaints about physical aches and pains, stomach cramping or nausea, problems with either eating or sleeping, frequent complaints about various illnesses, complaining of jaw pain (caused by clenching their teeth from repressed anger), sore neck (also caused by repressed anger), and marking themselves from self-mutilation (also caused by repressed anger or as an indication of borderline personality disorder, which is directly related to sexual abuse).

In psychological terms, survivors who have witnessed violence may demonstrate such diverse behaviors as feelings of powerlessness, anger, depression, shame, grief, deep despair or hopelessness, inability to trust others or decisions made by themselves, fear, low self-worth or self-esteem, problems with authority figures and peers, and acting-out behaviors, which may at times duplicate the violence that they have experienced and/or witnessed. Often these survivors will be overbearing and pushy toward others, especially toward children who are younger and less able to protect themselves. These survivors sometimes have a difficult time being affectionate. They may have learned that being affectionate means that you are weak and that others will take advantage of you. There may be problems such as encopresis (soiling their underclothing) or enuresis (wetting themselves). These conditions are found especially in younger children. Additional regressive behaviors may occur, such as thumb sucking and baby talk in younger survivors or foul and inappropriate language in the older child. These children may be seen as the "bullies" in the neighborhood, or they may be the *aggressors who identify* with the older and stronger children as a way to deal with their own vicitmization: they identify with the behaviors of their own abusers. Whether the child will be the victim or the aggressor depends upon the role with which the survivor most closely identifies. These children also are often the victims of horrible emotional and verbal abuse. They may go on to abuse others with these same types of behaviors. By projecting the abuse that they themselves have experienced onto others, bullies are able to deny the helplessness of their own situation. When others fear a bully, the bully has managed to regain a sense of power and control, even if it is only over other younger or weaker children.

The survivor often will not do well academically. It takes a tremendous amount of energy to contain the intense emotions that are related to violence and abuse. This energy could and should have been extended to the development of skills for such tasks as schoolwork. Survivors who have experienced or witnessed such violence usually perform much lower academically than they are capable of performing. Their poor academic performance feeds into their lowered sense of self-worth, which in turn further feeds into their poor academic performance. Thus begins an ever-widening cycle from which the survivor feels it is impossible to escape.

Sometimes, in an attempt to escape their intense fear and emotional pain, these survivors will make repeated attempts to run away. It is almost as if by fleeing from their current environment, the survivors feel that they can escape their most painful feelings. In reality, we are aware that survivors will take their pain and unresolved issues with them whereever they may go.

The survivors described are the ones most apt to develop substance abuse problems or eating disorders. By developing these problems, survivors are able to shift their focus internally to something over which they *do have some control*. They will minimize the amount of pain that they are experiencing and provide a sense of some relief, comfort, and self-nurture.

These survivors are also the ones who are most likely to replicate some type of violence that they have either witnessed or experienced. This *does not* mean that they *will* go out and kill or maim someone. It simply means that they have witnessed, sometimes repeatedly, the experience that "might makes right." The survivors have learned that the bigger or stronger person often wins arguments or gains whatever it is that they want simply through violence and brute force.

It is not unusual for these survivors to keep this sort of fear and knowledge of horrible abuse to themselves. Even the closest of family members may have no knowledge of what the survivors have experienced or witnessed. Mothers especially may have no knowledge of the survivors' most frightening experiences, especially if the survivors' fathers are the perpetrators. I have seen survivors go to extreme lengths to protect their mothers from the knowledge of the abuse that has transpired. The survivors may feel sorry for their mother because of the painful life that she has had. The survivors may believe at some level that their mother simply couldn't handle the emotional costs of such knowledge. This may be especially true if the survivor is the first born or the eldest daughter. The survivor becomes very parentified. If the mother is codependent or fragile, she may allow the child to bear the burden of the abuse, while all the time the mother may at some level have an instinctive knowledge of the abuse. This is not always the case, but it does happen quite often. How unfair it is to a child who has already been traumatized to be asked to handle emotional events that are too difficult to deal with at such a young chronological and developmental age. Most adults would be traumatized if asked to deal with this sort of trauma.

Our society must assume responsibility for some of the violence and abuse to which our children are exposed. Domestic violence occurs more often than any other form of violence in our society, yet we pay little attention to its effects on our children. Trying to find a treatment resource for dealing with children who have been traumatized by exposure to this type of violence is very difficult. Little funding exists for programs dealing with this problem. The funding is often from short-lived grants and able to serve only a very restricted population in terms of gender or age.

A serious concern for children and adolescents who have been exposed to this type of violence is that as adults they may choose partners who will also be abusive.

Fear is often triggered in the group by the experiences that are shared by one group member with the rest of the group.

> Randy was raped at gunpoint when he was twelve years old. Randy had not even told his parents the details of his rape when he began to participate in the adolescent survivors' group. From the beginning, it was apparent that Randy was very reluctant to share the details of his rape. The group was extremely patient and never pressed Randy to share what had happened to him.
>
> One evening, after several years in the group, Randy suddenly began to participate actively in the group and share what had happened to him. It wasn't apparent what had triggered Randy's sudden decision to tell the group about his abuse, but no one was going to refuse to listen to Randy's story after waiting so long for him to tell what had happened. The details of the rape were unspeakable. The fact that Randy was still alive spoke volumes about the courage that he possessed. It is not usual practice for group members to share all of the details of their abuse experience with the group. We have structured the group in this way so that group members will not feel more or less justified in being included in group discussion depending on the severity of their abuse. We want group members to understand that whether the abuse occurred once or one hundred times, each member deserves the same caring and support. Randy's sharing of all the details of his abuse began so quickly and came out in such urgency that it would not have been therapeutic to attempt to stop his disclosure. As Randy told his story, the group became more and more quiet. I have always had the ability to "pick up vibes" from other people's feelings. The room was so charged with terror and violence that I could feel the fear in the room. Members of the group denied that Randy's story upset them, but it was obvious that they were unsettled. It wasn't long after this group session that it became apparent that the group's members had increased their usage of drugs and alcohol. Group members who were sexually promiscuous began to act out sexually even more than usual. The fear that the group had shared with Randy was intense enough to spark an increase in their drug or behavior of choice in an attempt to quell the uncomfortable feelings and personal memories that the group experienced after hearing of Randy's abuse. This is not to say that it was Randy's fault that the group members increased their compulsive or addictive behaviors. Any other intense event could have

triggered a like response. I believe that their shared empathy for Randy and his horrible abuse reminded the group members of their own painful experiences. When the group members felt Randy's pain, they reached for a substance or behavior to try to "medicate" the emotional pain they were experiencing.

Sometimes trauma such as sexual abuse can *prevent* the survivor from experiencing fear in a way that most people would experience it. Walden is a good example of a survivor who has no sense of the danger of the behaviors in which he is engaging.

Walden was raped on at least three different occasions by men who were friends of Walden's family. Because Walden's mother is also a survivor who has not dealt with her issues, Walden has been exposed to more people who have potential to molest than most other people would be exposed.

Walden does not feel secure in expressing his anger toward his mother for not protecting him from the rapes. His mother is very fragile. She has made several suicide attempts in recent years. Walden is afraid that if he expresses his anger toward his mother, she will not be able to deal with his anger and will harm herself. Instead of directing his anger toward his mother, Walden has been directing his anger toward himself. Walden doesn't realize that this is what he has been doing. When he stays out all night (he is only seventeen years old) without telling anyone where he is or who he is with, Walden doesn't understand what all the fuss is about. When Walden began smoking crack cocaine and marijuana like other people would smoke tobacco, he couldn't understand why people were so concerned about him. When Walden was so desperate to get high that he prostituted himself, he didn't understand why others were upset with him.

Why is Walden so oblivious to the risky situations in which he places himself? Walden's fear of the *known* (in this case, drugs and prostitution) is much less than his fear of the *unknown* (what his mother would do to herself if he told her how angry he is with her for not protecting him from the rapes). Rather than risk harming his mother by telling her of his true feelings, Walden would rather risk harming himself. The risky behaviors also serve the purpose of keeping Walden's mind off of his feelings of grief and anger. What a sad way to try to keep a lid on his feelings. Both Walden and his mother would be much better off if he would risk expressing his feelings and sharing them with others who would be supportive.

Sometimes the survivor will be fearful of a situation that is very real and could have exactly the consequences that the survivor fears the most.

Jarod is sixteen years old. Jarod was sexually abused by a friend of his mother's when Jarod was only six years old. The sexual abuse was so frightening that Jarod told his mother what had happened as soon as he was safely away from the perpetrator. It was confusing to Jarod when he told his mother about the sexual abuse and she became very angry at him instead of the perpetrator. His mother began to cry and blamed Jaron for being a "bad" boy who would tell such lies about a close family friend—who was paying most of their rent and utility bills. Jarod's mother had also begun to develop a drug problem. Most of her drugs were being supplied by this friend. Jarod had no way of knowing or even understanding why his mother chose to side with the perpetrator.

Jarod was a very proactive little boy. Once he told his mother and nothing happened to stop the sexual abuse, Jarod told his teacher what had happened. His teacher immediately reported the abuse to the authorities. When the authorities investigated Jarod's claims of abuse, the police and Family Services knew that six-year-old Jarod's descriptions and details of the abuse were too clear and detailed to be a lie. When the perpetrator was charged and found guilty of numerous serious sexual offenses, Jarod's mother attempted suicide. Jarod was the one who found his mother and called the ambulance. She was taken to the hospital to have her stomach pumped of all of the drugs she had taken. Jarod's mother was so upset and confused from all of the drugs she had taken that she didn't notice the look of terror, sadness, and guilt on Jarod's face when she told the police that she had attempted suicide because she could not deal with the loss of her boyfriend. Jarod immediately felt that *he* was the one who had caused his mother to try to kill herself. From the time that he was six years old, Jarod was never able to go to his mother with any emotions of anger, complaint, or any other emotion that he felt might cause her to harm herself. Jarod felt that he had to walk on eggshells to protect his mother. Jarod was molested many other times while he lived with his mother. Her drug use escalated. As her drug problem became more and more serious, Jarod's mother's choice of friends became less and less wise. Her criteria for choosing a friend involved only one element: the friend must be able to supply her either with the drugs that she needed or the money to buy the drugs that she wanted. The only friends that could provide these services were people who were dealing and using drugs themselves. In her stupor, she felt no concern for what people of this quality might do to her children. By the time Jarod was sixteen years old, he had been molested by eight different perpetrators.

Despite all of the pain and anger that Jarod felt, he never confided to his mother about any of the other experiences of sexual abuse after he made the first disclosure and she had attempted suicide. Jarod never forgot the feelings of guilt and responsibility that he had felt then. Keeping a lid on rage and justified anger was easy compared to the thought of walking into his mother's bedroom and finding her dead because of something Jarod had told her. The years of silence finally took its toll. To keep his anger under wraps, Jarod began to steal some of his mother's drugs. At first it was just drugs to help him deal with physical pain. Then Jarod began to take pills to help him sleep, then pills to help him get up in the morning. Jarod's mother never noticed that he was acting differently, which caused him even more pain and anger. It was only when Jarod was strung out on heroin and arrested for solicitation for homosexual prostitution that his mother came out of her drug-induced haze long enough to ask Jarod "what the hell was wrong with him."

Jarod finally realized that no matter how much he gave to his mother or how many negative behaviors he chose to ignore, his mother was never going to care for anyone but herself. At this point, Jarod began to release all of the pent-up rage he had felt toward his mother. She took the onslaught of anger much better than Jarod could ever have hoped. She not only did not kill herself but, for the first time, she seemed actually to *see* what was happening to Jarod. She began to realize that her son was suffering as much if not even more than she was. This was a real turning point for their relationship. Although she was never able to become the attentive and nurturing mother seen on family television shows, she was able for the first time to look outside of her own pain and situation to see that she had responsibilities to parent her child. The more that Jarod was able to express his feelings without her harming herself, the less need Jarod felt to indulge in drugs. Jarod had finally turned the corner in his recovery. Although his fears about his mother attempting suicide if he confided his feelings to her did not materialize, the fears were based in reality.

The next chapter discusses how survivors who are exposed to constant fear, shame, and depression often begin to act violently in an attempt to maintain safety.

Chapter 7

Violence As an Outgrowth
of Shame, Fear, and Depression

No man can think clearly when his fists or his mind is clinched.

George Jean Nathan

Sometimes in an attempt to deal with the sense of shame that survivors feel from being sexually abused, and as a sort of defense against the fear that they experience at the loss of control in their lives, some survivors may become addicted to violence.

When most people think of violent behavior, they almost invariably associate males with such behavior. Although most often males do *appear* to be more apt to display violence, this does not necessarily mean that men are more violent by nature. It may be that males are socialized more often by society to be more free to display their anger instead of their feelings of sadness. In our society, women are much more free to display sadness and grief. Linda is an example of a survivor who has become accustomed to using violence as a way of dealing with the fear and the shame that she feels.

Linda grew up in a household where drug addiction was an everyday issue. Linda's stepfather has been addicted to drugs and alcohol for as long as she can remember. Linda was sexually abused by an older male friend of the family when she was twelve years old. Although Linda's mother was supportive when she made the initial disclosure, Linda's mother has never been able to fully forgive Linda for the inconvenience that the family went through while dealing with the legal complications after the disclosure was made.

Although Linda's mother had grown up in a family where her own father had also been addicted to drugs and alcohol, Linda's mother could not seem to find the strength or insight to leave her husband. As with most active codependents, Linda's mother kept hoping that her husband would see the light and change. While her mother was waiting for this miracle to occur, Linda's life was a living hell.

Linda felt a huge sense of shame from the sexual abuse and having to live with an active drug addict and alcoholic. Linda also experienced a tremendous amount of fear from having to worry each day if *this* was the day that she wouldn't be able to hide the bruises and welts from her stepfather's beatings. Although her mother knew of the physical abuse perpetrated by stepfather, she constantly minimized and rationalized it. "If only Linda behaved better" or "if only Linda didn't talk back to her stepfather so much" thought Linda's mother, then things would be better. Linda soon was seen as the family problem instead of Linda simply reacting to the abusive situation in which she found herself.

When Linda turned fourteen she began to smoke marijuana in an attempt to deal with all her other emotions. Linda had moved onto stronger drugs by age fifteen. As Linda progressed into her later teen years, she developed a reputation for being violent. Whenever anyone would anger Linda or even appear to be threatening in the least, Linda would quickly resort to violence as a way to deal with the perceived threat.

Once the pattern of reacting to stressful situations with violent behavior is established, it is difficult to change this behavior. Humans will act instinctively to protect themselves. If a survivor or any other child sees someone rewarded for violent behavior on a continual basis, then the likelihood of that child duplicating violent behavior increases. As long as Linda remains in her family home and her stepfather is not brought to task for his behaviors, Linda will most likely deal with her own stressors with addictions and violence.

Yale is an example of an adolescent who has had to develop a strong set of violent responses just to survive in his family of origin.

Yale is eighteen years old. When he was thirteen, he was raped by his stepfather's older brother. For years, Yale did not disclose the sexual assault because he knew that no one would believe him if he told of the assault. Yale was admitted to a psychiatric hospital for his third suicide attempt in two years. In a state of rage from being restrained by the hospital staff after hitting another patient in the hospital, Yale finally disclosed the sexual assault.

Yale was wrong about no one believing him about the assault. Yale's biological father did believe him. His biological father's response didn't help his situation much though. Yale's biological father reacted in the way that he had always reacted. First, his father exploded into a fit of rage and threats of what he would do to obtain justice for what had happened to *his child.* Then his father became aggressive and physical in an attempt to release his rage. At no time did Yale's father acknowledge that what had happened had not happened to *him personally but to Yale.* Yale felt as though he had caused the family problem but that the sense of sympathy and injustice belonged to his father. Because Yale had already developed a dependence upon drugs and alcohol, it didn't take long for him to explode physically when he was under the influence and challenged by another adolescent. After all Yale had been through, he wasn't about to turn down the opportunity to regain some of his sense of power and control if the opportunity was offered to him. For years, Yale had been the recipient of other males' superior strength and sense of rage. Yale was protecting himself against all the *potential* harm that he might face by being aggressive and violent *before* anyone else could harm him. Yale was simply recreating what he himself had experienced.

Sometimes a survivor will get so used to living a life filled with violence and anger that the survivor will go on to inflict this same pain onto others who then become the survivor's victims.

Spencer was raised in an area where it was necessary to be on guard all the time. When he was only seven years old, Spencer was raped by his uncle. By the time Spencer was fifteen, he was raping younger boys. Although Spencer appeared to be a hardened person, he was really ashamed of the way that he was hurting other people. Despite this sense of shame, he continued to assault others on a regular basis.

To deal with the pain of his own abuse and to try to deny the intense feelings that he had in regard to the assaults which he was committing, Spencer began to lie compulsively. He would lie about the smallest thing . . . even when telling lies wouldn't benefit him. Spencer became so good at telling lies that he had a reputation in his neighborhood as a con man. He became so proficient at telling lies that he even lied to himself about his own behaviors. His rapes became "consensual" sex.

Many of the sexual acts that Spencer committed were replications of his own victimization. He couldn't face his actions so he tried to hide his feelings by abusing substances. Eventually Spencer will have to deal with his feelings in regard to his own victimization and the pain that he has inflicted upon others.

When I was working with Spencer one day, he spoke of the sense of power that he felt when he was hurting someone and the victimization was at its worst. He described the sensation as being a "high." Spencer was actually describing blind rage. He would become so angry that he would not be conscious of what he was really doing. After the violence was over, Spencer would feel remorse and a real sense of shame at what he had done. He had not only become addicted to drugs but he had also become addicted to the sense of power that he felt when he was hurting others. Once a behavior has paid off in a positive way, it is very difficult to stop that behavior.

Having a sense of shame is not always overtly apparent. A sense of shame may be concealed by others' behaviors.

Helen is a fifteen-year-old survivor who was molested by her stepfather when she was eight years old. Helen disclosed the abuse when she was twelve years old. Although her stepfather was charged and sent to prison, he did not receive the maximum time that he could have received because Helen did not disclose the extent of the sexual abuse until her stepfather had been incarcerated for almost two years. It was at this point that Helen revealed that instead of fondling and touching her, he had actually had intercourse with her on a number of occasions.

One of the reasons that Helen did not tell her mother about the abuse when it first occurred was because Helen instinctively knew that mother could not deal with the stress that the knowledge of the abuse was bound to bring. Helen also felt a deep sense of shame concerning the abuse. Although Helen had asked her stepfather to stop the abuse, her body had still responded to her stepfather's touch. Helen felt that the abuse was as much her own fault as it was her stepfather's fault. No amount of trying to persuade Helen otherwise seemed to make a difference.

One of the behaviors that Helen has displayed on a consistent basis in group with the other adolescent survivors is a pervasive need to dominate and control the group. Helen tries to manipulate group members to talk about and solve her problems. Whenever someone else in the group tries to address his or her own problems, Helen will invariably say, "That's the same problem that I have, only mine is much worse. Let me tell you what it's like for me. . . ." Because Helen is very physically aggressive, others will not challenge her on her negative behaviors. I believe that, at some level, the other group members also understand how very desperate Helen is for attention. Somehow the group understands that although Helen can be obnoxious at times she is only a product of what has happened to her.

One of the persistent themes that I have seen with survivors who seem to have the greatest amount of shame is a need to control the situation and to control others in the situation. These survivors are also the ones most at risk for substance abuse problems. Many times these young survivors will also come from homes and families where there are multigenerational survivors with substance abuse problems.

Why would someone who has such a deep sense of shame try to control others? Most people would think that those who attempt to control others would be confident and secure in themselves. Nothing could be further from the truth. The person with a deep sense of shame fears one thing more than anything else: being exposed and being seen as being inadequate or flawed. As long as persons with the sense of shame can control the situation and the people in the situation, they can also have some sense of control over how they themselves are seen and what the situation they are in is like. Control is an insurance policy to these people, but this insurance policy also inhibits intimacy and closeness. To be intimate and truly close to another requires that survivors must be genuine and be themselves. To control means that they could never risk the exposure of their true selves. As long as they need to control, they are doomed never to be truly close to the most important people in their lives. The saddest part of this situation is that the original source of survivors' shame is often something over which they had no control: their own sexual abuse. Survivors pay over and over again in their lifetimes for the sexual abuse. First survivors are the victims of the original abuse and then as ado-

lescents and adults the survivors pay as individuals who are lonely
and isolated from others.

Healthy shame occurs when survivors know that they have limits
on their own behaviors and actions. If they do not listen to their internal sense of conscience and go against their own convictions, then the
sense of shame that they feel would be healthy. In fact, what many
perpetrators *should be feeling but usually don't feel* is a sense of
shame. Most perpetrators will rationalize their abusive behaviors or
minimize the harmfulness of what they have done to their victims.
Perpetrators will feel an internal increase in tension while they are abstaining from sexually abusing someone. The minute that they allow
themselves to sexually abuse a victim, they have released the internal
tension that drives their abusive behavior, but the release comes at the
victims' expense. Perpetrators fail to find any sense that the victim is
a human being with feelings. To allow the victim to have feelings
would require perpetrators to acknowledge that they have seriously
harmed another human being. Perpetrators' egos are usually too fragile to handle this type of guilt or shame. Perpetrators have carried
shame since childhood. Shame and unresolved anger combined are
the primary emotions the perpetrators usually mention as driving
their abusive behaviors. When perpetrators finally take responsibility
for their abusive behaviors while in treatment, they can then acknowledge that these emotions are at the root of their negative behaviors.
"Carrying" this shame and anger is so painful that perpetrators
project their sense of shame onto the victim through sexual abuse.
The cycle of abuse is then complete and poised to create a new generation of victims.

Some survivors become so traumatized by their sexual abuse that
they will begin to identify with their perpetrators by adopting behaviors that may in some way replicate behaviors that their perpetrators
have used against the survivors.

Mallory is a fifteen-year-old who has been sexually abused by numerous family members in her extended family. Mallory has been
sexually abused by so many in her family that she herself has trouble
remembering the exact details of what each perpetrator actually did
to her. Mallory does remember how awful the sexual abuse made her
feel and the sense of rage that she felt that others could do to her whatever they pleased, and she couldn't do anything to stop what was happening.

Although Mallory's mother had no knowledge of the abuse, Mallory is furious with her mother. She feels that her mother should have known what was happening. Mallory's parents were divorced. Her mother lived over a thousand miles away from Mallory's father and his family. The sexual abuse would happen to Mallory when she went on extended visits to see her father.

It wasn't long after the visits with her father had stopped that Mallory began to have episodes of intense rage. She would scream at her mother and threaten to kill her. At first, Mallory's mother didn't take her threats seriously. She felt that Mallory was not capable of any sort of physical violence. In fact, Mallory was a very loving and pleasant young lady. It was only when she became overwhelmed with the rage that she had never been able to express toward her perpetrators of abuse that Mallory would direct all of the force of her pent-up anger toward her mother. When Mallory held a knife to her mother's back and dared her mother to walk past the knife, her mother began to worry. Mallory would swing alternately between being so angry with her mother that she wanted to kill her and being so terrified that her mother would abandon her that she couldn't stand the thought of her being out of her sight. It was only when Mallory had threatened to kill her mother and eat the skin off of her body that the degree of anger and fear of abandonment that Mallory felt was truly apparent. She couldn't deal with the anger she felt because she feared that if she expressed this anger her mother would leave her. After all, Mallory had not been able to express her rage toward her perpetrators because she knew that when she treated the perpetrators well they still abused her. What horrible things would they have done if she had expressed her rage? What if mother was able to express the same kind of abuse and harm? Mallory's mother loved her so much that she never could have harmed her daughter. Because Mallory had been abused by so many people, she had no sense of whom she could trust. Symbolically, what better way to have her mother with her always than for her to devour a part of her mother's body? Would Mallory really ever have partaken of her mother's flesh? I don't believe that she was capable of such a thing, but, as therapists, we need to listen to what our clients are really telling us. We need to believe that when clients tell us that they are thinking of doing something this is a clear warning sign that they are at least considering this action. Mallory's thought process revealed how fearful she felt of further abuse or abandonment. Whether

Mallory actually was capable of such violence was not so much the issue as was the fact that she felt desperate enough even to consider committing such a violent act. In Mallory's case, her mother did take the threats seriously. She agreed to sleep with her bedroom door locked at all times. If Mallory even threatened to hurt her, Mallory's mother agreed to call the police immediately. This agreement was made in the presence of both Mallory and her mother so that Mallory could also participate in the decision-making process. I wanted Mallory to know that I cared about what happened to her also. She was told that calling the police would be an attempt to keep her from committing an act that all of us knew she would be sorry for. Mallory agreed that the plan was in both her mother's and her own best interests, although she did not like the door being locked to her mother's room in case Mallory had a nightmare. She understood that it was her own threats toward her mother that had caused the locked door. Mallory was able to honor her part of the agreement. The most frightening thing about this situation was that despite repeated hospitalizations and changes in medications, no professional could guarantee that Mallory would not harm her mother. The police could do nothing as long as Mallory was able to refrain from harming either herself or her mother.

Mallory was only replicating the sorts of behaviors that she had seen and experienced while living with her father and his family. Had it not been for all of the abuse that she had experienced at their hands, she never even would have thought of that type of violence. It was only by experiencing the extreme violence that Mallory began to develop the idea that "might does make right." This was not a conscious decision she had made. The decision was made because Mallory had decided that she would never again in her life allow someone else to control her or to harm her.

Children who have grown up in violent homes or who experience violence themselves exhibit the following characteristics.

1. *Hypervigilance for either their own safety or the safety of those to whom they are emotionally close.* These are the same children who jump if someone pats them on the back for a job well done or tries to give them a hug as a show of affection. Since these are the survivors who have known the effects of violence, they react as if any sort of physical touch will be hurtful.

Alex is a seventeen-year-old survivor who has had to protect himself against physical violence all of his life. Although Alex doesn't consider what happened to him as being sexual abuse (an older woman seduced Alex when he was eleven), it is clear that the sexual contact has caused Alex to have a low opinion of women. Alex refuses to go anywhere without a weapon. The people in his life who were the most trusted were the ones who physically harmed him. Not only did Alex experience physical abuse himself, he witnessed his mother being physically abused by a long series of live-in boyfriends. Alex blames himself because he feels that he should have been able to protect his mother. This theme of having to "parent a parent" is a universal theme with survivors. Since the violence against his mother began even before Alex was born, there was no way that Alex could have protected his mother. Still, Alex blames himself for his mother being harmed.

2. *A strong sense of depression.* These children feel that nothing will ever change for the better.

Carolyn is a fourteen-year-old survivor who witnessed her mother being beaten by all of the boyfriends that her mother has ever had. Carolyn herself has been beaten repeatedly by most of her mother's boyfriends. All of Carolyn' mother's boyfriends have been either alcoholics or drug addicts. None of these men have ever held a regular job. Carolyn's mother has always had to support both her children, herself, and the men in her life. Is it any wonder that Carolyn's mother was raised in a home where her own father was an alcoholic and beat not only her but Carolyn's grandmother as well?

3. *Difficulty either falling asleep or staying asleep.* Many of these children will be afraid to fall asleep because sleeping means nightmares of all of the terrible abuse they have witnessed or experienced. Much of the time the abuse happened late at night while the child was asleep. To be awakened from a sound sleep to screams and violence is to be aware that you must always be on guard to protect yourself.

Scarlett is a fifteen-year-old survivor who was molested numerous times by her stepfather. Scarlett has witnessed her mother pulled from her wheelchair and knocked across the room by the stepfather. Despite all of the beatings and abuse, Scarlett's mother refused to go to a shelter or prosecute her husband. Chances are that unless Scarlett sees her mother defend herself against the stepfather's abuse, Scarlett herself may pick a partner as abusive or even more abusive than her stepfather.

4. *Aggressive or intimidating behavior.* Survivors who have grown up in an environment of "might makes right" soon learn that the quickest and surest way to get what you need or want is to intimidate others. Not only is this type of aggressive behavior apparent in male survivors, but female survivors also demonstrate this behavior, especially with other females.

> Jamie is a fourteen-year-old survivor who was raped repeatedly by her biological father. Although Jamie is small-boned and petite, she can still intimidate girls twice her size. Jamie is tough because she has always had to be tough. In Jamie's world, it is survival of the fittest.

5. *Developmental delay.* The child puts so much energy into guarding against abuse that he or she has little energy left over for developmental tasks. Not only does the age of the onset of the violence and abuse determine the extent of the developmental delay but the length and severity of the traumatic events and the availability of a support system or lack thereof to help the child to deal with the abuse also factors in. Very young survivors who come into treatment after they have either witnessed violence or experienced violence themselves usually lag behind their peers.

> Shannon is a five-year-old survivor who was molested by her biological father. Shannon is so disturbed by all of the abuse that she has experienced that she can't sit still or follow any sort of directions. Shannon has done so poorly in kindergarten that she will have to repeat it.

6. *Poor school performance.* Whenever children or adolescents are having problems in their lives, it becomes apparent in their school performance. Studies have shown that being sexually abused dramatically decreases performance on standard IQ tests. When working with young survivors I'm amazed at how they often perceive themselves as being "dumb" or "stupid." These young survivors have no

sense of how truly amazing they are by virtue of being able to endure their abuse. On top of being able to survive the abuse, the survivors expect themselves to be able to thrive and perform academically just like their unabused peers.

7. *Suicidal ideation and behavior.* Survivors have one of the highest rates of suicidal ideation of those who are abused as children (Deykin and Buka, 1994). When we add physical violence into the mix I'm sure the rate goes even higher. I have seen young survivors drink bleach to attempt suicide, attempt to run their cars into trees, slit their wrists repeatedly, take overdoses of pills, and employ any other means of suicide possible all in an attempt to "kill" the pain of being sexually abused.

8. *Reexperiencing the abuse memories.* Some survivors have such difficulty dealing with their sexual and physical abuse that they often have flashbacks and nightmares of the abuse. Despite all sorts of strategies, the survivors will continue to exhibit post-traumatic stress disorder symptoms. It is this intense intrusion of the abuse memories that causes many survivors to attempt to "numb" themselves through the use of substances and behaviors. Despite the delay of dealing with the memories and feelings of the abuse, survivors must eventually deal with the abuse in order to heal.

9. *Generational transfer of behavior.* Survivors raised in a home where violence is a way of life learn to transfer this behavior from one generation to the next. I had a case in which a teenage male survivor learned to be as aggressive as his father.

> Octavio's father had felt "different" as a child because of his nationality. Octavio's father was also a survivor. To protect himself, he had to be physically aggressive. Although his son did not have the same physical threats in his environment (Octavio was molested by an uncle who used seduction as a method of getting the child to comply with the abuse), Octavio became as physically aggressive as his father.

Perhaps the ultimate expression of violence is the act of suicide itself. Nowhere else will you find the threat of suicide more prevalent than among survivors, particularly incest survivors. If the survivor comes from a family in which violence is a daily occurrence, the risk of suicide goes up dramatically. Perhaps because the incest survivor experiences betrayal at such an immediate level and is expected to keep the abuse secret, the survivor has anger that builds to such great levels that the anger must be expressed. Although I have never lost a client to suicide, I have had many clients who have attempted suicide numerous times. I'm never sure from one day to the next who in my caseload will attempt suicide.

Most major religions consider suicide a sin against God. The idea of going against God and committing suicide is the one clients struggle with the most. The idea that they will offend God if they commit suicide has kept many survivors from actually killing themselves. When survivors who consider suicide think about how this will be a rejection of the beautiful gift of life that God has given them, many have changed their minds and found at least some small reason to live.

> Pia is a forty-year-old survivor who was molested by each of her mother's boyfriends while growing up. Since her mother was overwhelmed trying to raise six children by herself after Pia's father deserted the family, Pia never told her mother about any of the molestations. Pia was the oldest of her siblings and had all of the responsibility for taking care of everyone else while her mother was constantly at work. Pia felt that she had nobody to lean on. As she became older, she herself picked men as partners who were abusive to her. During her lifetime, Pia has made between fifteen and twenty suicide attempts. Most of the attempts have involved the use of pills, but several have involved one-car "traffic accidents." Pia was very candid in the past about not having any reasons to live. It was only when her adolescent daughter began to follow in her footsteps that she realized the example that she was setting. Despite all of the horrible abuse that Pia had experienced, she realized that she and her daughter might both live if she could find a *reason* to live. Pia found this reason when she began to meet with other survivors in both the adolescent and the adult survivors' groups. By her own example of hanging in there despite all of the pain that life has given her, Pia is helping other survivors to find a reason to live.

As a therapist working with survivors, the predominate emotion I always sense is depression—the deepest depression that one could imagine. Underneath this depression lies an unexpressed rage about the unfairness of being treated as someone else's "toy."

Most survivors who attempt suicide would tell you that there are two main reasons why people consider suicide.

1. They have no sense of hope about the future. The way that things are now is the way that they will always be.
2. They have no control in their own lives or control over their own sense of emotions. Everything that has occurred in the survivors' lives has been at someone else's whim.

Yale Bradshaw (1986a) calls this the *lost self*. The lost self pertains to the idea that the survivor is not allowed to be the person that he or she was born to be. This idea coincides with Nakken's (1996) idea of the false persona that a person must present to be accepted by others in the world. According to Bradshaw, the lost self is always looking for something outside of itself to be the answer to the internal emptiness that the person feels.

Teenagers are at very high risk of suicide in part because they have not yet learned or developed the coping skills that would allow them to experience loss and bounce back from it. Suicide is the eighth leading cause of death among *all* people regardless of age, sex, or race. In people ages fifteen to twenty-four, suicide is the third leading cause of death. Suicide is the fourth leading cause of death among people ages ten to fourteen. I find these statistics alarming. How can children so young, who should have so much to live for, want to die? How many of these children are survivors who just can't deal with the pain of knowing that they weren't valued or nurtured by those who should have done just that?

Our adolescent survivors need to be watched most closely. Adolescent suicide rates are higher today because the stressors that teenagers face today are greater than at any other time. Our society appears to condone violence as evident by the current popular television shows and movies. Teens get the impression that whatever means justifies the ends are okay. Today more than ever adolescents have easier access to the means necessary to hurt themselves or others. If we add the depression that the adolescent feels from being a survivor, we have the recipe for violence.

The very things that would help prevent an adolescent from attempting suicide are the things *least* likely to happen if the adolescent is in an abusive environment. Still, if *someone* in the survivor's life cares about the survivor, the chances of suicide are decreased if that person will talk with the survivor about other coping skills besides suicide. For many survivors growing up in a physically abusive household the idea that there is a way of life in which they do not have to fear getting hurt or seeing someone that they love get hurt is a foreign idea. In these households the abuser usually has managed to maintain the abusive relationship through "promises" to change abusive ways. This change seldom takes place unless the abuser is willing to seek treatment and the other partner is able to stand by whatever conditions he or she has demanded in order for the relationship to continue.

The adolescent survivors with whom I work have their own methods of using violence in their everyday lives. It is not unusual to see these young survivors involved in gang activity. Gangs offer a way to feel part of a greater support network than ordinary members of society offers these survivors. Often these young survivors will join a gang in an attempt to reduce the degree of shame they feel. One young adolescent male survivor was made to participate in gang-related violence perpetrated upon some younger children. The cost of refusing to participate would have meant that the survivor himself would have been severely harmed. Once the survivor participated in this activity, he was part of the gang. The gang's acceptance helped to decrease the survivor's level of shame at what he had been forced to do, but at some level he instinctively knew how he had transgressed against his own value system. Once he had disclosed to the other survivors what he had done and gained their support in taking responsibility for what he had done, he was able to begin to deal with the guilt that he felt for the abuse.

As adolescent group members share their stories in the survivors' group, they are constantly on the lookout for someone to laugh at them when they display any sort of intense emotion. It is the ability to display rage and violence that keeps these young survivors safe from rejection and scorn. If everyone is afraid of them, they are not going to attempt to get close enough to find out their flaws and weaknesses. In most of the environments that these young survivors originate, weakness is a fatal flaw that they can ill afford.

Another interesting behavior that I have observed time after time in the adolescent survivors' group and occasionally in the adult survivors' group is what I referred to earlier in this book as "whistling in the dark." This is found most often in male survivors after they have been sexually abused.

> Jake was raped by his uncle for over ten years. Now that Jake is safe from his uncle's abuse, Jake will talk at length about how he would kill anyone who ever tried to touch him.

It is not unusual to see male survivors go to great lengths to demonstrate their prowess and strength in defending themselves once the abuse has *already occurred*. These attempts at bravado are what I consider to be attempts at regaining some of the power that has been taken from them. In fact, it is common to see young male survivors try to outdo each other with tales of gang-related activities in an attempt to compete for who is "king of the mountain."

Female adolescent survivors have a tendency to swing between two poles of emotion: extreme depression and uncontrollable rage. When survivors are depressed, they may withdraw from others and isolate themselves. Sometimes, in an attempt to allow themselves to feel, survivors will cut themselves. Once they cannot contain their intense emotions any longer, they may abruptly swing toward the other emotional pole where they may either attempt suicide or strike out in intense anger and fury. It is interesting that survivors who are full of rage seldom will strike out at the person with whom they are *really* angry. Survivors will grapple with the issue of (a) striking out at the person who has really made them angry or harmed them and taking a chance on that person abandoning them or harming them again or (b) aiming their anger at someone who is more safe and will be more likely to stand by the survivor after the anger has passed. Most times, this target will be the nonoffending parent.

> Kevin is a fifteen-year-old survivor who was sexually abused by his stepfather when he was quite young. Kevin's biological mother did nothing about the abuse and, in fact, was physically and verbally abusive to Kevin herself. For years, when Kevin was in group homes and foster care all he wanted to do was to return home to his family. After years of struggles with depression and anger, Kevin finally was placed in a foster home where the family really loved and cared for him. After only a short time in the foster home, Kevin's biological mother wanted him returned home to the family. Kevin wanted to believe that things

with his mother would finally work out. The tension of having to decide where he wanted to live was so great that Kevin began to alternate between episodes of depression and rage. These intense emotions were directed at either the foster mother (who would love Kevin no matter what he did) or at Kevin himself in the form of suicide attempts.

Sheri is a fifteen-year-old survivor who was molested by uncles, cousins, and brothers while she was growing up. The abuse was documented by eyewitness reports to the sexual abuse and by physical evidence. Sheri deals with the intense feelings related to her abuse by "not remembering" the details of what happened to her.

Sheri's case is fascinating because even though she has no conscious memories of what happened to her, she still has the rage, depression, and shame resulting from the abuse. Even when we attempt to suppress the feelings and memories of our abuse, they still manage to be evident in some way.

Kari is a sixteen-year-old survivor who was molested by a boyfriend of her mother's when Kari was quite young. Although no one ever sexually abused Kari after her mom's boyfriend had abused her, Kari lived a life that was full of neglect and emotional abuse. Instead of expressing the anger that she feels toward her mother for the abuse that she has experienced, Kari projects this anger onto other adult women that she feels are similar to her mother. Kari is constantly on the lookout for that "perfect" mother who will remove all of the harmful memories of the abuse and make things "okay."

Many survivors who are raised in families where violence is a way of life do not realize that the addiction to violent behavior is a progressive process like any other addiction. Abusers do not start out by perpetrating the worst abuse on their victims the very first time they offend. Survivors may grow up in families where the violent behavior is overt in the forms of beating, hitting, punching, throwing things, and countless other violent behaviors. The survivors who sometimes don't realize the impact that violence has had on their lives are the ones who grow up in covert violence homes. This is often the subtle type of violence such as extreme jealousy, a lack of emotional intimacy in the family, the withholding of emotional warmth, raging, threats, intimidation (both spoken and simply implied), sexual intimidation and coercion, verbal abuse, broken promises, and outright lies. The harmfulness of these behaviors occurs because the child begins to believe (since this is the primary example of what a relationship should be as the child is growing up) that this is the way in which all relationships should be conducted.

Since survivors see the abusive relationship up close they begin to identify with one of two roles in the relationship: (1) the partner who is abusive and narcissistic or (2) the partner who is abused, doesn't leave the relationship, and is often codependent. Without some sort of intervention, the parents of the survivor either will progress the intensity of the abusive behaviors or eventually will not be able to endure the abusive relationship any longer and will leave the relationship only to find new partners with whom to create the same dynamics. Survivors will copy the family-of-origin issues in their own relationships. The survivor will then identify with one of the two previous roles and either become the perpetrator or the codependent. Either way, the choice that the survivor makes is not a fulfilling one. Because most people who abuse were often abused themselves, we see the abuser as someone who is recreating his or her own abuse history and whose negative behaviors are almost always shame based.

Survivors who have been raised in abusive families in which the relationships between the parents or caregivers were violent or have demonstrated abusive behaviors will more quickly progress in group treatment because in group they will see the abusiveness of their family of origin mirrored in the abusive behaviors of the other group members.

Survivors are set up not only for addictions and compulsive behaviors but also to be partners of abusers. The characteristics of survivors who are apt to be abused include the following:

- a poor sense of personal boundaries (i.e., an inability to say no to others despite not wanting to do whatever is requested of them);
- an inability to express anger directly (so many survivors will direct their anger onto a target that has nothing to do with what has really made them angry);
- Adult Children of Alcoholics issues (i.e., codependency issues, rigid roles from which they can't seem to escape);

- low self-esteem;
- the survivors' own history of abuse, including physical, verbal, emotional, or sexual abuse;
- being forcibly isolated by their partners from contact with others outside of the survivors' immediate family;
- a history of depression;
- the use of food, drugs, alcohol, or any other addictive or compulsive behaviors in an effort not to emotionally "feel" their abusive history;
- the tendency to believe that willpower alone is the answer to life's problems;
- trying to make an impossible relationship work simply by "hanging in there";
- the idea that if only they work hard enough or are "good" enough, the relationship will work out; and
- taking the entire responsibility for whether a relationship will work or not.

Perhaps no other form of violence is so insidious as "raging." Raging involves behaviors such as pouting, screaming, manipulating, making threats, and attempts at emotional blackmail. I once knew a man who was able to control his entire family by simply taking a very deep breath. The family knew this signal meant that if he didn't get his way he was going to explode in anger and rage. Raging persons are expressing *any* strong emotion (whether it be fear, sadness, guilt, shame, or anger) through the use of rage. In families where raging occurs, the person who rages was usually shamed as a child. Raging enables abusers to balance their sense of shame and feelings of inadequacy. Even more notable is that chemical changes take place in the brain of the person who rages which appear to make the behavior very addictive.

A survivor who is raised in an environment in which adults express anger by raging has problems learning how to appropriately express his or her anger. Many survivors think of anger as a "bad" emotion and become afraid of their own anger. In reality, anger is a healthy emotion. It tells us that our boundaries have been crossed. It is what we *do* with our anger that can sometimes be inappropriate. Survivors must realize what has angered them, confront and deal with the situation, and resolve whatever issues lie beneath their anger. Most survivors fluctuate between two ways of dealing with their anger: denial or raging.

It is not unusual to see adult survivors inflict abusive behaviors upon themselves as a sort of punishment directed toward their abusers. These survivors might say, "Well, my husband doesn't care what happens to me, so why should I care?" "One more drink [or whatever it is that the survivor is doing to kill the emotional pain] won't make any difference. I deserve a treat after the way that everyone treats me!" What is sad about this type of behavior is that the person who has hurt the survivor usually isn't even aware that the survivor is attempting to retaliate through the use of the addictive or compulsive behavior. The abusive person simply uses the survivor's addictive or compulsive behaviors to justify opinions about the inadequateness of the survivor.

How do results differ in the sexual abuse of males versus the sexual abuse of females? Although both genders might experience the same sort of sexual abuse, the way individuals are free to express their emotions about the abusive experience is vastly different.

Male survivors usually find that once they disclose their sexual abuse to their male friends (and sometimes even to their male family members) they may be regarded as less "manly." I believe that male survivors often are the recipients of more physical abuse during the commission of their sexual abuse experiences. Men are often reluctant to disclose the physical torture that may have accompanied their sexual abuse because they fear that it will make them appear "weak." The memories that these male survivors carry are often as fresh to them today as when the original abuse occurred. The fear experienced by the adult male survivor when recollecting childhood sexual abuse is often as intense as the feelings experienced during the abuse. It is only when these adult male survivors are allowed to express their grief and are not forced to maintain their exterior demonstration of anger and violent behaviors that true healing for the male survivor can begin.

> Thatcher is a seventeen-year-old survivor who has had not only childhood sexual incest perpetrated by his stepfather but also numerous perpetrators of physical abuse throughout his entire childhood. Thatcher comes across at seventeen as being streetwise and extremely dangerous. Adults often cross the street when they see him coming because he looks as if he could and

would hurt someone. The truth is that Thatcher is just "whistling in the dark." He wants to keep others at a distance because he never intends to give anyone the opportunity to abuse him again. Thatcher wants everyone to be afraid of him so that they will leave him alone. The saddest part of his story is that for him to begin to heal he had to completely fall apart emotionally and be hospitalized numerous times. His depression was so deep that he tried to kill himself more than twenty different times before he could finally disclose his history of sexual abuse.

How do we help these young male survivors who may be addicted to violent demonstrations of aggressive behavior in a mistaken attempt to keep themselves safe? Sometimes the best way to reach these young survivors is by offering them services that increase their self-esteem and offer them the opportunity to have a brighter future. Obtaining a high school diploma is a big accomplishment for someone who has faced the incredible odds of many of these survivors. In families experiencing multigenerational sexual abuse, this young survivor may be the first in the family to graduate from high school. Job skills training helps increase self-esteem. Job Corps is one avenue that some of the young male survivors have chosen to work toward as a way of freeing themselves from a life of poverty and abuse. Something as simple as getting a driver's license offers the young survivor a way to feel competent and more independent. I have found that simply having a driver's license and access to a car increases the likelihood that the adolescent survivor will stay in treatment. Often this same adolescent will provide transportation to group for other group members who do not have transportation. Peer support groups are vital to the survivor's recovery. Unlike gangs, which can be violent and involve crime, peer support groups offer guidance solely based on the best interests of the survivor. Recreational centers in the community may also give male and female survivors a place to receive peer support along with adult guidance.

Giving these young males a positive support group enables them to feel that disclosing their abuse is a strength rather than a disability. Offering young male and female survivors a warm emotional bond with an appropriate adult role model can effect wonderful changes.

Sometimes the young male survivor can be his own worst enemy. At a recent adolescent group meeting Thatcher, the young male survivor mentioned in this chapter, was able to meet several members of the adult survivors' group. In his zealousness to attempt to get to know the adult group members, Thatcher began to tell them of all of his exploits and what he would do to anyone who ever attempted to abuse him again. The adult group members became nervous at hearing him give details of the violence that he would use if necessary. The adult group members didn't know of the extreme fear that Thatcher felt toward his perpetrators. Once we discussed the philosophy of "whistling in the dark," the adults were able to understand that Thatcher was simply trying to protect himself. The adults were then able to see the child that lay beneath his bravado.

Anger is perhaps the most difficult emotion for the survivor to express, especially among females. Society does not socialize females to think of anger as a healthy or appropriate emotion. When we add the concept of learned helplessness from being sexually abused to what society teaches us about the inappropriateness of feeling and expressing anger, it is then easy to understand why anger is such a difficult emotion.

Unexpressed anger will always find some way to express itself, even if it does not directly appear to be anger. There are numerous signs of unexpressed anger. Many times anger will covertly express itself as out-of-proportion irritability over small issues. Anger will also express itself through dreams or nightmares. Even young survivors will have dreams in which they have superhuman strength to slay the monsters. One of the signs of unexpressed anger that I see most often among survivors of both genders is foot tapping and other repetitive movements, especially jiggling their legs up and down in a continuous motion. Survivors will also keep their hands in tightly clinched fists. Often the survivors are not even aware of this behavior. Survivors will often grind their teeth or talk out loud during their sleep. I have noticed that I often sigh out loud. Sighing is a sign that something is being repressed, usually anger. Constantly being late is another sign of repressed anger. Of all of the survivors I know, I am more guilty of this than any other survivor in any of the groups. It is a standing joke in the groups that they always plan on starting at least fifteen minutes later than the stated time because I've never been able to start on time in my life. I'm working on this, but lateness has been a lifelong problem for me.

Inappropriate affect, smiling when you know that the person has been hurt, is another common sign of repressed anger. Active codependents quite often will also smile or show affect that is quite inappropriate to the painful situations in which they find themselves. I have seen survivors be insulted and continue to smile and nod their heads in a fashion to indicate that they have heard what was said to them. I am always amazed when this happens because what was said was so cruel or cutting, yet the survivors would never let on that they were hurt. Many survivors also like sadistic or flippant humor. I believe that this sort of humor gives survivors an outlet that is more socially acceptable for their anger. It is almost as if the survivors can express their anger vicariously through this kind of "slapstick" or "gallows" humor. Physical symptoms of anger include stomachaches and pains, stiff or sore muscles, and a constant sense of being tired, which indicates repressed anger. I am reminded how appropriate it is that we say someone is a "pain in the neck" when that person makes us angry!

Survivors who are most apt to also be codependent are those who are overly polite. These are the survivors who, no matter what life hands them, seem to be cheerful. People will be amazed at how well this type of survivor can hold up under the most unpleasant situations. The survivors' ability to create false personas that has allowed them to survive their own abusive backgrounds is what is truly being demonstrated. These are also the survivors who are most likely to develop depression or eating disorders as a result of never being allowed to express their true feelings.

Many survivors reading about unexpressed anger would not even be aware that they *are* angry. Survivors become experts at being out of touch with their true feelings and are not aware of what or how they are feeling. It isn't socially acceptable to express unpleasant emotions such as anger. Yet repressed emotions won't go away unless they are expressed.

Some very good ways exist to tap into the hidden anger that survivors carry. Being aware of places in the body where anger is most often felt is one of the best ways to realize unexpressed anger. This can be difficult for survivors because in order to survive their abuse they needed to "stay in their heads" and not feel the abuse in their bodies. Trying to make the shift from an intellectualization of the abuse to physically and emotionally feeling the abuse can be quite traumatic.

Because many survivors display hidden anger in psychosomatic ways (chronic headaches or stomachaches that have been determined by a physician to have no organic cause), it would be prudent to examine the possibility that perhaps emotions are at play in the physical ailments. Some good indicators that repressed anger could be causing the psychosomatic ailment could include laughing inappropriately at a situation (this can also be a sign of nervousness or being unsure of what to do in a given situation) or finding oneself with chronically clenched jaws or fists. Whenever a behavioral pattern becomes apparent involving withdrawal from certain situations or situations in which the person displays extreme changes in style or tone of speech, the person may be struggling with an intense anger-provoking situation and using repression as a means of dealing with the anger. Being able to accept feelings of anger without apologizing or justifying the feelings gives one the ability to accept the fact that anger is a part of life. Remember that it isn't the anger that is inappropriate, it's only what you do with the anger that might be inappropriate. If the survivor is able to stop hiding the anger and learn the subtle art of confrontation, chances are that the psychosomatic symptoms will decrease and often disappear.

Why would someone who has known the pain of being shamed want to go on to shame others or use rage and violence to control others? The answers are not simple or easy to understand, but I believe that the dynamics of shame are so painful and long lasting that those who experience the shame often use their rage as a way to "put off" the feelings that they themselves can no longer tolerate.

> Jay is a seventeen-year-old survivor. Not only was he raped as a child, but Jay experienced verbal, emotional, and physical abuse while he was growing up. Jay never knew from day to day what was going to happen to his family. Since he was so young when the abuse began, Jay was never able physically to defend himself against the abuse. Jay's family members taunted him as being a "sissy" because he cried when he was being abused. As a consequence of constantly berating him, Jay has grown up with the idea that the world is a very unsafe place and he must do to others *before* they do to him. Jay comes across as being rough and tough. Everyone, especially adults, is afraid of his rough demeanor. That is exactly the impression that Jay wants to make. Jay makes others feel the way that he has been made to feel be-

cause experiencing those old emotions of powerlessness and fear are simply too much for Jay to bear. Jay is addicted to a behavior that has helped him to endure the original abuse but now is very dysfunctional.

In 1992, Nathanson developed a model of the relationship between shame and anger that he called the *Compass of Shame*. The model shows that if survivors experience shame and are not able to make it a part of their lives in a healthy manner, then they may protect themselves against these very intense feelings of shame by doing several things. As suggested earlier in this chapter, survivors who experience the shame of their abuse may attempt to "put off" their shame onto another by victimizing that person. Shamed survivors may instead attack themselves (such as cutting themselves, using suicidal ideation, or attempting suicide). Other common tactics involve withdrawal from social situations altogether or avoiding situations similar to ones that provoked the original shame. Jay is a very good example of a survivor who attempts to put off his shame by attacking others and making them feel as he did when he was shamed.

> Jay perceives that the slightest criticism places him in a one-down position. In order to deal with such painful reminders of his childhood, Jay will find someone else upon whom to put off his painful feelings and make feel lower than Jay feels about himself. This putting off of feelings can involve verbal abuse and criticism or actual physical attacks and intimidation. The bottom line is that this behavior is always a result of Jay's own internal sense of shame and his inability to integrate these painful feelings resulting from shame as a part of himself. Jay's family has socialized him to believe that shame is something that only women should accept.

Sometimes shame can be very intense and individuals will still not consciously be aware that they are being shamed. This could happen when the children in a family have been shamed for as long as they can remember. How would they know that what is happening to them is not normal if that is all they have ever known?

Gene is an adult male survivor who exemplifies withdrawal.

> Gene was born into an immigrant family and learned early that life is difficult and always painful. As with many immigrant

families, Gene's family worked extremely hard to succeed. Success meant being as much like other Americans as possible. Any reminder that the family immigrated from another country had to be erased. Unfortunately, Gene's appearance was a constant reminder to the family that they were not "really" American. Gene's sexual abuse by an older male neighbor simply convinced the family that Gene would never be good enough. As a consequence, Gene grew up with constant criticism. After years of the family's put-downs and remarks, Gene simply began to withdraw from others. Being alone was better than being under constant attack. Gene's constant sense of shame was even apparent in his posture and appearance. Gene was stooped over most of the time, he never stood up straight and tall. It seemed as if Gene carried the weight of the world on his shoulders. Gene always wore drab, dark clothing that did not do his good looks justice. It was only when Gene began to work with other adults in group and see that he did possess a lot of good qualities that Gene was able to begin to appreciate himself.

Not every survivor who has been shamed will go on to shame others. Some survivors who can't integrate the shaming into their own psyches will be violent only when placed in certain situations. These survivors are seldom aggressive and have become aggressive only when they simply could not stand the pressure of the situation in which they found themselves. Some survivors—a very few, for most survivors would never want to harm anyone the way that they were harmed—are aggressive by nature. Extreme anger is a part of their everyday lives. These are the ones that I feel could go on to become sex offenders.

What separates those survivors who are capable of causing shameful and violent behaviors in others from the majority of survivors who would never want to harm another human being? In his book *Speaking with the Devil: A Dialogue with Evil,* Carl Goldberg (1996) talks about shame vulnerability, benign neglect, inability to mourn, linguistic difficulties in expressing feelings, and witnessing significant people who behave as if violence is a legitimate way of dealing with frustration and conflict as being factors that influence the way that people deal with shame. Nowhere are these qualities more apparent than with adolescent male survivors. Simply because of their young ages and limited life experiences, adolescent male survivors don't have the coping skills to talk about how their abuse has affected them. To allow others to know of their vulnerability resulting from their prior abuse would be seen by these young survivors as an invitation to abuse them again. In the homes of many of these adolescent survivors the most physically strong family members are also the ones who dominate the family by brute force. Since our family of origin is our introduction to how we *believe* that we are supposed to behave, many young survivors will carry these abusive behaviors into their own marriages and families. Goldberg goes on to list secondary conditions that determine the capacity for destructive behavior as being parental seduction (which would violate all of the child's boundaries), heavy exposure to media violence, identification with a philosophy of superiority (to justify abusive behaviors one must see the victim as being inferior to the abuser, perhaps as even being less than human), family conspiracy, and a conceptual inability to understand death as a permanent event (many adolescents fail to grasp the finality of death even though cognitively they understand people who die don't get back up and go on with their lives).

> Carlos is an adult survivor. Carlos's family of origin never knew that Carlos had been molested by an older neighborhood male beginning when Carlos was only ten years old. In Carlos's family, one didn't talk about feelings (linguistic difficulties expressing feelings). Since Carlos was not allowed to discuss his abuse, he could not mourn how he had been molested and how his family had always shamed him (shame vulnerability). The family often ignored Carlos's needs (benign neglect). Carlos had often seen his father berate and beat his mother (witnessing significant people behave as if violence is a legitimate way for dealing with frustration and conflict). Carlos's mother would often go on drinking binges for weeks at a time. During these times of heavy alcohol intake, his mother would often fall asleep on the sofa or at the kitchen table almost nude (parental seduction.) Carlo's mother would allow Carlos all sorts of additional freedoms and privileges if he would go to the neighbor's house to bring her back beer. His father enjoyed watching violent movies on a regular basis (heavy exposure to media violence). There was almost a family conspiracy to see Carlos as the family scapegoat. In fact, making Carlos the family "problem" enabled the family to unite around Carlos as the issue instead of addressing the family's true issues (family conspiracy). Carlos grew up

with the idea that men are better than women and should be able to dominate their family (identification with philosophy of superiority). Is it any wonder that although Carlos had experienced the most painful of childhoods he still went on to inflict the same sort of emotional pain on others in an unconscious attempt to not "own" his own emotional pain? Carlos fits the profile perfectly of someone who has been given all of the conditions to use violence as a way to deal with his own shameful experiences.

According to work done by David Lisak (1996), buried pain leads to perpetration. In my own practice, I have seen these dynamics over and over again. When victims are not allowed to grieve their pain and must hold in their anger, the likelihood of victims becoming perpetrators greatly increases. Lisak's work indicates that emotional pain is etched in the neuronal circuits. To get rid of this pain one must fully express how one feels and the degree to which one feels the pain. Because of what men are taught in our society (i.e., *real* men don't cry), men are more apt to constrict their feelings and perhaps have a greater incidence of becoming perpetrators. Male children are no different from female children where feelings are concerned. Male children feel fear and pain just as much as female children do. As a male child matures, he quickly learns that it is not acceptable for men to appear vulnerable or helpless. Men quickly learn to be scornful of other men who show their pain. Pain that is not expressed does not just disappear. More likely than not the pain will find a way to be expressed, usually onto a more vulnerable person, perhaps a woman or a child.

Jarrell is a sixteen-year-old male survivor. Although he has never given very many actual details of his rape by his older brother, it is clear that Jarrell felt very small and helpless. Jarrell has worked so hard at burying his feelings of being vulnerable that he has decided that he will never be in that situation again. Jarrell has begun to bully everyone around him. At times Jarrell even attempts to intimidate those who could physically harm him. He is so "macho" that even though others might be able to physically harm him they will not attempt to do so because he really puts on a good act. Jarrell's act is abusive because he causes other people to take his abuse, and they are too afraid to tell him how much it frightens them and how helpless it makes them feel. Until Jarrell is able to get in touch with his own feelings of vulnerability and helplessness and own these feelings, he will continue to victimize others.

A study (Goldberg, 1996) done of 1,500 men at the University of Massachusetts in Boston indicates that abused men who go on to perpetrate against others have higher scores on such characteristics as gender rigidity and emotional constriction. This makes sense when we consider Goldberg's (1996) research indicating that people who are abusive tend to have problems with expressing their emotions and appear to assume the roles of significant others in their lives who demonstrate abusive behaviors. The University of Massachusetts study also indicates that these same abused men tend to score higher on measures concerning lowered empathy and post-traumatic stress disorder (PTSD) than do men who do not go on to perpetrate against others. Again, this makes sense considering the idea that some people perpetuate the abuse that has been done to them indicating a lack of empathy for their victim. PTSD would tend to keep the original trauma that perpetrators have experienced fresh in their minds and require a way to deal with the resulting intense emotions. If the individuals can't express verbally the distress that they are feeling, perhaps they express it by acting out in an abusive manner. This would certainly fit in with the male survivors that I have seen who become abusive (not necessarily sexually abusive).

Gender rigidity indicates that the survivor is trapped by society's expectation of how someone of the survivor's gender *should* act. Although this study was done with abused men, I believe that women in such a study would achieve scores that would tell us that because society teaches women to be nurturing and "soft," women survivors would have much higher scores were traits such as codependency measured. The male survivor who becomes abusive is trapped by society's expectations of him, but there is a real benefit to this trap. Because he isn't allowed to express his pain, the male survivor who perpetrates will put his pain off onto his victims. Anger and aggression are allowable emotions for this type of survivor. Once his feelings are put off onto his victim the perpetrator can then deny his own pain and vulnerability.

When survivors bury pain and other uncomfortable emotions, they run the risk of projecting their feelings onto others. Because the survivors can't accept their own emotions in themselves, they need to project these same negative emotions onto others and then attack this emotion in them. In order to attack their own emotions that they have projected onto their victims, these survivors must have a much less empathetic ability to sense not only their own pain but the pain that they have projected onto others. I agree with Dr. Lisak (1994) when he says that in order for perpetrators to heal they must first go back into their own childhood abuse and feel their own pain if they are ever to feel the pain of their victims and develop some sense of empathy for others. This is a tall order for perpetrators, or they would not have needed to develop such elaborate defense systems in the first place.

In his research findings contained in "The Psychological Impact of Sexual Abuse and Content Analysis of Interviews with Male Survivors," Dr. Lisak (1994) discusses fifteen psychological themes that affect male victims of sexual abuse. The themes of anger and betrayal (expressed as disappointment, abandonment, or the breaking of trust) are common themes found in Lisak's work, as well as in the clients that I treat. Both male and female survivors may express these angry and sometimes violent feelings against the nonoffending parent for failure to protect the survivors. Again, it doesn't matter to survivors if the nonoffending parent says that he or she had no knowledge of the abuse. Survivors still feel that somehow the nonoffending parent should have picked up on signals that the abuse was occurring. Many times the anger toward the nonoffending parent can be much greater than the anger expressed toward the offending parent, probably due to the nonoffending parent being seen by survivors as less abusive and more a permanent part of their lives.

Fear is also a constant theme that can be expressed as flashbacks or other intrusive thoughts. Even though male survivors are socialized to be "macho" they still feel a sense of helplessness and isolation. Most male survivors will question if they were *really* victims or if they somehow took part in their own abuse. I believe this goes back to our society's image of the male having always to be strong and in control of the situation. The loss of innocence and childhood as well as negative peer relations further separates the male survivor from his peers. Masculinity issues cause male survivors to question their own sexual orientation. The male survivor may develop negative schema about himself and others which leads to further alienation and mistrust. Problems with his own sexuality and questioning if he is gay often are issues for the male survivor. The male survivor's constant theme appears to be one of self-blame, guilt, and shame.

Even very young survivors can become addicted to rage and violent acting-out behaviors in an attempt not to think about or feel the memories of their own sexual victimization.

> Robert is a five-year-old survivor who was sexually abused by his stepfather for over two years. When Robert first entered treatment he was so violent that he had thrown chairs three times his size across the room at his mother and siblings. His mother and stepfather were divorced. Although his stepfather had been emotionally, verbally, and physically abusive toward Robert's mother, she had no knowledge that his stepfather had been sexually abusing Robert. When Robert began treatment and felt more safe, he disclosed the sexual abuse. As treatment progressed, Robert's behaviors began to calm down somewhat. It was only when Robert would have to talk about the sexual abuse that he had experienced with his stepfather that Robert would begin to get so frustrated and angry that he could not control his rage. I believe that Robert's rage was expressed by physical violence because of the young age at which Robert's abuse began; Robert could respond to the abuse only in an emotional way. Robert's left brain could not express his anger verbally, as he did not have the cognitive skills for appropriate verbal expression. For days after he had discussed the stepfather's abuse, Robert would be difficult to live with. His mother would feel as if she and the rest of the family were walking on eggshells, all in an attempt to placate Robert. Robert's anger was holding the entire family hostage.
>
> The situation had become so difficult that the mother talked with me about having Robert placed in a children's group home. Robert's behavior was dangerous, especially to the younger siblings in the family home, but placing Robert in a facility was only a stopgap measure. For a long-term answer, we needed to go beneath the offensive behaviors and deal with the real issues that were driving Robert's behavior: the abuse by his stepfather and the sense of vulnerability that Robert could not tolerate. Although we were not able to criminally prosecute Robert's stepfather due to Robert's inability to be consistent in the details of the abuse (this was due to Robert's sense of fear and his age), we were able to obtain a no-contact order. When Robert realized that the stepfather was not going to be allowed to have any con-

tact with him and that he was safe from further abuse, Robert's behavior began to settle down.

Children as well as adults often begin to deal with traumatic events only when they feel that they are safe enough to deal with them. Robert's rage was a defense mechanism aimed at keeping people far enough away from him so that they would not push him too much and make him deal with the events that were too traumatic, events that he wasn't emotionally prepared to deal with. It wasn't long before Robert began to disclose more and more details of the abuse. Robert's behaviors remained stable and manageable as long as he was reassured that he was now safe from the stepfather. Robert no longer had a need to engage in behaviors that took the focus off of his internal emotions. It was now "safe" to feel.

Some survivors, especially those who have the most repressed anger, will self-mutilate. Most often a series of small cuts will be located on the inside of the survivor's forearms, but sometimes the cuts may be found on the other parts of the survivor's body where they are not so easily seen.

Cutting serves several different purposes. Cutting can be used as a way to block out feelings. When survivors are cutting themselves, they can focus on the pain that they themselves are administering. The survivor can determine the duration and the intensity of the pain. This self-administered pain allows the survivor to focus only on what is happening at that precise moment. It is much less painful emotionally to focus on "fresh" pain that is self-administered.

An interesting fact about self-mutilation is that although it is used to take the focus off of "old" pain-numbing becomes such a good defense against feeling emotional pain that to feel again the survivors must cut themselves and see their blood to convince themselves that they are still alive. The relationship between violence and shame, whether the violence is administered by others or by oneself, is one in which shame is at the core of the survivors' beliefs and feelings about themselves. Whenever this sense of shame is triggered, violence provides an immediate sense of relief from the feelings of shame. Violence also gives the survivor a sense of power. The power that may have been taken from the survivor during the abuse feels as if it has been restored. This scenario seems to be especially prevalent among male survivors. The survivors' need for power is in direct relationship to the emptiness that they feel inside.

A continuum of self-abusive behaviors occurs, beginning with cutting behaviors and leading to promiscuity, prostitution, substance abuse, and finally to completely giving up the survivor's sexuality entirely. At the end of the spectrum we have survivors who become "addicted" to masochism and sadism in an attempt to replicate what may have been unresolved issues in their own pasts. Does this mean that every masochist or sadist has been sexually abused? Certainly not, but *some* survivors will go on to reenact their own abuse in an unconscious attempt to make it "come out right." Those who are seriously into sadism and masochism (who actually hurt or allow themselves to be hurt by others) are to be differentiated from those person who are involved in S&M and B&D and do not physically abuse others against their will. AASECT (American Association of Sex Educators, Counselors, and Therapists) has a clear delineation between S&M and B&D that is consensual and not pathological versus the behaviors that involve what could be called coercive and "unhealthy" S&M and B&D.

> Kelly is a fourteen-year-old survivor who was molested by both her older brother and her father. Kelly is angry at both of them, yet she feels helpless to express this anger. Instead, Kelly has attempted suicide four different times because she feels that she should have been able to stop the sexual abuse. Even though Kelly was only ages seven to eleven years old when the abuse was occurring, she still can't understand that the abuse was not her fault and that she was too young and too dependent to have been effective in stopping the abuse.

Survivors blame themselves in an attempt to believe that they had at least some sort of control over the abusive situation. In reality, the survivor had no control at all. Some survivors become angry because in their family of origin, from an early age, they learned that their feelings mattered little to the family. What really mattered was keeping the peace no matter who was sacrificed or hurt. So many survivors grow up in this atmosphere that they are never able to change their way of relating to others, even when they are adults and have an opportunity to develop autonomy and a sense of power in their lives.

The next chapter explains why some survivors use drugs and alcohol as a way to obtain the "mood" that the survivors' reality can't provide.

Chapter 8

Drugs and Alcohol As Anesthesia

God, give us grace to accept with serenity the things that cannot be changed, courage to change the things which should be changed, and the wisdom to distinguish one from the other.

Reinhold Niebuhr

Although addictions are often the cause of much pain and loss in the survivor's life and the lives of the ones close to the survivor, addictions can also enable the survivor to endure the most painful of experiences and memories.

Addie is a forty-year-old survivor who was molested by both her father and her maternal grandfather when she was quite young. Although Addie's memories are not very clear, she knows that she has always picked men that somehow have reminded her of the male authority figures from her childhood. Although her partners may have not physically reminded her of her father or grandfather, her partners all have had two common traits: they are alcoholic and they don't value Addie. Addie has never been in an intimate relationship with a partner that did not involve violence or abuse. Addie has had partners try to strangle her. Men have beaten Addie so badly that she has suffered broken bones and needed to be hospitalized. Addie has abused alcohol, heroin, marijuana, LSD, and just about every known drug. Throughout all of her addictions, Addie was able to keep the memories of her sexual abuse by her father and her maternal grandfather at bay. Every time Addie would attempt to become clean and sober, the emptiness inside would become so overwhelming that she would relapse. Addie's health finally became so impaired that she *had* to quit abusing substances or she would have died. It was only when Addie was able to refrain from the use of drugs, alcohol, and relationships with abusive partners that her memories of her childhood sexual abuse began to surface.

Is Addie angry about all the years of addiction she has lived? Quite the contrary. Addie thanks God for her addictions. The addictions are what enabled Addie to keep the pain of the abuse distant enough so that she could function until she was strong enough to deal with the memories.

Kassidy is a good example of how a survivor's history of abuse can lead to a full-blown addiction.

Kassidy was molested the first time at age six by a friend of the family, a much older male. She was terrified to tell her mother of the sexual abuse because her mother was not able to deal with anything stressful. By the time Kassidy was in her teens, she had already witnessed her mother's attempts at suicide whenever anything difficult to deal with occurred.

Although Kassidy was very young, she understood enough to know that suicide was not something pleasant. Several years after the first molestation, she was sexually abused during an extended family visit by another much older male friend of the family. Kassidy's mother was oblivious to the sexual abuse due to her own alcohol abuse. Kassidy knew that her mother was too fragile to deal with all of Kassidy's sexual abuse experiences. Kassidy knew that if anything was to be done about her sexual abuse she would have to do it. She told a teacher about the abuse she had experienced. The sexual abuse was reported, but before the perpetrator could be arrested he died of a heart attack. Kassidy was left with the feeling that if she hadn't told of her sexual abuse, the perpetrator would still be alive. She was left with much guilt and unresolved anger. Kassidy had wished numerous times that the perpetrator would die because of what he had done to her. For a child, this death wish was real and had come true. Adults understand that "magical thinking" does not cause someone to die. Kassidy was too young to understand magical thinking, so on top of all of the trauma of the sexual abuse, she also had to deal with thinking that she had caused the perpetrator's death.

As Kassidy got older, she was molested several more times. Someone who has never experienced sexual abuse might wonder why she was molested so many times. One might even ask if she was a "willing" victim. Kassidy had developed a pattern of thinking that led her to feel helpless. Every time in the past that she had reached out for help, no one had been there to help her. Kassidy had developed a pattern of learned helplessness.

The pain of dealing with multiple rapes and molestations and parenting her own mother had taken its toll on Kassidy. She couldn't sleep, didn't eat for days on end, and was so depressed that all she felt like doing was crying or thinking about suicide. Even being in several different treatment centers for suicidal ideation and depression did little to help Kassidy deal with the results of her abuse.

One day, as she watched her mother smoke marijuana, Kassidy decided that if smoking pot helped her mother relax, then maybe it would help her also. From the very first time she smoked marijuana, she was destined to develop a problem with drugs. The marijuana gave her the relief that she had sought for years and had never been able to find. For the first time since all of her abuse began, Kassidy could think of things besides pain and sadness.

Soon Kassidy and her mother were using drugs and alcohol together. Although she continued to use the drugs, Kassidy felt a sense of shame at what she and mother were doing. Basically, she was a very "good" child. She had heard all of the talks at her school about the dangers of drugs. Kassidy knew that if anyone found out about the drugs that she and her mother were using, they would be in trouble.

The conflict between feeling that she needed the drugs to survive the emotional pain that she was in and knowing that society frowned on drug use caused more conflict within Kassidy. Soon she had progressed to much more serious drugs, such as crack cocaine and heroin. To obtain the money to buy drugs, she began prostituting.

Before Kassidy was eighteen years old, she became a prostitute. Kassidy had resorted to the most addictive drugs currently available on the street in order to kill the pain of her sexual abuse and the neglect of her childhood. Anyone from the outside looking at Kassidy would probably think that she was just another "junkie." In reality, she was simply attempting to live her life day to day with the worst emotional pain imaginable.

Young teenage girls are not the only victims of sexual abuse who resort to addictions to deal with their emotional pain.

> Ricky is a seventeen-year-old white male who grew up the son of an alcoholic father. Ricky's parents divorced when he was only five years old. His father had custody of Ricky, but Ricky

grew up being passed from one family member to another. Ricky's father was either working long hours or was in the bars "relaxing" from long hours. When Ricky's father did spend the occasional hour or so with him, the time would be spent telling Ricky how he was never going to amount to anything or be able to reach his father's expectations of what a son should be. Any shortcoming that Ricky had, his father would attribute to the negative qualities that his father found in Ricky's mother.

Ricky was introduced to drugs when he was only ten. An older neighborhood boy had offered Ricky some marijuana. Once Ricky began to smoke pot, it wasn't long before he progressed to harder drugs. Ricky had such low self-esteem that he really didn't care what happened to him. Ricky had been molested by one of the male friends his father had brought home one weekend. Ricky was so ashamed of the molestation that he had never confided in anyone about the sexual abuse.

It was only about a year or so before Ricky became a male prostitute. Not only did the drugs help Ricky deal with the pain of his father's neglect and disapproval, but the drugs helped to deal with the pain of the past sexual abuse and the knowledge of how Ricky now was actively offering his body to whomever had either drugs or the money that he needed to buy drugs.

The vicious cycle caused by sexual abuse and neglect had begun. The more that Ricky attempted not to deal with his abuse through the use of drugs, the lower his self-esteem became. The last time that I saw Ricky, it was apparent that for something to happen to cause Ricky to see the harm that he was inflicting upon himself, Ricky would have to stop using drugs long enough to feel the pain of what he was doing and the pain of his past abuse. Ricky is in so much pain that he will do anything to avoid those incredibly painful feelings. If a miracle doesn't happen soon, Ricky will probably die from either an overdose of drugs or a sexually transmitted disease.

The need to project violence and act macho is an attempt to push people so far away that they are not able to get close enough to abuse the survivor. I have seen female survivors use drugs and act tough in much the same manner.

Blossom is a twenty-five-year-old who was sexually abused by her stepfather. Prior to her stepfather's rape, Blossom was a virgin. The rape was so brutal and so traumatic that within just a month of the rape, Blossom was drinking alcohol and smoking marijuana.

Blossom's mother's family of origin made her the family scapegoat. Blossom's mother loved her very much and would have done anything to protect her. Blossom's mother had no knowledge of her rape. Blossom sensed that her mother was not able to protect herself from Blossom's stepfather's physical and emotional abuse. Because she feared that her mother could not handle the knowledge of the sexual abuse, she kept quiet about the abuse in an attempt to protect her mother from having to deal with something painful and upsetting.

This wanting to protect the nonoffending parent from the knowledge of what the offending parent has done is very prevalent in incest families. To keep a lid on her intense feelings of anger, fear, and sadness, Blossom needed to do something to relieve her pain. Drugs and alcohol served the purpose. Blossom had easy access to drugs and alcohol, as her mother and stepfather had their own issues with substance abuse. If Blossom had not had easy access to drugs and alcohol, she could have just as easily developed an eating disorder. Her substance abuse issues became so bad that she began prostituting to support her habit.

The process of addiction is so subtle that survivors often don't realize that they are in the midst of addiction until major damage has been done to their lives. When survivors begin the process of addiction it is often an unconscious attempt to quell the emotional pain that they feel from their abuse. The first thing that the survivor uses that "successfully" quells the survivor's pain and discomfort is usually the same thing that the survivor will return to time and again. Many times behaviors used to quell this pain are inherited from older family members.

Peggy is a seventeen-year-old survivor who was molested by an older male friend of the family. Peggy was also molested by her older brother. Both Peggy's mother and father are alcoholics. Although Peggy had sworn that she would never drink alcohol, she has a problem with alcohol abuse. The first time that she used alcohol Peggy couldn't believe how wonderful it felt not to have to worry about things for a little while. For the first time, Peggy was able to express the anger that she felt toward her two perpetrators. Of course, Peggy expressed this anger to her friends;

it was too risky to express the angry feelings toward the people who had really hurt her. After all, they might not love her anymore if she displeased them.

Peggy has been drinking off and on for about a year. It takes more alcohol now to get the same results that initially took only two drinks. Peggy doesn't drink to be sociable now. Drinking is used to "numb" all of the negative feelings that Peggy has regarding how her parents behave and how they often neglect her. Despite Peggy having a problem with alcohol, not one person has commented on her drinking or tried to intervene in stopping her behavior before it is too late. Although Peggy brags that she can hold her liquor, she realizes that no one cares enough about her drinking to try to stop her from drinking. It really hurts to know that it doesn't matter to her parents that she has been drinking and driving. Peggy hasn't even tried to hide the smell of alcohol on her breath when she comes home very late at night. On several occasions, Peggy has left empty beer cans in her car. Peggy's parents believed the flimsy excuse that Peggy offered—that the beer was left in her car by her friends—because they didn't value Peggy enough to set limits on her behaviors. Peggy has begun to think that since drinking was good enough for her parents then it is good enough for her also.

Carol is another example of a young person who has coped with her abuse by using substances. Carol is filled with guilt because she perceives she instigated her own incest. Carol will use almost any means to focus her attention away from her own feelings. Carol is only fourteen, but she has used and abused substances for several years in attempts to escape the negative feelings that her abuse has caused. Carol's uncle, the perpetrator, was insidious in his abuse of his niece. When Carol's uncle would rape her, he would tell her that if she told no one would believe her. Her uncle told Carol that she was "special" to him—that she was prettier, smarter, and much more mature than the other girls her age. Carol came from a family filled with chaos and economic strife. Although Carol's mother was a very loving person, she herself had never received the nurturing that she had needed from her own mother. Carol's mother was under much pressure and had much confusion in her life; she did not notice what was happening to Carol. Carol was so lonely and felt so guilty about the first few times that her uncle raped her that Carol needed to believe that someone loved her. Eventually, Carol began to "ask" her uncle to allow her to have sex with him. Carol didn't understand that she was desperate to feel loved and her uncle seemed to offer her the only "love" that Carol felt was available. Carol managed to contain the story of the rape and her feelings of worthlessness for several years. Eventually, the situation at home made it impossible for Carol's mother to care for Carol and her siblings. The children were placed in a residential group home. For the first time in several years, Carol was safely away from her uncle. The uncle dared not contact Carol for fear that he would draw attention to himself, raising suspicions.

When Carol realized that she was safe, she began to "feel" the effects of the rapes. She began to have nightmares and flashbacks, especially when she was under stress at school. Instead of talking about her feelings regarding the rapes, Carol began to act out. She began to do outlandish things such at drink alcohol or smoke marijuana at school and start food fights in the cafeteria. Although Carol didn't understand consciously that she wanted someone to notice her behaviors and ask her what was wrong, unconsciously Carol's behaviors were an attempt to call attention to how awful Carol was feeling inside.

Eventually Carol's behaviors became so outlandish and troublesome that school officials and the staff at the group home did notice that something was wrong with Carol. Unfortunately, it took almost six months for the authorities in her life to see that it was something that had *happened* to Carol that was causing these negative behaviors and not that Carol was a *bad* child. It took an additional several months for Carol to feel enough trust to disclose in therapy what she perceived as *her* seduction of her uncle. Carol did not see the rape as the abuse that it really was. Carol's uncle had been successful in his attempts to have Carol take on the sexual assaults as *her* responsibility. She gave no responsibility to the uncle at all for being the abuser or perpetrator of the abuse. Because she was in so much emotional pain, Carol had turned to alcohol and later to drugs as a way of keeping a lid on her feelings. Carol had such low self-esteem that she would continually make friends with the worst behaved peers in her classes. If there were people in her class that did drugs, slept around indiscriminately, or drank, Carol was with them. If her classmates shoplifted or got in brawls, Carol was right there with them. No matter what the negative behavior, if it offered a brief reprieve from the feelings of low self-esteem and guilt resulting from the rapes, Carol was involved.

What is most interesting about Carol is that she had no real idea of the connection in her life between the rapes and her negative behaviors. Carol, along with the authority figures in her life, simply saw herself as being a "good" girl who had turned out "bad." Carol didn't understand that the rapes had caused her to go from being a straight-A student to a student who was failing in every class. Each failure in her life that was a direct result from the feelings resulting from the rapes compounded the negative self-concept and low self-esteem that Carol experienced. Carol was in a cycle that simply kept widening with each negative occurrence in her life.

Trying to help survivors such as Carol realize that their negative behaviors can be traced back to the original abuse is a very difficult task because to do so, one has to get the survivors first to stop distracting themselves by abusing substances or using behaviors as a smoke screen. They must stop and *feel* the pain from the abuse. Notice that I did not simply say that survivors need to *acknowledge* the pain of their abuse. Carol knew on an intellectual level that she felt emotional pain resulting from the sexual experiences that she had with her uncle. What is required is an *emotional* acknowledgement of the abuse and its resulting harmfulness. In Carol's case, the pain of acknowledging that the only person that she felt had truly loved her in her entire life was also the person who had harmed her and exploited her the most was overwhelming. Drugs, alcohol, and anorexia eased Carol's emotional pain, which she desperately required to be able to function. Carol had the most difficult time realizing that these substances and behaviors were the most sure route to returning to finish the type of abuse that the uncle had begun. Without ceasing these behaviors, Carol was bound eventually either to ruin or end her life.

When many survivors finally understand the dynamics which lead up to sexual abuse and the addictive behaviors that result from sexual abuse, they are able to heal from lifelong patterns of abusive behaviors that the survivors themselves have caused and others have inflicted upon the survivor.

Doris is a forty-two-year-old survivor who has had a lifelong battle with addictive behaviors, including drug and alcohol abuse and food addiction. When Doris came into treatment, she was on a mission to "discover" all of the details of her childhood sexual abuse. As our work progressed, she began to understand that no matter what the details were, the results are the same: patterns of either self-inflicted or other-inflicted abuse. When survivors with good cognitive skills are given the framework for what causes sexual abuse, they often can use this framework to facilitate their own healing process. Doris was no different than the child and adolescent survivors with whom I work. She was blamed as an adolescent for the sexual promiscuity she exhibited and the substance abuse that she later employed to deal with the emotional pain of her abuse experiences.

It is a well-accepted fact that a very high number of prostitutes are incest survivors. Some research indicates that the percentage of prostitutes who are incest survivors is as high as 98 percent (Zierler et al., 1991). Even if these statistics are not entirely accurate, it is clear that sexual abuse, particularly incest with its betrayal of the victim's trust by a person who is closely connected to the victim, is extremely detrimental to the survivor. How can we blame our children and adolescents when they turn to drugs or alcohol to deal with problems that most adults don't have to deal with in an entire lifetime? Many times society is not even comfortable discussing subjects of a sexual nature. It has been only in recent years that society has begun to recognize that sexual abuse occurs as often as it actually occurs, yet society still is not ready to deal with the large number of cases of sexual abuse that occur. Whenever I tell people the type of work I specialize in, they begin to look very uncomfortable. No one wants to believe that people could be so cruel as to abuse a child in such a way, but if we as adults don't acknowledge that sexual abuse occurs as frequently as it does, we cause survivors to try to protect us from the discomfort of having to deal with the abuse by simply not disclosing that the abuse happened at all. Children must be protected and nurtured. It is the *parent's* duty to protect the child, not the child's to protect the parent. This situation happens all too frequently. Many times the parent will have an idea that the abuse might be happening simply because of the changes in the child's behaviors. The parent has a responsibility to investigate the cause of the child's changed behaviors. Often the parent will ignore the changes in the child's behavior because acknowledging the changes would require the parent to deal with the abuse and all of the subsequent repercussions. Some parents would rather remain comfortable and allow the child alone to bear the brunt of dealing with the perpetrator and the abusive behaviors.

Even survivors who have no conscious memory of their sexual abuse are not immune to the ravages that addiction can cause.

> Cherry is a woman in her thirties. When I first met Cherry, she was having numerous panic attacks. The attacks were so frightening to her that she would refuse to sleep with the lights off, even though she worked the night shift and slept during the day. Cherry was on a mission to try to find out exactly what had happened in her childhood to explain the symptoms that she had experienced almost all of her life. These symptoms included being afraid to go to sleep in her room at night, a chronic problem with urinary tract infections as a child, frightening nightmares on a regular basis, picking partners who were extremely abusive, a feeling of constant dread and hypervigilance, an inability to enjoy sex, and a problem with drug addiction that stretched from her early teens until the present. Although Cherry had managed to abstain successfully from using drugs for several years when I first began working with her, it was obvious that she still had numerous compulsive behaviors.

I'm very uncomfortable "helping" a client try to uncover repressed memories. I take the position that I am not a detective. The possibility always exists that the therapist could even unwittingly plant false memories. When Cherry wanted me to help her uncover what she was sure would be memories of incest, I had to explain to her the dangers in my doing as she wanted. Cherry understood, but still was disappointed because she felt that she really needed to *know* what had happened to her and what had caused all her past issues with addictions and the current problem of panic attacks.

It was helpful to explain to Cherry the underlying dynamics that cause sexual abuse, addictions, and compulsive behaviors and to allow Cherry to make her own conclusions. By simply discussing how sexual abuse has elements of coercion and violence underlying its structure and that addiction and compulsive behaviors are often what we use to anesthetize ourselves, Cherry was free to create her own hypothesis about what may or may not have happened to her. In other words, do we have to *know why* something has happened to treat the symptoms? Ideally we would like to know as much as possible about why a client has a problem. If by trying to find out why a client has a problem we might cause false memories, isn't it simply better to help the client to relax and work with the issues about which they are sure?

By simply allowing herself to relax and work with the issues she was sure about, Cherry was able to develop a plan to address the panic attacks. Within a very short amount of time, Cherry's symptoms were greatly reduced. If the therapist is able to help clients let go of their anxiety about knowing exactly what caused their symptoms and try to deal only with the symptoms they are sure about, this in itself will help clients relax enough to use whatever energy they have in a more functional manner. Therapists must be comfortable enough with their skills to realize that eventually clients will uncover whatever it is that they need to find out to heal themselves. Therapy is a *process* not an ultimate goal. Symptom reduction is something that occurs over a period of time. With the current emphasis on brief therapy and time constraints on client treatment, it is sometimes difficult for the therapist to remain calm about a client who is not progressing as quickly as the therapist would like. It is imperative that clients know that no matter how quickly or how slowly they are progressing, they are exactly where they are supposed to be in their treatment. When Cherry realized that the treatment itself was part of the healing and that there was no correct time table to the healing process, she began to make real progress.

What is it like for survivors who have used drugs or alcohol to deal with their issues without the addictions that have enabled them to suppress their feelings? The feelings are so intense and raw that they can barely deal with all of the feelings that emerge seemingly all at once. Their first response is to want to run from their feelings. After all, that is what addictions are all about: suppressing true feelings that are too painful to address. When survivors are in a secure setting, such as a psychiatric hospital, the intensity of emotions becomes overwhelming. This is when survivors finally realize that they must deal with every feeling that they have worked so hard to ignore. At some level, it is when survivors feel safe enough that they finally begin to disclose their abuse and deal with their feelings. Although survivors will not acknowledge satisfaction about unburdening themselves by disclosing the abuse and the related feelings, they are often glad that they have begun the process of disclosure and healing. It is only when people acknowledge what has transpired in an open and honest fashion that they can view their situation clearly.

Joel is an example of a survivor with an addiction to drugs and alcohol.

> Although Joel is only fourteen years old chronologically, he is much older mentally. Joel's father is an alcoholic who has a history of being in and out of the state mental institution for various mental disorders. When Joel's father drinks to excess, which happens on a regular basis, he becomes very violent. Joel never knows who will get hurt or when the violence will occur. His father raped him when Joel was only eight years old. Joel never told anyone until at age fourteen he was placed in a psychiatric hospital for his substance abuse and violent acting-out behaviors. When Joel was agitated from not using drugs or alcohol to quell his emotional pain, he lashed out at the staff who were trying to console him.

At a point such as this, it is important to reassure survivors that nothing lasts forever and that they are approaching the situation as a child would, by expecting things to improve immediately without any effort or time invested in recovery. Most survivors with addictions will be so angry and upset at this point that they won't want to deal with what is being said to them. Part of recovery is allowing the feelings to wash over the survivor—even the most unpleasant feelings, such as impatience and anger. Reminding survivors that they are exactly where they are supposed to be in their recovery normalizes a very tense and volatile situation—then wait until they are more rational and stable to try to address their issues. Quietly sitting with them and allowing them to experience their feelings is the most therapeutic action that the therapist can perform for clients at this time.

It is amazing to what lengths survivors will go to try to keep their family together. I have seen adolescent survivors follow their siblings into the worst kind of drug or alcohol use in an attempt to "join" with the family member. As so many other drug and alcohol counselors have stated before, the other members of the family will allow themselves to be only as healthy as the sickest addicted member of the family.

Can talking with survivors about their drug use when they are joining another family member in the usage change their behaviors? I have found that the fear of losing whatever is left of their family is so great that it is extremely difficult to try to stop the natural progression of addiction once the process has begun. Survivors will convince themselves that they are different from other people who have suffered the consequences of drug use. Sometimes survivors feel that it really doesn't matter what happens to them. These are the survivors who most often have a history of suicide attempts or suicidal ideation. Sometimes these survivors will actually tell the therapist that they just want to hurry up and die. Drugs are often the quickest and most available method of achieving this end. I have had survivors who are using the most lethal drugs tell me that they aren't suicidal. They have no concept of how dangerous and risky their behaviors are, at least on a conscious level. These survivors are in such pain that they will do almost anything to stop it.

> Dennis is a survivor who began to use drugs when he was only twelve years old. His stepfather dealt cocaine and marijuana. Dennis's stepfather had molested him, so when Dennis stole a large amount of his stepfather's drugs and sold them on the street for a large amount of money, Dennis knew that he was safe from his stepfather's rage. His stepfather would not risk Dennis disclosing the sexual abuse. When Dennis attempted to tell his mother about the sexual abuse, she refused to believe him and did not even bother to confront Dennis's stepfather with the allegations. Dennis began not only to sell drugs, at this point Dennis also began to *use* drugs, mostly in an attempt to try to escape the pain that he felt at seeing his mother side with his stepfather. It wasn't long before Dennis had a full-blown cocaine problem.
>
> Although Dennis hated using drugs and would often pray to God to take the addiction away, he couldn't stop using. It was only when the drugs caused him more pain and loss than the original pain of the sexual abuse that Dennis began to realize that the drugs weren't working. The pain from the sexual abuse was coming through anyway. It was at this point that Dennis began his recovery.

Even though survivors are truthful in telling the therapist that they may have no conscious memories of being abused, the compulsive behaviors may still be exhibited.

Donna, a sixteen-year-old, has engaged in compulsive behaviors on many different levels. When she was seven years old, Donna would wake up screaming night after night with terrible nightmares about "monsters" chasing her. As Donna became older, she would exhibit compulsive checking behaviors. Night after night, Donna insisted on checking under the bed and in her closet before she could even attempt to go to sleep. When she was twelve years old, Donna began to cut her forearms compulsively with a small knife that she kept hidden under her mattress. At thirteen, Donna began to experiment with drugs. Before she was fourteen, Donna was getting high on marijuana almost every day.

Working with Donna was like trying to fit together the pieces of a jigsaw puzzle. Donna was able to dissociate, but she wasn't aware that this wasn't something that everyone else couldn't also do. Donna had been using dissociation as a defense for as long as she could remember. It didn't seem unusual to Donna to have chunks of time that were unaccounted for or to have other people comment on how "different" or "strange" she seemed at times. Donna's behavior was also very subtle when she would dissociate. Since Donna was so guarded when working with a therapist the opportunity to observe her dissociation wasn't readily available. It was only after over a year in therapy that it became apparent that Donna was dissociating. As we began to get closer to the actual abuse history, Donna's compulsive behaviors became more apparent and necessary. Not only did they become more apparent, but her family's own compulsive behaviors also became more apparent. Donna's parents had divorced several years before Donna had entered therapy. As we got closer to the actual abuse that had caused the original compulsive behaviors, Donna's mother became more anxious. Soon the concern in the family for the mother's anxiety overshadowed the investment in Donna's treatment. Donna's father's anger and rage became more and more magnified until it also became so compulsive that Donna's problems took a backseat. The entire family system was trying to find a way to "balance" what was causing the family too much stress. It was only when Donna's drug involvement became so serious with her use of heroin that the family was *forced* to look at the possibility of an underlying cause for Donna's behaviors. As therapy progressed, the need to repress the feelings of anger and fear became less intense and Donna began to feel more safe. She was able to remember her maternal great-uncle coming into her room night after night and molesting her. Her uncle had often hidden either in the closet or under the bed before Donna had come into her bedroom. What Donna had unconsciously re-pressed surfaced as compulsive behaviors. Once the abuse was ex-posed and dealt with, Donna's compulsive behaviors began to de-crease. The compulsive behaviors had allowed Donna and her family members to shift their focus of attention onto behaviors that would keep the more threatening feelings and memories at bay. Once Donna felt supported in attempts to deal with possible abuse issues, she no longer had such an intense need to focus on compulsive behaviors. It is important for the therapist to listen to clients when they say that they have no memories of abuse. Although Donna had all of the signs of sexual abuse I couldn't *tell* her that she had been sexually abused. To do so would have been planting the memories of abuse in her mind. It was imperative that I allow Donna the time and the space to process her own memories and feelings.

Safety is always an issue when the therapist is feeling secure in a hunch that some sort of abuse has occurred. If the therapist's feeling is such that he or she feels the abuse is *still occurring,* then it is neces-sary to form a safety plan. On occasions such as this, I have told cli-ents that I'm not really sure what may or may not have occurred in the past, but that I really want to be sure that they are safe until we can find the answers to questions about the past. To keep the client safe, I will set the boundaries in the family as high as I possibly can, by which I mean that the family must put locks on all of the bedroom doors and use the locks on a consistent basis. No one is allowed to walk around the house unless fully dressed. Only one person at a time may use the bathroom. The bathroom door is to be locked whenever someone is using the bathroom. By making these rules the same for everyone in the family, the client is not singled out or focused upon. I will ask clients to keep a journal of their feelings. If they feel uneasy or fearful around someone, I will ask the clients and/or their care-givers to respect the clients' feelings and stay away from that person.

Many times it is the *caregiver* or *parent* who is the perpetrator. If the person that the client feels uneasy around is the caregiver or the parent and we have had no disclosure that this person has sexually abused the client, I will ask everyone in the family to come to a ses-sion to let the caregiver or the parent know that the child feels uneasy and uncomfortable and needs the reassurance of establishing more secure boundaries as mentioned earlier. I *do not accuse or confront anyone with my suspicions.* The only way that anyone would ever be accused of sexual abuse is if the *client* had clear memories of sexual abuse. Simply by letting the possible perpetrator know that the client has had feelings of fear is sometimes enough to keep the perpetrator at bay until clear memories surface. I understand that risk is involved in allowing the perpetrator to know that the client may be regaining memories, but the perpetrator has no real knowledge of what is said during sessions because of client-therapist confidentiality. The possibility always exists that the therapist can report suspicions to child protective services if the caregiver or parent terminates the client's treatment. If the client is a victim, the perpetrator will be aware of the possibility of the case being reported and will not be willing to risk addition charges. No easy answer exists to this situation. One thought that has always helped me in situations such as this is that even if the client has no clear memories, perhaps by being in treatment and knowing that help is available might allow the client to regain memories at some later date. The therapist walks a thin line between planting thoughts of sexual abuse and keeping the client safe.

What should parents do if their child develops a problem with drugs or alcohol? Many parents make the mistake of trying to talk with the adolescent who is still under the influence of drugs or alcohol. Waiting until the child is sober can be difficult, but trying to get someone who is drunk or high to listen to wisdom and consequences is next to impossible. It will help if the parents don't throw in the towel and believe that their child is worthless because he or she has used drugs or alcohol. People who have good self-esteem are able to overcome any number of negative behaviors. By talking to the child about his or her positive worth and the love that the parent feels for the child, the child may be able to see the damage that the addiction or problem behavior is causing. If the parents are well informed about drugs and alcohol use and are able to relate this information to their child in a nonjudgmental and nonhysterical manner, the child is more apt to listen and trust what he or she hears. Many organizations exist that parents can turn to for help when their child has become involved with substance abuse. Don't let pride stand in the way of going to meetings or looking for professional help. Alateen, Al-Anon, Alcoholics Anonymous, and Narcotics Anonymous are excellent examples of organizations that have helped countless numbers of people affected by drugs or alcohol.

When adolescents first begin their descent into substance abuse, they usually begin by abusing alcohol, followed by marijuana. If the adolescents have any sort of genetic predisposition to obsessive-compulsive disorder, they may also be at increased risk of self-mutilation and eating disorders. There appears to be some sort of problem with the neurotransmitters in the brain that causes persons with OCD to be more at risk of self-mutilation or eating disorders.

How does a therapist work in a group setting with adolescents who are dually diagnosed with issues relating to sexual abuse and addictive or compulsive behaviors? Although I can't tell you exactly how to facilitate a group for this population (or even if it is a good idea to attempt to address all these issues at the same time), I *can* tell you some of the things that have helped my cotherapists and me while working with this population. Because of the nature of sexual abuse and all of the betrayal of trust that it causes, some survivors simply will not be willing to establish a separate relationship with a therapist who specializes in treating addictions without the security of the therapist with whom they are working with their sexual abuse issues. The established practice of addressing substance abuse before other issues makes sense. When referring clients for substance abuse counseling, many times issues relating to sexual abuse are not considered important enough to address at that time. Many times the addictions counselor will see the client's addiction as the primary problem without realizing the behavior that is driving the addictive behavior, namely, the need to be "numb" as a result of sexual abuse. The clients in our groups that have made the most lasting recovery are the ones who addressed their sexual abuse issues in individual treatment and in the survivors' group while they were concurrently attending separate substance abuse treatment with addictions counselors. By simply aligning services, the survivors were constantly being supported by therapists while addressing either their addictions issues or their sexual abuse issues. Because of managed care, it is very costly and difficult to have a client hospitalized in an inpatient facility for the dually diagnosed. Coordinating services between the addictions therapist and the sexual abuse therapist is the best alternative. This coordination requires constant communication between the professionals. The professionals must not allow treatment to be "split" by one professional being played against the other. If the client is in treatment willingly (not court mandated), the chances of success greatly increases.

Because I am not an addictions counselor (I do not have a CAC or a CADC but I receive guidance from those who do have these credentials), I do not feel that I can adequately address the recovery from alcohol and drugs. If we understand the *purpose* of drugs and alcohol, it is easier to relate the abuse of these substances to all of the other abusive substances and compulsive behaviors in this book. The entire purpose of addiction is not to feel. The addict can act spontaneously only while under the influence of substances.

While facilitating a group of adolescent survivors with drug and alcohol problems, the therapist must remain nonjudgmental, but probably nowhere else will the therapist's own issues be so sorely brought to the forefront than when dealing with this population. The therapist will be tempted to tell the group members that they should know better, yet if the therapist behaves as an authority figure and lectures the group, they will simply identify the therapist as yet another parental figure and discard whatever wisdom he or she tried to share with them. The therapist can best reach these adolescent survivors by helping the adolescents process what has happened to them and letting the adolescents make their own decisions based on the facts that both the adolescents and the therapist are able to bring to the discussion. I have found that by telling the adolescents that soon they will be adults and will need to make decisions that will be in their own best interests and that now is the time to begin making these sort of decisions, is usually the first step in getting adolescents to think in a more adult manner. People recover only when they are ready to do whatever it takes to recover. If clients aren't ready to commit themselves to full and complete recovery, nothing the therapist can do or say will make that much difference. All the therapist can do is offer the expertise and help that is available. I have a plaque in my office at home that sums up this situation completely: "In nature there are no rights or wrongs, only consequences." How true this is!

What is it like running a group for adult survivors with addictions and compulsive behaviors? In one word, difficult. The therapist is usually dealing with issues that have been around a long time in adult survivors' lives. Adult survivors rely on these behaviors so much that it is much more difficult to change their behaviors. I have never tried to run an outpatient group for survivors with alcohol or drug addictions because the addictions are usually so severe that I don't feel that I am qualified to offer assistance. Numerous survivors in the adult groups have a history of drug or alcohol addiction. One of the adult group members had a history of using crack cocaine. While she was in the adult group, she was doing quite well. The other group members were offering her support and encouragement in her fight against her addiction and in dealing with her sexual abuse. The client stopped coming to group and relapsed several weeks later. One of the people who had sexually abused her when she was a child had died. The perpetrator was a family member toward whom the survivor had very mixed feelings. It hurt too much to deal with her feelings, so drugs provided the escape that she had found useful in the past. She was incarcerated for prostitution and dealing drugs. While she was incarcerated, her daughter, who was in foster care, was molested by one of the other children in foster care. The saddest part is that because her daughter has seen her mother turn to drugs when she couldn't deal with emotional pain, the daughter may also turn to drugs when she feels that she can't deal with her abuse. The cycle of abuse goes on.

The group offers adult survivors with a history of drug or alcohol dependence the sense of forgiveness, compassion, and community, which they may be receiving for the first time in their lives. The group can end the sense of isolation that the addiction/compulsion causes. The shared histories of the group's members allow the members to understand that they are not alone in the problems and the situations that they have encountered. The group has been able to offer economic and emotional support to members who are not making ends meet or are struggling with the loss of employment or housing. Last, because the adult group members all have children who have been sexually abused also, the adult group helps not just to deal with the adult's addictive or compulsive behaviors as they relate to sexual abuse, but also offers support to deal with the child's abuse issues and addictions as well. Many times I have walked into the waiting room to call everyone into the meeting room only to see group members clustered together, helping one another deal with problems and offering support *before* the group meeting even has started. Trying to end group meetings is sometimes a lengthy process because the group members will often stand outside of the building and talk for hours. It makes me feel so proud when I see how the group members are able to empower one another. Each group member has a special place in my heart.

In the area in which I practice, marijuana, cocaine, and ecstasy are the drugs that seem to be the most popular. Female survivors seem to be drawn to heroin much more often than other readily available drugs. The statistics in the area where I practice indicate that about 57 percent of heroin users are female. The majority of the heroin users in group are white and about fifteen to seventeen years of age. Since I specialize in treating sexual abuse, I can't be sure of the percentage of heroin users who are survivors, but some recent statistics indicate at least 70 to 75 percent of heroin users have a history of sexual abuse. This does not surprise me at all. People who value themselves do not take risks with their lives; those who abuse drugs such as heroin likely do not feel very good about themselves. Sexual abuse effectively sends the message that what happens to them doesn't matter. These are also the clients with the lowest self-esteem and greatest sense of shame.

> Angie is a teenager who "looks" as if she has the world by the tail, but nothing could be further from the truth. Angie is sixteen and lives in a group home. She was molested by two of her "stepdads" (her mother was never married to any of the men that she brought into Angie's life). Angie's mother had a drug problem and often neglected Angie. When Angie was twelve, she disclosed the sexual abuse to a teacher. Angie's mother refused to believe Angie's story, so Angie was placed in the first of a series of unsuccessful placements in foster care. Angie felt so alone that in an attempt to be accepted by others she began to use what she referred to as "herbs" with her friends at school. "Herbs" was what Angie's friends called marijuana. It wasn't long before Angie had progressed to drinking alcohol on a daily basis. When the family in which Angie was placed reported the alcohol use to Family Services, Angie decided that she would simply switch to something that the placements couldn't detect—heroin. Angie didn't have to inject the heroin with needles. She could snort the heroin, which somehow didn't make it seem so dangerous. Before long, Angie found herself prostituting to support her growing addiction.

Angie's story is not uncommon among the survivors with whom I work (Polit, 1990). Young survivors only fourteen or fifteen years old have talked in group about prostituting in the bus terminals of large East Coast cities in an attempt to support their addictions. These survivors have described what it was like to "do a train with several johns" in a bathroom stall in a bus or train terminal. One group member described what it felt like the first time she heard a "client" talk about the whore he had picked up and realized that he was talking about her. It is almost impossible to look at these beautiful, articulate adolescents and picture the horrors that they have experienced because of their addictions and sexual abuse histories.

Adolescent survivors with addictions will often give indications of their addiction problem. One of the first signs is usually a drop in grades. Problems may develop in the relationships in which the survivor is involved. Survivors with addiction problems may keep others at arm's length in an attempt to prevent discovery of their addictions. They may withdraw completely from their friends who do not use substances. Wild mood swings may occur as the survivor attempts to self-medicate and may be either overindulging or coming down. Behaviors may be very unpredictable with overreactions or "numbed" feelings. Physical symptoms such as weight loss or somatic complaints may be evident. Sometimes when the survivor's drug use has greatly escalated, behavior may actually appear to be psychotic.

It is important to understand that not all survivors who use drugs will have an addiction problem. Some survivors will try drugs and find out that they really don't get anything from the experience or don't like the experience at all. These are social users. The survivors who go on to abuse drugs or alcohol on a more consistent or predictable basis are term addicted. At the far end of the spectrum are the users who leave no doubt in our minds that they are abusing drugs or alcohol. The use of the substance has so seriously impaired their functioning that it is apparent that something is wrong. Unfortunately, this is when survivors first may be placed into treatment.

What has happened to a survivor's developmental progress when reaching this point? Almost every aspect of the teen's development has been affected. These teens are usually sexually promiscuous but not necessarily because they enjoy sex. Usually having sex is a way to make money to support addiction(s) (Dekker et al., 1990). These survivors have such low self-esteem that they are isolated and have very poor problem-solving and social skills. They may have sexually transmitted diseases as a result of either their sexual abuse or their

promiscuity. There is virtually no ability to trust others, so there is no
real sense of intimacy with anyone.

I can't think of one survivor in any of the groups who trusts easily.
Sexual abuse is a betrayal of trust; the ability to trust others is severely damaged. Survivors either trust almost everyone indiscriminately or they trust no one at all. Recovery means that the survivors
must deal with their feelings without the use of their "anesthesia" and
learn to trust their perceptions of others. If your sense of shame is so
overwhelming, if you have no faith in your decision-making abilities,
and you feel that no one understands your problems, recovery can be
a monumental task. It is no wonder that group is one of the most effective ways to help the survivor heal. When one sees that one is not
alone in facing a problem and that others have survived and even
thrived in spite of similar circumstances, the healing process can begin. Time and again, I am amazed by the ability to heal from the most
horrendous abuse. I respect the survivors with whom I work. They are
so courageous, especially when they begin to face their abuse without
the addictive or compulsive behaviors. It is encouraging to see individuals who have been underdogs all of their lives begin to blossom and
become empowered, and finally speak out not only for their own
rights, but also for the rights of others.

Not only are adolescent survivors at greater risk of substance
abuse, but they are also at much higher risk of early pregnancy due to
their introduction to sex at an early age. A study done by Stock and
colleagues in 1997 found that a history of sexual abuse is associated
with adolescent pregnancy due to an early engagement in sexual activity. This same study also found that survivors of sexual abuse are
also at higher risk of behaviors such as promiscuity, low self-esteem,
and becoming victims later in life of a forced sexual assault. A study
by Elders and Albert in 1998 also found that a history of childhood
sexual abuse is linked to high-risk behaviors and an increased risk of
early unplanned pregnancy. Various studies done in the mid-1990s
(Moore et al., 1995; Cooper, Peirce, and Huselid, 1994; and Advocates for Youth, 2001), have found connections between childhood
sexual abuse, adolescent pregnancy, and substance abuse. In 1995, a
study done by Moore and colleagues found that teens who use tobacco and alcohol at an early age along with their friends have more
permissive sexual attitudes and behaviors. In 1994, Cooper, Peirce,
and Huselid found that substance abuse is associated with increased

sexual risk taking at the time of first intercourse and at the time of first intercourse with a new partner. One has to wonder which comes first: do adolescents use drugs to kill the emotional toll of their sexual abuse or does the substance abuse cause lowered inhibitions, which then leads to risky sexual behaviors?

Many times just because a person has stopped drinking or getting drunk, his or her partner (many times a survivor) will believe that the partner no longer has problems related to the addiction. In many cases, although individuals are no longer actively drinking, they have become what is known as a "dry drunk." In such cases it is important to watch for signs of relapse, such as problems in eating and sleeping, mood swings, uncontrollable outbursts of anger, not attending regular meetings of AA or NA that were previously needed to remain sober, having the sweats, and anxiety often displayed as tremors or depression.

Forty percent of American high school students have used drugs by their senior year in high school. This is a huge number of adolescents. Keep in mind that this is not just high school students who would need to "numb" themselves because they have been sexually abused. If we add in the traumatic experience of sexual abuse, the percentage of students using drugs would go up dramatically. In a 1991 study, Johnson found that the breakdown of drug use was as follows: stimulants, 27 percent; cocaine, 16 percent; hallucinogenics, 15 percent; sedatives, 14 percent; inhalants, 14 percent; tranquilizers, 13 percent; opiates, 10 percent; and LSD, 9 percent. The adolescent survivors with whom I work generally use a much higher percentage of opiates and LSD. This difference in percentage may be due to the location of my home state (a state that is in a major north to south East Coast corridor) and the types of drug available to the adolescents.

In a 1994 study done by Lowry and colleagues, a large percentage of students who used drugs also had sexual intercourse with four or more partners without the use of condoms. In Spingarn and DuRant's 1996 study, young men involved with pregnant partners reported more use of cigarettes, alcohol, cocaine, and were more likely to drink and drive. Studies done by Stevens-Simon and Reichert in 1994, have found a correlation between sexual abuse and an increased risk for adolescent pregnancy. Boyer and Fine (1992), Moore and colleagues (1995), and Stock and colleagues (1997) found that the consequences of sexual abuse often included adolescents having their first voluntary sexual intercourse at a younger age, less use of contraception in subsequent sexual activity, a greater frequency of sexual activity, the presence of more mental health problems, and a greater number of sexual partners. I believe that this research demonstrates the problem that younger survivors have in trying to deal cognitively with sex once they have been exposed to it at too early an age. It is impossible to expect that an adolescent survivor could simply "turn back the clock" and be the same person as before the abuse. Developmentally, the adolescent is not prepared to deal with the possible ramifications of sex at too early an age (i.e., unplanned pregnancy, sexually transmitted diseases, and the emotional cost of such intense relationships).

The Alan Guttmacher Institute in 1994 released research indicating that 74 percent of women who had intercourse before the age of fourteen and 60 percent of women who had intercourse before age fifteen had been involved in *involuntary sexual activity*. The Guttmacher Institute's research also indicates that 32,101 pregnancies result each year from rape. This is an astronomical number of children who will be born to mothers who did not plan for a child. In many cases, the woman will keep the child even though the child is a constant reminder of the rape. Even though some mothers try to overcome the circumstances of the child's conception, they often are unable to accept the child once it is born. The saddest case is when the mother does not feel free to express how she feels about her pregnancy or about raising a child who is a constant reminder of sexual assault. Although it is not the child's fault, many times the child pays for the sexual assault and the child's conception.

The Washington State Survey on Adolescent Health (1998) found that girls who were sexually abused were more likely to lack parental supervision, have a history of physical abuse, miss more school, have decreased involvement with extracurricular activities, have lower grades, think more often of dropping out of school, have an increased likelihood of drug or alcohol use, have a poor body image, and have more thoughts of suicide or have attempted suicide. The University of Pittsburgh Medical Center's Western Psychiatric Institute and Clinic (Clark, 1997), found that the majority of adolescents with alcohol abuse issues may have been exposed to such traumatic events as physical and sexual abuse. Sexual abuse was reported more often in girls, whereas physical abuse was reported more often in boys.

Many survivors not only have problems with drugs or alcohol but often find themselves involved with partners who are also addicted to drugs or alcohol. If the survivor's partner does not have a problem with substance abuse he or she probably has codependency issues. A perfect fit exists between the addict and the codependent; one can almost predict that when we find the addict the codependent can't be far behind. Problems with alcohol or drug addiction can often be predicted in families where there is a lot of drinking going on, yet the family has no perception of how much drinking or drugs are being consumed.

R. VanPelt's (1988) *Intensive Care: Helping Teenagers in Crisis* talks about the "5 Stages As Adolescents Progress Toward Alcohol Addiction." The five stages include

- curiosity and the availability of alcohol;
- learning that alcohol makes them feel good with only slight guilt;
- seeking the mood swing and deciding to get drunk as the goal;
- preoccupation with the mood swing and getting drunk as the main goal;
- the addiction phase in which the adolescent drinks just to feel okay and needs larger and larger amounts to get drunk.

J. E. Meek's (1971) *The Fragile Alliance: An Orientation to the Outpatient Psychology of the Adolescent* describes the four types of adolescent drug users. The "experimenter" uses up to four or five times to gain acceptance. The "recreationist" uses to share pleasurable experiences with friends and not to achieve mood or mental effect. The "seeker" searches for altered states and uses regularly to achieve a sedative or intoxicant effect. The "drug head" uses hard drugs such as cocaine or heroin. This user is addicted.

If the adolescent survivors with whom I work were asked if they have an addiction problem, most of them would emphatically deny it. The truth is that almost all of the adolescents in group who use drugs will have problems with addiction at some point. In many families of origin of these adolescent survivors, drug or alcohol abuse has been a major issue. It is the pain of their abuse and the hopelessness of their situations that often causes the adolescent survivor to turn to drugs or alcohol. Many times, these survivors have such difficult lives that it is easy to understand why they turn to drugs or alcohol. How does one face the future when all that one has ever known is pain and sadness?

> Brynn, a sixteen-year-old survivor, was sexually abused by her older half brother for over ten years. When Brynn finally told her father and mother about the abuse, they didn't believe her. The family had fallen on difficult economic times because both parents have serious physical ailments. Brynn tried to find some help from extended family members, but they too had problems of their own and didn't pick up on the desperation in Brynn's situation. At fourteen, Brynn began to smoke marijuana. By sixteen, Brynn had tried LSD, cocaine, and heroin. It was only when Brynn became pregnant that she stopped using drugs for the remainder of the pregnancy. Despite Brynn's intentions to not use drugs again, she returned to drugs shortly after her baby was born. Brynn is a very bright young lady with a kind heart.

The chances of Brynn escaping the negative consequences of drug use are remote. It will probably be a long time before Brynn is able to see the negative consequences of her drug use. It will probably be even longer before Brynn understands how her drug use and her sexual abuse are connected. Only then will she have the best chance of beating her addiction.

How can we prevent adolescent survivors from turning to drugs and alcohol as a way of "numbing" themselves to the pain of sexual abuse? We need to teach our adolescents how to make wise choices about drugs and alcohol. We need to help our adolescents develop better problem-solving skills. Helping adolescents find ways in which they can be more comfortable in social settings and have confidence in their own social skills without the abuse of substances is important. Adolescents, as well as adults, need to accept the fact that things in life aren't always fair. It is what we *do* with what has happened to us that makes the difference between success and failure in life. Perhaps if we as adults try to place the adolescents' focus on the positives in their lives and the skills that they have developed over the years, we can encourage adolescents to continue to strive for success and healing. We need to encourage adolescent survivors to take responsibility for their current decisions. They cannot cling to their abusive history as an excuse to make additional mistakes in their futures. At some point, we must all take responsibility for our actions. Adolescent survivors need to learn not to run from their feelings even though the feelings may be extremely frightening. They need to learn to identify the differences among their various feelings. It is helpful if adolescents can learn which situations are apt to trigger episodes of substance abuse. By learning to reach out for help and support, the adolescent can avoid relapse. By learning to set and maintain healthy boundaries, adolescent survivors can verbalize troublesome feelings rather than *act out* those emotions. By learning cooperation and social interplay, adolescent survivors can accept and give criticism and praise in a constructive and healthy manner. By learning to accept healthy limits, adolescents can avoid future unpleasant confrontations which may also result in relapse.

Although the signs of drug or alcohol abuse will vary according to both the substance being abused and the person abusing it, some signs seem to be universal in identifing drug or alcohol abuse. These signs include staggering or poor coordination, the smell of alcohol on the survivor's breath, slurred speech, a "spaced out" appearance, dialated pupils, sexual promiscuity, a drop in school activities, attendance, or grades, a loss of interest in former friends, isolation or social withdrawal, a set of new and different friends, behavior problems and the inability to accept limits, a negative attitude, behavioral and emotional outbursts, uncontrollable anger, physical problems, eating or sleeping changes or problems, engaging in risky behaviors that previously would have been avoided, the smell of gas or household products on the adolescent, paint on the adolescent's body or around the mouth, or finding household products that contain inhalants missing, and finding alcohol missing from the household.

Most caregivers don't have a full understanding of the classes of drugs that the adolescent survivor can abuse. The depressant class of drugs includes such substances as nail polish remover, gasoline, tranquilizers, aerosol propellant, lighter fluid, cleaning fluid, barbituates, and assorted household products.

The stimulant class of drugs includes such substances as cocaine, Ecstacy, caffeine, amphetamines, nicotine, and methadrine. Of the adolescent survivors with whom I work these drugs are the most often abused. Some of the kids in the groups come from drug-abusing families. Some of the group members refer to their drug use as simply being a form of entertainment or "refreshment." Many times not only is the sexual abuse multigenerational but the drug use is as well.

The hallucinogenic class of drugs includes marijuana, LSD, mescaline, and any other sort of drug that distorts or creates altered perception. Of all the illegal drugs used in the adolescents' groups where I am employed, marijuana is abused most often. Most of the adolescent group members think marijuana is "harmless."

The narcotic class of drugs includes morphine, codeine, and heroin. Heroin is also used frquently by the adolescent group members. Several of the group members have turned to prostitution to support their heroin habit. The survivors who turn to heroin use are perhaps the most difficult of all to reach. Their drug addiction blinds them to the damage that they inflict upon their lives. Even the other survivors in the groups often can't reach them. Only when they are arrested and incarcerated for prostitution or illegal narcotics possession do they seem to "bottom out" and have a chance at recovery.

Traditional treatment of substance abuse states that the substance abuse must be addressed before any other work can be done. In the dually diagnosed, such as survivors with a drug or an alcohol problem, referring them to a drug or an alcohol treatment center often means that they do not want to connect with the substance abuse treatment agency. We lose the connection that we have in the survivors' group, and the client won't make the necessary transition to the substance abuse treatment agency. We have tried to address both the substance abuse issue and the sexual abuse issue within the adolescent survivors' group. It is too early in the treatment program to be able to give feedback as to the results. I suspect that we will find that whenever the adolescent has a very strong attachment to the survivors' group he or she will stand a better chance at recovery if treated for both the addiction and the sexual abuse within the same group. When we have referred clients out for substance abuse treatment alone, most of the referrals have not made the necessary connection. Substance abuse treatment alone doesn't seem to reach the underlying issues that can cause the survivor to relapse once the addiction is removed. Although the substance abuse treatment used alone has had some degree of success in stopping the substance abuse, the minute that these survivors are without the substance that has "numbed" their feelings, they are at much higher risk of relapse. We have observed this many times in the adolescent survivors' groups. Just because survivors stop abusing the substance does not mean that they will not find another outlet to abuse themselves. If the underlying issues are not addressed, they will find another way to "medicate" their emotional pain. Later on, you will read how survivors switch addictions and compulsive behaviors in an attempt to end their dependence on a certain addiction or compulsive behavior.

Gwen is a good example of an adolescent survivor who has been unable to deal with sexual abuse without an addiction or compulsive behavior of some sort.

> Gwen is sixteen. Starting at the age of six, Gwen was sexually abused by numerous adult family members and family friends. Gwen already demonstrates very codependent behaviors. Gwen's mother is also a survivor who has made numerous suicide attempts. Gwen has also made several suicide attempts. This scenario is very common in the families with whom I work. In many cases, parent and child communicate with each other through suicide attempts. Instead of simply telling each other how overwhelmed they are feeling and asking for support, either the parent or the child attempts suicide.
>
> One of the most painful issues Gwen must deal with is her fear that anger expressed toward her mother for failure to protect her from the sexual abuse will lead to her mother's successful suicide. To vent her intense feelings of anger, Gwen began to use drugs and often ran away. At sixteen, Gwen has a full-blown addiction to heroin. Gwen has prostituted within the last year in order to support her drug habit. The shame that Gwen feels for her drug use, sexual abuse, prostitution, and failure to be able to "parent" her mother is a constant source of pain. Gwen can find escape only in drugs. Discussing the sexual abuse issues without her addiction are sure to bring on a binge that will result in Gwen making another suicide attempt. The irony is that by dealing directly with the pain of her abuse and her feelings toward her mother, Gwen possesses the most possibility for recovery. The pain from Gwen's attempts to flee from her abuse history is greater than the pain of facing her abuse issues. Trying to convince Gwen to allow the feelings to sweep over her is almost impossible. Gwen is so terrified of emotional pain that she simply can't fathom allowing herself to feel the emotions resulting from her abuse.

Clients who have experienced the trauma of sexual abuse have already had too many dishonest people in their lives. If therapists cannot be genuine in their understanding of the ability of an addiction to bring individuals to their knees in shame and humiliation, then they should refer clients to someone else who is better suited to address those issues. Why do I make such an issue over this need for genuine understanding between the client and the therapist? There was a time when, as a therapist, I did not understand or want to work with addiction. I had little patience for the repeated relapses and failed attempts at change. It was easier for me simply to see the addict as being weak-willed. When I was made emotionally aware that my own weight issues were tied to an eating disorder that was a form of addictive or compulsive behavior, I seriously began to want to understand as much about addiction as I could. If the therapist doesn't understand the cycle of addiction and compulsive behaviors, then that therapist will have little patience with the addict's attempts at recovery and the inevitable relapses that so often occur. The therapist must be able to help the addict see beneath the addictive behaviors to the underlying issues that drive the behaviors. The therapist needs to understand that many times survivors will be addicted as a way of being able to hold onto their own sense of power. While addicts are in the process of addiction, no one else can *make* them stop the behavior as long as they deny a problem exists. For survivors who have never had any control or power in their lives, this new sense of power and control is heady stuff. It is only when a crack occurs in the denial system that the addict has hope of recovery. The pain that the crack in the denial system causes, taking away the addict's illusion of control, is enormous.

Delle is an example of a survivor who has struggled for several years to deal with her addiction to crack cocaine.

> Delle was sexually abused by numerous people as a child. As an adult, Delle was raped several times. Over a period of years, Delle learned to turn to crack as a way to deal with her pain from the abuse experiences. Now the crack addiction has become a bigger problem than the pain of the sexual abuse. As her drug use increases so does her sense of shame. Delle works very hard to place the blame for her addiction on anyone around her who makes her angry or who she feels gets in the way of what she wants.

When Delle realizes that her *real* power lies in her ability to take responsibility for using drugs, she will be able to make a lasting change.

Early in their recovery, most survivors are able to tell the details of their abuse experiences in an intellectual manner without any apparent feelings. After addicted survivors have been able to refrain from using a substance to numb their feelings, it is quite a different story. The feelings begin to pour out—sometimes in such quantities that the survivors worry that the feelings will overwhelm them. At this point true healing begins. Prior to this, survivors may have engaged in the creation of false selves at the expense of the loss of their genuine selves. Although false selves allow survivors to meet the needs of those around them, they do not allow them to express their innermost feelings. To survivors this may feel like the death of their spirit. Once the anger and pain begins honestly to emerge, the survivor will begin to get in touch with the person he or she was meant to be before the abuse occurred.

Often, sex addicts use drugs or alcohol as a way to facilitate their involvement in sexual addiction. Sometimes sex addicts will use drugs or alcohol to kill the pain of allowing themselves to be sexual. In her book *Women, Sex, and Addiction,* Charlotte Kasl (1990) states that codependent women will use drugs or alcohol to feel relaxed about their sexuality. Kasl explainess that women who are sex addicts but not codependent will use chemicals so that they may assume the role of seductress. Some survivors fear sex so much that the only way that they can engage in sex is to drink or use drugs so that they don't have to "feel" the sexual act. Other survivors use drugs or alcohol to allow themselves to become sexual. The substance abuse "numbs" the survivors and the repulsion that they feel for sex enough so that they can at least participate in the sexual act on a somewhat superficial level. Alcohol seems to be the most often abused substance.

> Maggie is a seventeen-year-old survivor who was molested numerous times beginning at age six. Maggie's situation is especially painful because one of her perpetrators was killed shortly after Maggie made her disclosure of abuse. In Maggie's mind, she killed her perpetrator because she hated him for what he had done to her and wished that he would die. To Maggie, the wish that the perpetrator would die became so closely intertwined

with her sexual victimization that she began to feel that she was responsible for the perpetrator's death. Maggie began to believe that if she enjoyed sex, she would be punished. Maggie's distorted cognition about her sexuality was based on the idea that if you enjoy sex, you must be dirty and disgusting. Yet Maggie craved the closeness and intimacy that sexual relations provide. To not feel the disgust and fear of acting sexual, Maggie began to use heroin and smoke crack before sexual encounters. Maggie felt that she was so disgusting that she could never be loved honestly by someone else, so she began to prostitute. At least when she prostituted Maggie could afford to pay for her drug addiction and would receive at least the superficial closeness that she craved.

Maggie has been in treatment both for her drug addiction and her sexual abuse. She has begun to address her issues: the first time that she felt like killing herself, Maggie called the twenty-four-hour crisis hotline and asked for psychiatric help. For Maggie, this was a tremendous step because she acknowledged that she deserved to live and that she could be loved for herself.

"Alcoholism is a devastating illness. An estimated 6.6 million children under the age of 18 years live in households with at least one alcoholic parent" (National Institute On Alcohol Abuse & Alcoholism, 1990). In view of this statistic, and considering that lowered inhibitions caused by alcohol or drugs is a direct contributing factor to sexual abuse, it is possible to grasp the true magnitude of the sexual abuse problem. Thus, sexual abuse is tied to substance abuse and can become multigenerational.

Children of alcoholics have certain characteristics that make them especially prone to become involved with either substance abuse or with a partner who abuses substances. Children of alcoholics (ACOA) tend to have either a sense of overresponsibility or a sense of underresponsibility. Those with a sense of overresponsibility are especially attractive to a partner who may abuse drugs or alcohol because the ACOA personality will take care of the addict. The ACOA with an underdeveloped sense of responsibility tends to be the life of the party, fun to be around, and very charming. These ACOA are usually drawn to the overresponsible person who will take care of them and allow them to abuse substances. Other characteristics of ACOAs include low self-esteem, impulsivity, constantly seeking approval or acceptance, being overly serious without a sense of fun, and being very self-critical. Since ACOAs have not had a typical childhood they can only guess at what "normal" is.

> Kirk's family owned a bar. When Kirk was seven years old, he was molested by several of his father's friends who had frequented his parents' bar. Kirk never told of the abuse because he was ashamed of what had happened. In Kirk's family, "real" men don't cry or ask for help. He grew up feeling that he had let both himself and his family down by being molested. As Kirk grew older and spent time working in his family's bar, Kirk found himself turning more often to alcohol to dim the pain from always feeling that he was "less than" others. As Kirk's addiction to alcohol began to grow, he felt that at times he could stand outside of himself and watch himself fight his addiction. Even though Kirk knew that he was the one who was fighting the battle with alcohol, it was as if he was outside of his body watching the battle between the part of him that wanted to stop using and the addict part of him that said it was acceptable to use.

Before Kirk was able to begin his recovery from alcohol addiction, he needed to gain some insight into the real issues that were motivating his behaviors. Simply having willpower was not the answer. He needed to learn coping skills for social situations in which he might encounter triggers that would induce him to drink. Recovery for Kirk, as well as for others with addictions and compulsions, seriously begins when the addict faces and accepts reality. Those who no longer drink but still have no healing of their underlying issues often feel as if they have no emotions. They are simply going through the motions of life. These survivors may be "dry drunks." They may not be actively drinking to dull their emotional pain but they still have the same pent-up issues.

Many codependents are very angry and bitter toward God for what they perceive as God's failures in the codependents' lives. Virtually all survivors come from a background in which serious and multi-generational codependency or addiction has occurred. Whenever addiction and codependency exist within a family, generations to follow will be affected—even if several generations of the family have not abused substances. By the nature of addictions and codependency, survivors are "set up" to develop their own addictions and compulsive behaviors simply to be able to deal with the pain that they have experienced in their families of origin.

The book *Love Is a Choice* was originally published ten years ago. At that time, statisticians had estimated that at least fifteen million Americans were either alcoholic or drug addicted. In the ten years since this book was published, the numbers have grown astronomically. What does the need to anesthetize say about the climate in which our families are being raised? What does the huge number of addictions and compulsions say about how we feel about our relationship with a higher power? In truth, if we employ addictive or compulsive behaviors we then make these addictions or compulsions our higher power. We begin to look outside ourselves to find the solace and peace that we so desperately need. Survivors are set up from the moment that they are born into dysfunctional families to become addicted or compulsive in an attempt just to survive their own pain.

Recent research has indicated that substance abuse occurs alongside other psychiatric disorders. An article by Kathleen Brady (1999) titled "New Frontiers in the Assessment and Treatment of Dual Diagnosis," presented at the 1999 American Psychiatric Association Annual Meeting, indicates that individuals with psychiatric disorders are nearly twice as likely to have a substance abuse disorder as those in the general population. In this article, Brady discusses the difficulty of working with the dually diagnosed individual and the problem that many clinicians encounter concerning the lack of skill and training in working with this population. Brady further states that as many as 25 percent of all clients in treatment for substance abuse problems have post-traumatic stress disorder. Many survivors with PTSD are able to escape the pain of their abuse while in the trance state. Perhaps those victims who aren't able to escape trauma through dissociation need to look outside themselves at addictions or repetitive compulsions to escape their pain. It appears that one of the most promising treatments for PTSD accompanied by substance abuse may be the use of antidepressants in the selective serotonin reuptake inhibitor (SSRI) family. Brady (1999) cites research done by David McDowell (1999) indicating that the common symptoms of both

PTSD and substance abuse might be the neurochemical pathways that both of the ailments share.

Brady states that although attention deficit-hyperactivity disorder is found in 1 to 3 percent of the population, it is found in 10 to 15 percent of those seeking treatment for substance abuse. Brady reminds us that Douglas Ziedonis (1999) has urged mental health providers and those treating substance abuse to collaborate treatment when seeing the schizophrenic substance-abusing client. Ziedonis urges this collaboration due to the lack of motivation for change that often occurs in these clients.

Another interesting point was made by Rounsaville (1999), who found that although lessened anxiety and personality disorders may lead to decreased substance abuse, decreased substance abuse did not necessarily lead to a reduction in anxiety and personality disorders. This seems to reinforce the hypothesis that substance abuse is a form of "anesthesia" for uncomfortable feelings associated with anxiety and personality disorders.

However one approaches the dilemma of survivors with addiction or repetitive compulsive behaviors, one point remains clear: sexual abuse is so emotionally painful that survivors will go to extreme lengths to numb their emotional pain.

The next chapter considers how some survivors will focus their attention on their weight or body image in an effort to minimize their emotional pain.

Chapter 9

Weight Issues, Eating Disorders, and Disturbed Body Image As Anesthesia

What some people call health, if purchased by perpetual anxiety about diet isn't much better than tedious disease.

George Dennison Prentice, 1860

Perhaps of all of the forms of "anesthesia" that survivors employ, few are more painful than eating disorders. Eating disorders go right to the heart of a survivor's need for comfort and a sense of predictability and control over an impossibly abusive environment.

Nelia is a thirty-one-year-old who was sexually abused by numerous men in her life. The sexual abuse that Nelia experienced began when she was only six years old and continued until she left her husband when she was thirty. Because Nelia came from an environment in which abuse was an everyday fact of life, she does not consciously realize the impact that the abuse has had on her life.

Nelia weighs 300 pounds. Because she has a petite bone structure, the weight that she is carrying is obvious to all who see her. Not only must Nelia deal with the feelings that the sexual abuse has caused, she must also find a way to deal with all of the criticism and scorn that society heaps upon her because she is overweight. Unfortunately, Nelia resorts to overeating as a way of self-nurturing and "anesthesia."

Does Nelia consciously realize the connection between her sexual abuse and her weight? Intellectually she is aware that a connection exists. She has not been able to refrain from overeating long enough to feel the pain that the abuse has caused and therefore to become emotionally aware of the connection between the overeating and the abuse.

Nelia proclaims that she is happy with her life, but as she is saying this, she is overeating. She has no conscious awareness of what she is doing when she is consuming large quantities of food. Overeating provides Nelia the ability not to feel the emptiness inside resulting from the perpetrators of her sexual abuse taking her personal power and invading her personal boundaries. To deal with the pain of the abuse without the shield that the excess weight provides is too much for her at the present time. The time will come when she will be able to face the feelings connected to her abusive past without the need to overeat. It takes time to feel safe enough in their current environment for survivors to face the pain of an abusive past.

Why doesn't Nelia just decide that since her past sexual abuse is the cause of her overeating she will just stop overeating? Even though she has an intellectual understanding of the connection between her sexual abuse and her overeating, she does not emotionally realize the significance of her sexual abuse history. It is only when survivors abstain from whatever substance they are abusing that they can feel all of the emptiness that they have worked so hard to deny.

Do survivors consciously know that the emptiness and pain from the abuse are inside them? Are they aware that this pain and emptiness is why they abuse substances and develop compulsive behaviors? I believe that most survivors never make the connection. Most survivors, unless they go into treatment, never realize that they are not "bad" or "weak" people. So many survivors spend their entire lives blaming themselves and having others blame them for the very self-abusive behaviors that enable them to survive their abuse and the abuse's aftermath.

I believe that when survivors compulsively overeat they are attempting to fill the void left in their hearts caused by the pain from abuse by someone who should have cared for them and didn't. Most times the survivor never becomes aware of this "hole" in the heart. Perhaps I should call this pain a "hole" in the soul. In his book *Soul Murder: The Effects of Childhood Abuse and Deprivation,* Leonard Shengold (1989) discusses how parents or those people in a position of authority can literally "kill" the creative part of the child that is full of potential. In essence, the abusiveness of the person in authority in the child's life drains the child of his or her innocence and spirit. The process of humiliation and degradation that brings about "soul murder" is the same process that a survivor undergoes when being abused.

> Annie is a survivor who has unknowingly attempted to fill the void in her heart with food. She was not overtly sexually abused as a child. Annie's father simply said and did many things that were covertly abusive. Her father would comment on how "developed" Annie was becoming and how womanly her shape had become. It didn't help Annie that she had developed large breasts by the sixth grade. Because Annie was so much more developed than the other girls her age, she felt alienated and alone. When Annie was in her early twenties, she was raped by a family friend. Annie never told anyone about the abuse. Annie went on with her life just as if nothing had ever happened. She married a man who was rather timid and shy. Annie told herself that the rape didn't matter because it was over and in the past.

Annie didn't realize that although the abuse had occurred in the past, it was far from over. Our minds and our bodies are so complex and intricate. Although we may tell ourselves that what has happened to us doesn't matter, our mind is unable to comply with our wishes.

To bury the memories of the rape and her father's intrusive behaviors, Annie needed something to kill the pain of the abuse and to take the focus off of the feelings related to the abuse. Annie was a "good" girl. She had been raised in a religious family and didn't want to disappoint her mother by making her mother deal with something as unsavory as the rape and her father's behaviors. The toll that Annie paid for denying the harmfulness of her abuse was enormous. The longer Annie denied her rage toward her rapist and her father, the more food it took to keep the lid on her feelings. Soon Annie became obsessed with the need to eat constantly. If Annie wasn't eating, she was planning *what* to eat. Annie would stockpile huge quantities of food. Her explanation for all of the excess food that she had purchased was that the food was on sale. When I first met Annie, I was amazed at how little she realized what her true feelings were. Annie claimed to be happy but her posture and outward appearance said exactly the opposite. Annie was doing exactly what she needed to do in order to live the life that she thought that she had to live. Annie wasn't even aware that she could make choices in her life. In fact, she had made the choice to carry all of her excess weight. I know that Annie would deny that she had "chosen" to gain and carry all of her excess weight; the truth is that simply because Annie was in conscious denial about the harmfulness of the abuse that she had experienced, she had unconsciously "chosen" to suppress feelings that had to be kept down by her weight. Annie's feelings below the surface were so powerful that to suppress them she had to expend huge amounts of energy to keep the feelings down. Food was a way of nurturing herself against the abuse and the hurt and abandonment Annie felt from not being true to her real feelings. It was only when Annie made the conscious decision to face her demons and deal with them that she was able to lose well over a hundred pounds and keep the weight off for the first time in her life.

Losing the weight was a wonderful thing, but it hasn't been without its cost. Facing her true feelings meant that Annie couldn't stay in the relationship in which she found herself. The relationship was based on Annie being a "mother" to her partner. Annie was her partner's caregiver in every aspect of his life. There was nothing for Annie to obtain from the relationship except some financial support. Survivors are so afraid of being alone that they will often choose an empty relationship rather than take the risk of being alone until someone who might really make them happy comes along. Survivors often "settle" for relationships or whatever else comes their way. If we were to ask Annie if she is happy that she made the choice to face her issues and deal with them, I'm sure that she would say yes. I'm also sure that for just a brief moment Annie would hesitate before answering. She would look at the listener and, with a twinkle in her eye, explain that change and growth is never easy and never without cost. In Annie's case, the cost has been realizing that the idea that someone would come along who could protect her and take care of her for the rest of her life was simply a "pipe dream." In reality, we all need to take responsibility for our own lives and our own happiness.

Perhaps more than any other issue that survivors fear none is more pervasive than having to fend for themselves in life. This fear makes sense when we realize that a child's biggest fear is abandonment. The child fears that he or she will be left alone and, unprotected, will perish. This fear doesn't go away simply because the survivor has become an adult. All of the experiences and feelings that the survivor had as a child are still inside the adult survivor. Whenever a situation arises that would be an issue for the child inside of the adult survivor, the adult reacts very much like the frightened child inside. Older survivors seem to have no knowledge that they now have the abilities and resources to overcome whatever obstacles they may face. Instead of facing their fears, many survivors will use eating disorders to keep the fears at bay or to take the focus off their fears.

The tragedy of this is that despite their attempts at denying their abusive pasts or their fears, the time comes when all of us must either deal with our issues or face the consequences of this denial. In Annie's case, the cost of the denial was a host of health issues. Once Annie began to deal with those issues, she lost the relationship with her husband. Perhaps if Annie had been able to deal with her own issues earlier in the relationship, the relationship might have been forced to change and grow. Annie will never know for sure. Annie is happy that she has faced her issues despite what it has cost her. She has said that, "Ignorance is not bliss; it's just ignorance."

Even when the survivor has no clear memories of the sexual abuse, the hurt and the anger still manage to leak through. Sometimes the anger is expressed years later and is directed toward people who have nothing to do with the abuse.

> Katie is a nine-year-old who was molested by one of her mother's friends. When Katie disclosed the abuse, her mother did not believe her and told her to forget about the abuse. Within a very short time, Katie began to hit her younger sisters. Soon this aggressive behavior spread, and Katie began hitting her classmates and causing disruptions in the classroom. When her parents would attempt to correct Katie's aggressive behaviors, the situation would escalate until Katie would become out of control and would have to be sent to her bedroom. Neither parent was able to acknowledge the part that the molestation had played in Katie's sudden aggressive behaviors. As Katie became older, her behaviors became more self-abusive. Katie began to use food as a way to deal with her unexpressed anger. Food was a safety valve for Katie's unexpressed anger.

According to John Bradshaw (1986c) several types of families seem to be most prone to eating disorders. Although these families may have some distinct differences, they tend to share some characteristics that are remarkably similar.

The overprotective family is so closely enmeshed that no one single member of the family is allowed to have individual reality. Any sort of negative feeling about the family or what is happening in the family is seen as being a threat to the family. This family has poor communication and conflict resolution skills. As with alcoholic families, the overprotective eating-disordered family has the motto of "not feeling and not talking." This type of family also tends to have members who feel that they are not good enough.

> Trina is a sixteen-year-old survivor who can't seem to do anything without her family's help. Trina's father goes everywhere with her. Trina's mother and father divorced when she was ten years old. Since her mother had a drug and alcohol problem, Trina had gone to live with her father. Her father felt so guilty for what he perceived as his failure to hold the marriage together and provide Trina with a mother that he began to overcompensate. Trina's maternal uncles had molested her. Both Trina and her father believed that since the uncles no longer had access to Trina, she would be able to put the abuse behind her and go on with her life. Although Trina did feel safer without the uncles having access to her, she began to gain large amounts of weight. She would not even participate in the most minimal of physical activities. When asked if she was angry about the abuse, Trina would always say that she wasn't angry and that she forgave her perpetrators. Whenever she would be pushed to delve into her feelings about the abuse and the divorce between her parents, she would quickly dismiss whatever questions were asked with the comment that the abuse was over with and she never thought about it anymore. It was only when Trina allowed herself to realize that she did indeed have anger in regard to the abuse and her parent's divorce that she was able to understand the role that food had played in holding down such intense and uncomfortable feelings as her anger.

Bradshaw believes 90 percent of eating-disordered women have been taught not to express anger. Our society seems to consider anger an unacceptable emotion. Anger is simply the feeling that someone has wronged us. It is what we *do* with the anger that may sometimes be inappropriate.

In chaotic families, no sense of consistency or predictability exists. Substance abuse or compulsive behaviors may occur by the caregivers. The younger and less powerful family members are sometimes victimized. The parents in the chaotic family are often either emotionally or physically unavailable to the child. In this sort of family, appearances are everything. The family is overconcerned about what others will think about what happens in the family. This type of family also has rigid roles.

In perfectionistic families, the father usually has all of the power. As with the chaotic family, the real emphasis is on appearances, the children's achievements, and the family's standing in the community. In the perfectionistic family, the anorexic is likely to develop the eating disorder in an attempt to exert at least some sense of control over something in the environment. Anger is perhaps the greatest taboo in this sort of family.

> Savannah is a sixteen-year-old survivor who was never allowed to express her feelings toward her parents. Every time her parents would do something that would make her angry, Savannah would be reminded that her mother had a weak heart. If Savannah dared to express feelings that the family found uncomfortable, immediately Savannah would be reminded that she could "kill" her mother by disagreeing with her. Savannah quickly learned that numbing herself by not eating was easier than stating her true feelings and getting into a shouting match with her entire family. When Savannah's weight dropped to 80 pounds and she became very ill, the family finally had to focus on Savannah's feelings instead of just their own.

In the family of the child suffering from reactive obesity, dining with the family is like being in a combat zone. Dinner is not a time for conversation and discussion. The child suffering from reactive obesity would most likely have a normal weight if it were not for the power and control games going on in the family. The child's weight is simply a reaction to the stressors found in the family. In families in which reactive obesity occurs, children are taught to eat everything on their plate, to eat quickly without talking, and to give total control and obedience to the father.

Survivors with eating disorders are either using their disorder as a means of "eating" their grief, anger, sadness, or fear, as in the case of the compulsive overeater, or they are using their anorexia as a means of not being able to feel at all.

Bradshaw describes the characteristics of the eating-disordered family as having a father who is often on the verge of leaving the mother, is emotionally cut off from others, and enforces rigid family roles. The father may or may not be a sexual addict but is often seen as being shallow. The mother often turns to the children as a source of comfort and treats them as confidants.

Anorexics often see their mothers as being totally dominated by their fathers. When the anorexic sees what she thinks being a woman involves, the anorexic makes the decision that she does not want to be a woman if that is what being a woman involves. Not eating provides a sort of boundary from the rest of the family and allows the anorexic to have a private self, separate from that of the family.

In families in which the survivor is very obese, it is often an attempt by the survivor to protect himself or herself sexually. Survivors may become so heavy that they seem not to have genitalia. Again, this is an unconscious attempt to create a boundary separate from that of the family. Although the eating disorder may result in large part from sexual abuse, the eating disorder itself can lead to a sort of "sexual" anorexia in which the survivor has no sexual life or identity at all.

Eating disorders, similar to other addictions or compulsions, are really based on a spiritual deficit. Early in life, survivors learn that they can count on no one but themselves. In an attempt to find nurturance and comfort, they turn to those closest to them and find nothing to end their emotional pain. It is when survivors attempt to self-soothe and turn to a nonhuman substance or behavior that they have begun the addictive or compulsive process. Addictions and compulsions are really about the alienation and sense of isolation that survivors feel. The stigma of sexual abuse or incest is only an additional burden that further separates survivors from others who might be able to offer support and comfort.

To recover from eating disorders, survivors need to do all of the same things as those who are recovering from eating disorders but who are not survivors in addition to being able to deal with their sexual abuse without the aid of the eating disorder. This is where conventional treatment has failed to address adequately the survivors' issues. Conventional treatment has stressed how you must first address only the addiction or compulsion. By addressing only the addiction or compulsion, the individual is figuratively tearing off a scab from a wound and taking nothing to ease the pain.

To heal from an eating disorder, survivors must first surrender to the fact that they have a problem that they cannot control. They have tried to use willpower in the past, but they need to accept that they are powerless over food. Survivors must find a support group or therapist that is understanding, nonshaming, and supportive of the survivors' attempts to recover. These people will perhaps offer survivors the first real support, which will replace the shamebased isolation that they have previously endured. Support groups allow survivors to receive the help that they so badly need, mirrored in the faces of the group's members.

Eating-disordered survivors must learn to accept themselves, faults and all. They must learn to care for and love themselves, perhaps for the first time in their lives. Imagine how difficult it is to learn to love or to care for yourself if you are the very first person who has ever offered this kind of unconditional care to yourself. How do you learn to give something that you have never previously received? Jung says that any time that we find a part of ourselves that we don't like or accept, that part of us "splits off" and creates a false persona. Sometimes we project this quality that we dislike about ourselves onto others in an attempt not to own it. Jung says that this part of us then becomes "primitive" and we may try to destroy this quality in others.

Survivors who have eating disorders must try to:

- Stop eating when they are not hungry
- Think of food as being neither good nor bad
- Listen to inner wisdom and respect the inner child
- *Not diet.* Dieting is a self-imposed form of rigid control that is bound to be part of the addictive or compulsive control-and-release cycle. This cycle implies that the survivor can return to previous eating habits when additional weight is lost
- Listen to and have love for the self and the body
- Be involved in healthy relationships that meet survivor's needs as well as the partner's needs
- Seek a spiritual connection that will end the survivor's shame-based isolation
- Attempt to find a balance in life. Begin to know limits and don't participate in the control-and-release cycle that leads to addictions and compulsions.

Changing one's habits as suggested is a tall order for anyone, but to the survivor with an eating disorder, it is almost impossible. Survivors are used to situations being all or nothing. In their families of origin, survivors either received all of the attention from the perpetrator when they were sexually abused (yes, it was negative attention, but it may have been the only attention that they ever received) or they received no attention at all. I have seen survivors attempt over and over again to recover from addictions by using willpower alone. Willpower alone just doesn't work. It is only when survivors have made numerous failed attempts at recovery based on willpower alone that they finally reach the end of their rope and seek help.

Eating disorders and mood disorders appear to go hand in hand. Depression is the most frequent emotion in clients with eating disorders. This situation is especially true for women. Statistics indicate that women may seek treatment more often than men do, causing the statistical gender discrepency.

A study done by Kruger, Shugar, and Cooke in 1996, "Comorbidity of Binge Eating Disorder, Partial Binge Eating Syndrome, and Bipolar Disorder" found that in the period between two and four a.m. there was a significant increase in the incidence of night-binging syndrome among those studied. This is thought to be important because it is also the time of day when mood swings in bipolar disorder are believed to be most likely to occur. This would lead us to believe that a strong biological component of eating disorders also ties the disorder to mood disorders. Bulimic behaviors are believed to have a mood regulatory function that relieves emotional tension for the bulimic client. The study indicates that although bulimic behaviors may decrease anxiety, these same behaviors have a tendency to increase guilt, shame, and depression. This same study also indicates that a percentage of eating disorders involve obsessive-compulsive disorder (OCD) characteristics. Perhaps this may indicate that OCD predates eating disorders. This same study indicates that 37 percent of anorexics also have OCD. Is it any wonder that so many survivors who have experienced the trauma of sexual abuse and the resulting depression later go on to develop eating disorders?

Food addiction seems to mirror the bond that is most symbolic of the attachment between parent and child. If survivors are anorexic, it is almost as if they will refuse to allow food to nourish them. Likewise, it is almost as if the survivor sees that the bond to the parent as toxic. If the child is bulimic, it is as if the child will initially accept the parent's nurturance and then will reject it. Food represents the feelings that the survivor is not able to express. Food becomes a way of setting limits of what the survivor will and will not accept emotionally, without the survivor ever having to vocalize these feeling.

In the survivors' relationships, their weight and eating patterns will mirror the way they are handling their relationships. When the relationship with a significant partner is fresh and new, it is not unusual to see survivors lose weight and also appear to be "fresh and new." Once the newness and freshness of the relationship ends, survivors may gain weight as a way of setting a boundary within the relationship without actually expressing how they feel emotionally. When and if the relationship ends, survivors may again gain weight, much like they have "gained" the acceptance that someone else can't "make things right" for them.

Sexual abuse seems to be highly correlated with eating disorders in women, probably because of the greater number of women who report being sexually abused. In her book *Losing Your Pounds of Pain,* Doreen Virtue (1994) quotes from R. Devine's article, called "Incest: A Review of the Literature" in *Sexual Abuse of Children, Selected Reading:* "Women who are involved in sexual activity before the age of 14 against their wishes are much more likely to have eating disorders" (p. 8). Virtue explains that in sexual abuse survivors, eating disorders occur two to four times more often than in the general public. Virtue cites research by Strober (1984) stating that adolescent overeaters have 250 times more life stress than adolescents who don't overeat. This statistic certainly disputes the commonly held theory that overeaters simply lack willpower.

Virtue believes that compulsive behavior is a way to avoid intimacy and demonstrates a lack of emotional mothering as opposed to physical mothering. Virtue states that as children mature they try to fill the void from this lack of emotional mothering with food or material goods. Once the high from the addiction to food or material goods has worn off, the addict is faced with the realization of what he or she has done and begins to feel the self-disgust that will only lead to future indulgences of the addiction.

Some food addicts come from families in which there wasn't *enough* food to eat. These addicts begin to equate food with love. Whenever these food addicts feel an emotional emptiness, they will turn to food as a means of filling the emptiness. Survivors grow up feeling perhaps the greatest emotional emptiness of all. Because of the role reversal involved in incest, survivors often must forego their childhood so that they can parent their parents. Incest survivors grow up feeling that they must take care of everyone else and be responsible for everyone else's happiness.

Virtue describes the "Raggedy Ann Syndrome" in which those who have eating disorders feel that others can see through them or see them as damaged goods. If the damaged goods feeling has resulted from sexual incest, the survivor is apt not to disclose the abuse in an attempt to protect everyone else and to keep the family intact. This type of self-sacrifice is bound to lead to anger and resentment. If such intense feelings are not vented, they are often turned back toward the survivor in the form of self-abusive behaviors (e.g., compulsive overeating or other eating disorders). When survivors with compulsive eating behaviors express their anger toward the appropriate people, the weight will begin to drop off. Reality is the best way for the survivor with compulsive overeating to begin to lose weight. Reality means seeing things as they really are, as painful as that might be for the survivor. Survivors must acknowledge the pain in their lives and the disappointment and betrayal that they have experienced. Using their weight as a barometer, survivors can judge how successful they are in dealing with their emotional issues.

> Susie is a fifty-year-old incest survivor who has fought being overweight almost all of her adult life. It wasn't until Susie finally acknowledged how damaging her father's betrayal of her in the form of incest was that Susie began to be able to deal with her depression and weight. Once Susie had lost a considerable amount of excess weight, the anger that she had always managed to ignore began to come out toward anyone who would make her the slightest bit angry. Susie needed to allow herself the luxury of being angry and feeling good enough about herself to realize that she deserved better treatment—both from others and from *herself.*

Many survivors with weight issues will say that they can't believe that sexual abuse is the cause of their overeating because the abuse happened only once or happened so long ago that they can't remember very much about the abuse. One instance is all that it takes to cause addictive or compulsive behaviors to begin, because one single life experience is significant enough to change a person's perception of the world and his or her safety in that world. Survivors who have not been physically sexually abused but have experienced emotional sexual abuse or emotional incest have difficulty seeing themselves as abuse victims due to the lack of physical harm. Emotional sexual abuse can be something as simple as dressing a young child provocatively or parents discussing their most intimate physical relationship with the child. The truth is that these survivors may be just as damaged by their emotional abuse. It is the fact that someone did not value these survivors as human beings which causes the damage that leads to weight issues. Survivors need to acknowledge that all the food in the world is not going to fix what is wrong or missing or erase the abuse that they have experienced. Only reparenting themselves and learning to set boundaries that will cause survivors to value and protect themselves in the future will lead to weight loss and being able to maintain that weight loss.

The next chapter discusses how survivors develop codependent behaviors, often along with other compulsive or addictive behaviors, in an unconscious attempt to prevent abandonment and loss of valued (but sometimes destructive) relationships.

Chapter 10

Codependency As an Addiction

In its broadest sense, codependency can be defined as an addiction to people, behaviors, or things. Codependency is the fallacy of trying to control interior feelings by controlling people, things, and events on the outside. To the codependent, control or the lack of it, is central to every aspect of life.

Love Is a Choice (1989)
Robert Hemfelt, Frank Minirth, and Paul Meier

In my personal experience, codependency is the worst ailment that results from childhood sexual abuse. According to Dr. Timmen Cermak (1986), codependence involves (1) a distorted relationship to power, (2) a confusion of identities, (3) denial, and (4) low self-esteem. All of these signs make it seem as if it would be simple to detect when one is being codependent, but nothing could be less simple or obvious to the person who has not yet discovered or accepted the label of being codependent.

A distorted relationship to willpower lies at the heart of co-dependency, yet because of our society's mistaken belief that all one needs to overcome addiction or compulsion is enough willpower, one may never realize that the willingness to surrender to what one can never hope to control is the answer to the miseries of codependency. Probably more survivors struggle with codependency than any other single issue resulting from sexual abuse, yet codependency is often taken lightly.

Liana is a thirty-nine-year-old survivor who has a serious weight problem. Liana is more than 150 pounds overweight. Her doctor has repeatedly warned her about the risks associated with her weight, yet Liana is much more worried about her friend Ellen's smoking, her cousin Elsie's marriage problems, or her sister Diane's pregnancy. Liana has become addicted to other people's problems in an attempt not to have to deal with her own issues. She is looking for a solution to her own problems in something or someone outside of herself.

Many times female survivors focus on their addiction to a boyfriend, acting as if he is the answer to the pain in their lives. Male survivors may be codependant upon their relationships also. Despite having serious problems, these female survivors will be so tightly entwined with the men in their lives that the survivors have no identity of their own. The survivor becomes so focused on the boyfriend that she has no real idea of her own wants and needs. If asked what her boyfriend felt or needed, the survivor could go on at length about those facts. The codependent's self-worth is tied so tightly to the partner's success or failure or the partner's happiness or unhappiness that it is almost as if the two are simply one person.

The codependent focuses so intensely on the relationship with the partner that he or she becomes addicted to the partner and the relationship. Again, it is the addiction that allows survivors to take the focus off of the really painful emotional issues that lie at the root of their emotional pain and focus it onto others. Survivors are able to shift their focus off of their own pain through the use of repression, rationalization, and projection. In other words, to continue to focus on others' needs or desires, codependents must be able to deny what is really causing the pain in their lives. Codependents identify with their partners and try to be there emotionally for the partners just as the codependents unconsciously wish that someone had been there for them. Since codependents have such low self-esteem, they usually end up with people who have a strong need to feel special—the narcissistic personality. Who is more narcissistic than someone totally caught up in a chemical addiction? It is no wonder that we see so many codependents who are involved in a relationship with an active drug addict or alcoholic. By focusing all of their energies on their addiction of trying to "fix" their partner's addiction, codependents are able to deny their own pain. Trying to "fix" their partner is really a form of manipulation that allows codependents some sense of control in their lives.

Codependency is the most frequent outgrowth of sexual abuse. Because of the isolation from others and their own authentic selves and their lack of a sense of power greater than their own willpower, codependents can virtually die from the addiction to others. When codependents fail despite repeated attempts to control the feelings and behaviors of their chemically dependent significant other, the codependents see themselves as failing once again. This sense of failure only reinforces the low self-esteem that the codependent already possesses. It is only when the codependent surrenders and develops a *willingness* to let things be as they are meant to be that the codependent is able to begin to recover from the addiction to the chemically dependent partner. None of us has any control over any behaviors besides our own. Even having control over our own behaviors is an awesome task!

When codependents make the assumption that they are responsible for meeting others' needs to the exclusion of their own needs, they are expressing a fear of being abandoned or left alone. Since codependents were never allowed to have their own feelings in childhood, boundary distortions and anxiety exist from not having a sense of personal feelings or needs. When codependents pick up on the feelings or needs of others, they make the partner's feelings or needs their own feelings or needs, since codependents have no sense of their own needs or feelings. The codependent will quickly switch from a terrible fear of abandonment to feeling overwhelmed by intimacy with others. No happy medium exists for the active codependent.

The similarities between the active codependent and the chemically dependent are quite striking. Both the codependent and the chemically dependent operate from a sense of strong denial. The chemically dependent denies the harmfulness and the degree of the addiction or the compulsiveness of the behaviors. Active codependents can't seem to grasp that they are *giving control* of their lives to someone else. Active codependents think that if only their significant other, whose behavior they are trying to control, would do as they wished, everything would be fine. Codependents see no roles that they play in the drama.

Both the codependent and the chemically dependent act out of constricted emotions. Both are apt to experience one of two extremes: (1) either their emotions are completely labile; they seem to have no control over them at all and may display sudden explosive outbursts, or (2) their emotions are so constricted that they appear basically to be without emotion. In fact, they may both claim to feel "numb." Some active codependents become so out of touch with their own feelings and emotions that they complain that they don't feel as if they are "real" or that life feels as if it isn't "real." Therapists refer to these conditions as derealization and depersonalization. Both of these conditions are part of the dissociation continuum and are related to post-traumatic stress disorder.

Both the chemically dependent and the active codependent are likely to be depressed. Imagine the enormous amount of energy it requires to contain such denial and repress your feelings. No wonder the codependent and the chemically dependent are both depressed. They have little energy left over for any stronger emotions. If you were to ask active codependents if they were depressed, chances are that they would respond that they are *not* depressed. The codependent acts out of the need for strong willpower. Feeling that they are unable to control a situation or their own feelings creates such anxiety that, in the codependents' eyes, they appear to be a failure.

Both chemically active dependents and codependents feel the need to be on the alert constantly and to be very sensitive to the moods of those around them. Because many chemically dependents and codependents have come from backgrounds in which substance abuse and trauma may have occurred, they may often suffer from post-traumatic stress disorder.

> Peter is a fifteen-year-old survivor who has a problem with marijuana. Although Peter is now in a group home, he still remembers vividly all of the times that he had to sleep with "one eye open" when he lived with his father. Peter's father is an alcoholic who would beat Peter on a regular basis. Peter was molested by several different male perpetrators who had been drinking buddies of his father. Peter tried to tell his father what had happened, but his father would become very angry whenever Peter would go to him with problems. Peter soon learned to keep his problems to himself. Peter can't seem to relax even though he feels that in the group home he is in a much safer environment. Peter says that he could never take his safety for granted. He is constantly on guard for the slightest indication that he is about to be physically harmed or sexually assaulted.

The chemically dependent and the codependent both use compulsive behaviors as a way to shift their focus from painful topics or situations with which they would rather not deal. Although the compulsive behaviors may shift their focus over time, the one constant is that there is *always* a compulsive behavior. Sometimes survivors will become so fixated on not being compulsive that they will compulsively fixate on the idea that they *are* compulsive. Although this sounds very complicated, Evan's example will explain.

> Evan is a twenty-eight-year-old survivor who has been in treatment for his drug addiction for over ten years. During this ten-year period, Evan has been in both inpatient and outpatient treatment. He has been in treatment for the dually diagnosed because he has drug issues, depression, and a lengthy history of sexual abuse. Does Evan worry about all of these problems? No, Evan simply worries that he is compulsive. Evan is compulsively worrying about being compulsive. He can't see that he needs to do something about the drug addiction, the depression, or that he needs to try to heal from the sexual abuse. Rather than admit to himself that he feels helpless and overwhelmed by these problems, Evan has become stuck on worrying that he is compulsive. When asked what he is going to do about his compulsive behaviors, Evan simply laments about how he is compulsive. By trying to tackle his problems head-on and devise a plan of treatment, Evan would have to risk confronting his feelings.

Feelings are too risky for the chemically dependent and the co-dependent. It is much safer simply to lament over being compulsive. Compulsive behavior is the result of an internal battle between what the person really is (the core personality) and the addict part of the person. Until the core personality becomes the outward and inward parts of the person, the false persona will exist. The false persona leads to compulsive and addictive behaviors.

> Wynne is a sixteen-year-old incest survivor who seems too good to be true. She is very kind, very gentle, and always giving of herself; except when she has occasional outbursts of angry and destructive behaviors. Without warning, Wynne will erupt into anger that is totally out of proportion to the situation in which she finds herself. Wynne is able to contain her angry feelings for long periods by using rigidly controlled socially correct behaviors. Whenever too much anger has built up, she simply can't control the anger or who the anger is directed toward. Wynne

seldom expresses her anger toward those with whom she is actually angry. The anger almost always is directed toward someone Wynne is not close to or with whom she doesn't care about having a long-term relationship.

It is not unusual to see the codependent, as well as the chemically dependent, have a real problem with abusing some sort of substance whether it is drugs, alcohol, or food. Some codependents have problems not only with codependency but with substance addiction as well. This occurs frequently in older survivors.

> Tatum is a forty-year-old survivor who has a food addiction as well as a codependent relationship with her live-in boyfriend. Tatum's boyfriend has not worked in three years and is an alcoholic. Her main focus in life is trying to "change" her boyfriend's behavior. Tatum believes that if her boyfriend stops drinking, her life will become perfect. She has not even begun to address her own issues regarding her food addiction or her history of sexual abuse.

Similar to many other codependents and those who are chemically dependent, Tatum has free-floating anxiety. She is constantly anxious about something but can't quite put her finger on what the cause of the anxiety is. Other codependents, as well as those who are chemically dependent, suffer from several different forms of anxiety disorders, such as chronic anxiety, panic attacks, or what is termed "existential dread." I have seen many survivors begin to experience panic attacks when they begin to cut back on the substance that they are abusing.

> Denise is a twenty-six-year-old survivor who recently has been successful in dramatically cutting back on her use of cocaine. As Denise's use of cocaine has decreased, her feelings of anxiety have greatly increased. There are times when Denise literally feels as if she can't breathe. The anxiety level when Denise begins to regain the feelings that she has "numbed" with cocaine are at these times simply overwhelming. I have asked her to try not to run from the feelings, but to let them wash over her knowing that they are only feelings and that they will pass. Denise has such a difficult time feeling these emotions. Even the reassurance that she has lived through these experiences and that the

feelings cannot hurt her is often not adequate to reassure Denise that she will be okay. The look of terror on her face when the feelings begin to affect her is heartbreaking to watch.

Finally, both the chemically dependent and the codependent share the characteristics of being involved in chaotic relationships (usually with each other), often experience medical illnesses that are caused by stress (one can only imagine how stressful it is living in such a chaotic environment), and, as in the main premise of this book, are the victims of physical or sexual abuse.

The theme of codependency often emerges when working with survivors. The codependent survivor's intentions are basically kind-hearted. The survivor sees or senses that someone is in emotional pain. Figuratively, it is comparable to seeing a dog hit by a car and rushing over to comfort the dog. The dog is in such pain that it will most often bite the person who attempts to provide it comfort. The same dynamics lie beneath the relationship between the chemically dependent and the codependent. The main difference is that the codependent tries to use manipulation (usually an unconscious attempt) to control the behaviors of the chemically dependent in an attempt to provide some sense of predictability or stability that will benefit the codependent.

Recovery from codependency is a lifelong process. It would be wonderful if codependency was something that we could work on and heal from knowing that at least one problem is solved for good. However, codependency is a lifelong pattern of relating to others that requires constant vigilance. Certain types of people or situations are triggers for codependency. The most common way to know that codependency has been triggered is that one does things that he or she doesn't really want to do and later feels resentful or angry about having done them. If individuals find themselves in relationships in which they are constantly willing to wait, hope, or try harder to please someone, this is a good indication of codependency. If one person holds all the cards in the relationship, this is another indicator. If one is constantly drawn to people who need to be taken care of or "fixed," this is an indication of a codependent relationship. If one has a history of a lack of security or love in the family of origin and tries to recover this lost love and security in adult romantic relationships, this also indicates codependency. The extreme fear of abandonment that all codependents share, however, is the true hallmark of codependency.

How does a survivor go about healing from codependency? Of all of the problems resulting from my own incest experiences, codependency is the most difficult and pervasive problem with which to deal. Being in the helping professions has not made it any easier to deal with, but it has made me more aware of my tendency to be codependent. It is a daily battle not to try to "fix" clients and instead to let them find their own paths to healing.

I believe that healing from codependency is facilitated by using a twelve-step program. CODA is the twelve-step group specifically designed to help one heal from codependency. One of the first steps toward healing is the acknowledgement that a problem exists over which one is powerless. Asking for help is the first prerequisite toward healing. Being seen by a therapist who is knowledgeable about codependency and the seriousness of the disorder is of the greatest importance. Support groups such as CODA also are invaluable. One needs to make recovery the primary focus of his or her life. It is so easy to put off taking care of something that can be as subtle as codependency. In fact, sometimes our society makes trying to heal from codependency seem like a selfish act. Who among us isn't taught to place others first and ourselves last? To place ourselves first is seen as selfish, but how can we give to others when we ourselves are depleted?

Developing a sense of spirituality is also very important. Realizing that another source of power is greater than our own allows us to see that we don't need to control everything. Spirituality allows us to feel the connection to others and removes the sense of isolation that addiction and compulsion causes. Spirituality allows us to be nurtured and takes us outside of ourselves.

Try to stop controlling or manipulating others. If you really want someone to change, let the person make his or her own decisions and face the natural consequences of the behavior. Trying to control someone is not going to facilitate the change that you want. Controlling will only delay the process of change that *the person* must decide that *he or she* wants. Allowing others to live their own lives also gives you the freedom to live your own life.

Focusing on individual faults and shortcomings allows one to grow and make the changes needed in order to be the person that one was meant to become. It is not unusual to see codependents tell the person who they are trying to change the very things that they themselves should be doing in their own lives. I see this as a form of projection. Codependents must focus inward and feel whatever emotions they are masking in their own lives. Running from the pain won't solve anything. Making sure that they have met their own needs is also very important to the recovery of codependents. Codependents need to begin to realize that they are entitled to all of the good things that life has to offer. The only thing keeping them from getting the things that they want in life is their own self-limiting ways of thinking.

To recover from codependency, one must develop greater self-esteem. The best way to gain this sense of self-esteem is to really know and accept yourself as you are. Codependents also need to accept others as they are, not as the codependent would like to see them become. As our self-esteem increases, this improvement will be noted in the quality of our relationships. With increased self-esteem, no longer will we tolerate those who don't treat us well, because we will feel that we deserve better treatment. Our values in life will change as well. We will not value being tied to another's whims or moods, but we will base our choices on what we know is right for us instinctively. We will be able to determine what is right for us by our sense of peace of mind and serenity, not by whether someone else loves us or not. For survivors, this is perhaps the most difficult task of all because they never had the appropriate love and nurturance that they needed in childhood. By asking them not to look for this love in others, we are telling them that they will never have it unless they get it from themselves. To heal, survivors need to accept the losses they have experienced and grieve those losses. The good news for survivors is that once they are able to find the love, acceptance, and nurturance they need *within* themselves they no longer have to look to others to find what they need. Survivors learn to care for their own needs, to become protective of themselves, and to see their needs as a responsibility that they themselves must meet, not that they should expect others to meet.

How does the process of recovery from codependency progress? Are there certain steps that the survivor must take in order to heal properly and completely? Although there is no one "right" way to heal from codependency, numerous authorities on codependency say that there are certain concrete, discrete steps that indicate that the codependent is on the right path to healing. As with other twelve-step groups, survivors must first admit that they are powerless over their codependency. This is perhaps the most difficult step of all because the denial is a primary defense mechanism that powers all of the other dysfunctional addictions. To heal from codependency, survivors must focus on themselves and see themselves clearly and fully. Survivors need to see how they are sometimes their own worst enemy by the behaviors that they employ and the partners they choose. This is the stage in which codependent survivors hit bottom and see the crack in their denial system. Codependents fully realize that something is very wrong in their lives and must be changed. Codependent survivors need to accept that they, along with everyone else in this world, have limits and cannot control everything and everyone. Once codependent survivors reach this point, they will often grieve the illusions that they had of power and control. It is only when codependent survivors realize that they have no real power or control that they are able to be healed. Not only must they accept that they have little control or power, but they must also accept that they have a compulsion to control that must be fought their entire lives.

The next stage of healing involves dealing with the core issues that have led to the codependent survivor's compulsive behaviors. Early core issues usually involve long-repressed emotions. The only way that codependent survivors can begin to deal with these repressed emotions is by abstaining from using the addiction that dulls the pain of their core issues. In this case, it would be childhood sexual abuse. The final stage of healing involves being aware of what one is doing instead of being in denial. Being honest and not keeping secrets is very important at this stage. Possessing a sense of spirituality is a significant feature at this point of healing. It is the sense of spirituality that will help the survivor keep the isolation and withdrawal, which perpetuates addictions and compulsions, at bay.

Although the above scenario seems complex, if we examine a case history it becomes quite clear that there is a natural progression to healing that makes sense.

> Naomi is a fifty-year-old incest survivor. All of her life Naomi has taken care of others—first her siblings and her parents, then later in life her clients. (Naomi is a social worker.) Naomi has an underlying sense of depression that she has never been able to understand fully or describe to others. Naomi really doesn't understand that others don't live with the sense of impending

doom that she does. Naomi believes that everyone is as "sad" as
she is.

In a desperate attempt to keep things in her life on a more predictable level, Naomi will try to care for and please everyone.
Nothing is too much work or trouble if it means that others will
like her. Did I mention that Naomi weighs 325 pounds and is
only five feet two inches tall? Naomi constantly snacks on
candy and whatever else is within arm's reach whenever she
gets "upset." Naomi gets upset a lot.

When Naomi's doctor told her that she had to lose weight or
she might have a heart attack, she made a real effort to cut back
on her eating. At the same time that Naomi was losing weight,
she began to deal with her parents' death from a car accident.
Her father had been Naomi's perpetrator. As the weight began to
drop off, Naomi's depression deepened and she finally reached
out for the psychological help that she had needed for a long
time. When Naomi was able to continue to refrain from overeating while she worked on her core issues, the chances of Naomi
never regaining the weight greatly increased. Naomi was eventually able to admit openly that she had suffered sexual abuse
and what it had cost her.

John Bradshaw (1986a) refers repeatedly to addictions and compulsions as stemming from the rigid roles that we must assume to be
accepted in life versus the true person that we really are on the inside.
Bradshaw states that addictions and compulsions are really about survival. They are ego defenses that allow us to be out of control when
we are forced into being in rigid control. Some examples of these
rigid roles are *the adapted child, the lost child,* and *the family hero.*
Adapted children are those who control their feelings to be accepted
and loved in their surroundings. These children are intuitive. They
know instinctively that if they express their true feelings they will be
ousted from the family, so they adapt to survive.

I can personally identify with this role. I am the oldest of five children. Instinctively, I knew that both of my parents had experienced
very difficult lives through no fault of their own. As children, both of
my parents had grown up in abusive and punitive families. I have no
doubt that if my parents had grown up in families that were not struggling so much to make ends meet financially their childhoods would
have been much easier. Somehow I knew when my mother asked me
at age twelve if my father had ever "touched" me, that she needed for

me to say "No." She was trying so bravely to face her greatest fear: one of her children being molested. I knew that disclosing the abuse would be costly to my family. My mother had no job skills and five children for whom she was responsible to provide the necessities of life. My father was struggling to support five children and a wife with his limited education and no help from extended family. I couldn't make things even more difficult than they already were by disclosing the abuse, so I said, "No!" I was adapting to what the situation called for to keep my family intact.

This is an example of what Bradshaw (1986a) refers to as "the child's parent's adapted child interacting with the child's adapted child." When a situation occurs in which the child's parent's adapted child interacts with the child's adapted child *no adult* is in charge at all. The parents are operating out of the fears and insecurities of their own inner adapted children. When parents also operate out of their own inner adapted child, there is no honesty or sense of reality to the interaction between the parents and the child. Most children who have had to become adapted have had to do so because their parents were adult "adapted children."

The lost child is usually the family scapegoat. This is the child that no one really notices. This child is usually fairly well-behaved and at times seems to blend into the woodwork. It is only when he or she does something very wrong that the child is noticed.

The family hero is usually a high achiever who feels that although others can rely on him or her, he or she doesn't have the right to depend on others. In my clinical experience, the family hero often has a lot of repressed anger toward others, particularly parents.

Perhaps the most troubling aspect of codependency for survivors is that because of the need for them to develop a "false persona" to survive the abuse, they never develop a clear sense of themselves. In other words, these survivors were never able to discover or express their true selves when they were developing children because of the need to adapt and survive their abusive environment. The survivor as a child has difficulty developing a sense of worth or of power. Children and adolescent survivors become so skilled at doing or being what others tell them to be that they have no sense of their own inner lives, of what they like or dislike, or of a true sense of self-esteem. The way that survivors develop a sense of success when they are codependent is by those most important to them *telling* them what is or is not valid to think or to feel.

When survivors have had to give up so much of their own sense of self to survive in a hostile environment, the emotional costs are huge. Most codependents suffer the following effects of codependency in varying degrees: feeling alienated and apart from others (even those in the most intimate relationships with them), eating disorders, addictions, drug and/or alcohol abuse, a sense of emotional numbness with tension stored physically in the body, losing touch with their own sense of reality and sexuality, feelings of anxiety or depression, fearing the future and constantly agonizing over the past, being terrified of abandonment, not knowing what they really want or feel, and a generalized dread of the future. Codependency can be seen as an emotional divorce from one's true self: to adapt to an abusive environment survivors must dissociate from their true selves. To express true emotions and values is too risky for the survivor. The constant fear is that they will not be loved if they allow their true feelings to be known.

I am surprised at the little weight that the diagnosis of codependency is given by professionals—except for those professionals in the addictions field. The amount of damage done to the survivor because of codependency is enormous. The loss of one's own sense of power, the fear of attempting to avoid one's inner emotional pain, the need to be rigid so that the survivor can manage to get through at least one more day, the need to rationalize relationship issues, and the amount of minimization and denial that the codependent must use in order to continue with such abusive relationships is overwhelming. To those who are on the outside observing the codependent's behaviors, it is difficult to understand the degree to which the codependent will go to remain in what seems to others a totally abusive relationship. To codependents, the abusive relationship may appear to be the lifeline that ties survivors to their own sense of personal worth. Without the partner that the codependent has determined is his or her "reason for living," the codependent feels unable to survive. Even the sense of shame that the codependent may feel due to the abusiveness of the relationship will often not be enough to stop him or her from seeking to continue the abusive relationship.

Codependency can be expressed in two ways that appear to be opposites of each other but in reality are complementary to each other. Both of these addictions are directly related to being a sexual abuse survivor. Alyse is an example of a survivor who has become a sexual

addict as a way of taking back control and becoming addicted to her
own sense of power.

Alyse was sexually abused by her biological father when she
was four years old. When Alyse was seven years old, her older
brother witnessed her father's sexual abuse. Shortly after witnessing his father sexually abusing Alyse, her brother began to
sexually abuse Alyse also. Alyse's mother had died when Alyse
was an infant. Alyse became so frightened that there was no one
to protect her from her family's abusive behaviors that to endure
the sexual abuse she needed to see herself as being the one with
the power. To see herself as having power, Alyse began to use
sexual attraction as a means of manipulating what her abusers
were already taking from her by force. At least if Alyse was the
one determining *when* the abuse would occur and *where* it
would occur she felt that *she* controlled the events. Soon Alyse
became addicted to her own sense of power and began to solicit
sexual relationships with older men. Before long, all of Alyse's
relationships with men were centered primarily on having sex.
The relationships would end as soon as the men began to "love"
Alyse. Alyse would feel she needed the excitement of a new conquest.

Tanya's way of dealing with the incest that she experienced by
her father was to give her power away to others in the form of
codependency. Tanya's mother was very frail when Tanya, the
youngest of seven children, was born. Tanya watched her mother
drink herself to death as a way of dealing with the abusive relationship her mother had with Tanya's father. Tanya's father was
physically, emotionally, and verbally abusive to Tanya's mother
and all seven of the children. Tanya felt helpless as she watched
her mother slowly die from alcoholism. Tanya's lack of power
began to invade all parts of her life. When in school, Tanya
would wait for another student to answer the teacher's questions, even though she knew the answer. Tanya simply had no
faith in her own abilities. As the sexual abuse continued, Tanya
found that the only way she could survive the abuse was to use
her sexual value to attract the power of others. In other words,
because Tanya felt that she had no power of her own, she felt
that she should keep in the good graces of those who *did* have
power.

Both Tanya and Alyse came from similar backgrounds but they developed opposing ways to deal with their own abuse issues. Alyse and Tanya did share some common behaviors. Both were most likely to engage in their addictions when a current event would trigger shameful beliefs they held about themselves from their abusive pasts. If anyone acted as though, in Tanya or Alyse's eyes, they were inadequate or disappointing, Tanya and Alyse would quickly revert to their addictions as a way to smooth the situation over and reassure themselves that all was well.

Erin is a survivor who has become a sex addict. Erin's inner feelings regarding sexual acts that her boyfriend has requested were never expressed until recently, when the acts became so repulsive and demeaning that Erin simply could not comply with them.

> Although Erin loves her boyfriend very much, at some level she has begun to despise him because of the sex acts in which he has asked her to participate. These sex acts include group sex and "swinging" with other couples. Erin has looked all her life for the love and caring that she never received in her parents' home. The sexual abuse that Erin experienced early in her childhood has left her afraid to trust others. Erin believes she would be abandoned if she ever dared to disagree with others. For awhile, Erin did swing with several other couples that her boyfriend met through pornographic magazines. When Erin was diagnosed with a sexually transmitted disease and didn't know from whom she had gotten the disease, she knew that she could no longer comply with her boyfriend's requests. The shame and disgust that Erin felt at the sexual acts she had allowed her boyfriend to pressure her into performing were finally greater than Erin's fear of abandonment.

Although Erin felt a sense of power and control over her boyfriend and her other partners when she was being sought out for participation in the sex acts, the "good" feelings were short lived and really an illusion. Erin's fear of being abandoned if her boyfriend knew her real feelings about their sex life were not based on reality. Erin's boyfriend loved her enough to put an end to the swinging activities once Erin finally voiced her true feelings. Whether the relationship between Erin and her boyfriend will last remains to be seen. The underlying sense of shame and disgust that Erin feels for compromising her

values is bound to have an impact on her relationship with her boyfriend.

> Azura complies with her boyfriend's sexual requests simply be-
> cause she doesn't want to be abandoned. Azura has used drugs
> to keep suppressed the intense and painful feelings that she has
> in regard to her childhood incest. The intense anger that she felt
> at her mother's failure to protect her from her older brother's
> sexual abuse (despite repeated disclosures of the abuse) was
> buried under the effects of the drugs Azura has used over the
> years. Azura has begun to use sex to hold onto *someone else's
> power.* She sees herself as being completely powerless, so she
> employs sex to hold on to her partner. By doing so, Azura also
> holds on to her partner's power. She has such a great sense of
> shame and anger that the relationship with her partner never can
> be truly intimate or truthful.

Survivors can switch between sexual addiction and sexual codependency without being aware that they have made a basic switch
in their method of thinking.

> Elsie is a twenty-nine-year-old survivor who has used her sexu-
> ality to obtain both her own power and the power of those upon
> whom she depends. Elsie was molested by her stepfather, her
> older cousin, and a day care employee when she was a small
> child. Elsie watched her mother's involvement in abusive rela-
> tionships and swore that she would never put up with such
> abuse. When Elsie was fifteen, she became pregnant by her boy-
> friend. Elsie's boyfriend was as abusive as any of her mother's
> partners had ever been. The marriage between Elsie and her
> boyfriend was very rocky and after ten years they divorced.
> Elsie could not bear being alone, so she soon began to involve
> herself in relationships using her sexuality to entice men to be-
> come involved with her. After Elsie was sure of a man's com-
> mitment, she would grow tired of the demands that the man
> would place upon her. Elsie soon would begin the process of
> looking for another conquest. Early in the stages of the relation-
> ships, Elsie would be totally dependent upon her partner's ap-
> proval of her. Nothing would be too much trouble for Elsie
> where "her man" was concerned. For Elsie, each new relation-
> ship was *the* relationship. Denial and minimization were constant

themes in all of Elsie's romantic relationships. In the beginning stage, Elsie would use her sexual power to involve her partner in a relationship. As the relationship began to develop, Elsie would use her sexuality as a tool to pull her partner closer to her because of Elsie's intense fear of abandonment. At this stage, Elsie would give all of her power to her partner. As she became more sure of the relationship and began to tire of it, Elsie would switch back into her sexual addiction and would begin the process of looking for the excitement of a new partner—sure again that *this* new partner would be the answer to Elsie's problems.

What is especially interesting in Elsie's story is the childlike quality of Elsie's relationships. The dependency that Elsie places upon her partners to meet all of her demands is overwhelming to her partners. Anyone involved in a sexual relationship with Elsie feels as if they were Elsie's parent. In fact, Elsie places demands upon her partners that *would* be better suited to the demands of a parent-child relationship. Elsie is like a child in an adult's body. Elsie is looking for the unconditional love from her partners that she never received from her parents. A partner in a romantic relationship can never give the unconditional love that a parent could give. Partners in a romantic relationship are also looking to have their own needs met within the relationship. A partner will place conditions upon the relationship that a parent never would. Until Elsie understands these dynamics, she is doomed to keep repeating her search for the "perfect" partner.

When the survivor makes the switch from codependency to addiction, the fuel that causes the switch is anger.

Synne is a forty-five-year-old incest survivor. When Synne became involved with her husband, she identified with his painful childhood and decided that she would take her husband "under her wing." Synne would focus all of her efforts toward helping her husband heal from his own issues. One might be inclined to think that Synne's husband would be thankful that he had a wife who cared so much about his welfare that she focused all of her attention on him. Nothing could be further from the truth! Her husband had never developed an appreciation for Synne's feelings and efforts because Synne valued herself so little. As the years went by, she developed a compulsive overeating disorder and became grossly overweight. The unexpressed and unacknowledged anger that she had kept in due to never having any of her own needs met was the fuel that caused her to switch from codependent behaviors to food addiction. The excess food that Synne consumed gave her the comfort that she craved because of the pain of her life.

I believe that prostitution has many of its underlying roots in the switch between codependent behaviors and sexual addiction. Whenever codependents begin to take back their power that they have given to others in the form of codependency and begin to use their sexual addiction as a means of exerting their own power over others, they have crossed the line from codependency to sexual addiction and sexual codependency. Many of the adolescent survivors with whom I work often say that they might as well make some money using sex because for years they have had their sexuality taken away from them anyway. That is a difficult argument with which to reason. These young survivors are correct that they have had their innocence taken away by force or coercion. They have been exploited and abused. The most difficult thing to get them to understand is that by resorting to prostitution they are allowing their abusers to continue the abuse that they originally began. The only difference is that now it is the survivor who is doing the abusing.

When survivors are in the midst of sexual addiction, they have no time for anything else in their lives. Work, friends, family, and any other relationship or interest will fall by the wayside. The only focus that survivors have is on the sexual conquest and relationship in which they are involved. The pursuit of the intended partner is all consuming. Sexual addicts themselves will have no idea how the pursuit of their partner will appear to those outside of the relationship observing the entire process. To onlookers, the pursuit looks like complete insanity. What the observer is seeing is an intense effort to shift the focus of the survivor's attention away from an internal emotional emptiness that is all-consuming and painful, toward what appears to the survivor to be *the* answer that the survivor has always longed for: unconditional unending love. Only a higher power could provide something so unique.

Codependency is a powerful tool for numbing oneself. Rationalization is one way that many codependent survivors manage to tolerate the most awful relationships all in an attempt not to be abandoned and to numb their feelings.

Rozeanne has been married for fifteen years. Her husband has been physically violent a number of times during their marriage. He has been verbally and emotionally abusive. All during their relationship, Rozeanne has told herself that her husband is really trying to change and that *real* change takes time. Fifteen years is a long time—long enough for most people to get the point that if change were going to happen, it would have happened and would be observable at least to some degree. Rozeanne has much built-up anger and resentment toward her husband, but she is in complete denial about her true feelings. She tells others that her husband is working hard to change, but that things keep getting in his way. She talks of his abusive childhood and his learning disability. Rozeanne's relationship with her husband is a very clear replica of her relationship with her own mother. She has such anger at her mother for her mother's failure to protect her, yet Rozeanne has never consciously acknowledged this anger—to her mother or even to herself, for that matter. She constantly rationalizes her mother's failure to parent.

Until Rozeanne manages to acknowledge her own true feelings, she will be doomed to be caught up in codependency in an attempt to avoid abandonment. What is sad is that you can't be abandoned if those you fear will abandon you have never been there for you anyway.

Some sexual addictions become so painful that the addict would gladly give up sexuality in an attempt to know peace of mind. These sex addicts are so consumed with their addiction that everything else in their lives has little meaning. Without their use of addicted sex, life itself has little meaning. Family, friends, and interests have no real meaning to them. Their consuming passion is always for the next sexual conquest.

Although many survivors would not want to hear this, our childhoods do indeed have a huge influence upon our futures. Although survivors would like to think otherwise, being logical and rational in our thoughts does not always keep us from unconsciously picking people and situations that allow us to recreate our childhood conflicts that have not been resolved so that we can finally get things to come out "right."

All survivors are driven by the compulsion to try to solve the issues from their pasts. The major difference between codependents and other survivors is the manner in which they try to kill the pain from their abusive pasts. After the abuse, most survivors are left with low self-esteem. Codependents not only have low self-esteem, they also allow their happiness to hinge upon the feelings of those upon whom they are "addicted." Codependents feel responsible for others. Until codependents have dealt with their own issues, they are living a life that swings from one extreme to the other. One minute they will feel that they are on top of the world. This usually lasts as long as the other partner is happy. The moment that the object of the codependency is unhappy, codependents feel a sense of responsibility for resolving the unhappiness. If the object of codependency wants out of the relationship, codependents can be masters of understatement and denial. No matter what the situation, codependents can find a way to minimize or negate the truth of the situation. All codependent behaviors are an attempt to avoid the emptiness they felt when they were children.

Many codependents feel that if only the original situation could reoccur, they could somehow "fix it." The reason that so many people who come from abusive families go on to choose partners so much like those who abused them in their childhoods is that the abuser and the abusive behaviors feel familiar to these survivors. Sometimes survivors will feel that they were somehow responsible for the dysfunction in their family of origin. When survivors believe that this is true, they will often feel that they don't deserve anything better than abuse.

Codependency sounds as if it is all a negative experience, but there are some real payoffs to codependency also. When codependents rescue or care for someone else (usually an addict of some sort) they get some reassurance that the addict will not leave them. Abandonment is the greatest fear of the codependent. If codependents acknowledge the pain in which they find themselves, the chances are that they will no longer feel the sense of anesthesia that they had originally sought. Acknowledgment of their own pain causes codependents to break through their own denial and lose whatever benefits they received from their anesthesia.

Codependency is really a form of self-punishment when we consider how much pain and dysfunction codependency causes. So many codependents are depressed, largely because codependents do not acknowledge their true emotions, especially anger. The sense of loss of self-identity, lack of a proper childhood (in which the codependents should have but did not receive the nurturance and care that they needed), and a lack of a sense of fulfillment all contribute to cause codependents to seek happiness and fulfillment outside of themselves.

The codependent family looks very much like a typical incest family. The parents can be immature and lean on their children to do the parenting. There may be addictions: most often the father has some sort of addiction either to drugs, alcohol, or pornography and the mother has a food addiction. Both parents have poor self-images and usually low self-esteem. One or both of the parents may be survivors. Many times the marriage is an unhappy one, although to outsiders it may not appear that way. Appearance means a lot to these families. Many incest families either have no relationship with a higher power or the family is rigidly religious. Religious families often have very rigid and literal opinions about how one should "look" and "behave" if one is *really* a "good" family. Either way, the family is enmeshed and demands rigid roles of the family members.

Unhealthy codependent relationships have characteristics that are very easy to spot once you are aware of the dynamics that are involved. Survivors who have been educated about the signs of an unhealthy relationship always seem surprised that they were not aware of the unhealthiness of the relationship while they were involved in it. Signs of unhealthiness consist of the following: one partner feels that he or she *must* control the relationship; one partner is involved in the relationship in such a way that he or she is always one-upping the other partner and appears to be the "wise" one or the one who is in the role of adviser; the partners will alternate being in crisis as a way of keeping distance between them in the relationship and avoiding real intimacy; and one partner will be able to promote severe emotional trauma or pain in the other partner, usually as a defense against an intense fear of intimacy.

Healthy relationships are much different from these relationships. In a healthy relationship, the partners are not "fused." Each partner has his or her own identity and separate friends. Each partner is complete within himself or herself. Although each partner will want to be involved with the other, neither partner *must* be with the other. If need be, each partner could live without the other. In other words, they *want* to be together, but they don't *need* to be together. Each partner fosters the growth of the other and attempts to adapt and grow with the partner's changes. The partners are mature people who know that life is not always easy. The partners expect tough times and try to adapt to the stressors in their relationships. If they are married, there is a sense of "our" marriage rather than "my" marriage. Both partners value their relationship above all else and schedule time to nurture it. The partners try to listen to each other and, because of this, have good communication skills, which enrich and deepen their relationship.

The roller-coaster ride that some partners experience is a good indication that the relationship is an "addicted" relationship. Whenever one person is addicted to another, there will be an inequality of power in which one of the partners will be so overdependent upon the other that there will be resentment and anger. Whenever one feels that someone else has the ability to determine one's happiness or the lack of happiness, the relationship is bound to result in anger and resentment. One partner's need for the other to make him or her feel complete is also an indication of an addicted relationship. To have a truly healthy relationship, both partners must be complete individually. The inability to accept one's partner as both good and bad and to expect him or her to make one whole is immature and leads to disappointment and unhappiness.

In addicted relationships, there is a heightened sense of jealousy that is very similar to the relationship between the child and his or her primary caregiver. In neediness, a child acts as if there is never enough love to go around. The caregiver literally becomes all that is capable of giving and sustaining life in the child. As adults, we can get our needs met in many ways. In an addicted relationship, the sense of jealousy and neediness is apparent by the threat that the addicted partner feels to the object of the addiction having any interests outside of the relationship. Addicted partners will feel complete happiness if the objects of their addictions meet their needs, and complete despair if their needs are not met. The decision to either leave the relationship or to remain will result in chaos and indecision. The decision to stay in the relationship results in despair and hopelessness. The addicted partner sees no choice but to stay or leave. They do not realize that the power for change is in the hands of the addicted partners: they can either choose to accept or refrain from accepting the way the current relationship exists.

Survivors addicted to a relationship have given their personal power away in an attempt to receive the promise of the "perfect" relationship that will meet all of the childhood needs they never had met. This is an empty promise: no one else can ever meet all of our needs.

> Mick is a seventeen-year-old survivor who is addicted to his relationship with his sixteen-year-old girlfriend. Mick is powerless whenever his girlfriend is angry with him. He will do or become whatever it is she wants in an attempt to hold onto his addiction to her. Mick is in a very uncomfortable situation because his girlfriend is aware of the power that she has over him and uses it to manipulate him. If Mick were to take a few moments and look back at all of the previous relationships that he has had in his young life, he would discover that he is always attracted to the same types of people. All of Mick's girlfriends have manipulated Mick's fear of being abandoned. Mick's earliest memories of fearing abandonment began when his mother abandoned him when he was four years old. Mick's mother had already begun to use Mick's fear of being abandoned as a way to get Mick to "behave" when he was very young. Mick's self-esteem is so low that he doesn't believe that anyone could ever love him for himself. Mick constantly tries to "win" his partner's approval. Instead of seeing his partner's manipulation for what it really is, Mick sees his partner's manipulation as being a sign that the partner is better and stronger than he is. In all his relationships, Mick sees his partner through rose-colored glasses. Mick sees his partners as he wishes they were instead of how they really are. Mick constantly has the hope that if only he can win his partner's approval and love, his life will be wonderful.

If Mick, as with so many other addicted survivors, would only look at his relationship with his partners in a realistic manner, he would see that his partners seldom act in accordance with what they say they feel (i.e., saying that they want to spend time with Mick, then never making time for him), saying that they both value the relationship when it is clear that Mick puts much more time and effort into the relationship. His partners never make any real attempts at changing the relationship to make it more fair or equal.

Because of Mick's addiction to his partners and fear of abandonment, his partners have learned to control the relationship by threatening to leave if they don't have things their way. Some survivors learn to manipulate their addicted relationship by turning the tables on their partners. Addicted survivors will act as if they are so weak that their partner will feel too much guilt or fear to leave the relationship. The cost of this type of behavior is very high for the addicted survivor.

Whatever gains the survivor may make by retaining the codependent relationship are lost due to low self-esteem. Other codependent survivors will make themselves so pleasing and helpful to their partners that the partners feel they "owe" the survivor loyalty and remain in the addicted relationship.

> Marcella is a forty-two-year-old incest survivor. Marcella is able to anticipate her husband's needs constantly. Before he says that he wants something, she has gotten it for him. Marcella's husband has had several affairs in the past six years. Marcella's family and friends wonder how she is not aware of these affairs. He is not discreet about hiding credit card receipts for motels and gifts for his girlfriends, yet Marcella never acknowledges that she is aware of what is happening. In reality, she has been aware of the affairs almost as soon as they began. As long as she doesn't acknowledge that she knows of the affairs, she can pretend that they don't exist. Marcella is able to hold onto the relationship with her husband because her fear of abandonment is greater than her need for self-respect and independence. The cost of this type of relationship is that her self-respect is so low that she can never share her true feelings with anyone. Marcella has not grown as a person for years because her main focus is always on keeping the relationship going with her husband. Her satisfaction with life is almost nonexistent because she never knows from day to day what she is going to have to do next to keep their relationship intact.

Survivors involved in a codependent relationship need to ask themselves if the companionship in the relationship is worth what it costs them in terms of self-esteem and self-respect. Does the relationship offer the respect, caring, trust, support, shared interests, sexual involvement, fulfillment, and time investment that the survivors need and want? If the relationship is much more costly to one of the partners than to the other, it is probably a codependent relationship. If survivors are able to look back at their histories and see a series of other relationships that were similar in nature, then the chances are even greater that it is a codependent relationship. If codependent survivors cannot be realistic and see any of their partners' faults, if they feel that they can never be as good as their partner, or if they can never confront their partners with any complaints that they may have about their partner's negative behaviors, then the chances are almost certain that it is a codependent relationship. Some addicted survivors are so afraid of losing the comfort, predictability, and familiarity of an addicted relationship that they will remain in the relationship despite the most negative of consequences.

Relationship-addicted survivors can help themselves by recognizing that being involved in a codependent relationship keeps them from finding a relationship with real commitment and intimacy. It is important for survivors to learn to recognize and stop the self-defeating behaviors that cause them to continue to seek addicted codependent relationships. Survivors need to find their sense of self-worth that is not directly tied to belonging to someone or being in a relationship with someone. If survivors can remind themselves of the pain involved in the addicted codependent relationship when they are tempted to return to the relationship, they may be able to refrain from returning and instead may find someone who will treat them much better and with whom they may have a truly intimate and satisfying relationship. Most codependent survivors think as a child would, in the sense that they want *what* they want *when* they want it. Thinking as a child would (i.e., immediate gratification) is something to which many survivors are accustomed. The more secure that survivors can be in the core concept they hold of themselves, the less likely they are to become addicted to a codependent relationship.

> Ryder is a thirty-year-old incest survivor. When Ryder told his parents that his older brother was molesting him, his parents didn't believe him. Ryder was abused by his older brother from age eight to age thirteen. He grew up with no clear idea of who he was or what he wanted in life. His primary goal was to please whomever he was involved with at the time. Ryder's greatest fear was that he would find himself alone someday with no one to "take care" of him. He never realized that he was very capable of caring for himself. He had been so involved in trying to placate others that Ryder never realized what a capable adult he had become. It was only when we began to talk during sessions about the things that Ryder liked about himself, what he thought

his strengths were, what he believed about himself, and what he wanted to do with his life that he began to get a clearer picture of himself. The road to higher self-esteem and competence is not a straight incline. Ryder has times when it seems much easier for him to allow others to make his decisions, but he knows that ultimately he is responsible for his own happiness. He has worked very hard at building a support network so that one single person is not the only person who can help meet his needs. Ryder sought therapy when he found that, despite repeated attempts to break off his dysfunctional relationship with his partner, he was so afraid and insecure that he kept running back to the relationship despite knowing that the relationship was harmful. After working in therapy for some time, Ryder realized that his attraction to the dysfunctional relationship was really an attempt to try to receive the nurturing that he had never received from his parents and siblings. His way of trying to build a relationship was really keeping him from finding a truly positive and freeing relationship in which both he and his partner could achieve their full potential. As Ryder begins to feel better about himself he will demand better treatment in his relationships.

The most difficult thing for a relationship-addicted survivor to do is to refrain from immediately entering another dysfunctional relationship once a previous relationship has ended. The time spent without a partner is an excellent time in which to address core issues that lead to repeatedly picking the same dysfunctional type of relationship.

Healing from codependency is not impossible, but healing does involve an entirely new way of thinking about oneself and one's relationships with others. For the codependent, the most difficult task of all is to let others face the natural consequences of their own behaviors. Codependents want to "fix" or "take care" of others. Codependents need to let others take care of themselves. Codependents need to stop trying to change others and begin to take responsibility for their own lives, to get in touch with their own feelings, and to think of things the way that they *are* and not the way they *should* be. All of this is a tall order for individuals who are desperately running away from their innermost feelings. If codependents can put only half of the effort into making changes in their own lives as they do in trying to change the lives of others, they will succeed.

Making the kinds of changes that are necessary to heal from codependency is not always met with the welcome that one would expect from the people closest to the codependent. Whenever anyone in a system makes a change in behavior, those closest to that individual are also affected. The enabling that codependents have facilitated is often difficult if not impossible for the addict to give up. Without the codependent's efforts to stabilize the relationship, the addict must then begin to suffer the repercussions of the codependent's withdrawal from the enabling behaviors. Sometimes codependents will be reluctant to stop the enabling behaviors because they may feel that they are not worthy of love without earning it by taking care of others. A childhood full of abuse and neglect messages will often confirm this self-perception held by the codependent. The strongest drive toward codependent behaviors comes from within the codependents themselves. It is the codependents' core beliefs that they are unlovable or undeserving that fuels codependent behaviors. Until codependents go back into their childhood and grieve the losses that they have experienced and feel the emotions that they have avoided, codependent behaviors will continue. Trying to overcome our addiction to someone is very difficult because in our minds the person to whom we are addicted holds the key to all of the unmet needs that we have experienced since childhood. As with other addictions, a compulsive need exists to have the object that we think will fulfill all of our needs (even if the relationship is not healthy for us), the physical and mental withdrawal symptoms of not having the person meet our needs, and the sense of loneliness and emptiness that we feel from not having our addictions met. If we are legally bound to this person, as in marriage and/or with children, then practical reasons exist why we must have at least some contact with our "addiction." This situation makes breaking the addiction somewhat more difficult, but still not impossible when one considers the cost of such a relationship.

The feelings that we have about ourselves also have much to do with our ability to break the ties of an addicted relationship. If we feel that we will never be able to find someone else or that no one else will ever find us attractive, then we are much more likely to stay in codependent relationships. The need to become attached to someone originates early in our development, with our primary caregiver(s). If this attachment is not securely made, we will seek the attachment with someone else in our lives. I have worked with many survivors who will look to their partners to meet this need for a secure attachment. The intensity of the survivors' need to become securely attached to their partner is so intense that the partners often feel as if they are being suffocated.

> Delores is a fifteen-year-old survivor who was molested not only by her biological father but by numerous family friends. Delores received no emotional support whatsoever when she disclosed the abuse to her mother. All of her young life Delores has craved a family that loved and cared for her. Each new boyfriend who becomes involved with Delores is frightened off because of her huge need for reassurance that the partner will never abandon her and will always take care of her. The slightest attention that the partner pays to schooling or sports is seen as an attempt to abandon Delores. Hope is present, though, because Delores has become aware of and acknowledged how her behaviors have driven off the very people that she was attempting to keep close to her.

Why do survivors such as Delores become greedy and attached so early in a relationship? Most survivors would tell you that either one or both of their parents did not provide them with a safe, emotionally warm environment in which they felt loved and wanted. The degree to which their current need for attachment exists is determined by the degree in which the primary caregivers failed to meet the survivors' childhood emotional needs. The more anxious and needy the parents of the survivors, the more anxious and needy the survivors will be as they mature.

The person to whom survivors become attached as they become older shares some characteristics that may unconsciously remind the survivor of the parent to whom the survivors needed a more secure attachment. This is why women who have fathers who are alcoholic will often marry men who become alcoholic. It is an unconscious attempt on the survivors' part to replicate their childhood situation and "make it work out this time." What survivors are usually not aware of is that this early sense of being in love and "walking on air" ends very quickly when they begin to see the qualities that demonstrate that the other person is really human and may share all of the frailties the survivors have sworn to avoid in relationships.

What are the indications that someone is "addicted" to another person? How do the signs of being "addicted" to a person differ from the signs of healthy love? In a healthy relationship, both partners value their time together, but at the same time they are able to utilize and value their time apart. In a codependent relationship, one or the other of the partners can't tolerate even a short time apart. A short time spent apart seems like an eternity that will lead to being alone forever. Codependent partners can't find any value or worth in any other interests or activities except for the object of their codependency. As very young children, all of us experience the knowledge that without our parents or other adult caregivers we would perish. If we as adults have not resolved these feelings, we are apt to seek partners who will feel familiar to recreate these unresolved feelings so that we can resolve them. The problem is that almost inevitably we pick partners who feel familiar *because* of their inability to fill our needs for a more secure attachment.

> Jenica is a seventeen-year-old survivor who is so "hungry" to be securely attached to someone that every person she meets becomes the "answer" to her problems. Jenica's mother came from a very dysfunctional home in which she also was never securely attached to her caregivers. Any time that either Jenica or her mother are in a situation that has the "feel" of their family of origin's surroundings, both Jenica or her mother are apt to be attracted to whomever is available as a caregiver in an attempt to resolve the issues of insecure attachment. Jenica is more apt to be drawn to a motherly figure as she is only seventeen. Her mother is more apt to be drawn to an adult man who reminds her at some unconscious level of her father with whom she had a terribly abusive relationship.

Neither Jenica nor her mother had a caregiver who adequately reflected their sense of themselves. Both Jenica and her mother had caregivers who were depressed and distant. As children, we need caregivers who will give us feedback as to the kind of person we are. Young children are fragile. They are impressionable and believe adults when adults tell them that they are stupid, smart, industrious, lazy, ugly, or pretty. It is so important that parents love and value their children! Survivors are at a disadvantage to begin with because they are usually born into dysfunctional families. In this type of family, the child's worth is never clearly mirrored back by the parent because the parent often can't tell where he or she (the parent) ends and the child begins. Often the child is so distant emotionally from the parent that the parent has no real idea of the qualities that the child may possess. The parent may see the child as a negative extension of the parent. The parent may see the child as someone who the parent wanted to be. Either way, children see a distorted reflection of themselves and have no real solid basis on which to build their own self-image.

So many survivors believe that the person to whom they are addicted *makes* them feel sexy, smart, or attractive. The truth is that survivors themselves have always had the ability and capacity to be all of the qualities that they feel the object of their codependency (addiction) brings out in them. It is the feeling of attachment that codependent survivors feel to the object of their codependency that brings about those feelings.

> Maisie is a fifty-year-old incest survivor. For most of her adult life, she was grossly overweight and depressed. It was when she fell in love with a colleague that she began to lose large amounts of weight and change her style of dress and the way she relates to others. For several years, Maisie believed that her colleague had "made" her change her appearance because of the love that she felt for him. Finally she realized that *she* was the one who had made all of the changes in her appearance and in her life. It was the *attraction* for her colleague that sparked the changes, but the desire and the ability to be different had been *inside* of Maisie the entire time. She realized that the good things that attracted her to her colleague were in fact simply extensions of Maisie herself. Initially, Maisie was very angry and distraught when the relationship didn't turn out the way that she wanted. She blamed her colleague for "causing" her pain. It was only when she was willing to delve back into her childhood issues that she realized how much the colleague reminded her of her father, who had sexually abused her and had been emotionally remote and controlling. Because of her intense attraction to the colleague, she was willing to give him all of her power. When he didn't act the way that she thought he should, she became very angry and resentful. The colleague was supposed to know exactly what it was that Maisie wanted from him without her telling him. Maisie really was angry because she had placed all of the power for her happiness in the colleague's hands. He had

never asked for such responsibility. Once she gave her colleague such power and control over her happiness, she became resentful when the colleague didn't respond as she wanted or expected. Maisie also feared that her colleague would become abusive toward her as her father had been.

The real danger in the relationship was that Maisie herself would allow the relationship to become abusive because she would not demand the respect and consideration that she deserved. Our relationships are a good indication of how we feel about ourselves. When we respect ourselves, we expect others to respect us also. We won't stay in relationships where we are *not* respected.

The next chapter discusses how codependency and sexual addiction combine to form, for some survivors, a lifelong pattern of exploitation and manipulation.

Chapter 11

Sexual Addiction
and Sexual Codependency

Sexual addiction can result from childhood sexual abuse. Sexual addiction can be displayed in numerous ways, but the result is almost always the same: Survivors will be exploited as a result of their own behaviors. The fact that the sexually addicted survivor is the one who invites the self-abusive behavior is even more tragic. Karma is a good case in point.

Karma is a sixteen-year-old incest survivor. All three girls in her family were sexually abused by the father. Although Karma is very angry at her father for the incest, she also feels an intense loyalty toward him. She also feels very guilty for the testimony in court that ended up sending her father to prison for forty-five years.

Sexuality is a difficult issue for Karma and many of the other survivors who share similar characteristics with her. She feels very little real regard for men. All of the men that she has trusted in her life have somehow managed to let her down. Karma feels that all men want is sex. She has never had the opportunity to enjoy sex. Sex for her had always been a form of exploitation. Now that she is an adolescent and has developed mature feminine attributes, Karma has decided that she will use these attributes to *her* advantage.

Karma walks with a decidedly seductive gait. Her clothing is always either very low cut or extremely formfitting. She wears midriff tops that show her navel and waistline. Red lipstick and makeup are always applied in the most advantageous manner. Every attempt is made to draw attention to herself and her appearance. Karma will sit in such a manner that any man who is in her vicinity cannot help but notice her feminine charms.

Unfortunately, she is noticed, but the attention is always an attempt to take advantage of her physical appearance. Not one man so far has realized how intelligent or caring she can be. Karma will not allow a man to recognize any other ability that she possesses other than her ability to arouse sexual desire.

Karma is not really aware that she is putting out signals which indicate that *she* doesn't value herself for anything but what she can provide sexually. She feels that it is the men who can see only the sexual value that she possesses. She limits what the men *can* find attractive about her because she never allows the men to see how smart, witty, or capable she is—she fears that they will find her lacking or inadequate.

The adolescent males in the groups are always commenting on Karma's appearance. She appears to thrive on their attention. When the subject of her seductive behavior is brought up in group, she adamantly denies that she has ever put out "vibes" to invite men to exploit her. It is interesting to see how the males in the groups attempt to protect Karma from the knowledge of the part that she plays in her own sexual addiction. When asked outright by Karma if she sends signals that indicate she is sexually addicted, the males in the groups attempt to dodge the question. Finally, the male group members tell her that she does indeed come across as liking their sexual remarks and innuendoes. After Karma has been *forced* to recognize and acknowledge the sexual addiction, she begins to open up to the groups and state that she has frequently thought of becoming an exotic dancer or a stripper. Although she says that stripping or dancing offers "easy money," the dynamics of her sexual addiction lie much deeper and are much more complex than simply trying to obtain easy money.

Sexual addiction has its very origins in the attempts by survivors to turn the tables and regain the power that sexual abuse has taken from them. When the survivor is the one initiating the sexual overtures and setting the limits of the sexual activity, the survivor feels a sense of control and power. It doesn't take long for the survivor to become addicted to this sense of control and power. At the same time that survivors feel that they are regaining the power that the abuse took away, they are simply colluding with their original abuser—the survivors are "finishing" the abuse that their abusers began. It is so difficult for the survivor to acknowledge this fact. The survivor wants so badly to regain the lost sense of power and control that their abuse cost them. Survivors will attempt to try to regain the sense of safety and security that "being in control" offers them, even if it is only an illusion. What a sad commentary for our society that there are so many people who are willing to take survivors up on their offer of self-abusive sexuality and help survivors further abuse themselves!

The definition of sexual addiction used by the National Council on Sexual Addiction and Compulsivity is "Sexual addicts engage in persistent and escalating patterns of sexual behavior acted out despite increasingly negative consequences to self and to others." Behaviors such as sexual harassment, voyeurism, child pornography, pedophilia, stalking, exhibitionism, and professional misconduct are all defined by the National Council on Sexual Addiction and Compulsivity as sexually addictive behaviors. The council lists offending sexual addictive behaviors as including compulsive masturbation, multiple affairs, consistent use of pornography, unsafe sex, sexual anorexia, multiple or anonymous partners, phone sex or cyber sex, sexual massage, escorts, prostitutes, and prostitution. Many sex therapists would disagree with the listing of these behaviors as being offending and addictive. I believe the fine line that determines whether the behavior is offensive is the *intent* behind the behavior. If the intent is consensual and harms no one, it is a very different matter than exploiting someone for one's own sexual gratification.

Sexual codependency can be seen as the partner of the sexual addict feeling "turned off" or not being sexually attracted by the behaviors that the sex addict is requesting participation in, yet participating anyway out of fear of being abandoned or losing the relationship that the sexual codependent has with the sexual addict. Because of the sexual abuse that they themselves experienced, they often feel unloved and devalued. Sexual codependents will stay in a relationship that other healthier people would quickly abandon simply because of the feelings of blame that they will assume for the failures in the relationship. Sexual codependents will see the failed relationship as yet additional proof that they are not lovable or are unworthy.

> Francine is a forty-five-year-old incest survivor who is married to her third husband. Over her lifetime, Francine has had so many extramarital affairs that she long ago lost count. Because of her numerous sexual encounters, one would assume that Francine enjoys sex more than most people. The truth is that

Francine engages in sex for only two reasons: (1) to hold onto the person with whom she is involved and (2) to attempt to manipulate her sexual partner into doing something that Francine wants him to do.

Debbie is a forty-eight-year-old survivor who was molested as a child by her paternal uncle. Debbie is married to a very prominent physician in her hometown. Everyone in Debbie's small town knows of the numerous affairs that Debbie's husband has had. Women involved in the affairs have telephoned and stopped by the office to tell Debbie that it was over between Debbie and her husband because of the "love" between the other woman and Debbie's husband. Debbie is fully aware of how her husband views sex and commitment. The emotional pain caused by her husband's sexually addictive behaviors is enormous, yet Debbie continues to stay in the relationship and engage in unsafe sexual practices with her husband despite her knowledge of the affairs and the possible health consequences because she is afraid of "losing" her husband. How can you lose someone who you have never really had to begin with? Not only is Debbie's physical health in danger, the loss of her self-esteem that accompanies the sexual codependency is so pervasive that it is a part of Debbie's every thought and activity.

Perhaps no other situation is so disturbing as when young survivors become pregnant in an attempt to have someone who will love them who they can also love. Most survivors, especially incest survivors, begin to feel the "emptiness" of the abuse by the time they are in their teens. Instinctively they know that they will not be able to fill the emptiness that they feel without the interaction with someone outside of themselves. At this point the survivor is apt to begin the next generation that will continue the cycle of the abuse unless someone offers the survivor genuine nonsexual affection.

Stephen is a seventeen-year-old survivor who has been sexually active since he was ten years old. Recently, his fifteen-year-old girlfriend told him that she is pregnant. Stephen's girlfriend is also a survivor. Neither Stephen nor his girlfriend consciously decided to have a baby. Underneath both of their needs to be close to someone outside of their families was the desire to find someone who would be with them "always."

Most adults realize that the need for someone to remain with us always is a need that can be found only within ourselves or in seeking a higher source of spiritual power. Teenagers who have never known anything but abuse have learned that sex and physical intimacy is how people get close and stay with each other. To young survivors, sex *is* intimacy because they have learned this from their abuse experiences.

When teenage survivors finally begin to realize the seriousness of having a child and the reality of the sacrifice and commitment involved with raising a child for eighteen years, the young survivors experience a rude awakening. The young survivors who are more fortunate begin to realize just how much their own sexual abuse has cost them, and they begin to deal with the pain of their issues. Less fortunate survivors have no sense of how damaging their own sexual abuse has been. These survivors are often the ones who become involved in relationship after relationship in an attempt to fill the void created by the lack of genuine affection and nurturing experienced during childhood. Many times they become biological parents of child after child. By biological parent, I mean that they will provide either the sperm or the eggs necessary to parent a child, but they will have no real knowledge of what emotional or physical needs the child may require or will not stay around to support or be involved in the child's life.

Many people do not realize that there is a difference between love addiction and sexual addiction. Love addiction involves romance. It is not unusual to see someone who has love addiction lose interest in a partner once the realities of life become apparent in the relationship. Love addicts are more interested in the idealized component of the relationship rather than the day-to-day hassle of maintaining a real relationship.

Love addiction also involves relationship addiction. Love addicts will go from relationship to relationship. It is as if they are terrified of ever being alone.

> Jeralyn is a seventeen-year-old survivor. In the year that she has been in treatment she has had over twenty boyfriends. As soon as she begins to get really "close" to her newest boyfriend, Jeralyn becomes cool and distant. Almost always she will find some fault with her boyfriend that will allow her to drop him and to move on to the next relationship. Jeralyn is constantly looking outside of herself to someone else to provide the happi-

ness that she desires. If she was to ever go for any length of time without a romantic interest, she would begin to feel the effects of her past sexual abuse issues. Constantly looking toward a new conquest is Jeralyn's way of keeping the focus off of her painful issues.

Sexual addiction is a part of love addiction, but sexual addiction itself has several other additional components than does love addiction. In love addiction, the addicts are really more interested in the "high" that they get from their involvement with a new love interest and the prospect that perhaps this time they will find someone who will make them happy at last.

> Tony is an eighteen-year-old survivor who constantly looks to his girlfriends to provide him with the self-esteem and caring of which life has deprived him. Tony will make many demands and be so needy that no real woman could ever possibly live up to the expectations that Tony has of a relationship.

It is not unusual to see love addicts consumed with and constantly reading romance novels. Often love addicts will be so consumed with their addiction that they will read romance novel after romance novel in an attempt to satisfy the unmet need that they have for romance and affection. Love addicts are looking for the love that they never received in their abusive childhood.

> Nancy is a twenty-nine-year-old survivor. Nancy's family of origin was very cold and cruel toward her. She grew up on a farm and knew only hard work. Nancy's father was an alcoholic who became very mean when he drank. Nancy was a target for her father's cruelty and anger whenever he was drunk. Nancy's mother was an emotionally distant woman who had little time for what she considered frivolous things, such as combing a little girl's hair or telling her daughter a bedtime story. Nancy grew up never knowing parental affection. Now that Nancy is grown she is unable to stay in a relationship for long. The first time that her boyfriend becomes less than "perfect," Nancy will lose interest in him and move on to someone else. Nancy reads one romantic novel after another. None of the real relationships that Nancy is involved in could ever hope to match the emotional intensity of the romance novels that Nancy absorbs. None

of the men with whom Nancy becomes involved could ever hope to be as sensitive, handsome, or wealthy as the heroes in Nancy's romance novels.

The characteristics of a love addict include:

- a lack of nurturing during childhood in the family of origin;
- a basic lack of trust;
- depression;
- a deep sense of pain that the love addict shows no one;
- equating intense emotion with a strong relationship, which in actuality may be just codependency;
- a feeling of worthlessness when not in a romantic relationship;
- participating in a series of consecutive relationships;
- confusing sexual attraction with love;
- manipulative behavior, especially in romance; and
- an inability to view this behavior as an addiction.

I believe numerous movie stars might fall into the category of being love addicts. Women who give sex to get love might well fit these characteristics. It is said that women give sex to get love and men give love to get sex. There may be more truth to this statement than we realize.

Some readers might wonder what the harm is in letting a person have dreams of an idealized romance. What is the harm? The truth is that these individuals are cheating themselves because they will never find a relationship that will meet their expectations. No real relationship could stay "fresh" and "new" all the time. There will be bills to pay and conflicts between the partners. A real relationship involves working through such issues and problems.

Sexual addiction is similar to love addiction, but in sexual addiction, the real emphasis is on the sex. Affairs are the drug that provides the "high" for the sex addict. Because the sex addict goes from affair to affair and partner to partner, sex addicts never develop a sense of intimacy with their sexual partners. People are viewed as objects who can provide the "fix" that the sex addicts require to keep their minds off of the internal pain and issues of their past hurts.

Ryan is a seventeen-year-old survivor who has slept with more women in his seventeen years than do most men in an entire lifetime. Ryan has slept with women three times his age. Ryan doesn't consider it abusive that he was molested by a female friend of his mother when he was only seven years old.

In our society, young men who are sexually abused by an older female don't often realize that their experience *is* abusive. The young man and his family will often view the sexual experience as part of being masculine. The experience itself may have been overwhelming and frightening for the young man, but our society says that men should "get all the sex that they can." Usually the young man and his family will keep the sexual abuse a secret in fear that the man will be stigmatized and labeled by the experience if the family objects to the sexual abuse.

Sexual addiction is really a conspiracy; the partner of the sex addict will simply turn his or her head to the sexual addiction in an attempt to keep the relationship with the addict intact. The nonaddicted partner may stand by as the addict has numerous affairs and will never confront the addict about the damage the addict is inflicting on both the relationship and the nonaddicted partner. The nonaddicted partner is really addicted to the sex addict. Most times the non–sex addict is really an enabler and a codependent of the sex addict. Recent studies indicate that 70 percent of people are unhappy with their sex lives. Most people do not understand how important intimacy is to a good sexual relationship. If sex was only about the physical part of the sexual act, then it wouldn't matter about feeling trust and genuine liking for sexual partners. Without genuine affection, trust, and shared values, sexual relationships never achieve full potential.

Numerous survivors in the adolescent groups which I have facilitated are sexually active. Some of the adolescent survivors will have sex with many partners in an attempt to find someone who will care for them and make them feel loved. When we look for happiness outside ourselves, we are setting ourselves up for disappointment. By allowing someone else to determine our happiness, we have no control over our emotional state. Survivors have been taught to equate sex with love through their sexual abuse, especially if the abuse involved an incestual relationship.

In her book *Women, Sex, and Addiction,* Charlotte Davis Kasl (1990) equates *addiction* with the five following criteria: (1) powerless to stop at will, (2) harmful consequences, (3) unmanageability in other areas of life, (4) escalation of use, and (5) withdrawal upon quitting. Survivors of childhood sexual abuse whom I have worked with often exhibit all of these characteristics. Yet these survivors are not aware that the sexual experiences are addictive. These survivors will brag about how many people they have slept with and what a wonderful time they had. When the survivor is alone with me in treatment, a different story will often emerge.

When survivors confuse sex with intimacy, they are on the path to sexual addiction. Sex without intimacy is simply sex for the physical release that the sexual activity provides.

Adele is a forty-year-old survivor who was sexually abused by her biological father during most of her childhood. Adele also watched as, one by one, her brothers and sisters were also sexually abused by their father. Adele's mother was very weak and passive from the responsibility and work that came with raising the seven children to whom she had given birth. Somehow Adele knew even at an early age that telling her mother of the abuse would be too much for her to handle. Adele experienced great emotional pain as a child and adolescent. She had such low self-esteem that she believed everyone could tell what had happened to her simply by looking at her. Whenever Adele had gym class she would be the last girl to disrobe and take the mandatory shower. Adele was also the first girl in her gym class to dress and leave the locker room. Carrying the weight of such a powerful and damaging secret as incest is a huge burden. Adele began to overeat to comfort herself. Before long, Adele had a compulsive eating disorder. Adele's weight ballooned to 250 pounds when she was only nineteen years old. She was so lonely. Adele envied the lifestyles of other girls who had boyfriends, pretty clothes, and time for fun and friends. When several popular boys from Adele's class asked her out on a date, she was so excited! It seemed that finally someone had seen beneath the weight and quietness to the "real" Adele who was waiting to emerge. After the boys had raped Adele and left her in the high school parking lot bleeding and bruised, she believed that *she* must be the problem because both her male classmates and her father had abused her. Adele's self-esteem was so low that she never realized that what had happened was not her fault, that she was the *victim* of sexual crimes.

As time went on, Adele began to comprehend that she had more power than she had ever thought. Adele's case illustrates how some survivors will use their abuse experiences to further abuse themselves. Since she had something that men wanted, namely sex, all she had to do was give them what they wanted. *This* time she would be paid for what she provided. Before long Adele had slept with almost the entire football team. She had gotten a reputation as being easy. Adele soon became addicted to the power that her sexuality afforded her. Adele enjoyed sex very little. Her bouts in bed had little to do with Adele's pleasure or genuine closeness with another human being. It was the control that Adele had over the men with whom she slept that kept her sleeping with man after man. As Adele grew older, her pattern of sleeping with men to obtain control over them became a set way of dealing with her sexuality. Adele was never able to establish any sort of genuine intimacy with her sexual partners because she never allowed them to become close to her emotionally. Whenever Adele sensed that a man was getting too close to her and might have the ability to harm her, she quickly picked an argument and moved on to the next partner. Adele could never find herself worthy of true love or intimacy. Adele would sabotage her own happiness because of her fears of being hurt as she was during her childhood.

Kasl quotes Ken Keyes' book *Handbook to Higher Consciousness* when Kasl talks about addictiveness rather than the addiction model so often described by most professionals. In addictiveness, anyone could have the ability to be attached to anything. Kasl uses sexual addiction and addictiveness to describe what addictions bring individuals: fear of nonfulfillment (they must have a lover to be happy), jealousy (that someone may steal their source of fulfillment), anger when someone thwarts them (anger because they won't have sex with the addict), boredom when they make no progress toward satisfying their addiction (being bored because they have no current lover), worry if they don't have a steady supply (worry if someone won't be sexual with them), and finally unhappiness (when the world does not provide them with the addiction). Survivors are looking for happiness outside of themselves. The real source of happiness is always inside.

Sexual addiction is perhaps one of the most misunderstood addictions that I see in survivors, especially when the addiction mirrors the very abuse that the survivor experienced originally. In the following section, I will discuss survivors who become so addicted to sex that they go on to victimize others using sex as the weapon. Society must take a large part of the responsibility for the current problem with sexual addiction. Because of society's reluctance to discuss anything of a sexual nature, topics such as sexual abuse have been pushed into the background. Victims of sexual assault or sexual abuse have been reluctant to disclose their abuse for fear of being labeled by the stigma surrounding sexual abuse. Many of the survivors with whom I work talk about feeling "dirty" after they had disclosed their sexual abuse. Because society does not realize the seriousness and the scope of the problems surrounding sexual addiction, funding sources for treatment have been sparse. Society must realize that relapse occurs frequently among the various addictions. In this respect, sexual addiction is no different from any other addiction. Just because a sex addict can't afford intensive treatment doesn't mean that society can afford to allow the addict to be given poor quality treatment. Society will pay the cost of lesser treatment either in financial costs or in the cost of additional victimization. If the sex offender cannot be placed financially into the correct treatment to prevent future victimization, then it is better to deny treatment and place the offender in a correctional setting until the proper treatment can be afforded. The risk to future victims is simply too great to settle for less costly but less effective treatment. Society must be able to discuss sexual addiction and sexual abuse to allow the perpetrator and the victims to bring this sensitive issue out into the open and stop the isolation that surrounds this problem. In no way should society ever feel guilty for holding perpetrators accountable for their abusive behaviors. Perpetrators are master manipulators, skilled at putting the responsibility for their abusive actions off onto anyone else willing to accept the responsibility.

When an offender has entered treatment, we must prepare the offender to be always on the alert for relapse. Treatment is no guarantee that the sexual addict will never be attracted to abusive sexual behaviors again. The offender must avoid situations and people that would be triggers for his or her offending behaviors. It is not the responsibility of the victims to have to avoid the perpetrators, for how does one know ahead of time just by looking at someone that he or she is an offender? The solution for sexual perpetrators is constant supervision and monitoring of their behaviors for the remainder of their lives. If it becomes clear that the offenders are not serious about trying to control their abusive behaviors, then society should also make it clear that this sort of noncompliant behavior will not be tolerated. Society simply can't count on laws and notification of offenders living in the local area as a total defense against sex offenders and sexual addicts.

Our courts and judges, therapists, and law enforcement agencies must work together to develop a safety net of treatment knowledge, accountability, and consequences so that the offender can be adequately made aware of the lifelong severity of this addiction and society's nontolerance of the addiction.

The safety of the community must always be a priority in this type of treatment of sexual addiction. Although it is wonderful if treatment can also nurture the sexual addict, we must not lose sight of the fact that sexual addiction is one of the underlying themes of sexual abuse. It is not fair to risk the safety and well-being of future generations of victims by coddling the perpetrator simply because he or she may consider treatment too harsh. The perpetrator needs to always examine his or her behaviors and constantly look for situations in which relapse may occur. If the perpetrator is not able to develop some sort of empathy for others, recognize what buried feelings and hurts lie beneath his or her own behaviors, and become fearful of his or her own ability to relapse and reoffend, then the perpetrator is a continued risk to the community. Roger is such a person.

> Roger was raped by his oldest brother throughout his childhood. When Roger told his parents about the abuse, nothing was done to stop it. Roger buried all of his feelings about the abuse and began to put those feelings off onto others whom he then perceived as being "weak" and "sissies" because they could not handle painful situations as well as Roger felt that he could handle them. When Roger became a father and faced many new and different pressures all at the same time, he began to sexually abuse his oldest daughter. Roger's negative behaviors went steadily downhill from this point on. It wasn't long before Roger became totally addicted to pornography and casual sex with prostitutes and other men that he met in "peep shows." Roger soon had sexually abused numerous other children who came into contact with him. Roger could be so nurturing and pleasant that those around him had no sense of what a dangerous person he could be. Until the day that he died, Roger continued his sexual addiction and sexually abused countless numbers of innocent children.

Roger never was able to acknowledge the harm that his behaviors caused. Roger's victims were isolated in their sense of shame and society's reluctance to discuss what it perceives as a "dirty" secret. Secrecy is the breeding ground for sexual addiction and sexual abuse. The entire treatment process of sexual addiction and sexual abuse *must* not tolerate any type of secrecy.

Sexual addiction can take many forms. Some sexual addictions are more approved of by our society than others. For example, young men who are coming into their sexual maturity are praised for "getting all that they can get" sexually. The partners of these same young men are often criticized for the same sexual behaviors for which their male partners are praised. Society's double standard is often used as a way to control unwanted pregnancy and to determine a woman's value as a prospective marital partner. Although a man might have sex with a woman, society encourages women to be virginal when they marry. What happens to young survivors who see their abuse as taking away their value as a prospective marital partner?

In the adolescent groups that I have facilitated, I have often seen survivors who have been sexually promiscuous use sexual acting-out behaviors to establish their worth as a person. If the survivor can no longer be valued for their virginity and purity, then they may begin to think that at least they can use their knowledge of sexual matter to their own advantage. The problem with this line of thinking is that the survivor's knowledge is often based on *abusive* sexuality. Survivors often find themselves abused repeatedly.

Sexual addictions are among the least talked about and probably least understood of all of the addictions. Since our society is unwilling to take an honest and open look at sexuality, the general lack of knowledge and understanding about sexual addiction is understandable. If the sex addict is a female, the stigma tends to be even greater. Men who are sexually addicted are able to use society's view of male sexual excess as "just being a guy." Women who are sexual addicts and are in their addiction process are frequently termed "sluts," "whores," and "tramps."

Sexual addiction is sad because the addiction is often mistaken by the sex addict as "love," but in reality love has very little to do with the addiction. What passes for love is really a progressively negative and intrusive behavior that takes away all of the addict's self-esteem. Sexual addiction has little to do with true intimacy. Intimacy is the ability to let down your defenses and accept and be accepted just as the two partners *are* right at that moment. Intimacy involves trust and respect. Sexual addiction can involve some of these qualities but most often involves exploitation and use of power or manipulation.

Perhaps of all forms of sexual addiction, none is more harmful to both the addict and the victim than childhood sexual abuse. If the sex addict is in a position of authority to the child (such as a parent, step-parent, or other authority figure) then the child not only experiences the abusiveness of the sexual abuse but also the betrayal of trust so important that the victim may never be able to fully trust anyone again. Pedophilia is destructive not only because of the damage that it does to the victim but also because of the severity of the addiction it-self. Of all of the sexual addictions, I personally feel that pedophilia is the least likely to effectively respond to treatment. Currently, the most effective treatment for pedophilia is to have the offender be-come aware of the triggers that could cause relapse. The pedophile should then avoid those triggers. Pedophiles are very skilled at ma-nipulation, not only of the victim but of the entire legal, judicial, and psychotherapeutic systems. Because pedophiles may lack the funds for the long-term treatment necessary to effectively attempt to treat their addiction, many pedophiles are released from the legal system with only a slap on the wrist. Countless other children then become victimized.

When doing group work with incest survivors, Kasl (1990) had to refer about 50 percent of the group members out for chemical de-pendency evaluations. That roughly corresponds to the same number of incest survivors I see with addiction problems in the adolescent survivors' groups. Kasl states that about 30 percent of the incest sur-vivors in the groups which she facilitated also had eating disorders. I have found similar numbers of eating disorders in the survivors' groups. If we think of the purpose of addictions, this number is under-standable. All addictions or compulsions serve the purpose of taking the focus off of painful emotions and memories. It is surprising to me that the statistics don't indicate higher percentages of addictive be-haviors.

There are numerous reasons that addictive sex is not healthy for ei-ther the sex addict or the addict's partner. One of the main reasons for the unhealthiness of the sexual addict's relationships is the fact that neither partner feels closer emotionally after the sex act has been completed. The dynamics of addicted sexual relationships involve se-crecy and feelings of shame when the sex act is over. Both partners may feel saddened by their slip into behaviors that they know at some level they are not able to openly share with others. The climate surrounding addicted sex serves to further isolate the addict. Sometimes the secrecy and the shame of the sexual addict's behaviors will cause the addict to remember earlier memories or feelings surrounding the original sexual abuse experiences. Sex addicts may in fact remember earlier abusive experiences while they are in their sexual addiction. All of the sexually addictive behaviors are an attempt to "numb" the addict's feelings of unpleasant and painful memories.

As with addictions to drugs or alcohol, sexual addicts feel that if they can't have sex they will be incomplete. Each new sexual adventure gives meaning to the sex addict's life—for a short time. Any attempts at real intimacy pale in the light of reality and the need to work on a real relationship. As with drug and alcohol addictions, the relief that the sex addict gets from each new sexual conquest is temporary and must be repeated with new partners over and over again when any sense of boredom or routine begins in the relationship. The constant need for excitement and conquest takes the focus off the addict's internal pain and sense of being unconnected to what should have meaning in the addict's life.

> Terri is a thirty-two-year-old incest survivor. Terri has had numerous perpetrators in her life. All of the perpetrators were father figures to Terri; most were her mom's live-in boyfriends. Terri was molested for the first time when she was five years old by her "daddy," Paul. Terri has had drug and alcohol problems for most of her adolescent and adult life. It was only when Terri's addiction became so bad that the state took away her three children alleging neglect that she began to address her drug and alcohol addiction. Terri has been clean and sober for over three years now. She has also managed to keep her weight at a stable level. Terri's weight has always increased considerably every time she attempted to refrain from using drugs and alcohol. Now that she has become clean and sober and has her weight under control, Terri has begun to get involved in a series of very short-lived relationships with men. Each relationship promised to be the "one thing" that would make Terri's life complete. Each relationship was also exploitative and abusive. Terri's relationship with her children has deteriorated as they have watched Terri bring a long series of men into the family home. Terri will introduce each new man to her children as their

new "daddy." Although the children don't verbalize their feelings about their mother's involvement with this long string of "daddies," the children are embarrassed when they hear noises coming from their mother's bedroom and when their friends ask who the new man was that they saw leaving the house early in the morning *this* week. The children are so grateful that their mother is not drinking or using drugs that they don't talk about what it is like to see their mother with a different lover at least once every couple of weeks.

According to Kasl (1990), the criteria for addiction involves such things as feelings of powerlessness over a person, substance or behavior, harmful consequences from indulging in the addiction, other parts of the addict's life becoming unmanageable, increased usage from the addiction as time goes by, and feelings of pain when withdrawing from the addiction. Terri fits all the criteria for being addicted—not only addicted to drugs and alcohol, but addicted to sex and codependent behaviors. When Terri's feelings of shame and unexpressed anger are triggered by something in her current life, she immediately begins to look for ways to quell her emotional pain. Since she can't use drugs, alcohol, or food, Terri turns to sexual addiction to focus her attention on something she feels she can control. The addiction could just as well be gambling, spending, shopping, or any other behaviors. Behind many addicts' behaviors lurks unexpressed anger. Until Terri deals with her feelings, she will continue to use behaviors and substances to help keep a lid on them.

It is difficult for survivors to distinguish the difference between a healthy relationship and a sexually addicted relationship. A good indication of the health of a potential relationship is for survivors to look at the level of their own self-esteem. Self-esteem levels have a tendency to attract *like* self-esteem levels. As the survivor's level of self-esteem increases, so will the quality of the relationships in which the survivor is involved.

Ryan is a female incest survivor in her thirties. Ryan couldn't understand why her teenage daughter, who is also a survivor, kept choosing boyfriends who were abusive and addicted. Ryan didn't understand that her daughter was only copying the behaviors that she observed in her mother's relationships with her own partners. Ryan's self-esteem was low due to her own abuse experiences, causing Ryan to choose a partner with the same low level of self-esteem. When Ryan went to college and got the support from her friends that she had never received from her family her self-esteem increased. She realized that she was *never* going to get her partner to change his negative behaviors until she herself believed that she *deserved* better treatment and would not settle for less.

When survivors are able to reach this point in recovery, it is a momentous discovery for them. This is also a very empowering discovery because the survivors begin to realize that the quality and the health of the relationships that they have with others has been in their hands all along.

A good indication for survivors that they are involved in an unhealthy relationship is when they find themselves involved with someone who has many qualities that the survivor finds unattractive, yet they continue with the relationship. Many times it is the qualities that we strongly dislike in others that will mirror the same qualities that we don't like in ourselves. The other person demonstrates the negative aspects of ourselves of which we may not even be consciously aware. If survivors will attempt to focus on their own negative behaviors instead of the negative behaviors of others, they may then begin to make enormous strides in improving the quality of their own lives.

What forces exist in survivors that cause them to become addicted or codependent? I believe that neediness and the inability for survivors to acknowledge their own insecurity is at the root of their addictive behaviors. In the case of addicts, they are attempting to receive the nurturing they may have never received as a child *without* having to give anything in return. Addictions don't ask for anything in return as would a person in a relationship, but the addiction eventually will take all of the gifts that survivors have to give to themselves or to their relationships with others. In the case of codependent survivors, they are seeking someone whom they can become completely dependent upon and who will never abandon them. Survivors are seeking security and completeness through their addiction to another person. It is this dependence upon another person that can cause the survivor to develop rage toward the very person upon whom the survivor is dependent. The survivors begin to hate the person upon whom they are dependent because this person has the ability to determine whether they will be happy or not. It is only natural that the survivors will begin to resent the power that they themselves have unwittingly given to the recipient of their codependency. The individuals upon whom survivors are codependent have been given power by the survivors either to give value to the survivors by staying with them or by "destroying" the survivors by "abandoning" them. Abandonment is a fear that has deep-seated roots in the survivor's childhood beginning with the survivor's own abuse experiences.

Another way to determine whether the relationship involves sexual codependency or sexual addiction is by the ease with which the survivor feels able to survive the breakup of the relationship. If survivors begin to notice a pattern in their relationships in which they leave when the partners do the slightest thing the survivors find unappealing, then the chances are that the survivors have been involved in "brittle endings" that are typical of sexually codependent or sexually addictive relationships. Once the addict no longer has a use for the codependent, the addict will simply end the relationship. In sexually addicted or sexually codependent relationships, a wide swing occurs between the need for closeness (which is really enmeshment) and detachment. Survivors who are sexually codependent or sexually addicted will seek a level of closeness with their partners that is suffocating. When the relationship becomes too close, the survivors will begin to fear abandonment because the relationship has become too important for the survivor. It is at this point that survivors may cause an argument or find fault and try to change their partners in an unconscious attempt to create distance and safety for themselves. This cycle is reminiscent of borderline behavior. An additional cause for concern for survivors is their attraction to partners who will reinforce their core negative beliefs resulting from their childhood abuse experiences. These beliefs may include such thoughts as "I am unlovable," "I don't deserve to be treated better," or "Things never happen the way that I want them to happen." Again, it is only when the survivors begin to address the core issues resulting from their own abuse experiences that lasting recovery can occur.

What are some of the ways that survivors create distance in their relationships? If we consider the fact that survivors are constantly seeking security and validation through their relationships with others, yet are terrified of the power that their fears of abandonment give to the survivors' partners, then we can begin to understand the tremendous power that the survivors' relationships hold. Some survivors will attempt to keep score of who hurt whom. Survivors will hold onto pain from long ago and will attempt to administer what they feel are equal retributions. The survivor may begin to engage in thinking that will fluctuate between absolutes of what is "good" and what is "bad." In an attempt to create emotional distance, the survivor will magnify every flaw that the partner has. The sad part of the survivors' quest for emotional intimacy is that if they are ever able to find someone who is caring and appropriate as a partner, they will find this relationship so unfamiliar and uncomfortable that they will be apt to "numb" themselves emotionally and not be able to engage in the relationship. Many times the survivor will also think that this kind of relationship is boring and lacks "spark."

What is it like to be involved in an addicted sex relationship? At the time that the addicted relationship is occurring, the addict will not fully realize the negative consequences. Addicts may lose all interest in their work or career. All of their attention and energy will be focused on maintaining the addictive relationship. It is not unusual to see addicts lose control of their money or financial status. Other relationships in the life of the addict no longer have any significance in comparison to the relationship with the addict's "addiction." If the addict is a parent, the attention paid to the addict's children may be eliminated or at least severely compromised. Any interests that the addicts would normally pursue, such as education or hobbies, lose their importance. Nothing is important but the person who is the object of the addict's fixation.

Sex addicts don't necessarily enjoy sex more than other people. In reality, the sex addict is *compelled* to act out sexually. The addicts themselves may not be able to understand why they are acting out sexually or why constant thoughts either of having sex with someone or compulsively masturbating fill their minds and push out other avenues of interest. Sex addicts have no comprehension of the risks they are taking in terms of pregnancy, their safety, or sexually transmitted diseases. The addict feels their life is out of control. Constant chaos and drama occur in the sex addict's life. To deal with this pain, the addict may resort to other addictions such as alcoholism, eating disorders, or abusing drugs. Many times sex addicts will have so much pain in their lives that suicide is a constant thought. Instead of feeling closeness after having sex, addicts feel shame and disgust at their own behaviors.

Besides being addicted to sexual behavior, some sex addicts are *also* sexually codependent. These are the addicts who don't really enjoy sex but are involved in the sexual acts just to please their partners. These addicts can't tell their partners that they are not enjoying the sex for fear that the partner will abandon the relationship. Many times these are the addicts who fake orgasms. When the addicts begin to dread the sex act, they will then begin to make excuses not to engage in sex. Codependent sex addicts will use what should be an honest expression of love and commitment as a weapon to punish their partners. Sometimes addicts will punish themselves by engaging in sexual acts that are degrading. The sexual behaviors may be so degrading that the addicts can't share what is happening with anyone else in their lives.

Sex addicts may begin to pile layer upon layer of addictions in an attempt to avoid the emotional pain of the original abuse. The addictions begin to form a structure of need in which the addicts will decide which one addiction is more important to maintain than the others. All of the addictions share the common characteristics of being founded upon the idea of a spiritual emptiness that cannot be filled. Whether the addict uses escapes that are physical such as excessive exercising, overworking, or overspending, or passive escapes, such as watching television, abusing drugs or alcohol, or simply "vegetating" in bed, the results are all the same. Finding connection and meaning in life is the real answer for the addict.

Trying to define sexual addiction can be quite difficult. How much sex is *too* much sex? Who determines the standards of our sexuality? How much authority do we allow society in determining what is appropriate sexual behavior and what is not? In the *Diagnostic and Statistical Manual of Mental Disorders* (1994) (DSM-IV), sexual addiction is not mentioned as a psychiatric disorder in itself. Maybe one of the best definitions of sexual addiction is that it can be used in place of real intimacy to express other feelings that the person may not be able to express such as anger, depression, or anxiety. One of the most easily identifiable hallmarks of sexual addiction is that each time the addicts engage in the behaviors, they swear that they will not do so again, yet they are continually pulled back to engage in the behaviors despite serious negative consequences either to themselves or to others.

Although men are most often identified as sex addicts, women also can be found with addictive sexual behaviors. Women are more apt to be involved in "love addiction." As with almost every other addiction, love addicts come from childhoods lacking nurturing and attention. Often love addicts talk of feeling alone and isolated even when they were with their families as young children. It is usual for love addicts to appear as if their world is perfect. At first glance, there is no sense that love addicts do not have their lives in order. Only when one observes love addicts for a period of time does one see how love addicts go from one relationship to another, always in search of what they are certain will make them whole. Although love addicts may have anger due to their lack of a nurturing childhood, they are seldom in touch with their innermost feelings. The love addiction is the lid that keeps their pot of anger from boiling over. Love addicts believe consciously or unconsciously that without a relationship, they have no real worth. Love addicts use sex as a way to manipulate their partners to get them to do as they want.

Although it is the sense of self-love and connectedness to others (spirituality) that is the "cure" for addiction, some survivors will turn to religious addiction as a way of establishing the "rules" that will provide structure and predictability to their lives. The following chapter examines the difference between having a sense of spirituality and religious addiction.

Chapter 12

Religious Addiction versus Spirituality

That man is a success who has lived well, laughed often and loved much: who has gained the respect of intelligent men and the love of children; who has filled his niche and accomplished his task; who leaves the world better than he found it, whether by an improved poppy, a perfect poem *or a rescued soul; who never lacked appreciation of earth's beauty or failed to express it; who looked for the best in others and gave the best he had.*

Robert Louis Stevenson

I personally find spirituality one of the most difficult terms to explain. I believe this is because spirituality is a vague term that can be interpreted many different ways. The word spirituality is based on the Latin *spiritus* which means "spirit." Because of the term *spirit* many people, as evidenced by the reactions of the adolescents in the survivors' group example at the beginning of this book, think that spirituality must be connected to religion. Although some who are religious could be said to possess spirituality, religion and spirituality are two different concepts.

I view religion as being an organized body of members who believe in a common set of beliefs, practices, and laws regarding their particular faith. Spirituality encompasses much more than a constructed belief system or system of rules. People can believe in many different faiths and still be deemed spiritual. Spirituality concerns the core of the person, that place within where one has experienced the ultimate reality. For survivors, this sense of spirituality may be realized the first time they believe they are worthy of better treatment and refuse to allow others to abuse or exploit them. By demanding better treatment, survivors begin to become connected to those outside of themselves and develop a sense of "richness" in their world and their experiences. Survivors develop a sense of connectedness to the spiritual part of their lives. They begin to realize that their experiences do not need to be in vain. They can still acknowledge the harmfulness of what has happened to them without allowing the harmfulness of the abuse experience to ruin their lives. The survivor is not aware that the gift of spirituality is *always* within us. Being spiritual is the basis of being human. It is being treated less than human by their abusers that leads survivors to lose their sense of spirituality and connectedness.

The capability of the human spirit to heal always amazes me. I have seen people heal from the most terrible abuse and blossom with forgiveness and self-knowledge. I have always wondered what enables some survivors to go on with their lives and thrive despite the most terrible obstacles, while other survivors cannot seem to move beyond their abuse. I believe this sense of connectedness called spirituality can enable survivors to flourish. It is the belief that a higher power of some sort exists, whether it be God, nature, or the power of love for one another that connects all of us in such a way that all things work for the common good. I get the sense that some sort of divine "rightness" exists in the universe—perhaps a sense of divine justice—that governs what ultimately happens. Perhaps we could define spirituality as being connected to working toward the good of all, including ourselves. Maybe spirituality is the act of learning to value oneself. The saying that one cannot love others until one is able to love oneself is very true indeed.

Of all topics, religion is perhaps the one I attempt to avoid most often. How can one find fault with someone who is devoutly religious? Isn't religion a good thing? The answer lies not in to what extent one is "devoutly" religious. I have seen families torn apart when the religious ideology of one family member differs from the religious ideology of another family member.

Perhaps the best example I can give to explain religious addiction is the case history of a client named Russ.

> Russ was a forty-year-old survivor. Russ had been raped repeatedly by his oldest brother beginning when he was quite young. Russ also witnessed all of his brothers and sisters being raped by this same brother. When Russ as well as his siblings told their parents what the oldest brother was doing, nothing was done to stop the abuse. Russ's parents were simply too overwhelmed

with their worries and responsibilities to put a stop to their eldest son's abusive behaviors. Russ's family was so addicted to their religion that even though the family was starving, the parents still gave everything that they owned to their church. When Russ complained as he got older that his parents didn't take care of their children, Russ was severely punished. Religion to Russ meant punishment and humiliation for everyday childhood behaviors. Finally, Russ was asked to leave the church. The parents never punished the older brother who had raped Russ and his siblings because the brother never criticized the family's religious practices.

Probably no other addiction is as supported, yet causes as much pain as religious addiction. Religious addicts are truly convinced that they are doing what is best for both themselves and for everyone else. The pain from the rigidity of their belief systems and the self-righteousness with which they chastise others is all in an attempt to find control outside of themselves. Religious addicts really need to change the qualities and the characteristics that reside within themselves. Instead of listening to religious dogma, the religious addicts must accept responsibility for their own behaviors and beliefs. It is by turning to religious addiction that religious addicts seek to avoid the consequences of their own choices. When religious addicts blindly follow the creeds and dogma of others, they are giving away their personal power because they believe that someone else knows what is best for them. It is the blind adherence to rules that sets the religious addict up for making black-and-white, either/or choices. The rigid role that religious addicts set for themselves and for others allows no room for real emotion or genuine personality. To the religious addict, everything must "look" right. Whether things *are* right is another matter and not of primary concern.

Spirituality is not present only when one is worshiping a higher power. Spirituality and sexuality can often be seen as having many common ties. Some believe that the act of consensual, loving sex can be seen as an attempt to become one with our higher power. It is as if a loving sexual union is the seeking of the completeness of ourselves, of regaining that part of us that is missing, and to experience what we might have been. What a tragedy sexual abuse is when we compare it to the qualities of sex that are found in a truly loving and intimate sexual act in which the partners have deep caring ties to each other.

Our society often tends to try to separate our lives into discrete "compartments," when we do certain activities only at certain times. The truth is that *all* of life is tied together. Something seriously amiss in one part of life will become apparent in others parts of life also. If we have no sense of spirituality in our lives (i.e., connectedness to each other, a sense of belonging to something that is greater than ourselves), our lives and our desires become the only force driving our behaviors. We cannot develop a concern for and interest in our fellow human beings except for whatever purpose they can fulfill for us. We begin to see others as objects to rank simply by the return we can get by how much time we have spent with them. We have no sense of connection and caring; at some point, behaviors that we might have otherwise considered to be less than acceptable become quite acceptable. Spirituality makes the difference not only in how we see ourselves in the grand scheme of things but also how we see others.

What are the symptoms of religious addiction in survivors? Father Leo Booth (1991), in his book *When God Becomes a Drug,* lists the following symptoms:

- inability to think, doubt, or question information or authority;
- black-or-white simplistic thinking;
- shame-based beliefs that you aren't good enough or aren't doing right;
- magical thinking that God will fix you;
- rigid and obsessive adherence to rules, codes of ethics, or guidelines;
- uncompromising judgmental attitudes;
- compulsive praying, going to church, or quoting scriptures;
- unrealistic financial contributions;
- believing sex is dirty and our bodies and physical pleasure are evil;
- compulsive overeating or fasting;
- conflict with science, medicine, and education;
- psychosomatic illness (sleeplessness, back pain, headaches, and hypertension);
- progressive detachment from the real world, isolation, and breakdown of relationships;
- manipulating scriptures or claiming to receive special messages from God;

- trancelike state or religious high, wearing a glazed happy face; and,
- cries for help; mental, emotional, or physical breakdown or hospitalization.

Many of these behaviors could also pertain to other physical addictions, such as alcoholism, drug addiction, or food addiction. Although religious addiction is found frequently in incest families, very little attention is given to the harmfulness of religious addiction. When we begin to think of our bodies or our sexuality as sinful and dirty, the physical and emotional urge to relate in a sexual or romantic manner to another does not go away. The need to express our emotions and our sexual desire is instead driven underground. Without an outlet to express such intense physical needs as our sexuality, a person living in an atmosphere of addicted religion sometimes will turn to a child. If we take a close look at the characteristics of survivors who become addicted to religion, it is easy to see how each of the many characteristics of religious addiction are designed to take the focus off what is going on inside the person. The focus is then placed on an external structure that gives individuals a greater feeling of control and a guarantee that they are "following the rules" and will get a reward. If only real life were that simple. All of life contains risk. Survivors who become religious addicts are looking intently for reassurance that if they do what the rules say, life will be good.

Playing by the rules is no guarantee that everything will go well. Bad things happen to good people all the time. Perhaps it is the sense of predictability that the survivor who becomes a religious addict is seeking. Life is not fair, and learning to be flexible and develop coping skills goes a long way toward dealing with the uncertainty that life brings to all of us.

According to Father Leo Booth, there are several types of people at greatest risk for religious addiction. Adult children of alcoholics (ACOA) are at risk, especially if they are survivors of sexual abuse. Many times ACOA sexual abuse survivors will try to "cleanse" themselves with religious addiction. The abuse teaches survivors that their bodies are "dirty." The same could be said for homosexuals, asexuals, those with severe body image problems, and those with sexual dysfunction or sexual identity issues: the sick and the elderly (due to the idea of being rewarded and atoning), minorities and the young (need to belong and not feel vulnerable) and people with other addictions (this type of person may already have developed an addictive personality).

Booth cites two types of families that may be seen as being religiously addicted: the blue-collar family and the country-club family. Since I work in three clinics in a large nonprofit mental health organization that services a large population of families that are struggling financially, I have seen a greater percentage of blue-collar families. In the blue-collar family that has a survivor with a religious addiction, the father is apt to be quite domineering with episodes of unpredictable rage and violence. He may either be an active alcoholic or not be actively drinking but be a "dry drunk" with all of the same dysfunctional thoughts and behavior patterns as the active alcoholic. This father may also sexually or physically abuse his children. I have seen instances of sibling incest within these families. Sometimes the father will use religion to cover his bigotry toward other ethnic groups who he may blame as being the cause of the family's financial difficulties. This type of behavior occurs often.

The mother in the blue-collar family with religious addiction is often either passive or worn down from the stress in her life, or she may also be a religious addict who is full of rage and very rigid and controlling. Many times the wife herself was a childhood victim of sexual or physical abuse. Both types of mothers, passive or controlling, often have eating disorders, with compulsive overeating being the most commonly seen eating disorder.

Country-club families are much more concerned with how those outside of the family perceive them. The father in this type of family is a perfectionist and often a workaholic. Money is the commodity that buys the family prestige and position in the community and the church. The mother in this family often lives through her husband's achievements with no real self-worth of her own. This type of mother and father may both have weight issues and constantly battle overeating. Sometimes this type of wife will use sex as a way to manipulate her husband. Families with survivors with eating disorders and religiously addicted families have much in common. Any time there is a situation that demands a rigid role from someone that does not allow the person to express honest feelings, that person is ripe for an addiction.

Redmond is a sixty-year-old survivor who was raped all through his childhood by his older brother. When he disclosed the abuse as a child, nothing was done either to stop the abuse from continuing or to punish the older brother. Redmond's sense of shame resulted in such low self-esteem that he thought that the only way he could ever achieve any type of approval in his family was to become prominent in the family's church. He was the one who always sang the loudest in church, gave the most money, quoted the most scripture, and judged others the most harshly. The community and Redmond's church family weren't aware that he had been sexually abusing his oldest daughter since she was five years old. Although Redmond's wife denied that she knew about the abuse, when her daughter disclosed the abuse at the age of thirty-five it was clear that the mother had suspected long ago that something was wrong in the family. The mother never even questioned her daughter about what the sexual abuse had consisted of. Redmond and his wife had maintained their relationship through an unspoken agreement of peace at any price. The rules of "don't talk and don't feel" were clearly evident in the family. When their daughter disclosed the incest, she broke the rules and forced the family to deal with years of secrets and denial. The family could not tolerate the consequences of the daughter's disclosure. The daughter was abandoned by the family as a means of retaining the semblance of a family that was left.

All too often this is price that the survivors must pay when they disclose their sexual abuse. Nothing tends to polarize a family more than allegations of sexual abuse. In families having religious addiction in addition to sexual abuse, the disclosure of the sexual abuse breaks the denial of everything "looking" good. The rule of not thinking, speaking, or feeling has been broken. Emotions are at an all-time high. Because the religiously addicted family has depended on simplistic, black-and-white "rules," often the family has not developed the coping skills that enable them to realize that nothing in life is simple. Rather than admit that the family has serious problems that need to be dealt with, the family finds it preferable to reject the survivor. Often survivors will recant their allegations of sexual abuse in an effort to be reunited with their families. The survivors again develop a false persona to avoid being abandoned by their family. What a sad price to pay to remain part of the family—losing one's true self.

In the next chapter, we will learn how the survivor can become addicted to any number of assorted addictions and compulsions, all in an attempt to become "numb."

Chapter 13

Assorted Addictions and Compulsions Commonly Seen in Survivors

We speak of alcohol and drugs as being addictive. So is work. Driving, ambitious people become slaves to work—and the resultant stress can cause serious problems. All work and no play doesn't make Jack a dull boy: it makes him a dead boy. This isn't to argue that hard work should be avoided, just to suggest that the hard driver allow some time for diverting recreation. It can be his best life insurance policy.

J. D. Ratcliff

Luther's addiction is more difficult to see than most addictions. His addiction is socially acceptable. In fact, our culture in the United States encourages and rewards his addiction. Luther is a workaholic.

Luther is a sixty-five-year-old survivor who was molested by an uncle at age five. Luther puts in seventy to eighty hours a week at his job as a surgeon. All of his patients and co-workers are amazed at how hard he works and what a wonderful job he does. Luther is constantly met with praise and admiration for his selflessness and concern for his patients. Luther *really* is a good surgeon, but his overwork is an addiction nonetheless. Working the seventy to eighty hours a week that he works allows him to focus all of his attention on his work and not to deal with his personal issues.

Luther was raised in a family in which he met with constant criticism. Nothing that he did was ever good enough. The harder he would work to obtain his family's praise, the higher his parents would set their standards. Luther was destined to fail no matter how proficient he was at whatever task he undertook. This sense of failure was a constant theme in his life.

Luther married a woman who was never satisfied with what he was able to provide, despite the economic success that he achieved. From morning until night, Luther's wife would find fault with the life that he provided her. Luther began to stay away from home more and more in an attempt to relieve the pain of constantly being judged and coming up short with the demands of the most important people in his life. His anesthesia of choice was work. Work offered the solace that he needed to be able to get through each day with his constant sense of failure. Luther's clients and co-workers offered him the sense of achievement that the other aspects of his life couldn't provide. Over-working became such an addiction that eventually work was the only thing in his life. The relationships that should have been central to his life, such as with his wife and children, began to suffer. Luther was unable to change his behaviors in time to avoid the damage that would eventually cost him the closeness that he wanted with his family. Eventually, work became all that he had in his life. Economically, he was judged a success. Emotionally, Luther was so alone that work offered the only emotional connection he experienced.

Luther's situation is perhaps one of the most painful situations that an addiction can cause. Because our culture rewards Luther's addiction both emotionally and economically, the cost of his addiction isn't clear until the damage is already done. His relationship with his children will take the rest of his life to repair. Luther's children will probably never forget all the times that they needed to be with their father and he let them down. His sense of failure is reinforced once again, because he knows now that he honestly didn't meet his children's needs.

Luther will have to battle his addiction to overwork for the rest of his life. Every time that he becomes stressed and begins to feel the pain of not being able to meet the demands placed upon him, he will once again feel the pull to overwork.

To heal from the painful feelings of his childhood and his marriage, he must face the pain of feeling *less than* without resorting to overworking to numb the pain. Luther must realize finally that the pain he has experienced is not his fault. He must comprehend that the fault resides within the dynamics of his family of origin and was carried on in his choice of a marital partner. The real sadness in Luther's situation is that he has experienced little of the goodness that should have been available to him in life. He was *born* already more than adequate. It was his parent's expectations of what he should have been that were so out of line. Until Luther can grieve the loss of all of the years of futile attempts at trying to please his parents and his wife, he is destined to repeat the cycle of overworking and overcompensating.

David is another example of how our society can reward an addiction until the addiction is so out of control that the damage it causes is almost irreparable.

David was molested by his older brother throughout most of his childhood. David works in a discount store. He has risen in the ranks at his company to a managerial position. David is truly an excellent worker. He doesn't mind putting in long hours. David's expectations of his own performance are no less than what he would expect of his employees' performance. However, David's expectations are virtually impossible to meet. To accomplish all of the tasks that David feels are necessary, David and his employees would have to be "perfect."

In fact, David tries hard to meet the standards of being "perfect" because perfection is the anesthersia that will offer David comfort and predictability for the first time in his life. David's father was a very harsh and demanding man. David met with constant criticism from him when he was growing up. David's father ruled the household with an iron fist. David's mother was very insecure and dependent upon her husband for economic stability. David's father used the mother's dependence as a way of controlling the entire family. When David's father would become abusive toward David, the mother was unable to defend David against his father's abuse. David's mother couldn't even defend herself against her husband's abusiveness. David's only defense against his father was to try to control the environment in which he lived in order to try to avoid anything that might displease his father and set in motion the next round of abuse. Constantly trying to predict and avoid situations that would cause his father's displeasure became the focus of David's life. This need to control became a pattern in David's life that carried over into his work life and marriage.

David had seen the molestation by his older brother as being "mutual exploration." David's brother was almost ten years older than David and much larger in stature. The difference in power and the use of intimidation between the brothers was such a significant factor that the sexual acts were not consensual and offered no sense of affection. The sexual acts were exploitation on the offender's part. Because of

David's abusive past, particularly where his father was concerned, David did not see the situation for the abuse that it really was. David felt that the situation was not a significant factor in his life. He was so accustomed to abuse that the experience felt "familiar."

Until David is able to confront his denial of the abuse by the older male authority figures in his life, he is doomed to repeat his addiction to perfection both on his own part and the part of his employees that work for him. David even expects perfection from his wife and his children. To heal from his addiction to "perfection," David must abstain from his need to focus all of his attention on perfection and predictability and grieve the relationships in his childhood that forced him to need the ability to predict and control an intolerably abusive home life. David must first let go of his need to control and manipulate his environment at work and at home without the use of impossible standards and demands. David will need to realize that he was born more than adequate. It was David's father who was the one with the inadequacies—namely, inadequacies as a father. David and all of the people who fell under his control were also the victims of David's father's inadequacies.

Because David's need for perfection and control brought about results in the business world, he was rewarded both economically and emotionally for years. It was only when his behaviors became so obviously abusive that David was forced to deal with them.

Survivors will employ any number of behaviors in an attempt to numb themselves to the pain resulting from their sexual abuse. Carol is an example of an adult survivor who has given herself the false impression of safety by using anger to keep at bay anyone she perceives as being dangerous.

Carol was raped by her uncle from age ten until age fourteen. During this time, not only was Carol's uncle sexually abusive, but he was also physically abusive. Numerous family members were aware of the abuse, but no one had enough courage to confront the uncle about what he was doing to Carol. Carol's uncle was a very angry man who had a reputation for being physically violent when he did not get his way.

When Carol was an adult she was raped by another older male in the family. Carol was not physically able to fight off this attack, and saw herself as being "weak" because the older and stronger male had succeeded in raping her. Carol's behavior changed after this attack. Gone was the compliant and pleasant young wife. In her place was a woman who used her anger and threats of physical harm in an attempt to provide some stability and safety in her world. Although Carol was a slender and slightly built woman of average size, she was able to make herself seem much larger and very intimidating by using threats and innuendoes. In a sense, Carol was able to provide stability and safety in her world by using anger. Carol's use of self-blame after the second rape was an unconscious attempt on her part to give herself some sense of control over what had happened. If Carol could blame herself for the second rape, then she could see herself as being in control. If Carol saw herself as in control, then the situation wasn't as unsettling and threatening as one in which she had no control. Unfortunately, self-blame did little to help Carol's self-esteem. She constantly viewed the second rape as being "her fault," causing her marriage to suffer as a result. Carol felt that she had betrayed her husband by being "unfaithful." Carol's use of anger served the purpose of keeping others at a safe distance. Anyone that Carol felt could potentially harm her was an enemy. Carol would find a way to express anger at these people in an attempt to attack them before they attacked her. Male or female, what mattered was whether the person was able to get close to Carol. If the other person did get close to Carol she feared that the person might reject or harm her. Carol often rejected or harmed others before they got too close to her.

This use of anger served the purpose of keeping Carol safe and offering her some sense of predictability and control in her environment. The cost of this tactic was very high because Carol also alienated the people that she really cared about. Her husband and children were afraid to get close to Carol. They had witnessed her anger and rage so many times that they never knew when the rage would be turned against them.

The rewards of Carol's rage provided a false sense of control and safety. The costs were the loss of the people to whom Carol most wanted to be close. The rage also kept Carol from getting in touch with her true emotions of fear and helplessness. Until Carol is able to drop this defense of rage and address her vulnerability and the unpredictability that life offers her, she will not be able to heal completely.

Healing for Carol is so frightening that it will take all of her courage to drop her defenses long enough to face the fact that life is unpredictable and that none of us is able to totally control what happens to us. Belief in ourselves and the fact that we will be able to deal with whatever life throws our way allows us to function in an often unsafe and unpredictable world.

> Elese is a forty-five-year-old incest survivor who has an addiction to rage and anger. She learned at an early age that to survive she had to be tougher and meaner than any of her siblings. Elese was molested by her older brother for more than ten years. When she finally disclosed the sexual abuse, no one in the family believed her. The sexual abuse stopped only because her brother feared that Elese would become pregnant as a result.
>
> Elese's addiction to rage served her well. She was able to keep others at a distance so that she might feel safe, but the addiction also kept others from ever being truly intimate with her. Elese was never able to have a good sexual relationship with her husband. In truth, she was afraid of sex because of her abuse history. One would never know that Elese feared anything because she seemed so intimidating. Elese's children were also afraid of her. Whenever the children got into trouble or were afraid, they would go to their father instead of Elese. Elese's anger kept her from having to deal with the unpleasantness of life, but she was never able to grow and learn from those events either. It was only when her middle daughter made a suicide attempt and blamed Elese's rage as the cause that Elese was able to see how destructive her anger truly was. Today she is working on her anger issues. Without the anger to protect her, Elese feels very vulnerable. She must develop new coping skills for the times when events trigger her childhood abuse issues, but it will be time well spent.

One of the most difficult things for a nonsurvivor to understand is why the survivor would turn to self-mutilation after the survivor has been through such pain and abuse already. In a study done in 1995 by Yaryura-Tobias, Neziroglu, and Kaplan, it was indicated that the limbic system is involved in both self-mutilation and menstrual changes. It appears that the pain of both the self-mutilation and the menstrual cycle cause the body to release endogenous endorphins that produce pleasant feelings, control dysphoria, and maintain an analgesic effect. In this study, 70 percent of the clients reported a history of physical or sexual abuse. The study also found that clients with obsessive-compulsive disorder and eating disorders may also display self-mutilation. It is interesting to note also that in clubs where members engage in bondage and discipline and/or sadism and masochism, a large number of the participants may be obsessive-compulsive. Perhaps the participants that are obsessive-compulsive are attracted by the preplanning of the "scripts" before these scenes are enacted. In preplanning the "plays" that will occur, the participants are able to determine just how much pain they will allow and how far the role-play will go. This structure may allow the obsessive-compulsive partner to reduce the anxiety that they may feel. Perhaps the feelings of discomfort or pain that are felt during these "plays" may also release the endogenous endorphins which bring about pleasurable feelings. Prescribing treatment with fluoxetine can be helpful in decreasing self-injurious behaviors. This is not to say that the participants in S&M or B&D find their sexual activity to be injurious. In fact, I believe that most of the participants would say that their sexual activity and participation happens by mutual agreement in a very structured and safe environment. Although Prozac, the most commonly recognized fluoxetine, is helpful in treating obsessive-compulsive disorder, self-mutilation, or depression, it can cause sexual difficulties in about 20 to 30 percent of the men to whom it is prescribed.

It is important to realize that self-injurious behaviors can be addictive. Self-injurious behaviors have not only a psychological but also a biological component. We need to understand that beneath self-injurious behaviors may be a biological predisposition to the behavior that will drive the client toward the behavior if enough psychological stressors are present. Without psychological stressors, the person might never turn toward self-injurious behaviors. The pull of the feelings of relief or sometimes pleasure that the person receives from these self-injurious behaviors can be as addictive psychologically and perhaps even biologically as other more well-recognized addictive behaviors.

Shopping seems to be an innocent enough pastime. *Seems* is the operative word. When a survivor is engaged in a compulsive activity, that activity never is what it seems to be. Shopping may be simply one more way that survivors attempt to fill their internal void as a result of their abuse. Many times the emotional "high" that they feel while compulsively shopping is much like the high that drug addicts get when abusing their drug of choice.

While compulsively shopping, survivors are taking the focus off internal feelings. This need for constant activity is a very good way to keep the survivor's mind busy to avoid "feeling." Again, the survivor is using a behavior or a substance as a means of anesthesia.

> Rusty is a thirty-year-old incest survivor. As indicated by her name, Rusty has beautiful long red hair. Rusty has a heart of gold. There is not a request that someone makes of Rusty that she does not seriously attempt to fulfill. Rusty has been so emotionally damaged in her life that she identifies with the pain that others feel. Rusty will try to do whatever it takes to help others from feeling the pain that she has felt. It is this compassion for others that has gotten Rusty into so much financial trouble. Rusty and her husband have an annual income well over six figures, yet they are in danger of losing their home because Rusty can't seem to curtail her spending. Rusty has so much credit card debt that her husband has taken all of her credit cards away from her. Because Rusty and her husband have been able to make the minimum payments on the cards that they do have, other credit card companies keep sending Rusty new credit cards.

Until Rusty abstains from her compulsive spending and "feels" the emptiness that is inside of her from all of the love and nurturing that she did not receive as a child, she is doomed to keep using compulsive behaviors to numb the pain. Even if Rusty is able to refrain from overshopping, the chances are that she will substitute another behavior for her overspending. All compulsive behavior is an attempt to find control outside of ourselves. It is really inside change that is needed. Survivors need to learn to reparent themselves, to give themselves the love that they may not have received as children, and to find other less compulsive ways to have needs met. Survivors who employ compulsive behaviors or abuse substances need to accept responsibility for their actions. Many times these survivors will attempt to avoid facing the consequences of their behaviors or choices by deciding to allow someone else to do their choosing. When they give power away in this manner they may be able to avoid the pain of facing their choices, but they substitute facing the consequences of the choices that they have allowed someone else to make for them. This sense of minimizing abilities and maximizing the abilities of others is damaging to survivors.

Sometimes survivors feel so much self-hate that they will choose behaviors that are actually a slow form of suicide. Compulsive over-spending can be seen in this light considering the health costs in-volved in the constant wear and tear on the survivor's nerves and pro-ductivity. Who can be fully confident and productive when being constantly harassed by creditors? It takes tremendous energy to per-form daily functions when our minds are occupied with worry. Little energy is left over for taking care of one's health or emotional well-being. Most survivors don't even realize the cost of such worry. These survivors are not used to taking care of themselves anyway.

Part of the recovery process is letting go of our self-will. In the United States, we are raised to be self-sufficient and independent. Willpower is valued and is seen as being the answer to many prob-lems. We are taught that if we try harder and work longer, we will eventually be able to overcome the obstacle. By admitting that we *are* powerless over something we are able to finally begin to successfully deal with it.

Compulsive shopping is a very good example of this situation. Survivors who shop compulsively often find themselves with items that they have no use for or can never expect to afford. Still compul-sive shoppers continue to spend, hoping that somehow they will be able to fill the emotional void left by their abuse. No amount of goods will ever be able to fill the void inside themselves. To recover from compulsive shopping, first the addicts must admit that they cannot control their addiction by themselves. As with other addictions and compulsions, group support for compulsive shopping or spending is invaluable. Other ways to help deal with this compulsion include de-veloping a plan of what one can afford to spend and staying within that budget; setting a goal to get out of debt and trying to establish a time frame for accomplishing this; paying off existing debts before any new debts may be incurred; always paying bills before any money can be spent on frivolous items; only using secondary income for things that are wanted but not needed; and listing debts some-where that is easily observable so that the compulsive shopper is al-ways aware of financial standing.

All of these suggestions sound like common sense and would be relatively easy to accomplish. Because compulsive shoppers are apt to spend when having uncomfortable feelings, it is important to try to construct an advance plan for times when shoppers are least able to think clearly and wisely.

> Kitty is a sixty-one-year-old incest survivor. Although Kitty has never had counseling to address her sexual abuse issues, she has become aware over the years that her compulsive shopping is related to her feelings of loneliness and depression. Kitty is over $70,000 in debt for clothing and jewelry that she has purchased. Most of the items that Kitty has bought remain in her closet with the price tags still on them. Kitty could wear a new outfit every day for the next several years and still not wear all of the items that she has purchased. Kitty cannot resist a good "sale." Coupons mean that she *must* purchase the item. Kitty can barely meet her mortgage payment each month. At times, Kitty has been three months behind in paying her telephone bill; she was in danger of having the phone turned off. Kitty has had her charge cards rejected numerous times either for a late payment or a nonpayment of her bill. Still Kitty continues to shop, trying to find the one item that will make her feel better.

Until Kitty refrains from spending and instead allows herself to feel the negative feelings that she is attempting to avoid, Kitty cannot begin to deal with her abusive past.

It is this need to avoid negative feelings that motivates Kitty's spending behaviors, yet to the casual observer this may not be apparent. Kitty's extended family sees only that Kitty has everything a woman could want and yet she is not happy. Kitty's family has no idea that her abusive past is motivating her behavior. Most people will simply criticize Kitty's behavior instead of understanding the deep need for connection and nurturing that is within Kitty. Only those who are wise to the real dynamics behind Kitty's behavior will be able to really understand her desperation. A support group of peers in similar situations is important for Kitty's recovery. When Kitty is willing to acknowledge her problem with spending to members of a compulsive shopping support group, she will be able to benefit from the group's support.

One could almost point to any behavior as a symptom of having been sexually abused. However, some signs are so indicative that they almost always occur in conjunction with sexual abuse. Some of these symptoms of sexual abuse also lead to addictive or compulsive behaviors if carried to the extreme. Many survivors have such difficulty with eating disorders and disturbed body image that they will compulsively exercise or weigh themselves. Other survivors are just as compulsive about not exercising at all. Some survivors are chronically in financial or legal trouble. Sometimes this trouble will stem from overspending or gambling debts. Other survivors have ongoing relationship issues in which they can never trust another person and are always suspicious of any sign of kindness or concern toward them. Some survivors are so afraid of abandonment that they are compulsive in their need to "please" so that they won't be left behind. Some survivors have such contempt toward the gender who abused them that they can never find anything good to say about that gender.

Survivors may be so damaged by abuse that they avoid involvement with anyone else; they are completely isolated in a life devoid of joy or companionship. Conversely, some survivors fear being alone so much that they are compulsively social but yet never develop a real sense of intimacy with anyone. Everything in their lives is superficial.

Some survivors are fearful of losing control because they never had any sense of control previously; they become compulsive about being in control. This type of survivor expects everyone else to adhere to the standards of the survivor. When others are unable to conform to these standards, the survivor looks at these others with contempt, as if they failed a "test" that had been given to them.

Being compulsively late is another common trait of survivors. Some survivors become so wrapped up in what they are doing that they lose all sense of time. Although compulsively late survivors promise that they will become more punctual, and actually *do* make efforts to become punctual, these survivors never seem able to make lasting changes in their tardiness.

Some survivors are compulsively neat. Before their guests can even finish a meal, the compulsively neat survivor may have cleared the table of all dishes and silverware without even realizing how detrimental this behavior is to the conversation and companionship of the guests.

I've seen many survivors who seem to be compulsively avoiding the emotional pain of their sexual abuse. Survivors will recount over and over again what their abuse was like, but each time the story will be completely devoid of emotion. It is almost as if they are reciting their grocery list; the most horrible abuse history may be told in flat unemotional terms. When I've asked these survivors if the abuse was emotionally painful for them, they will reply in a monotone that, yes, indeed the abuse was the most horrible thing that they have ever experienced. They will act surprised that I wasn't aware how horrible the abuse was. When I comment on how unemotionally they recounted the story, they will seem totally surprised.

Christine, a sixteen-year-old incest survivor who has experienced some of the most horrible sexual abuse imaginable, was never able to talk about her abuse except in a monotone with no sense of emotional connection at all. When I would point this out to her, Christine would say, "I told you that it was awful." Yet when Christine repeated one more time how awful the abuse was, she still had no sense of emotional connection to the abuse. Christine separated herself from the emotional feelings that the abuse caused. Speaking in a flat tone was how she was able to separate her emotions from feeling the pain of her abuse.

Some survivors become almost the complete opposite of Christine in that they compulsively overreact emotionally to anything that they find upsetting in the least.

> Bree is a forty-year-old survivor who seems to be trapped in a cycle in which she almost always reacts emotionally before she has taken any time to think rationally of what is happening and how best to handle the situation. Bree is so on the edge emotionally that she jumps whenever anything even slight happens. Her sense of insecurity requires that she be prepared for any situation that she might find distressing.

Some survivors become compulsively compassionate to the extent that they empathize with others so completely that they no longer are able to protect themselves adequately. These survivors may feel sorry for their perpetrators so that they are never able to experience and feel the necessary anger that leads toward acknowledgment of the harmfulness of the abuse and finally forgiveness and healing. If these survivors do not fully remember the abuse and place the blame for the abuse in its proper place (with the perpetrator), they may turn the blame and anger inward toward themselves and become self-abusive. Many survivors have a tendency to minimize their abuse in an attempt to deal with the resulting pain, but this type of survivor goes to the extreme in an attempt to try to feel some sense of control over the harmfulness of the abuse. When anger toward someone who has harmed them is buried this deeply, the survivors may be so totally unaware of their own feelings that when they are extremely overweight, are self-mutilating, or become involved in many dysfunctional relationships, they have no idea why they are constantly being hurt. It is only when survivors are able to get in touch with their anger concerning the abuse and feel this anger in some part of their body that they become aware of the strength and the depth of their pent-up anger.

There are as many possible addictions and compulsive behaviors as there are survivors. To try to name all of the conceivable addictions and compulsions is impossible. If the survivor has made repeated attempts to refrain from continuing negative behavior, but still continues the behavior, then most likely the survivor has an addiction or a compulsive behavior.

The following chapter discusses how, many times, survivors may believe that they have overcome an addiction or compulsive behavior only to find out later that they have simply substituted one addiction for another.

Chapter 14

Switching Addictions

People spend a lifetime searching for happiness; looking for peace. They chase idle dreams, addictions, religions, even other people, hoping to fill the emptiness that plagues them. The irony is the only place they ever needed to search was within.

Ramona L. Anderson

Since the unconscious purpose of addiction or compulsion is to take the focus off the survivor's unpleasant thoughts, memories, or feelings, the only criterion that limits the addiction or compulsion is the choice dictated by the survivor's likes and dislikes. Furthermore, *if* survivors have a problem dealing with their abuse issues, the problems might be expressed in one of the following ways:

1. *The survivor might become codependent.* Codependency is really an addiction to a person, but because so many survivors become codependent and codependency is not often viewed by our society as being necessarily negative, I believe that codependency deserves a category all of its own. In my personal life, codependency is the biggest problem I have ever had to address.
2. *The survivor might go on to become a perpetrator.* This does not happen the majority of the time. Most survivors are far more apt to be victims later in their lives in other abusive relationships, but a small percentage of survivors do become perpetrators in an attempt not to feel their own pain and victimization.
3. *The survivor may develop addictions or compulsions.* Survivors may initially not appear to suffer any negative effects from the sexual abuse but will develop addictions or compulsions that will enable them to deal with the memories and feelings tied to their abuse histories.

Survivors may appear to have conquered an addiction or compulsion, but in reality have simply switched to another less apparent or troubling addiction or compulsion that has not yet become problematic. For example, many adult female survivors who have codependency issues will have a weight problem until they meet someone for whom they may have strong sexual feelings. It is not unusual to see these survivors lose large amounts of weight and become addicted to their relationship with the person that they find sexually attractive. These survivors have simply switched their addiction from food to a person. If the relationship with the person to whom they are attracted does not work out, they are likely to regain all of the weight that they lost plus even more.

Survivors also can move from one type of eating disorder to another. Beth was a fourteen-year-old incest survivor when I first met her. She was anorexic, weighing only 97 pounds at five feet six inches tall. As therapy progressed and Beth dealt with her difficult abuse issues, she began to binge eat. Beth's feelings of anger and powerlessness were expressed as anorexia. Control came when Beth decided that no one could make her eat if she didn't want to eat. As Beth began to get in touch with her anger and all of the losses that she had experienced, she became depressed. Depression was expressed as anger turned inward which came in the form of binge eating. Not only did Beth move back and forth in her feelings, she also moved back and forth in her eating patterns.

Whenever a survivor conquers a particular addiction or compulsion, this does not mean that the survivor is immune to another addiction that may have previously enabled him or her to deal with another issue. To prevent the use of addictive or compulsive behaviors, core issues must be addressed.

> Corby is a fifteen-year-old incest survivor who has had to provide care for her mother emotionally all of her young life. Corby has been addicted to disrupting her classes, acting out in very angry ways, and abusing drugs. She finally was able to disclose the incest and express her need for her mother to be a parent to her, rather than her being the parent to her mother. Corby then was able to begin to control her own negative behaviors.

Some parents use behaviors such as helplessness, tears, anger, and threats of abandonment to keep their children from expressing their own needs. This is harmful because the child is robbed of a childhood not only by the sexual abuse but by the parent's inability to parent appropriately. In situations such as this, the parent is appealing to the child's developing sense of codependency. Addictions and compulsions are often distractions that keep the child from dealing with painful issues, both past and present. I wouldn't be surprised to see research results indicating that the survivors who have the most painful abuse memories and abuse histories also might have the most severe addictions and compulsions. I would guess that the more painful the memories and feelings that a survivor has, the more of an addictive or compulsive behavior the survivor would need to employ to deal with those feelings and memories. Perhaps this is why the survivors with whom I work who have the most intrusive abuse memories also tend to abuse the most addictive and harmful drugs and substances. For example; survivors in the groups who have had more than one perpetrator or who are in an out-of-home placement seem to need a "stronger" and much more addictive drug, such as heroin, than survivors who had much less intrusive sexual abuse, abuse of a shorter duration, or sexual abuse by a non–family member. Survivors whose sexual abuse involved abuse of a shorter duration, sexual abuse that was less intrusive than actual intercourse, and sexual abuse which did not involve incest seem to abuse drugs such as marijuana or alcohol. This is not to imply that marijuana or alcohol are not harmful also, but that the survivor who abuses heroin seems to "need" some sort of "heavier" anesthesia to help dull the pain of their memories and emotions. Perhaps some sort of ratio exists where the more damaging the abuse is the greater the need for stronger "anesthesia." Considering the biological aspect of addictions and the release of the body's natural endorphins, it makes sense that the greater the emotional trauma, the greater the need for a stronger substance to dull the pain of the abuse.

When a survivor switches from one addiction to another, it is an example of "generalized addiction." To me, this term means anyone who uses one addiction or any other addiction in its place as a way of "numbing" unpleasant emotions is a generalized addict. One could argue that we all do this to some extent, and this is true. The difference between the addict and someone who occasionally abuses a substance or behavior is that the addict's life is negatively impacted by the addiction or compulsion, and the addict is powerless to stop the addiction or the behavior. It is not uncommon to see survivors switch addictions to try to find some sort of validation that can ultimately come only from within themselves. It is common to see survivors switch addictions when they come close to core issues while being treated for a substance addiction.

> Thea is a good example of a survivor who used food all her life as a way to deal with the pain of her incest. When she was in her midforties, she was able to lose a considerable amount of weight. Thea lost her excess weight when she became romantically involved with a colleague at her place of employment. When her colleague left the company, she began to switch her addictions to overspending, overworking, and sexual addiction.

Thea was unconsciously attempting to "numb" herself to the constant ache inside that resulted from the knowledge that she was abused and abandoned. In her mind, the pain originated from the loss of her romantic partner at her job. What Thea didn't realize, at least on a conscious level, was that the loss of her romantic partner only was a replication of the loss of the trust and caring that she had experienced when her father had sexually abused her as a child. The ache resulting from the abuse and abandonment by her father was a dynamic that was triggered by any relationship that Thea had with a male partner in which the partner was not able to be there for her either emotionally or physically. Ironically, Thea picked men, at least on a subconscious level, who were certain to abuse or abandon her because in their families of origin the men's needs were not met and therefore she played the role of caregiver.

There was no quick fix for Thea's situation. When she decided to focus on her own behaviors and address her own issues she began to gain control of the situation. If she had chosen to focus only on the faults of her partners, she would have had no control over the outcome of her romantic problems.

Relapse is always part of the recovery process. For survivors, relapse is seen as a sure sign that they are *less than* or that they are doomed always to fail. If survivors can realize the emotions and beliefs that lie beneath their addictive or compulsive behaviors, they will understand that they are not flawed. It is the survivor's *experiences* that shape the survivor's *self-perceptions*. The messages that the survivor has received in the past develop a *self-fulfilling proph-*

ecy: the survivor becomes the person he or she perceives as already being.

Recovery requires that survivors develop a new way of viewing themselves and others. The survivor needs to develop a new yardstick to measure self-worth. In recovery, the survivor's yardstick is based on ability to trust a power higher than the addiction or compulsion.

Part II addresses how the survivor makes the shift from "willfulness to willingness."

PART II:
THE RECOVERY PROCESS

Chapter 15

Establishing Healthy Boundaries

"Good fences make good neighbors."

"Mending Wall"
Robert Frost

Few things are more difficult for the survivor to understand than the notion of "good" boundaries. Even after dealing with my own incest issues for over forty years, I still struggle with boundary issues. The problem that most survivors have is that from the moment that they were sexually abused, they received a lesson in the "subjectiveness" of boundaries and the rationalization of the violation of those same boundaries. Since children base most of what they learn and how they see the world on the behaviors in their family of origin, survivors begin relationships one step behind those who come from families where boundaries are clear and healthy for *all* members of the family.

The relationships that addicted survivors develop are often replicas of the relationships that they had with their own parents. When the addicted survivor's parents don't acknowledge their own frailties and imperfections, especially if one of the parents is the child's perpetrator, the child begins to believe that his or her perceptions of events are wrong. The child begins to think that it isn't okay to make mistakes, that one needs to deny one's own imperfections. Criticizing and sitting in judgment of others becomes acceptable behavior. Using criticism and shame is also a way to keep others from seeing the addicted survivor's flaws and offers the survivor the opportunity to control others. Children of such parents may either become angry and unruly because they feel that they cannot measure up to such perfect and impossible standards or they become very judgmental and shaming, just like their parents were to them. Unless addicted survivors are able to stop pointing their fingers and instead look inward toward their own flaws, they will never be able to have a truly intimate relationship with others or with themselves.

Addicted survivors need to reparent themselves. It is imperative that they learn that they don't need to be "perfect" to be loved, that they are fine the way they are. It is necessary to develop self-love and self-esteem in order to be strong enough to demand that others treat us well. The pain of acknowledging unmet childhood needs will propel the survivor toward real intimacy and caring in relationships.

Addicted survivors attempt to maintain relationships in many ways. It is not unusual to see addicted survivors set ultimatums in an attempt to manipulate those with whom they are in relationships. Some addicted survivors will make many promises to change their behaviors if only their partners won't leave. Other addicted survivors will try to be so perfect and pleasing that their partners will stay no matter how they might really feel about the relationship. Whatever tactic the addicted survivor uses to remain in a relationship with a partner, unless the survivor has the ability to be genuine and to let the partner see the real person beneath the addiction, no real intimacy can develop in the relationship.

Many survivors have such problems with boundaries that the survivor is either too close with the partner or else the survivor cannot tolerate any real closeness at all. The solution is to try to find the balance between independence and interdependence that allows for closeness but not enmeshment. To be able to find the proper balance in relationships requires honesty about negative as well as positive feelings and one must not play the caregiver in intimate relationships. For the addicted survivor, this is the most frightening task of all.

Because addicted survivors will go to such lengths to avoid abandonment, they usually attract people who have a desire for control. Those who attempt to control the survivor will succeed only as long as the survivor is not in recovery. Once the survivor begins the process of regaining those parts of the self that were lost to the abuse, the structure of the survivor's relationships changes. To be in recovery, the addicted survivor must quit blaming others for the state of his or her life. Even though the addicted survivor has been abused, the abuse is not a lifelong excuse for negative behaviors and choices. Instead of finding fault in others, addicted survivors need to work on their own faults and deficits. Addicted survivors need to engage in improving themselves without using one-upmanship as a means of making others feel small. Addicted survivors must leave others to their own realities, while formulating their own standards and expectations.

I have seen two discrete types of survivors.

> Lucky is a sixteen-year-old survivor who sits in judgment of anyone who is different from him. If others are of a different race or religion, they are sure to meet with scorn and ridicule. Lucky feels so inferior due to the sexual abuse that he has experienced that he needs to make others feel even smaller in an attempt to bolster his own ego.

> Lady is a fifteen-year-old incest survivor who tries so hard to please others that there is no way that she would ever be abandoned. Just out of guilt others would stay with her. Lady will use others' pity and guilt to manipulate them to continue their relationships with her.

Neither of these survivors will ever be able to have a truly intimate relationship because they are not complete within themselves. When we find happiness within ourselves we are able to find happiness with others.

Boundaries are so difficult for survivors that some barely have any boundaries at all. These are the survivors who are constantly over-committed and resentful that they never have any time for themselves. Some survivors are so impaired regarding boundaries that instead of establishing boundaries they will instead choose not to let anyone get close to them. These survivors will set thick, impermeable barricades around themselves emotionally so that no one can hurt them or cause them to feel strong emotions.

> Maguire is a forty-one-year-old survivor who has chosen to isolate himself rather than ever to take the risk again of becoming close to someone and being rejected. Even though he will not be hurt by others, the results are the same: Maguire is alone and unhappy.

Learning to establish proper boundaries is a major part of the recovery process for survivors. The boundaries that we internalize protect us emotionally and spiritually. Without these boundaries, survivors are doomed to become angry and resentful of those who may unwittingly take advantage of them.

In their quest for intimacy, survivors attempt manipulation to achieve that which they think they could never be worthy of: a genuinely caring relationship with another. In his book *Man the Manipulator,* Shostrum (1968) discusses several different types of manipulation. In *active and competitive* manipulation, the individual will attempt to control and win at all costs. Such survivors use shame and negative judgment as ways to manipulate others. *Passive or indifferent* manipulators will attempt to be so pleasing that others could never abandon them or will act as if they don't care if they are abandoned. Either way, they do not have the real caring and intimacy that they crave if they must manipulate others to remain in a relationship.

It is not unusual to see survivors with poor boundaries become involved in physically abusive relationships. Although the traits of an abusive partner are not difficult to spot, many survivors are so accustomed to abusive treatment that they don't pick up on others' abusive traits. Many times the male partners of female survivors will feel the need to control the survivor due to the lack of control in the male's family of origin. Perhaps the male partner witnessed domestic violence in his own family. Whatever the reason, physically abusive partners will use whatever means necessary to assure themselves that they will be able to control their partners.

Survivors who marry men who are physically abusive often come from families with domineering and self-centered fathers. Usually the mother in such a family will be passive and often codependent. The survivor in such a family sees women as being powerless and ineffective. The female survivor quickly learns that to be female is to be under someone else's control. These female survivors grow up never knowing their own sense of power. They either know compulsive behaviors (which equate to total control of their environment) or no control at all (which equates to addiction).

The most important new skill that a survivor must learn while in the healing process is that of setting healthy boundaries. As a survivor myself, setting boundaries is one of the most confusing things I ever tried to do. I can never quite figure out whose standards to use when I try to determine which boundary is appropriate. Other survivors tell me that they have the same problem, so perhaps we should start out by defining exactly what a boundary is.

Boundaries basically state that there is a point where the individual begins and the rest of the world ends. The individual's space is his or her boundary. If someone invades this space without permission, whether the invasion be psychological, physical, or spiritual, then that person has invaded one's boundaries. Nothing violates one's boundaries as severely as sexual abuse. Incest especially is not only an invasion of one's boundaries, but is also probably the largest betrayal a parent or family figure can perpetrate upon a child. A person who grows up in a family with poor boundaries finds it difficult to understand what others mean when they tell the individual he or she has "poor boundaries." If our family's boundaries are poor, then we spend a lot of time in an environment that is not an accurate representation of how the world is supposed to be. Is it any wonder that survivors go out into the world and become targets for all sorts of harmful behaviors both by others and by the survivors themselves?

One of the most harmful aspects of incest families is the role reversal that exists between the oldest daughter and her mother. In such situations the child effectively becomes the "parent's parent," and has no opportunity to learn to say "no" to taking care of others. The daughter seems to sense, without the mother ever having to say a word, just how needy the mother really is. This pattern of the child taking care of the mother becomes a sort of "template" for how the daughter will relate to all of the most significant other relationships that she has in her life, unless she is lucky enough to begin to deal with her issues. I have worked with many survivors who feel it is disloyal to their parents to find any sort of fault with them no matter how horrendous the parents' behaviors might have been. This is when I talk with survivors about how to realize how inappropriate a behavior is without losing the love that they feel for their parents. This is a sort of "hate the sin, but love the sinner" type of situation. Most survivors seem able to relate to what I am saying when they realize that not approving of a parent's harmful behaviors doesn't mean that they can't value the positive things about the parents.

The varying degrees to which survivors are able or unable to establish boundaries indicate just how severely they may have been sexually abused. I believe that it makes sense to expect a survivor who has never known any boundaries as a child to have more difficulties establishing boundaries than someone who had some sense of boundaries while growing up. Boundaries are really what defines us as people when we become adults. Boundaries are also an indication of how well we are able to protect ourselves and value ourselves. Some survivors are so fearful of being violated again that they will set boundaries so high and imposing that no one can ever get close to them. Although this may help the survivors protect themselves, it also keeps them from ever having any really intimate relationships with anyone.

Whenever the survivor does become intimate with someone, that relationship will likely bring great joy and possibly great pain. The degree of joy and pain will be determined in part by how well the survivor is able to set and maintain appropriate boundaries. These boundaries should allow intimacy and closeness with others yet still protect the survivor from being violated or used. Even for those who have never been abused this would be quite a balancing act. Imagine what it is like for those who have never had their boundaries respected.

The first step in establishing appropriate boundaries is to notice that someone or something is attempting to violate a boundary. Again, this is difficult for survivors because they always tend to accept as "normal" that to which they are accustomed. Most survivors do not feel uncomfortable having a family member ask them to do something that the member is quite capable of doing for himself or herself. The closer in relationship the person doing the asking is to the survivor, the more apt the survivor is to accommodate the request without questioning it.

We need to pay attention to the feelings that arise in us when someone asks us to do something for them. Does the request make you feel as if you are being included in something, or does the request make you feel that you are just doing something for someone else and that you are not taking joy in the task? Does the request make you feel resentful or used, or does it make you feel that you are a part of something that you relish? If feelings of selflessness or resentment arise, this is a sure sign that the survivor is allowing someone to violate his or her boundaries or to use the survivor.

The subjective part of whether a boundary is appropriate is the next hurdle one must cross. Seldom do others take no for an answer without some sort of negative response. For survivors, any negativity feels like rejection or abandonment. Many times survivors who originally said no to a request will quickly change their minds at the first sign of someone's disapproval. Getting feedback from others who can be objective can give the survivor some guidance about the appropriateness of the boundaries that the survivor has established. Survivors will discover that although they may have not been able to express in words what made them uneasy about the request, the feelings of discomfort were a good indication that the survivor's boundaries were about to be violated.

For survivors who are new at trying to establish appropriate boundaries, it may be helpful to say that more time is needed to think about the request. This response will get the person off the hook long enough to think about whether he or she really wants to comply with the request.

When I am requested to do something that I'm not sure I want to do or is not really appropriate to do, I say that I want to meet with the person later to talk about the matter when I can concentrate on the request and give the request my full time and attention. After I have said this, if the person still insists that I answer immediately, I know that the person is not thinking of my welfare at all. At that point, I have no problem saying no. I tell the individual to speak to someone else who can answer the request immediately. Some survivors have found that saying they have another engagement is enough of an answer. If those who are making the request question what the engagement is, you are under no obligation to answer. You could always say that you will tell them for sure tomorrow when you have your calendar available. Although this kind of answer sounds flimsy, for some survivors this is the first step they can take toward establishing some sort of protective boundary. Setting boundaries is not an overnight affair. It takes time and patience. Because survivors know how it feels to be hurt, they have such empathy for other people's pain that they would never want to harm someone else. Sometimes saying no to someone's request (e.g., lending a sum of money that the borrower could never possibly repay) *is* being helpful. Imagine if your higher power gave you everything you requested exactly as you requested it. How many times have you wished for something only to be thankful later that you didn't receive it? If we take the focus off the other person's welfare and place the focus back on our own welfare, we will realize that not agreeing to everything that is requested of us is also being helpful to ourselves as well as the person making the request.

How should survivors react to someone who has violated their boundaries? Instinctively most people would become angry or would in some way inform the person who had violated their boundaries that they had infringed upon them. Survivors often won't let someone know that they are angry or hurt by the other's behaviors. It is not unusual to see survivors hold in their feelings of anger and resentment and let those feelings fester so long that when they finally release their pent-up feelings, a major explosion occurs. Many times the explosion is totally out of proportion to the other person's offense.

Survivors can take a series of steps to ensure that they talk about their feelings as they occur. First, the survivors should decide that they are no longer going to allow others to infringe upon their boundaries. The survivors might look back over the past to see how allowing others to cross their boundaries has cost and hurt them in many ways. Just the realization that they have lost so much by not defending themselves is often enough to get the survivor motivated to make the necessary changes where boundaries are concerned.

It is helpful if survivors have a few remarks prepared in advance for those times when someone may violate their boundaries without warning. Some stock remarks might be, "I'm not comfortable when you _____." "That's classified information!" (said with a smile). For times when someone insists on talking about a sensitive subject that you would rather not discuss, you might say, "It's obvious that we don't see things the same way. Let's agree to disagree!" For those people who continue to insist on discussing something survivors do not wish to discuss, the message must be stronger, "I'm uncomfortable discussing that. It's private information, and it would be inappropriate for you to continue to press me to discuss it." The survivor should learn not to be concerned about hurting the feelings of someone who won't take no for an answer.

The next step would be for the survivors to say just what they mean instead of using words that soften the message. If survivors don't want to do something they should say they don't *want* to do something versus *not being able* to do something, so that no misunderstanding occurs. When the message is soft, the other person is likely to interpret the message in the way the person *wants* to hear it rather than how it is *really* meant.

Another step that the survivor can take in setting healthy boundaries is to see oneself as the parent of the child that he or she once was. Just because the survivor was not protected as a child does not mean that one cannot learn to reparent oneself as an adult. Survivors need to learn how to look after themselves in the way a good parent would look after a child. If the adult survivor is a parent, this is easier, because anything that would be harmful to one's child would not be beneficial to an adult either. At first, taking care of themselves will seem so uncomfortable that survivors may feel that they are being selfish. Being selfish is *not* taking care of yourself for so long that eventually someone else has to step in and do it for you.

When the survivor begins to waver and feels about to allow someone to take advantage, it is helpful for the survivor to find a physical way to come back to reality. Many survivors are so out of touch with their innermost feelings that the physical touch is a real reminder of the present time and situation. So many survivors become experts at removing themselves emotionally from the situation that the physical touch will "ground" them.

Survivors who are using these skills for the first time will feel uncomfortable. Others who are accustomed to the survivor being a "doormat" may not like the changes that the survivor is attempting to make. The survivor should be prepared for complaints about changing the status quo and should realize that, although these changes are uncomfortable at first, eventually the changes will lead to better emotional health for both the survivor and the relationships in which the survivor is involved.

Sexual abuse invades the survivor's boundaries on so many levels that the harm incurred is monumental. Because of the damage that sexual abuse causes, survivors often are set up for a lifetime of allowing themselves to be abused. It is disturbing to hear someone who has had a very comfortable life make negative remarks about survivors who are prostituting or using an addiction to make their lives bearable. No one would choose a life of degradation or abuse unless he or she had been accustomed to abuse and degradation.

For sexual abuse to happen, the perpetrator begins to see the victim as being of lesser importance than the desires of the perpetrator. The victim becomes an object that will satisfy the perpetrator's whims. Treating someone in such a callous manner crosses all psychological, spiritual, and physical boundaries that a person possesses. The brief time that it may take to perpetrate sexual abuse may result in a life-

time of agony, self-abusive behaviors, addictions, and compulsive behaviors. What a price to pay for a moment of sexual gratification.

In the next chapter, we will explore how the basis for all addictive
and compulsive behavior begins as an emotional emptiness inside the
survivor. This emptiness is really a spiritual issue.

Chapter 16

Addictions As a Spiritual Issue

Grace has been defined as the outward expression of the inward harmony of the soul.

William Hazlitt

A condition I have observed in my work with survivors is the sense of isolation among those with addictions or compulsions. Nothing is more humbling than addiction or compulsion. Others may attempt to offer advice or to understand what addicted or compulsive survivors' plights are like, but in reality no one can fully understand except the survivors themselves.

It is lonely to be a survivor, especially if one has an addiction or a compulsion. At first, the addiction or compulsion is the survivor's best friend. As the disease of addiction progresses, the abused behavior or substance turns into the survivor's worst enemy. In the meantime, the addicted or compulsive survivors have shamed themselves or estranged others so much that they have become totally withdrawn and isolated. This isolation reinforces the addictive or compulsive behaviors.

Being connected means that the addicted or compulsive survivors begin to learn to value others but to also value themselves. Self-love is very difficult for survivors. Affirmations can help, such as, "I am worthy of love," or "I am capable of change." I always remind addicted or compulsive survivors to learn to love others fully by first learning to love themselves. Self-acceptance is a crucial element in learning to love oneself. Thinking of themselves as being a cocreator with God or with their higher power is one way that survivors can begin to address change and learn to value themselves. Becoming a co-creator with a higher power is the beginning of empowering oneself. By taking responsibility for the choices that one makes in life, one begins to realize that change is possible and, in fact, probable. Taking responsibility might include calling a sponsor, attending a meeting, calling a support group when things get tough, or simply allowing quiet time to contemplate or meditate. Learning to take good care of oneself is a form of self-love. Taking the time to write down feelings or thoughts is also a good way to get in touch with and take care of oneself.

Another way that the addicted or compulsive survivor can attempt to develop a greater sense of connection not only with a higher power but also with other people is to visualize how the survivor *wants* things to be. Sometimes visualizing a situation will help the survivor to make the event happen. I always tell survivors who have nightmares to try to imagine how they want the dream to end *before* they go to sleep. Running from the dream tends only to make the outcome remain negative or sometimes even to become worse. When survivors have the dream, they should allow the dream to run its course but instead of attempting to wake when the dream begins to frighten them the most, they should attempt to remain asleep. If the survivors have been doing visualization work, the dream will often end with the visualization that the survivors have been practicing during their waking hours. If the survivors have also been writing down their feelings and have written down how they want the dream to end, this tends to reinforce the chances that the dream will have a satisfactory ending. Discussing the dream in detail with someone that they trust and talking about the desired ending is another way to reinforce the dream losing its power over the survivors.

Recovery from any addiction requires that the person surrender one's will to a higher power. What does this mean exactly? It means that the survivors must acknowledge that he or she can't make things happen with one's own willpower. Addicted and compulsive survivors think that if they try harder or are more disciplined, things will work out the way they want. Each time that survivors attempt "total discipline," they are doomed to fail. When survivors realize that a higher power is at work in the universe and they surrender to this divine will, they may then be able to make lasting change. Choosing to use the gifts that we have been given in helping others also takes addicted or compulsive survivors out of themselves and into a connection with something greater than themselves. I believe that when survivors feel an overwhelming need to change, they are being drawn by the very purpose that they were brought to earth to serve. Survivors can be drawn to this need to change whenever they come into contact with a situation that encourages them or angers them to a large extent. The very things that they have the strongest feelings toward, both positive and negative, are indicators that their purpose for existence may have been touched. If the survivors follow this strong emotion and become totally involved in something that causes them either to move out of their isolation and self-involvement or causes them to completely lose track of time, they have most likely found their life's purpose. It is the positive connectedness to something greater than ourselves that is a sign of surrendering to the divine will. All of this change requires placing trust in someone or something—the most difficult task for survivors to accomplish.

One of the most interesting thoughts I have ever read comes from *The Purpose of Your Life* by Carol Adrienne (1998). In this book, the author states that "who we are becomes an expression of who we have decided to be" (p. 33). The author goes on to state: "Our external world is a direct representation of our internal world" (p. 34). The author's ideas put more responsibility on the choices that we make about how we will perceive what has happened to us rather than just what has happened to us. She discusses the randomness of life and that although we have free will, we are not in control either. She discusses how once we decide exactly what we desire, it is only after we surrender to our higher power to determine what is best for us and work for our highest good that we are able to achieve our desires. The author makes an interesting point when she states that it is how we live, not what role we live, that determines our purpose in life. It is the small moment-to-moment choices that we make that set our course. Even pain has a purpose: it keeps us in touch with our purpose and tells us when we need to surrender to a force greater than our own willpower.

Addicted and compulsive survivors have such a sense of being adrift on life's ocean that they often can't find a reason why they should even *try* to change. It is inside us—that small voice that talks to us about the feelings we have about the events and people in our lives—that guides us. Sometimes survivors are so full of willpower that they refuse to listen to that voice. Being able to open our hearts to others and join in sharing their lives is a sure indicator that we are developing spirituality. Being open does not require us to fix or change others, simply to be a human being, not a human doing. The author discusses the purpose of our lives being to "develop our capacity to love" (p. 30). This is very difficult for survivors because this is the one thing that they themselves have never experienced or been given as children. By surrendering to the will of a higher power and trying to do that which the survivors truly love, the survivors are taking large steps toward their life's purpose.

Survivors are often great at surviving catastrophic events, but they have difficulty at thriving afterward. By accepting what has happened to us, allowing ourselves to experience all of the feelings that are connected to events without using a behavior or substance to numb these feelings, and realizing that our feelings are transient and not a permanent state, we as survivors can go on to cocreate a wonderful life with our higher power.

If survivors will take the quiet time necessary to look at the beliefs they may have about themselves or their lives, they may find that it is their beliefs that may actually be preventing them from having the kind of life that they desire much more than the actual events in their lives. If survivors can look at their feelings and try to use them to direct them toward what will make them more connected to life, experience their feelings no matter how uncomfortable, take quiet time to contemplate or meditate, and have the courage to trust that change is possible and even desirable, chances are good for positive renewal and change.

Carol Adrienne (1998) lists negative patterns of behavior. They are:

- lacking good judgment
- overaccommodating or people pleasing
- craving recognition
- talking too much
- being suspicious or secretive
- withholding love
- resisting authority and showing cynicism
- being self-righteous
- unwilling to commit
- committing to something that will never work
- always thinking that there is something better than what you have
- assuming others must meet your needs

- leaving when things get tough
- fearing change

All of these characteristics cause survivors to be their own worst enemies, yet they are the behaviors that they may have been taught during childhood. Some of these behaviors may have allowed the survivors to endure their childhood abuse. Spirituality is the force that pulls us closer to that part of us that tells us that even though we may be afraid, we can still accomplish that which is best for us if we let go and allow the forces that are at work in the universe to do their intended work.

Although it is difficult to heal from all of the addictions and compulsive behaviors that survivors turn to in order to become "numb" to the pain of their sexual abuse, all is not lost. In the following chapter, we will learn how we can use the Twelve Steps as a recovery aide.

Chapter 17

Using the Twelve Steps for Healing from Sexual Abuse, Addictions, and Compulsive Behaviors

Lord, I confess that I am not what I ought to be, but I thank you, Lord, that I'm not what I used to be.

Maxie Dunnan

Recovery is not a straight incline leading directly to a desired goal. Recovery does, however, follow a somewhat predictable path. Initially survivors may simply take a look at their childhoods and how they have impacted their current life. As survivors survey the painful emotional issues from their childhoods, a sense of loss and grief is felt for what could have been but never was. Many survivors will relapse at this point. Trying to look at an issue as painful as sexual abuse and know that the past can never be changed is enough for some survivors to say that they don't even want to begin to deal with the abuse.

Survivors who are able to begin to address the painfulness of their abuse history may begin to see how the abuse has impacted all parts of their lives. They may begin to see patterns in their behaviors across the board. For example, some survivors will begin to see that the abuse and their addictive or compulsive behaviors always placed the survivor in a "one-down" position in which the survivor was doomed to be taken advantage of or be the scapegoat. Those survivors with drug or alcohol addictions are especially vulnerable to being in a position where they are *always* wrong no matter what they do. I have heard alcoholics tell the most outlandish stories which later turned out to be completely true. One alcoholic told me, "Even the biggest liar will tell the truth sometimes." Even the worst alcoholic has some redeeming qualities. Society, in its haste to be judgmental, forgets that addictions don't make a person worthless. It is the addiction that is hiding the addict's true personality or positive qualities.

As survivors address their histories of abuse and their addictive or compulsive behaviors, the next step in recovery will be to understand the role that the addictions or compulsions have served. The addicted or compulsive survivor will begin to understand that although the addiction or compulsion served the purpose of "anesthesia," life has become so painful with the addicted or compulsive behaviors that true recovery is not possible without abstaining. When survivors abstain from the addiction or compulsion, they are at highest risk of relapse. Seeing the most painful experiences of life through clean and sober eyes can be so traumatic that some survivors find it impossible. For those survivors who do manage to go forward with their recovery without the use of "anesthesia," there is a period of grieving their losses—the loss of childhood, the loss of innocence, the loss of the illusion of protection and security, the loss of self-esteem and self-worth, and countless other losses. As survivors look over the wreckage of their lives, some are able to develop a new sense of themselves. Survivors may begin to appreciate their sense of strength and purpose. These survivors are attempting to take responsibility for their own lives and their own happiness. Taking responsibility for their choices and accepting the consequences for their behaviors is a totally new experience for these survivors. For those survivors who manage to accept this sense of responsibility, a new way of looking at life emerges. These survivors truly understand the difference between the terms *victim* and *survivor.*

Addiction itself can be seen in a more positive light if we realize that it may be the one thing that enables a survivor to endure the very worst abusive situations and go on to live a life that can later be full and rewarding. It is how the addiction is addressed and dealt with that determines how the survivor will fare later in life.

Addiction may be a lifeline to a survivor. Addiction may have been the tool that has kept the survivor's feelings and memories at bay. Addiction or compulsive behaviors are no longer functional when frequent and longer periods of use are required for the feelings or memories to be kept under wraps. When most survivors are ready to stop abusing their chosen substance or behavior, they will report that the behavior or substance no longer brings the comfort or feeling of euphoria that it once brought. At this point, the therapist has the beginning leverage that can ultimately lead to recovery. For the first time, the client *feels the pain without the numbing effects of the addiction or compulsive behaviors.* It is crucial how the client's treatment is addressed at this point. Once the crutch of the addiction or compulsive behavior is removed, survivors are very apt to relapse when they begin to feel the pain of their abuse. The therapist needs to hold steady and reassure the client that this too will pass—that the client has already lived through the abuse of the past. It is now simply a matter of experiencing the emotional pain of the abuse that has kept the client trapped in addiction or compulsion.

Many clients will panic at this point. If the therapist has a close bond with the client and the level of trust is high enough, the therapist will be able to reassure the client that although it is so uncomfortable to feel this emotional pain there is no way *around the pain. The client needs to go through the experience of the emotional pain without the numbing effects of abusive substances or compulsive behaviors to heal.* The therapist also needs to be realistic with the client and acknowledge that recovery from addictions and compulsive behaviors often involves relapse. Each try at recovery may bring more and more success if the client is willing to trust that recovery is possible and even more desirable than the transitory rewards of addictions or compulsions.

A sense of hope is so important to the client (and the therapist also) at this point. Humans can't live effectively without a sense of hope. Remind clients that they were able to endure the emotional pain of the abuse originally. If they can hang in there and endure the emotional pain a little bit longer and more fully address their issues, *this* may be the time that they fully recover. This incentive to try and try again may be what clients need to fully address their issues and make real progress toward full recovery.

The sense of hope that is so important in working toward recovery is probably one of the more difficult points for the survivor to grasp. How can someone who has been constantly disappointed and hurt by life get the necessary courage to hope one more time? This is the point at which twelve-step programs are the most helpful. If the clients see that others have also been through experiences similar to their own and yet can still have a sense of hope, maybe the clients can also begin to hope. Socializing with others with similar issues who don't resort to addictive or compulsive behaviors provides role models that give survivors techniques to deal with their emotions. For perhaps the first time in their lives these survivors have a firm basis on which to begin to build trust and their own sense of competency.

The process of recovery from addictions or compulsions is ironic. The recovery is complex and difficult, but recovery is really very simple once survivors are willing to let go of their need to control. Recovery simply means that survivors need to learn to nurture themselves and meet their own needs. Although this sounds simple for most of us, for survivors it is probably the first time that their needs have ever been fully considered. Some survivors don't even know what their needs *are*. Our basic needs are for security, trust, a sense of predictability, some sort of structure in our lives, a sense of self-worth, privacy and boundaries, a sense of our own reality, and a need for stimulation. Because their needs as children were not considered important, survivors learn to be "needless." Survivors learn only a sense of what others need from them. Recovery for survivors first involves getting in touch with their feelings, thoughts, opinions, desires, and wants.

Some survivors become compulsive about healing the "right" way. They want to know if they are healing quickly enough, completely enough, and thoroughly enough. No one right way exists to recover from whatever the compulsion or the addiction is.

1. *Survivors decide that they are finished hiding from their issues and make a decision to heal.* The survivors with whom I work have so many issues that this step can be very complex and time-consuming. By attending counseling, group therapy, support groups, and dealing with their own painful memories, these survivors have begun the healing process.

2. *Survivors begin to panic when they begin to "feel" memories.* Without the addiction or compulsion, survivors are in so much pain that they panic. They begin to question why they even decided to try to recover if the pain is so intense.

3. *Memories that may have been buried begin to surface.* The difficult part at this point is that along with memories the feelings are also beginning to return. Once Donna from Chapter 8 began to regain memories of her stepfather sexually abusing her, she had such intense emotional pain that she began to cut herself on the forearms and left scars that will probably remain with her for her lifetime.

4. *Acceptance that the abuse* really *happened occurs.* When individuals experience trauma such as sexual abuse, they will want to believe that this horrible event really could not have happened. Survivors who have begun recovery from the addictions or compulsive behaviors *want* to doubt their own memories or perceptions. This is a critical point for them. Even though it hurts badly to believe that the abuse happened, attempting to deny the abuse or the harmfulness of it will lead only to further addictive or compulsive behaviors. In order to heal the emotional "wound," the wound must first be completely cleaned out. Accepting the knowledge that the abuse did indeed occur is the way to "clean" out the wound.

5. *Disclosing the abuse occurs. The first time a survivor tells another human being about the abuse, the survivor has taken an enormous step toward healing.* Telling another person takes away some of the shame of the abuse and some of the isolation of keeping the secret. Sometimes just walking into a group of survivors for the first time and realizing that you are not alone is enough to begin the healing process. As survivors stay in a group together, less and less need occurs for the addiction or compulsion.

6. *The victim comprehends that the abuse was not his or her fault.* Of all of the steps toward healing, this is the step that survivors keep coming back to. After working with a survivors' group for a year or more, I will casually ask the group members who was to blame for their sexual abuse. The survivors will say that intellectually they know that the abuse was the perpetrator's fault, but somehow they still feel that the abuse was their own fault because they should have done more to prevent it. This step is also difficult to accomplish because if victims understand that the abuse wasn't their fault, it means that the perpetrator didn't value them or their feelings. Also, understanding that it wasn't the survivors' fault means that they do not have full control over their lives. Not having control is very anxiety provoking for the survivor. In fact, a lack of control was what led survivors into their addiction or compulsion originally.

7. *The victim begins to connect with his or her inner self.* This is the child who was not cared for or valued appropriately. Older survivors need to develop compassion and understanding for all of the mistakes that they as children may have made in attempts to find nurturance and comfort as a result of the abuse. Adult survivors need to develop

forgiveness for themselves, greater anger toward the abuser(s), and higher levels of intimacy with others.

8. *The victim begins to have faith in his or her own emotions and memories.* Because so many survivors are shame-based and feel that they are flawed, they need to learn to trust their own feelings and perceptions. This new sense of self-trust is the basis of what will enable them to act with confidence when they are faced with problems and feelings that would have previously caused them to relapse into their addiction or compulsive behaviors.

9. *The survivor accepts and grieves his or her losses.* Because survivors have used their addictions and compulsions to deaden their pain, this may be the first time that they begin to realize the full extent of the losses that they have experienced. Being able to grieve their losses and feel their pain allows them to deal with what has happened, let go of their pain, and move on with their lives.

10. *Anger is directed toward the appropriate people.* If anger is directed at the perpetrators and others who may have harmed the survivors, the anger will be the force that will move the survivors forward in their recovery process. If the anger is self-directed, the survivors will most likely relapse into the addiction or compulsive behavior.

11. *The survivor considers the choice to confront.* Although disclosures and confrontations can be helpful, they are not necessary for every survivor. Confrontations and disclosures can be limited in their scope also.

> Harmoni was a thirty-two-year-old survivor who was molested by her biological father for over ten years as a child. Although she was extremely angry at her father for the abuse, every time that she would attempt to tell him of her anger the family would tell her that her father's health was so bad that any situation that would upset him could possibly kill him. Despite her anger, Harmoni began to think that her family was right. She told herself that what had happened was done and over with and that she could go on with her life.

Although Harmoni had intellectually acknowledged her anger, she had not allowed herself to feel and express the anger. Strong emotions don't go away simply because we will them to do so. Until she is able to fully acknowledge her anger and express it, she will never be able to free herself from her eating addiction.

12. *The survivor considers the choice to forgive.* I don't believe that forgiveness is a prerequisite for healing. Once survivors get to the point that they are able to acknowledge the harmfulness of the abuse and fully express their feelings, whether forgiveness takes place is not of primary importance. It is really the icing on the cake if survivors are able to forgive, but how can they forgive people who won't even acknowledge that they have caused harm? Placing the burden of forgiveness on the survivors when the perpetrators will not acknowledge the abuse is an additional punishment for the survivor.

13. *The survivor may have a sense of being connected to something larger than himself or herself.* A greater power offers us comfort and determines what our lives are all about. This greater power doesn't have to be religion; it can be nature, a support group, prayer, or any other means of letting survivors know that they are not alone in their pain.

14. *The survivor may feel the need for closure.* If recovery were up a straight incline, the survivor would not be able to deal with the intensity of the recovery. Recovery is a gradual incline with a series of steps that may be revisted until finally the survivors feel that they have adequately dealt with their issues enough to allow them to move on with their lives.

One of the most therapeutic ways to heal from addictive or compulsive behaviors is to be able to accept what has happened in one's life. Acceptance is also one of the most difficult states to achieve. Who among us has not wanted to change what has already happened in our lives? Who among us has not wanted to change other people? Thinking that things or others "should" behave a certain way is a surefire path to addictive or compulsive behaviors.

Recovery from compulsions and addictions means being able to be open-minded toward accepting people and situations as they *currently* exist. Acceptance means realizing that all of us are works in progress. We are all on a journey to "becoming." When we are able to accept this in others we are less likely to judge ourselves unjustly or too harshly. Even though we may look grown up on the outside, a small vulnerable child is still within each of us. That small child still controls much of our current behaviors, especially our reactions to people and places that threaten or frighten us. Many times inappropriate behaviors are really behaviors that are based in fears that we still carry from our childhoods. Accepting these fears in others as well as in ourselves enables us to understand and deal with those people and situations in our lives of which we may have previously thought ourselves incapable of dealing.

In recovery from compulsions and addictions, we need to learn to tell the difference between those things that we can change and those things that we cannot change. For the survivor, telling the difference between the two can be very difficult because as survivors one of the first survival tactics that one learns is to be constantly sensitive to the moods and the actions of others and to try to anticipate what might happen in an attempt to control an otherwise out-of-control environment. For survivors, control has been the key in the past to being able to survive an otherwise intolerable situation or life experience. It is ironic and difficult for survivors to understand that by acknowledging our inability to control people and situations we begin to gain some control. By learning to focus on what is good for ourselves and focusing on controlling the only thing we do have any control over (our own behaviors), we do manage to gain some control over our lives. By letting go of the need to control we allow others to face the natural consequences of their behaviors instead of us trying to manipulate situations or people to meet our needs.

Acceptance and letting go is difficult, yet it is the only way that we can appreciate all of the choices that we have available to us in our lives. Although we can't control the behaviors of others, we can control what behaviors we will accept from someone else. If someone is hurting us, whether it be physically or emotionally, we can't change their behaviors toward us no matter how much we may threaten, cajole, or bribe. We can decide that we are in a situation that is harmful to us and therefore remove ourselves from the situation. We can accept that although we may not know what the future holds we are aware that the present is not beneficial to us and that we need to make some changes to take proper care of ourselves. In other words, by accepting the situation as it really is we enable ourselves to make the changes that *we* need to make to take care of ourselves. It is by our reliance on a power higher than our own that we can look to the future, knowing that what is happening now is what is meant to be happening, that we don't need to know all of the answers. We do not have to anticipate or manipulate. All we need to do is accept that things are happening for a purpose and that we are part of that which will always work for the good. All of the drugs, alcohol, food, gambling, shopping, spending, or whatever compulsive or addictive behaviors we may wish to employ will not change what is. Addictive or compulsive behaviors simply delay the inevitable: the need to accept what is.

How does one know when one has truly accepted what is? One will be able to enjoy the moment without living constantly in the past or living only for the future. One will find a sense of peace and regain a sense of spontaneity. One will worry less and feel connected more with others. There is less of a desire to judge others and an acceptance of others with all of their flaws when one has begun to develop acceptance. One feels a real sense of being connected to both others, to nature, and to one's own life. By accepting what is, we are able to feel the love for those around us without always waiting for them to love us in return or to disappoint us with their inability to love us as we think they should. By accepting what is, we can learn to find all that we need to meet our own needs within ourselves. We don't have to look toward others to guess what their needs are and expect to have to meet those needs. With acceptance, all that we need to do is to meet today's demands. It is much easier to try to meet the demands of only today rather than to look down the road toward all of our tomorrows.

Is there a generic method of healing from addictions or compulsions? I believe that there are several guidelines that we can follow that will allow us to heal more quickly. The first step is to observe if there is indeed a behavior that is having a negative impact upon one's life. A very good first step is to track this behavior and see what it costs. The survivor should try to refrain from using compulsive or addictive behavior to dull senses whenever stressed or down. The survivor should try to learn what underlying feelings or emotions are beneath this compulsion or addiction, and should try to discover what role(s) family of origin may have played in the establishment of this addictive or compulsive behavior. Finally, the survivor must try to accept that all of the food, alcohol, drugs, spending, gambling, etc., will never remedy what was missing in the family of origin. Accepting that what is done is done is the only way to begin healing as an adult survivor.

One of the most difficult issuess for survivors to deal with is change. Survivors want predictablity and calm. After a childhood of chaos and pain, no one would want to initiate upheaval and unpredictability. Survivors can successfully deal with the idea of recovery involving change if they can learn to focus on the issues currently at hand. In other words, make a plan and stick to it with concrete measurable steps. If the addiction is compulsive overeating, the survivors might make a commitment to themselves that every day they will exercise at least two times for twenty minutes, eat low-fat and low-calorie snacks instead of sugary foods, and reward themselves with something soothing, such as a hot bath, at the end of the day.

It is not unusual to see survivors indulge in their compulsive or addictive behaviors to an even greater degree during times of crisis in their lives.

> Lacey, a twenty-five-year-old survivor, found out that her boyfriend had been cheating on her. Lacey began to eat huge quantities of the richest chocolate ice cream she could find. Lacey had just managed to lose over forty pounds. By focusing her attention on an addiction to high calorie sweets instead of the real issue of the pain of betrayal from her boyfriend, Lacey was attempting to use a familiar way of dealing with intense pain.

When the survivors have passed the crisis stage and are no longer in crisis, they may be able to share their feelings and begin to deal with the underlying causes of their addictive or compulsive behaviors. If they are not able to deal with the underlying causes, chances are that they will sabotage their own recovery process.

Survivors in recovery must establish changed behaviors in a focused and concrete manner. The changes in their behaviors must be concrete, measurable, and consistent. For example, if the survivors are very codependent and can never confront others about the anger they hold, they might make the commitment to voice their real feelings about something at least three times a day. Although this may sound simplistic, it may be very difficult for a survivor who wants nothing more than to please others.

I cannot emphasize enough the importance of support groups. Not only can one find the necessary emotional support that is required for effective change in these groups, one can also find support from daily reading from an inspirational booklet, daily readings from a personal inventory, daily prayer or meditation, daily journal writing, and daily solitude. Nothing is more difficult for the survivor than solitude. Being abandoned is what survivors fear the most. Solitude and abandonment can feel very familiar to survivors unless they can plan ahead of time what they can do to benefit from the solitude. Being alone does not need to mean being lonely.

Survivors may "compete" for the title of being the one who is the "most sick." I have seen this competition among survivors who are anorexic. I have had numerous anorexic survivors tell me that when they were hospitalized they would compete with other patients to see who was the thinnest and the most ill. One of the brightest young ladies told me that she believed that inpatient anorexics should not have roommates because having a roommate allowed for much more intense competition between the anorexic patients. There also seems to be a sort of hierarchy between anorexics and bulimics, with anorexia thought to be the "best" illness. This same young lady talked with me about how bulimics will brag about no longer needing to induce vomiting by putting their fingers down their throats. Some bulimics brag they can vomit "at will." It appears that the "high" that many survivors with eating disorders experience early in their compulsion soon becomes a behavior that they are unable to stop. This young lady remarked that sex addicts are not confronted about their addictions nearly as often as other addicts because society in general is not comfortable discussing sex. This remark was very interesting and right on target.

According to this young lady and other "experts" from the adolescent groups, the most important thing in recovery is to have someone care enough about you to show you "tough love." My young experts are firm in their beliefs that there must be consistent consequences. Any ultimatums must be carried through. These young recovering survivors asked me to tell others that addicts are masters of manipulation. When addicted survivors are finally forced to deal with confrontation about their addictive behaviors, they get a small taste of what their own negative behaviors have been like for everyone else. My young experts tell me that recovery begins when they stop pointing fingers at others and begin to look at their own behaviors. Even though these recovering survivors are young in chronological years, they are wise beyond belief because of all they have learned from their experiences.

This book is not intended to be the authority on how to properly heal from addictions. Rather, it demonstrates how other addicted survivors or survivors with compulsive behaviors have dealt with their own issues and problems. This book cited examples of both the positive and the negative choices that addicted or compulsive survivors have made in their attempts to try to deal with their own abuse. I believe very strongly in twelve-step programs. Some clients tell me that they simply don't find twelve-step meetings helpful. Some of these clients have been able to heal fully without the use of twelve steps. I believe that somehow a higher power has stepped in to help these survivors whether they went to the twelve-step meetings or not.

Whatever the addiction, a pattern exists in the way people heal. Although I have provided suggestions for healing from each addiction, the general steps are the ones that fall under Alcoholic Anonymous's Twelve Steps. Survivors with various addictions or compulsive behaviors also asked me to include in this book tips on strategies that helped them heal.

Compulsive overeating is understood quite well by survivors in both the adult and the adolescent groups. Survivors are very well aware that the scales don't lie. If your weight is increasing, you are eating more than you need to eat to maintain your current weight. The ability to measure makes the weight a reality that must be dealt with on a realistic level. Keeping a food diary has helped those with compulsive overeating. Attending support groups such as TOPS (Take Off Pounds Sensibly) and OA (Overeaters Anonymous) has been very helpful for some group members. Weight Watchers has also helped some members. I believe that it is the connection that we make with others who are struggling with the same demons that helps us deal with the isolation and shame that have been caused by the addiction.

One tip that a survivor in recovery for anorexia asked me to share was that "No amount of starving yourself is going to make things right in your life." Real control over things was letting go of the idea that you could control situations and people by not eating and realizing that there was a greater force in the universe that would handle things. Whether the eating problem is compulsive overeating, binge eating, anorexia, or bulimia, all of the underlying dynamics are the same: unresolved feelings and pain. If headaches, sleeping problems, sore or stiff back, or neck pain, sadness, or other somatic problems are also among the complaints of the survivor, then the odds greatly increase that they have issues that they have not addressed.

Whenever the attempt is made either to turn to food or to turn away from food in an addictive or compulsive manner, the survivors have to ask themselves what they are *really* feeling. If the feeling is not genuine hunger then survivors need to consider that an emotional problem is probably the cause.

Recovery for the food addict means not reaching for food, especially something fatty or sugary, simply because the food is available. The food-addicted survivor should try to "feel" whatever the feelings are. Genuine signals of hunger include a growl in the stomach or a time span of several hours between meals. Many food-addicted survivors have never allowed themselves to feel genuine hunger, so abstaining from food at least once until they feel the physiological signals of genuine hunger is a good way to get an idea of what they should be looking for before they reach for another sandwich or piece of cake.

Once food-addicted survivors determine what genuine hunger is and moderate their appetites, chances are that they will be able to lose some weight. Although it varies with each individual, once food-addicted survivors have lost a substantial amount of weight, they will tap into feelings that they never consciously realized they had. Usually an incredible amount of anger and rage lies beneath this weight. For some survivors, this anger is so frightening that they will immediately begin to reach for food again. A support group can be especially helpful at this point in the survivor's recovery. If the survivors have someone that they can call for guidance and to listen to their feelings, the chances greatly increase that they will be able to weather the storm. As the survivors become more confident in their skills to refrain from using food as anesthesia, they will feel more secure and have less need to use food in an addictive manner.

Along with the anger that has been held in for so long comes a soothing sense of peace and self-nurturance, but also a sense of sadness for what could have been but will never be. Once someone has been sexually abused, life will never be the same. The past can't be changed, but it can be used to advantage and learned from so that the pain experienced is not wasted. This single point has helped countless survivors deal with the pain of their abuse.

Although anorexia and bulimia are different eating disorders, at least in the form that they take of repressing the addicted survivor's emotions, the recovery process contains many of the same elements. Keeping a food diary is helpful not only to determine (in the case of the compulsive overeater) what the survivors have eaten, but also, in

the case of anorexics, for what they haven't eaten. By using a food diary, bulimics can also assess what they have eaten then purged to give
them a sense of the degree to which they are using the bingeing-and-
purging cycle to deal with their emotions.

Whatever the eating disorder, the survivors need to try to stop and
view their past with as much objectivity as possible. I have clients
imagine another child in their place when the abuse occurred so that
they can realize just how powerless they were and what few options
they had when the sexual abuse occurred. This technique helps the
survivor realize that they really had no control in the situation and
therefore have no shame or sense of blame for what happened. When
survivors imagine another child in their own abuse situation, I ask
them how much responsibility this child had for what happened. It is
usually only when the survivors are able to imagine someone else in
their situation as a child that they allow themselves to feel the sadness
and the anger that they have held in for so long. Survivors need to
keep focused on the source of the pain and the anger, the perpetrator.
Anger is the very core of healing from sexual abuse. Survivors need
to understand that although their anger is great it does not mean that
they will suddenly "lose control" and be overwhelmed by their anger.
Hating the perpetrators often gives way to sadness or pity for what the
perpetrators have allowed themselves to do to innocent children.

Any twelve-step group is a wonderful resource for the recovering
survivor with an eating disorder. If survivors can substitute the eating
disorder in a twelve-step program where any reference is made to another addiction, survivors with eating disorders will be able to imple-
ment the steps much the same way.

Some commonsense actions can be taken by the survivor with an
eating disorder to keep from relapsing. Sometimes putting off eating
something that would be detrimental to the survivor's weight goals is
enough to cause the survivor to not engage in the negative behavior. If
the survivors could take a hot bath or go for a walk they might recon-
sider engaging in behaviors that will not be helpful to their recovery.
Writing down the foods that are eaten or the feelings experienced is
another good way to put off harmful behaviors. Survivors with eating
disorders need to take actions that will get them in touch with their innermost feelings.

Healing from shame is one of the single most important tasks that
will lead to recovery. It is so important that addicted or compulsive

survivors learn to be patient with themselves during recovery. Some survivors will become angry with themselves because they think that they are not healing correctly or fast enough. To heal from shame they first have to understand that they *have* been shamed. Because shame is such an uncomfortable emotion, survivors will go to great lengths to try to avoid the pain of feeling it. Some examples of trying to avoid feeling shame include denial (some addicted or compulsive survivors will deny or minimize that they were ever sexually abused because it is too humiliating); denying or minimizing a family problem (a parent may have had a drinking problem but it wasn't *that* bad); denying or justifying their own abuse (my dad beat me but it was only for my own good); denying their own feelings (denying being sexually abused because it caused embarrassment); or denying their own actions (I only hit my wife with my open hand, and she *made* me do it.)

To recover from shame, addicted or compulsive survivors must first notice which one of these ways they try to avoid feeling shame. Survivors must then fully experience their shame without using any of the previously used tactics of avoiding their feelings. The final step is realizing that by nature we all feel shame. By using denial, inflated ego, flaunting our shame to make a display of it before anyone else notices it, raging to keep others from getting close enough to notice our shamefulness, or by simply withdrawing from others, we only perpetuate our sense of shame. When fully aware, it is clear that our shamefulness is not an integral part of us but a part of our abuse speaking to us. Once we stop running from shame, face it, seek support, and deal with our feelings, we are well on the way to recovery.

Survivors in particular can heal from shame by sharing their feelings of inferiority and loneliness with a support group. Questions that they might ask themselves would be: Have they been treating themselves like those who have abused them in the past treated them? Have they made an effort to take better care of themselves and to be gentle with themselves? Have they isolated themselves with their shame, or have they at least attempted to share those feelings with someone they can trust? Have they attempted to attend support meetings? Have they admitted that they have shame instead of trying to deny those painful feelings? Instead of striking out toward others in anger to distance others from them, have they attempted to control their feelings of rage and work through the reasons for the anger?

Survivors should let themselves know that it is okay to be human because no one is perfect and the survivor shouldn't have to be either.

By seeking the support of others, by forcing themselves not to accept their shame but to bring those intense feelings out into the open, by setting measurable steps to gauge their progress toward shame reduction, and by seeking out positive people, the shame that survivors feel can be overcome.

How does the shamed survivor deal with shame that goes back for generations? Family-of-origin issues are sometimes so deeply ingrained that they seem impossible to resolve, but this is not true. Messages of inadequacy, family secrets, acts of physical, verbal, or sexual abuse, and the constant fear of rejection and abandonment lie at the root of family-of-origin shame issues. All of these create feelings of shame so intense that survivors would rather be alone than risk that others might view their inadequacies or flaws.

How does the shamed survivor go about changing such deeply held beliefs of inadequacy and defectiveness? It is imperative that shamed survivors take the time to examine their situation and determine the origin of the shame. The shamed survivor needs to try to look at the shaming messages as objectively as possible and determine how much validity each message has. Many survivors will accept a shaming message simply because it came from a parent. Since parents are sometimes more abusive toward the survivor than anyone else, it is important that the survivor try to have someone with more objectivity determine if the parent's shaming message is valid. Even if some validity is evident to the shaming message, the survivor needs to realize that change is always possible. Affirming and positive messages can cause survivors to begin to value themselves.

> Eddie is a fifteen-year-old survivor who was molested by a much older adolescent boy at age seven. Eddie has never been able to get over the shaming messages from his stepfather. When his stepfather found out about Eddie's molestation, instead of being supportive, his stepfather told him it was his own fault that he had been raped because Eddie was somewhere that he wasn't supposed to be. Eddie's stepfather then went on to call him a little "fag." At age seven, Eddie wasn't sure what *fag* meant, but he knew from all of the other unpleasant things that his stepfather had said to him that it couldn't mean anything

good. When Eddie was fourteen and in foster care he began to receive treatment. After treatment for a suicide attempt, Eddie learned the truth about sexual abuse: the blame always lies with the perpetrator. Eddie began to realize that the shaming message may have come from a parental figure, but that didn't automatically mean that the message was truthful and accurate.

Sometimes shamed survivors are the ones who are doing the shaming. Shaming others is often an unconscious and sometimes conscious attempt to defend against one's own shame by appearing superior to others or by making others appear to be "beneath us."

Because of their low self-esteem and sense of not being worthy of better treatment, many shame-based survivors are involved in relationships that are abusive in the sense that their partner continues to be shaming. For the survivor to recover while still in a relationship such as this, the survivor must first be willing to admit that the relationship *is* shaming. For some survivors, this may be the first time they are willing to admit that they deserve better treatment. This is a huge step toward recovery. If the survivor is the one doing the shaming in the relationship, others not involved in the relationship may be the first ones to point out the survivor's shaming behaviors. The partner being shamed may protest the survivor's negative behaviors but the survivors themselves may have such shame that they cannot accept the responsibility for additional shameful behavior. An outsider may have the objectivity required for the survivor to accept his or her own negative behaviors.

Recognizing the damage that the shameful behavior has caused is another step toward healing from being shamed or shaming someone else. Survivors have a tendency to minimize negative things that happen to them because minimizing and rationalizing has gotten them through their abuse. Survivors must take an honest and painstaking inventory of the harm that the shaming behavior has caused and make a pledge to not engage in allowing others to shame them or for them to shame others. Recognizing and not allowing shaming behaviors is a constant task that the survivor must be willing to undertake. If survivors are involved with people who refuse to discontinue shaming them, then the survivors may have to terminate those relationships and replace them with relationships in which they are valued and nurtured. Accepting the concept that survivors deserve good treatment is very difficult but can be done if the survivors use positive affirmations and develop the courage to confront others who attempt to make themselves appear superior by shaming the survivors.

When confronting shaming behaviors in others, the survivor must be able to tell the shaming persons what it is about their behaviors that the survivor finds so offensive and then must be able to tell the shaming persons the behaviors that the survivor would like to see replace the negative and shaming behaviors. Although when confronted about their shaming behaviors others may be reluctant to accept responsibility for the negative behaviors, survivors should not allow this to stop them from demanding better treatment. Over a period of time change will occur, usually in small steps at first. As survivors develop more self-confidence, they will be able to identify shaming behaviors much more quickly and react more strongly to demand better treatment.

Point out to those who are doing the shaming that they not only are harming others by their negative behaviors, they are also harming themselves. Very few people want to be around someone who constantly berates or browbeats them. Those who shame others learn eventually that such negative behavior drives people away. By accepting others as they are without criticism, the persons doing the shaming will learn that they can expect a much more intimate relationship filled with true closeness, allowing both partners their own integrity and sense of self. The more each person in the relationship cares for himself or herself in a positive way, the more positive qualities each will bring into the relationship. If only one partner in a relationship has control through shaming behaviors, no growth takes place in the relationship, only tyranny.

When shame-based survivors find themselves slipping back into shaming behaviors or thoughts, they should immediately see a sign saying "STOP." They should attempt to remind themselves of the good qualities they possess, such as "I am lovable," "I deserve respect," "I am worthy of good treatment," or whatever other affirmation that will help them realize that whatever sense of shame they are experiencing is not representative of their true worth. By allowing people who are positive and caring into their lives and by experiencing love (sometimes for the first time in their lives), the survivors will soon develop ways to change their self-defeating thoughts.

Codependency is difficult to overcome because it is ingrained in survivors from an early age. By the very nature of role reversal in incest families, child victims quickly learn that they must be the family caregivers. Having a secret as powerful as incest places a terrible burden on a child. If the children tell the secret, they risk breaking up the family. If they do not tell the secret, they risk continued victimization. No one should be forced to make such a sad and potentially destructive choice.

Unlearning codependent behaviors requires constant vigilance on the part of the survivor. Codependent behaviors are so subtle that they crop up almost without any warning. It is only when someone who has not experienced abuse points out codependent behaviors that some survivors become aware of what they are doing despite their best intentions to refrain from codependency. One of the first rules that codependents learn at CODA (Codependents Anonymous) is that they are not to give advice or engage in cross talk during meetings. By not allowing advice giving or cross talk, CODA keeps the active codependent from becoming focused on other group members' recoveries instead of focusing on his or her own recovery. The rules of CODA also suggest that the group members not continue to engage in "he or she did" complaining. Codependents need to take responsibility for their own behaviors and decisions. By talking about what others did to them, codependents give their sense of power away to others. Codependents should try to get in touch with what they themselves are really feeling and not look to others to tell them what to feel, as happened previously in their lives. The codependent should refrain from people pleasing, which includes such behaviors such as giving gifts to other group members or offering special favors or services in an attempt to manipulate others into liking the individual. By listening more, codependent survivors can begin to generalize what they hear other group members experience and deal with and apply it to their own lives. Codependent survivors need to learn to become assertive but not aggressive—not trespassing on others' boundaries. Paying attention to body sensations is a good way to judge how well codependents are doing with their recovery. Vague aches and pains, such as frequent headaches and stomachaches, can be a sign that codependents are not expressing their true feelings. Feelings are stored in the body so the attempt to simply suppress and ignore feelings is a waste of time. Sooner or later the feelings will be expressed whether it is by our addiction or compulsion. How will codependents know when they have recovered? In my own personal opinion, there is no real full recovery from codependency. Codependents must simply monitor their behavior every day to watch for relapse.

What type of recovery behaviors will help the survivor who is sexually codependent? If the survivor is a female, she should attempt to stop faking orgasms. Obviously a male survivor wouldn't have this problem. Partners can't help remedy what is wrong if they don't even know that something *is* wrong. By bringing the issues out into the open, the female survivor gives her partner a chance to help her explore her own issues and sexuality. If survivors do not feel in the mood for sex, they should be able to say so. Engaging in unwanted sex is manipulative and appeasing. The risk is always there that not being sexually fulfilled could damage the relationship, but honesty is the true basis for real intimacy. In time, if the survivors are given the opportunity, they may begin to actually enjoy and initiate sex.

Survivors who are sexual addicts need to understand what driving forces lie beneath their behaviors—namely, their abusive pasts. Sexual addiction doesn't occur because the addicted survivor is "horny" or feeling "sexy" more often than other people do. Sexual addiction is about using sexual behaviors to take the focus off more painful issues. To heal from sexual addiction, the survivor must first understand that sex itself is neither good nor bad. In the case of the sexual addict, it is the way in which sex is used that is harmful to both the survivor and the survivor's partners. To heal from sexual addiction, survivors must first acknowledge that their sexual behaviors are harmful. The harm may be indicated in numerous ways, such as unsafe sex practices and the possibility of sexually transmitted diseases, unplanned pregnancies, not paying attention to the survivor's activities and responsibilities besides sexual behaviors, and the inability to establish truly intimate and fulfilling relationships.

Survivors who are sex addicts should take an inventory of their past relationships to determine if there is a pattern to their harmful behaviors. Once sexually addicted survivors have acknowledged the harmfulness of their addictions and looked for a pattern to their behaviors, they must then look for ways to avoid triggers that would cause them to act out in a sexually addictive manner. At this point, the support group is invaluable. Trying to recover from addictions alone is difficult, yet addicts often refrain from seeking the support of others. This may be because addicts understand that once others form a support group around them the chances are much improved that they will give up their longtime friend, the addiction. Living life without addiction is a very frightening prospect. The addict must grieve the loss of the addiction and all of the pain that the addiction has both helped the addict get through and also the pain that the addiction has caused. Again, as with all addictions, addicts must learn to deal with their underlying issues without their addiction. This is a tall order.

Research studies done by Cohen and Densen-Gerbert (1982) and Rohsenow and colleagues (1988) indicated that a substantial number of drug and alcohol addicts (30 to 44 percent) had been sexually abused. An astonishing 70 to 80 percent of girls and women in treatment for substance abuse have a history of childhood sexual and/or physical abuse, according to Mary E. McCaul, PhD, of the Departments of Medicine and Psychiatry at Johns Hopkins University in Baltimore (Moon, 2000).

Once survivors have decided to address their sexually abusive pasts, twelve-step programs can be very helpful. To use the Twelve Steps of Alcoholics Anonymous as an aid in healing from sexual abuse, one need only replace the word *alcohol* wherever it appears in the Twelve Steps with the phrase *sexual abuse.* An excellent book on the use of the Twelve Steps as a way of healing from sexual abuse is *Recovery from Sexual Abuse and Incest* by Jean Gust and Patricia D. Sweeting (1992).

Many survivors' groups that I have facilitated have endlessly debated what the difference is between a victim and a survivor. I believe that one can tell when they have made the shift from victim to survivor when they no longer wring their hands helplessly crying about the raw deal that life has handed them. Survivors know that although they have experienced something horrible, they have *survived* the experience and have become stronger. I compare the experience of changing from victim to survivor to the experience of having scar tissue after surgery. Regular tissue that is unblemished and has never experienced any harm is smooth and often flawless. Scar tissue, on the other hand, is rough and often raised. The difference between the two is that scar tissue is much stronger than undamaged tissue. Much of the same could be said for survivors. Survivors have been scarred by their sexual abuse but they also are much more aware of their strengths when they are in recovery than those who have never had such a traumatic experience. The Twelve Steps are empowering because a negative experience can be turned into an experience that the survivor can use to advantage.

As survivors begin to recover, they must first accept that they cannot go back and change what has happened to them. Survivors can use their experiences both for their own personal growth and to help other survivors. Examples of this become evident in survivors' groups. The adult group members have taken adolescent group members under their wings and given them the nurturing that the adult group members themselves never received as children. The older, more established group members have guided the younger adolescent group members toward healthy choices and recovery during adolescent group meetings.

Survivors need to accept that they will never be who they might have been without the abuse. Once they are able to understand that part of themselves that the abuse took away, they can become who they were *meant* to be. This is difficult for the adolescent group members to understand. They want to go back to the way they were before the abuse. They need to accept that this is not possible and that maybe something even better can come out of what has happened if only they will do the necessary work and learn to trust a power that is mightier than their own. Once survivors have begun recovery, they will no longer need to resort to people pleasing as a way of getting others to love them. The survivors will learn to love themselves and therefore others will love them. Survivors in recovery learn to have faith in themselves and the choices that they make in life. Survivors in recovery learn that they can take care of themselves. Let's take a look at this process called recovery.*

Step One: We admitted that we were powerless over our past sexual abuse and our lives had become unmanageable.

Most survivors would tell you that they don't need a twelve-step meeting to tell them that sexual abuse had really impacted their lives

---

*The Twelve Steps are reprinted with permission of Alcoholics Anonymous World Service, Inc. (AAWS). Permission to reprint the Twelve Steps does not mean that AAWS has reviewed or approved the contents of this publication or that AAWS necessarily agrees with the views expressed herein. AA is a program of recovery from alcoholism only—use of the Twelve Steps in connection with programs and activities which are patterned after AA, but which address other problems, or in any other non-AA context, does not imply otherwise.

negatively. What most survivors don't realize is *how* negatively the sexual abuse has impacted their lives. Survivors don't often understand that eating disorders, abusive relationship after abusive relationship, sexual addiction, drug and alcohol addiction, sexual anorexia, gambling, codependency, dissociation, flashbacks, and countless other addictions or compulsions have their roots in childhood sexual abuse. The survivor may have learned to numb the effects of the sexual abuse by minimizing the seriousness of the abuse or the harmfulness of the abuse. The survivor may have dealt with the sexual abuse by simply denying that the abuse ever happened or that it mattered that much even though it *did* happen. Some survivors will become very intellectual and calmly discuss the abuse as if it had happened to someone else. Whatever defense they use, the goal is always to break the abuse down into small enough pieces that the survivors can live with it. As adults, to heal from sexual abuse survivors *must* accept that the abuse was very harmful and that there was nothing as children they could have done to change it.

Each step has its own issues that survivors will be addressing as they work on that particular step. Survivors working on Step One need to address the current issues that are causing their problems. Whatever addiction or compulsive behavior the survivor is engaging in will be of primary importance. Survivors also need to look at issues such as harmful behaviors or relationships for which there seems to be a pattern. The constant need for control in their lives is an issue common to many survivors. Someone who has never had control or predictability before will be very reluctant to give it up once they have found it. Some survivors have been so damaged by their sexual abuse that they have no desire for intimacy or sexuality. Whatever current problematic issues survivors have will need to be addressed in Step One. Most likely these issues will be causing as many problems as the original abuse caused for the survivors.

Step Two: We came to believe that a power greater than ourselves could restore us to sanity.

Survivors have a big problem with trusting others. Asking survivors to trust that someone or something can help them recover is very difficult, but, as Gust and Sweeting (1992) suggest, if only survivors are *willing* to begin to accept the idea of learning to trust this will be a sign of progress. I always tell survivors to trust their instincts, that little voice inside each of us that tells us when we are taking the right path in our life. This little voice will direct us toward acceptance of what *is*. Once survivors learn acceptance they can go on toward peace and tranquility. Without acceptance there is no peace. Gust and Sweeting (1992) refer to a "spiritual awakening" that is a mental change resulting in changes in our attitudes and actions. They state that once our attitudes and actions change, so will our behaviors. Survivors often want to change other people. I tell them that the only sure way to change others is to change the ways they act; others will change in response to their changes.

During Step Two, survivors may have issues that include anger at their higher power for allowing the sexual abuse to occur and anger toward those who were supposed to be protecting them as children and yet allowed the abuse to occur. Trying to identify a power greater than ours that will restore us to sanity is difficult if the survivors already believe that God "allowed" the abuse to happen to them in the first place. The survivor must realize that humans have free will. Our higher power will always work toward the good. Human beings have the ability to choose between good and evil. The people who hurt us chose evil. Survivors could work toward identifying what their higher power could be like if they were to believe in one. What characteristics would the higher power possess? Would the higher power be able to fill the emptiness inside of the survivors? Could the belief in a higher power offer the survivor hope that there is a plan and that life has meaning? As survivors progress in their recovery, they will find the answers to all of these questions.

Sondra is an example of an adult survivor who wasn't able to stop compulsively overeating until she began to believe a power greater than herself was at work in her life.

> For all of her life Sondra had felt anxious. She always felt ill at ease, as if something horrible were about to happen, yet she never could quite identify what it was that was wrong. When Sondra finally developed enough trust in her higher power, she was able to let go of outcomes for the first time in her life. Sondra no longer had to try to manipulate others to have them do what she wanted them to do. She didn't need to pretend to be someone that she wasn't just so that others would love her. Sondra knew that things would finally work out right without

manipulation. This was the first time that Sondra was ever able to have a sense of peace in her life.

Step Three: We made a decision to turn our will and our lives over to the care of our higher power as we understood that power.

Some survivors have a set pattern established early in their abuse experience in which they automatically react to situations that resemble past abusive experiences. It is almost as if the survivor is on "automatic pilot." These survivors have learned simply to react without exploring how the current situation may differ from their past experiences. Research tends to indicate that perhaps the neural pathways in the survivor's brain have formed a circuit that prevents the survivor from reacting to a situation after giving the situation careful thought and consideration to simply reacting without any thought process at all. If survivors are able to understand this pattern of behavior and make some changes in the way they see things, they can make lasting changes in both their behaviors and their lives.

Since survivors may have dealt already with any number of addictions or compulsions before they decided to address their core issues of sexual abuse, this step asks the survivors to turn the sexual abuse and all that it means over to a higher power. This step means that the survivors know that no matter how much they are asked to deal with in their life, they will always be okay because of their belief in a higher power. Survivors may look back on their abusive past with sadness, but they will live life in *this* moment, fully aware of the joys and sorrows that this moment brings. Living in the moment allows survivors to realize how they really feel about things. This may the first time in their lives that some survivors are able to connect an event with their feelings about the event. At this point the survivors know that they can trust both themselves and their higher power.

Issues that survivors may need to address while working on this step include letting go of controlling everything and everyone in their lives. Trying to change a lifetime of thinking and behaving a certain way can be overwhelming, but it is worth the effort. Survivors need to treat themselves gently as they begin to change patterns of negative behaviors. The biggest challenge when working on this step is trying to discover where one's own power ends and the extent of the higher power's power begins. Some survivors have never had a sense of their own power because they gave their power away by their dependence on everyone else in their lives but themselves. For these survivors, trusting a higher power will be difficult because almost everyone else that the survivor has ever trusted either has let the survivor down or has used the survivor for their own benefit.

> Jean is an eighteen-year-old survivor who was molested by her father when she was six years old. Jean began to use drugs when she was thirteen years old just to "fit in" with the other kids in her rough neighborhood. All of Jean's life she has had to take care of herself. Jean was never able to depend on anyone else to look after her. The few times that Jean turned to her mother to help her when Jean disclosed what her father was doing to her, her mother simply accused Jean of telling lies, then had gotten drunk with her friends. When Jean started to attend Narcotics Anonymous for the first time, she saw and heard people who trusted others and a higher power. These people didn't need to control everything in their own lives. Somehow they were able to believe that life could turn out okay if you just trusted that life *would* turn out okay. Of course, Jean saw these people were also willing to do the work that this process required. All in all, Jean thought that these people seemed at peace with themselves and with others. As Jean worked on the steps she found that she too was able to learn to trust again and to believe in herself. At seventeen, Jean began a new life.

Step Four: We made a searching and fearless moral inventory of ourselves.

Since so many addictions and compulsive behaviors are shame based, letting others see and know the "real us" is difficult. For so long we have believed that if others knew the real us they would reject us. We felt that we simply could not bear another rejection so we hid our real selves under a mask of what we though others needed or expected us to be. For the first time, we are willing to allow ourselves to see the "real" us without the defenses or excuses we have used for so long. We are willing to admit both the good and the bad that we are. We can now accept responsibility for our actions because we know that we can make the choices and decisions that are good for us. We can use the things that we have learned to avoid painful experiences that repeat past hurts. We can look at past behaviors and choices and see where they have led us. We can begin to work toward healthier behaviors for the future.

Gust and Sweeting (1992) suggest actually writing down this inventory. I agree with them wholeheartedly. I have found that the simple act of writing down what our thoughts or our goals are reinforces the impact that they make upon us. The authors suggest creating three columns. One column should be for the person who has hurt you. The next column might be why you are angry at this person. The third column might be how the act that this person committed has impacted upon your life. The authors also suggest writing an inventory of all of the things that you fear or an inventory of your sexual life. These inventories will help survivors get a clearer picture both of where they have been and where they are going. Some survivors may be surprised to learn that they are repeating patterns that have existed in their families for generations. This realization may be the first time that the family has had the motivation to make changes.

Issues at Step Four might include setting boundaries for future protection, dealing with intense subjects, such as determining how healthy the survivor's sex life is, and how to appropriately deal with anger, and the constant need to be on guard just in case the "next" bad thing happens. Some survivors can never accept when things are going well. The survivor is constantly on the lookout for the other shoe to drop. This step encourages the survivor to deal with the here and now in a realistic way without the use of substances to numb themselves. Although it is not necessary for all survivors, some survivors at this point may wish to confront their perpetrators. I always tell survivors that there is no right or wrong way to handle the feelings one has toward those who have harmed them. Survivors all have their own ways of handling what has happened to them.

> Sally is a thirty-eight-year-old incest survivor who was molested by three paternal uncles while she was growing up. Sally never told her parents about the incest because she felt that her parents could not handle what had happened. Sally did not want to be responsible for tearing the family apart. Sally's father was employed by one of the uncles. Sally's uncle told Sally that if she told what he had done to her, he would fire her father and her family would starve. Sally has spent all of her life trying to keep the peace. Sally will never express anger for fear that others will abandon her. Sally's husband has been emotionally and physi-

cally abusive to her all through their fifteen-year marriage. Sally has never defended herself against the abuse. As Sally began working the steps, she realized that she deserved better treatment. She began to demand that her husband not hurt her physically; when he did abuse her, Sally pressed charges against him. Sally began to demand that her husband speak to her with respect instead of contempt. As Sally began to set boundaries for what she would and would not accept, she began to realize that she had had the power to treat herself well all along. Sally would never again allow anyone to take her power away.

Step Five: We admitted to our higher power, to ourselves, and to another human being the exact nature of our wrongs.

Telling one's deepest secrets is a risky behavior even for someone who hasn't been sexually abused. Imagine if you are a survivor who has experienced horrible abuse and you go on to tell someone for the first time what has happened to you. The fear that others will turn away from you in disgust or revulsion is almost enough to cause you to become paralyzed. Yet it is only when we share the dark corners of our minds that we are ever able to become free of the shadows that haunt us. Survivors should choose carefully the person to whom they choose to share their secrets; not everyone can handle such heavy secrets. Yet if survivors choose wisely, they will find that sharing the secrets that they have kept hidden for so long is a very freeing experience. Sharing everything that has been done to harm them and that which they have done to harm both themselves and others allows survivors to put the past in its proper perspective. Again, authors Gust and Sweeting (1992) suggest that survivors write down the inventory as a means of impressing upon them the burden that they are releasing.

Issues that might be addressed at Step Five include learning to trust that even though we may have had awful things happen to us or may have caused awful things to happen to others, there are still people who see us as being lovable. We can learn to trust that not everyone will turn away from us if they see and know the real us. We may have problems accepting ourselves after we finally admit the wrongs that we have done. We need to learn to accept both the good and the bad within each of us. We need to learn to forgive ourselves before we are able to fully accept the soothing balm of forgiveness from others.

Connie is a nineteen-year-old incest survivor who became a prostitute in New York City when she was fifteen years old. Connie has done so many things that she is ashamed of that she can barely look at herself in a mirror. When Connie became involved in Narcotics Anonymous for her heroin habit, she tried several times to do Step Five. Each time Connie attempted to share her experiences with someone, Connie became so afraid that others would reject her that she was unable to tell anyone of those shameful experiences. It was only when Connie met another young woman with a history much like her own that Connie was able to find that although the experiences she had had were awful, they were not unspeakable. By talking about all of the things that Connie had experienced, she was finally able to let go of the need to hide the person that she really was inside.

Step Six: We were entirely ready to have our higher power remove all these defects of character.

Change is never easy. When we are trying to make changes in behaviors that have served us as a lifeline for a long time, change becomes even more difficult. If we use the things that we have written down as being defects in our character, we will have a template to use to decide which behaviors we need to change. Part of change is accepting reality. Accepting reality means not seeing things as we *wish* them to be but seeing things as they *truly* are. No room exists for the way that things "could" have or "should" have been. Change means dealing with what is in the here and the now. Letting go of the old ways of dealing with problems is scary, but it can also lead to even greater rewards if we have the courage to reach for new ways of seeing both others and ourselves. Most people tend to think of change as negative, but change can be positive and bring rewards that we have never dreamed of if we can change the way that we think. If the old behaviors (character defects) were working, we wouldn't need to look for new ways of handling things. This reminds me of the AA saying "Insanity is doing the same thing over and over again and expecting different results." Character defects are the same. It is only when we are willing to remove these behaviors that have not served us well that we can expect better results from our behaviors.

Issues to consider under Step Six include not picking and choosing among our negative behaviors, but being ready to let go of all of the

negative behaviors. As long as we are engaging in one negative behavior, we cannot be really free to experience life at its fullest. It is
only normal to want to hold on to all our smallest vices, but small
vices are still vices. Telling a small lie still means that we are telling
lies. Putting up a fight to keep from changing is to be expected because change is frightening.

> Audrey is a fifty-year-old incest survivor who has been ex-
> tremely dependent upon others all of her life. Audrey has de-
> pended on her children for guidance on how to parent them. The
> children have really parented her. Audrey has never been able to
> either feel or act her chronological age. She is a very kind per-
> son, yet her inability to be fully responsible for her own behav-
> iors has impacted negatively upon those to whom she is closest
> emotionally. Audrey views this behavior as being a direct result
> of her sexual abuse. She hasn't seen yet that she also plays a part
> in the behavior because she has a choice about how she handles
> the abuse and what it has done to her.

In order for Audrey to rid herself of this character defect (not being
able to take responsibility for her own behaviors) She must first acknowledge that she does indeed "own" this negative behavior. Once
she sees the behavior and recognizes that she does have the power to
change the behavior, Audrey could begin to take responsibility for all
of her own actions.

Sometimes defects in our character, such as addiction, can also be
seen in a positive light after we are in recovery. Nothing makes us realize our own mortality or develop compassion as completely as addiction. If we could be thankful for our recovery, yet at the same time
also be thankful for what our defect has taught us (as in addiction to
drugs or alcohol concerning our true inability to ever *truly* have control over anything), we will be doubly blessed. Letting go of our defects is our greatest test in our belief in our higher power. Wanting to
rely solely on our own willpower has always been the one way that
we dealt with problems in the past. Letting go of our willpower and
trusting something that we have no control over makes us feel powerless. It is this powerlessness that will ultimately give us the power that
we seek.

Step Seven: We have humbly asked our higher power to remove our shortcomings.

Step Seven requires that we seek assistance from our higher power. We don't have to do things all on our own, yet it is also important that we do those things that we need to do in order to also help our higher power in the process of changing us into the kind of people we are meant to be. This step asks the survivor to differentiate between willingness and willfulness. Willingness is the ability to do that which is helpful. Willfulness is doing what we desire even when we know our actions may hurt either ourselves or someone else.

During the process of addressing this step, survivors must ask themselves what goals they want to reach. What behaviors make up their shortcomings? How do the survivors plan on making changes in their shortcomings? Can survivors be objective enough about the negative behavior to be willing to try to change the behavior, yet also forgive themselves for this negative behavior in the past? What can survivors learn about themselves by examining their shortcomings? Can survivors be gentle with themselves if they are not able to achieve the change that they seek the first, second, third, or more times that they try to remove these shortcomings?

> Abira is a twenty-year-old survivor who has tried numerous times to stop drinking. She has relapsed time after time. Sometimes the relapse would come after a year or more of sobriety. Abira is brutal in her self-criticism. She has no compassion for her relapses, which only leads to additional drinking binges to keep from feeling the shame of relapse.

Until Abira is able to stop trying to use willpower to quit drinking and is able to rely on a higher power for help, she will most likely continue to relapse. It is only by surrendering to her addiction, realizing that she is powerless over her addiction, and asking a higher power for help that will enable her finally to be able to quit drinking.

Step Eight: We made a list of all persons that we had harmed and became willing to make amends to them all.

Survivors have problems with the idea of being required to make amends to those they have harmed because survivors are so accustomed to being the ones who have been harmed by someone else. It is when survivors begin to understand that sometimes they have harmed themselves the most and therefore need to make amends to themselves for this behavior that they can begin to grasp the meaning of this step. Survivors should include everyone on this list. Even those people with whom the survivors no longer have contact or who have died should be included on the list. If the perpetrator has been punished for the abuse, the tendency may be for the survivor to feel sorry for the perpetrator. This is the point at which the survivor needs to realize that *all* of us must learn to take responsibility for our own actions.

Audrey was a survivor that we mentioned in Step Six. It would be important for her to list her children under the people to whom she would need to make amends. Audrey needs to understand that her irresponsibility has caused her children to miss their childhoods. Until she can acknowledge that her behaviors have robbed her children of their childhood, a wall will remain between Audrey and the emotional closeness that she desires with her children. Real intimacy requires honesty and openness.

Step Nine: We made direct amends to such people wherever possible, except when to do so would injure them or others.

Saying that we are sorry to others when we have never had others apologize to us for the harm they caused is sometimes so difficult that it is impossible. Yet hanging onto old hurts and grudges only harms us in the long run. By letting go of these old hurts we are not only able to forgive others and let them move on with their lives but we are also better able to go on with our own lives. This step also requires survivors to go beyond simply saying that they are sorry. The survivors need to take concrete actions to try to remedy whatever it is they have done to harm someone. Trying to set things right between us and someone that we have hurt can be uncomfortable because it causes us to admit that we have made a mistake. Survivors often have low self-esteem. To admit that we have erred and to try to make amends is acknowledging that we have again messed up something. If we can learn to address this situation from a different viewpoint, we might be able to see our mistake as a way to learn and grow from a negative experience. We need to accept the fact that some people will not be able to let go of their anger at us and accept that we are trying to right a wrong that we have committed. When this happens we need to be able to walk away from that person knowing that we have done everything possible on our part to make things right. We have no control over how another person sees things or how they behave. It is enough simply to focus on our own behaviors and try to live our own life in the best and most peaceful way that we can.

One of the most healing parts of this step is the knowledge that by treating others fairly we can also expect that others will treat us fairly. If we find that someone is harming us, we don't have to stand by and take their abuse. We can learn to stand up for ourselves and use our boundaries to protect ourselves. Perhaps of all of the people on our list to whom we need to make amends we need to make amends to ourselves the most. We need to learn to treat ourselves better, how to nurture ourselves, but most of all learn to love ourselves.

When making amends, it is preferable to try to make the amends face to face. This allows survivors to take full responsibility for their actions and to show the injured party that there are new changed behaviors. If being with the injured party on a face-to-face basis is not possible, then a letter will suffice. If the injured party is dead, we could have a conversation with our higher power about how we have learned from the experience, how we are sorry about the negative part that we played in harming the other person, and can follow up by demonstrating new improved behaviors in the future. By not minimizing, denying, or rationalizing our past negative harmful behaviors we learn to take responsibility for our actions. Owning our own fragilities and making amends to those whom we have harmed with those fragilities is the most difficult part of recovery, but it also indicates the most potential for lasting positive change.

When working on Step Nine, we need to ask ourselves if we have actually begun to *make* changes and not just think or talk about making changes. Change is not realistic if all the survivor ever does is think about what they want to do. Letting go of the past and all of its negative behaviors is a good way to begin to learn to forgive ourselves for our past mistakes so that we can in turn learn to forgive others. Many times survivors who have begun to accept responsibility for their own behaviors and to make changes in their lives will become frustrated or angry at other people who aren't as motivated to change as they are. It isn't the recovering survivor's job to control the behavior of others. Thinking that we are in charge of others' lives is codependency in its truest sense. Survivors must be honest with

themselves as to whether they have tried as hard as they could to locate each person on their list to try to make amends. Sometimes we
are so uncomfortable with certain people and our histories with that
person that we may not put our full effort into trying to locate that
person and deal with subjects that may make us uncomfortable. The
steps require total honesty in everything that we do.

Step Ten: We continued to take personal inventory; when we were wrong, we promptly admitted it.

Survivors sometimes have trouble with the idea that they must do
something forever. To some survivors it seemed as if their abuse
would last forever. Other survivors were so terrified of the horrors
that the next day's abuse might bring that forever seemed to be an im-
possibility. For survivors to find lasting recovery they must take an inventory of their behaviors over and over again. Gust and Sweeting
(1992) recommend that the survivor take an inventory on the basis of a
spot check (perhaps a moment-to-moment kind of inventory), a daily
check (especially helpful if done at the end of each day), a weekly inventory, and an annual inventory. Each inventory not only reminds us
how we might have slipped up but also reminds us how far we have
come in our recovery. If we are holding onto things that might cause
us to slide backward (Gust and Sweeting mention qualities such as
fear, dishonesty, selfishness, and resentment), we may be able to
catch these behaviors before they have become ingrained habits
again.

> Shelby is a thirty-year-old survivor who is so filled with anger
> and resentment toward his father that he has inadvertently be-
> come much like his father. When Shelby was seven years old he
> told his father that his older brother was molesting him. Shelby's
> father was an alcoholic who could not deal with anything that
> caused him to feel intense emotions. Instead of dealing with the
> situation, Shelby's father told him to stop telling lies and al-
> lowed the molestation to continue. Although Shelby doesn't
> have a drinking problem, he has an eating disorder which causes
> Shelby to weigh almost four hundred pounds. The anger and the
> resentment that Shelby feels toward his father and his brother is
> certainly understandable. The problem is that instead of telling
> his father and brother how he feels about the abuse and trying to
> protect himself by the use of legal positive boundaries, Shelby

turns his anger toward himself. Shelby eats until he can't possibly can't eat anymore.

Vivian is so afraid of the possibility of being hurt by men that she will not allow herself to become involved in any romantic relationships at all. Day after day Vivian leaves her job as a secretary and goes home to any empty apartment. Although her sexual abuse happened twenty years ago, the fear that resulted from the abuse is as fresh in her mind and heart as if it had happened just yesterday. Vivian has come to the realization that she is an adult now who should be able to protect herself. She still allows her fear to rule her life.

Craig is a fifty-four-year-old survivor who doesn't understand that even telling harmless white lies is dishonest. Craig is a salesman who has become so good at manipulating customers with promises and false representations that he often tells a lie when telling the truth would be just as easy. To Craig, this is just "good business." Craig doesn't understand that his behavior is very much like the behavior of the older male neighbor who molested Craig at age eight. The neighbor had told a series of small white "lies" to groom Craig for the sexual abuse.

Shelly is a thirty-year-old survivor who is so selfish that she refuses to consider how hoarding sweets and high calorie "goodies" has caused her weight to increase to three hundred pounds. Shelly would rather eat these high-calorie foods all by herself rather than openly eat and share the goodies with others. Shelly doesn't connect how never having enough of anything in her family of origin has led her to believe that she must take what she wants when she can get it.

Chen is a nineteen-year-old survivor who doesn't know how to say "no." Chen never has enough money to buy food for the entire week because he will give whatever money he has to the first person who asks for it.

Both Chen and Shelly have problems with their boundaries. Using the inventory on a regular basis would be helpful for both of these survivors.

There are some red flags to which survivors should pay special attention because they indicate the possibility of relapse. Probably the one red flag I see that indicates relapse most frequently is the survivors who deny the power of their addiction or compulsion. These are the survivors who become angry or defensive when asked about their addiction or compulsion. It is almost as if they feel that by not talking about the negative behaviors, the behaviors will simply not exist. Denying the strength of their feelings is also another strong indication of possible relapse. Survivors who deny that they are feeling strong emotions when it is obvious that anyone else would at least be feeling *some* emotion is an indication that the survivors have closed down and are bottling up feelings. I also am concerned about survivors who stop going to their support group meetings. Talking about their addiction or their compulsions is the best way to keep recovery a priority in our lives. Ignoring the power of an addiction or compulsion is the surest way to relapse.

Being absolutely honest with others and with ourselves is a priority in recovering from whatever issues we may have. Any time we start engaging in minimization, denial, or in deluding ourselves, we are simply asking for relapse. We need to address past situations to try to find a pattern to these negative behaviors. Perhaps past situations have included times when we wanted others to try to change to become the person that we wanted them to become. We need to listen when people tell us what they feel or what they want. Many times we hear only what we want to hear. Although both genders engage in "wishful hearing," I find that women are especially apt to look for men to whom they can give guidance to be the men that they could be "if only they would change." By accepting people as they really are, we give them the choice to be what they want to be without failing us if they don't meet our expectations.

Autonomy is an important issue in the recovery process for survivors. We need to feel good about the progress we have made and not always beat ourselves up because we have not arrived at perfection. Just the fact that the survivors have made the decision to address their issues and begin the healing process is something to feel good about. Survivors can also feel good about setting boundaries and sticking to them. Learning to trust our higher power to work toward our good is a daily reminder that we don't need to manage our recovery all by ourselves. Just making the minute-to-minute decision to seek our higher power's guidance is a major step in the right direction.

Kari is a forty-year-old incest survivor who has learned that all of the worry and anticipation in the world cannot prevent bad things from happening. Kari has learned that by seeking contact with her higher power whenever she is unsure of how to react or handle a situation, she can find the strength to deal with whatever life throws her way. Since so many survivors have a fear of abandonment, finding faith and refuge in a higher power who will never desert the survivor is a great comfort. Survivors such as Kari have learned that they don't need to cling to old behaviors such as manipulating or pleading in order to retain dysfunctional codependent relationships. As soon as Kari finds herself engaging in her old codependent ways, she acknowledges her behaviors and promptly goes about changing whatever she needs to change. Recovery doesn't mean that the survivor won't ever make a slip and fall back into old negative patterns of behavior. Recovery does mean that when survivors make a slip, they will promptly address the slip and do what is necessary to remedy the situation.

Step Eleven: We sought through prayer and meditation to improve our conscious contact with our higher power as we understood that power, praying only for the knowledge of our higher power's will for us and the power to carry that out.

One of the most rewarding parts of my day is getting up early before anyone else in the household is awake and spending some quiet time alone to contemplate what happened the day before and what I would like to see happen today. By reviewing what the previous day brought and how I handled the situations in which I found myself, I can gauge how my recovery is going. By asking my higher power for guidance in the situations in which I could have handled my recovery in a more positive manner and thanking my higher power for the support that I received in the situations in which I was able to follow my recovery plan completely, I learn to trust and become close to my higher power. Learning to trust my higher power and nurturing myself by giving myself the parenting that I didn't receive as a child, I know that I can be assured of being loved and cared for simply because I am deserving. I don't need to be a people pleaser to be loved. Gust and Sweeting (1992) make an interesting point when they say that, "Prayer is *talking* to our Higher Power. Meditation is *listening* to our Higher Power" (p. 145). I think that this is a beautiful way to explain the difference between prayer and meditation. By using prayer, we bring our concerns and cares to our higher power. Meditation is the means that our higher power uses to answer our cares and concerns. Our higher power gives us the tools to know that which is his plan for us and that which is our willfulness. All we have to do is take the time to listen and distinguish between the two.

Some survivors can't seem to plan each day to have some time to spend in meditation and prayer. It is helpful simply to talk to our higher power whenever we feel confused or stressed. The simple act of just talking with our higher power enables us to begin to become accustomed to trusting in something greater than ourselves. As time goes by, the survivor will begin to value this special time more and more. Survivors will learn that although they might not always want to hear a negative answer, eventually we may be grateful for the prayers that *seem* to go unanswered. Learning to accept our higher power's will is a big part of simply learning to trust a power greater than our own.

When Georgia, a thirty-six-year-old incest survivor, discovered that she had cancer, she was so angry that she slid back into all of her old patterns. Georgia began to engage in self-abusive behaviors such as drinking and using drugs. When other group members reminded Georgia that she didn't have to deal with her fears all alone and that there was a higher power that would never desert her even in the darkest of times, Georgia began to trust in her higher power. Today, Georgia will tell you that without the love and the support that both her group members and her higher power provided, she would not have survived all of the fears surrounding the discovery of her cancer. Georgia would tell you that she can handle whatever life hands her with a little help from her friends.

Step Twelve: Having had a spiritual awakening as a result of these steps, we tried to carry this message to others and to practice these principles in all of our affairs.

In reality, recovery is never finished because we recycle the steps over and over again as we do our inventory on either an as-needed basis, daily basis, weekly basis, or annual basis. Gust and Sweeting (1992) discuss change in our personality as being a spiritual awakening. I believe that Gust and Sweeting have really captured the essence of recovery in this statement. Change is an unavoidable part of life. Since change is unavoidable, why not make the change be *positive* change? By telling others of our ability for change for the better once we learned that we could trust a power greater than ourselves, we give others the courage and the faith to attempt to change for the better also.

I would like to address the point that making this change should apply to *all* parts of our lives. I have worked with survivors who can quote all of the Twelve Steps yet still manage to manipulate the steps for only those situations in which the survivor wants to use them. Recovery means using the Twelve Steps as a guide for *every* part of our lives. Individuals are thieves if they steal once a day or once a year. The difference is only in the degree to which they steal. So it is with the Twelve Steps. One cannot be faithful to recovery if one doesn't attempt to make the steps an everyday part of life.

By telling others how our lives have changed since we began to address our recovery with the Twelve Steps, we can become beacons of hope. A picture truly is worth a thousand words. Other survivors will follow our example when they see the changes that we have been able to make in our own lives. By being able to face life without addictive or compulsive behaviors, others will see that they too can find a life filled with peace and joy.

The focus of this book has been on helping the survivors of sexual abuse who have addicted or compulsive behaviors begin the process of recovery. The presence of a higher power has been the backbone of recovery for countless self-help groups. I have no need to question the existence of a higher power. I have no need to go on pilgrimages or retreats or quote scripture to be made aware of the presence of a higher power. This power is present in the faces of all of the survivors with whom I have had the privilege of working. I thank God every day for this privilege.

Appendix:
Letters from the Survivors' Groups

Being raped was the worst thing that ever happened to me. To have it happen over and over again makes it even worse. I never thought that there was anything that could bring me any lower. I felt like I could never ever trust anybody again. Didn't want to, for that matter, since it happened so close to home. I separated family and friends as strangers on the street. So you feel you don't have anyone. Then, because of the sexual abuse I took during my life, I hardly let anyone in close to me or was able to depend on anyone. But then it seemed like overnight "it" came in my life like a bulldozer and took my feelings away. "It" was the best thing I have been able to feel. So I thought. "It's" an addiction. Yeah, it took my nightmares, my bad thoughts, and all of my pain—for a short time. "It" became the only thing I look forward to seeing and feeling. Then "it" showed me its true colors as did the perpetrators in my past. Now because of "it" pretending what it was, I am worse than before "it" bulldozed its way into my life. "It" now is the very worst thing in my life. I never thought it could be any worse. It has such a hold, much worse than the perpetrators had. Now my so-called ex-best friend won't leave.

"It" has caused me to hurt people who want to be there and love me. And being a survivor, we never want people to feel the pain we felt. "It" makes us do that whether we want to or not. You become mechanical, a robot. You lose any self-esteem you have, caring for yourself, or anyone else. You lose your life, your dreams, and your existence, but you still walk and roam around in pain from having a "friend" that you really didn't know you wanted. It just happens over night. Addictions strip away any decency you ever had, any love you have for people or for yourself. "It" takes you to the darkest place you thought you had seen when you were raped. I swear "it's" the worst hell you can see!

Dawn

341

When Sandy asked us if we wanted to write what the groups had done for us, I said, "Damn straight I will." People do not understand how much of a family we are. I mean, with the rude things our perpetrators have done to us, especially with it being a family member, as it is in my case. Since it was my father, I look toward other males to get the things I need, but not in a sexual way as it may sound. Someone will give my boyfriend a hard time in the sense of telling him he'd better not hurt me (or he'll break out the shotgun, for instance).

As funny as it sounds, a lot of girls don't realize what it is like to have a father to protect them from the bad things that guys can do and to have a feeling of being loved and protected. That's something that I never will have. Instead of protecting me, he turned out to be the one to hurt me. I struggle every day from saying "I love him" to "I hate him" to "I feel sorry for him" and then back again. My life has been to hell and back and it is still on that journey. He didn't destroy me; he just put an obstacle in my way. Damn it! The obstacle isn't going to stop me! I have a compassionate heart, and it's hard to think that I think these things about him, but it's how I feel. I know it isn't my fault that he put his hands on me. I'm his daughter, not his toy, not his girlfriend, not his wife, *his daughter . . . his daughter!!!!* You don't do that to your children. In the group, I'm the one who is usually the quiet one, the comforter. The group members really don't know my situation, but I know they do. They know how I feel because they are my family. Because they know the horrible feelings of disgust and anger we all have for people who hurt children, these people who take away a very important part of our life—our trust. From them doing this we aren't the only ones that suffer, our boyfriends or girlfriends or even our spouses suffer. You may have killed our beliefs of how important we are but not forever. We built up that trust in our groups that Satan himself can't take away. So there is no way in hell they're gonna take it away again. It saddens me that most of my friends have turned to alcohol, drugs, prostitution, or all three because no one believed them or they feel worthless. We are children, teens, and young adults, but we are also people. The person who is the head of the overall groups, the one who makes the decisions of where, when, and why we meet has split us. We've temporarily lost "our family" due to this person who, when I really think about it, is just as bad as one of our perpetrators. Our invaders took away our self-esteem, our family (in some cases), and in the higher authority we have been taught to respect and trust for so long. It is impossible to get rid of us simply because other people deny we exist and try to put us in the closet in a hush-hush situation that gave the perpetrators the go-ahead to continue this evil behavior. Some people look at us like we are just a "bug" to squish under their feet. We annoy some people. If it wasn't for people like "us," other people of authority wouldn't have their jobs. We have nothing to be ashamed of.

If you are reading this, remember if you or your child or friend needs help, go and get that help. My group has helped me bring out these feelings that need to be out. People who don't like recognizing the problems that we make them face are just one of our easier stepping-stones. I would also like to say that even though it may seem as if I'm a mean or violent person, that is totally not like me. Help us and yourself by standing up and getting help for your abuse. Shout loud and proud that we are not going away and that we are people who have been victimized. Until someone in power has the guts to stand up and help us prevent this, we will be here forever! We are not going to let ourselves be victimized by anyone who feels uncomfortable dealing with sexual abuse or with our issues. We are not going to be victimized again by anyone, especially anyone who thinks that we should simply put our abuse in our pasts! We never asked to be molested or raped! So stop telling us to go away and start facing the reality that it happens in your "perfect" little world. Because you can go ahead and pretend that we're not here, but when it happens to those people that *you* care about, we will have compassion and sympathy for the victim. Don't expect any sympathy for the people that tried to tear us down. *It happens everywhere. Wake up, people!* This is the message I'm trying to get through to people who don't understand sexual abuse and how it hurts: "If survivors ruled the world, it would be a much better place." This is from our group family.

Thanks for taking the time to read this.

Rozanda

Love

Love is a fucking made up piece of shit,
That humans made up to make their lustful affairs unwrong,
Instead of love, I prefer a fucking bong,
Smoke it up until nothing is worth living for,
Walk out the door and your friends say what did you do that for?
Then you get a fucking 35 caliber
And blow your fucking brains out
And you say,
"Oh, well, now my ass is going to hell."

C. J.

Support Groups and Resources

The following is a list of support groups and other resources that may be helpful to recovery. While these groups and resources may be quite helpful, they are not meant to take the place of professional help. The best possible chance for full recovery is to include support groups and outside resources with professional expertise.

Al-Anon Family Group Headquarters
1372 Broadway (at 38th Street)
7th Floor
New York, New York 10018
800-245-4656

Alcoholics Anonymous World Services (AA)
P. O. Box 459, Grand Central Station
New York, New York 10163
212-686-1100

American Anorexia/Bulimia Association, Inc.
133 Cedar Lane
Teaneck, New Jersey 07666
201-836-1800

Co-Dependents of Sex Addicts (COSA)
9337-B Katy Freeway, Suite 142
Houston, Texas 77024
612-537-6904
<http://www.shore.net/~cosa>

Incest Survivors Anonymous
P. O. Box 5613
Long Beach, California 90805
213-422-1632

Narcotics Anonymous—World Services Office (NA)
P. O. Box 9999
Van Nuys, California 91409
818-780-3951

National Association for Children of Alcoholics (NACOA)
31706 Coast Highway
South Laguna, California 92677
714-499-3889

Obsessive-Compulsive Anonymous
P. O. Box 215
New Hyde, New York 11040
516-741-4901

Overeaters Anonymous—National Office
4025 Spencer Street, Suite 203
Torrance, California 90504
213-542-8363

Prostitutes Anonymous (PA)
P. O. Box 131
Kennard, Nebraska 68034
800-537-7681

Recovering Couples Anonymous (RCA)
P. O. Box 11872
St. Louis, Missouri 63105
314-830-2600

Sexaholics Anonymous
P. O. Box 300
Simi Valley, California 93062
818-704-9854

Sex & Love Addicts Anonymous (SLAA)
P. O. Box 6500010
West Newton, Massachusetts 02165-0010
617-332-1845

Victims of Incest Can Emerge Survivors (VOICES)
In Action
P. O. Box 148309
Chicago, Illinois 60614

Bibliography

Adrienne, Carol (1998). *The Purpose of Your Life.* New York: Eagle Brook, An Imprint of William Morrow and Company.

Advocates for Youth (2001). Child Sexual Abuse II: A risk factor for HIV/STDs and teen pregnancy. Available online at: <http://www.advocatesforyouth.org/publications/factsheet/fsabuse2.htm>.

Alan Guttmacher Institute (1994). *Sex and America's Teenagers.* New York: The Alan Guttmacher Institute.

Alan Guttmacher Institute. "Sexual Abuse Increases Teenage Risk-Taking and Thus, Pregnancy." <www.agr_usa.org>.

Alcoholics Anonymous World Services, Inc., "The Twelve Steps."

Allender, D. B. (1992). *When Trust Is Lost: Healing for Victims of Sexual Abuse.* Grand Rapids, MI: Radio Bible Class.

American Medical Association (1992). *Diagnostic and Treatment Guidelines on Child Sexual Abuse.* Chicago: AMA. March.

Badgley, R. F. (1984). *Sexual Offences Against Children,* Volumes 1-2. Ottawa: Canadian Government Publishing Centre.

Bagley, C. (1985). *Child Sexual Abuse Within the Family: An Account of Studies 1978-1984.* Calgary: University of Calgary Press.

Bagley, C. and Ramsay, R. (1986). Disrupted childhood and vulnerability to sexual assault: Long term sequelae with implications for counseling. *Social Work and Human Sexuality,* 4: 33-48.

Benson, P., Williams, D., and Johnson, A. (1987a). *The Quicksilver Years: The Hopes and Fears of Early Adolescence.* New York: Harper and Row.

Benson, P., Williams, D., and Johnson, A. (1987b). "Addictions and More." <webmaster@addictions.net>.

Berne, Eric (1964). *Games People Play.* New York: Grove Press.

Booth, Father Leo (1991). *When God Becomes a Drug: Breaking the Chains of Religious Addiction and Abuse.* New York: Torcher/Putnam Penguin Publishers.

Boyer, David and Fine, David (1992). "Sexual Abuse As a Factor in Adolescent Pregnancy and Child Maltreatment." *Family Planning Perspectives,* 24(1): 4-11, 19.

Bradshaw, John (1986a). *Bradshaw On: The Family.* PBS. Part Five, Bradshaw Cassettes, 8383 Commerce Park Drive, Suite 600, Houston, Texas 77036.

Bradshaw, John (1986b). *Bradshaw On: The Family.* PBS. Part Seven, Bradshaw Cassettes, 8383 Commerce Park Drive, Suite 600, Houston, Texas 77036.

Bradshaw, John (1986c). *Bradshaw On: The Family*. PBS. Part Six, Bradshaw Cassettes, 8383 Commerce Park Drive, Suite 600, Houston, Texas 77036.

Bradshaw, John (1988). *Healing the Shame That Binds You*. Deerfield Beach, FL: Health Communications, Inc.

Brady, Kathleen (1999). "New Frontiers in the Assessment and Treatment of Dual Diagnosis." American Psychiatric Association Annual Mtg., May 19, 1999. <http://medscape.com/Medscape/CNO/1999/APA/story.com>.

Briere, J. N. (1992). *Child Abuse Trauma: Theory and Treatment of the Lasting Effects*. Newbury Park, CA: Sage.

Briere, J. and Runtz, M. (1988). Symptomology associated with childhood victimization in a non-clinical sample. *Child Abuse and Neglect*, 12: 51-59.

Brownlee, Shannon (1996). The biology of soul murder. Fear can harm a child's brain. Is it reversible? *U.S. News and World Report* November 11. <http://www.usnews.com/asnews/issue/11trau.htm>.

Calam, R.M. and Slade, P.D. (1989). Sexual experiences and eating problems in female undergraduates. *International Journal of Eating Disorders*, 8(4): 391-397.

Cattanach, M. and Rodin, J. (1988). Psychosocial components of the stress process in bulimia. *International Journal of Eating Disorders*, 7(1): 75-88.

Center for Disease Control and Prevention (1995). *Youth Risk Behavior Survey*.

Cermak, Timmen (1986). Diagnosing and Treating Co-Dependence. Minneapolis: Johnson Institute Books.

Clark, Duncan (1997). Adolescent alcohol abuse tied to trauma. *Journal of the American Academy of Adolescent Psychiatry*, December. University of Pittsburgh Medical Center's Western Psychiatric Institute and Clinic.

Cohen, F.S. and Densen-Gerber, J. (1982). A study of the relationship between child abuse and drug addiction in 178 patients: Preliminary results *Child Abuse and Neglect*, (6): 382-387.

The Commonwealth Fund (1997). *The Commonwealth Fund Survey of the Health of Adolescent Girls*. New York: The Commonwealth Fund.

Consuer, A., Rivera, F. P., Barnosk, R. and Emanuel, I. 1997. Maternal and perinatal risk factors for later delinquency *Pediatrics*, 99(6): 785-790.

Cooper, M. L., Peirce, R. S., and Huselid, R. F. (1994). Substance use and sexual risk taking among black adolescents and white adolescents. *Health Psychology* 13(3): 251-262.

Covington, D.L., Dalton, V.K., Diehl, S.J., Wright, B.D., and Piner M.H. (1997). Improving detection of violence among pregnant adolescents. *Journal of Adolescent Health*, (21): 18-24.

Cristie, R. and Florence L., Glis (1986). *Statistics in Machiavellianism, Social Psychology*. Edited by Festinger and Schaster. NY and London: Academic Press.

Danica, E. (1988). *Don't*. London: Women's Press.

Dekker, Anthony et al. (1990). The incidence of sexual abuse in HIV-infected adolescents and young adults. *Journal of Adolescent Health Care* 11(3).

Devine, R. "Incest: A Review of the Literature" *Sexual Abuse of Children, Selected Reading.* Washington, DC, U.S. Department of Health and Human Services.

Deykin, Eva and Buka, Stephen (1994). Suicidal ideation and attempts among chemically dependent adolescents. *American Journal of Public Health,* 84(4).

Diagnostic and Statistical Manual of Mental Disorders, Fourth Edition (1994). Washington, DC: American Psychiatric Association.

Elders and Albert (1998). *History of Childhood Sexual Abuse Linked to High Risk Behaviors and Early Adolescent Pregnancy.*

Erickson, E.H. (1950). *Children and Society.* New York: Norton.

Erickson, E.H. (1959). *Identity and Life Cycles.* New York: International Universities.

Everstine, D.S. and Everstine, L. (1993). *Trauma Response: Treatment for Emotional Injury.* New York: W.W. Norton and Co.

Fanning, Patrick (1992). *Self-Esteem.* Oakland, CA: New Harbinger Publications, Inc.

Farrell, A.D., Danish, S.J., and Howard, C.W. (1992). Risk factors for drug use in urban adolescents: Identification and cross validation. *American Journal of Community Psychology,* 20: 263-286.

Farrell, A. D., Danish, S. J., and Howard, C. W. (1992). "Addictions and More." <webmaster@addictions.net>.

Feldmeth, J.R. and Finley, M.W. (1990). *We Weep for Ourselves and Our Children: A Christian Guide for Survivors of Childhood Sexual Abuse.* New York: Harper/Collins.

Finkelhor, David (1984). *Child Sexual Abuse: New Theory and Research.* New York: Free Press.

Finkelhor, D. and Browne, A. (1986). Initial and long-term effects: A conceptual framework. In D. Finkelhor and A. Browne (Eds.), *Sourcebook on Child Sexual Abuse.* Beverly Hills, CA: Sage.

Forward, Susan and Joan Torres (1986). *Men Who Hate Women and the Women Who Love Them.* Bantam Books.

Gelles, R.J. and Strauss, M.A. (1988). *Intimate Violence: The Definitive Study of the Causes and Consequences of Abuse in the American Family.* New York: Simon and Schuster.

Gilchrist, L.D., Hussey, J.M., Gillmore, M.R., Lohr, M.J., and Morrison, D.M. (1996). Drug use among adolescent mothers: Prepregnancy to 18 months post-partum. *Journal of Adolescent Health,* 19(5): 337-344.

Glacier, Stephen (1997). Random House Books, New York, Random House *Word Menu.*

Glassner, Wm. (1984). *Take Effective Control of Your Life.* New York: Harper Row.

Goldberg, Carl, (1996). *Speaking with the Devil: A Dialogue with Evil.* New York: Viking Penguin Books.

Goldberg, Carl (1996). Psychological factors in malevolence in men. *SPSMM Bulletin,* The Society for the Psychological Study of Men and Masculinity, Division

51, The American Psychological Association. <http://www.indstate.edu//spsmm/newslet/Goldberg.html>.

Groth, Nicholas, W. and Hobson, Gary T. (1982). The child molester: Clinical observations. In J. Conte and D. Shore (Eds.), *Social Work and Child Sexual Abuse,* Binghamton, NY: The Haworth Press, Inc.

Gust, Jean and Sweeting, Patricia (1992). *Recovering from Sexual Abuse and Incest: A Twelve-Step Guide.* Bedford: MA: Mills and Sanderson Publishers.

Halpern, Howard M. (1983). *How to Break Your Addiction to a Person.* New York: Bantam Books.

Halpern-Felsher, B.L., Millstein, S.G., and Ellen, J.M. (1996). Relationship of alcohol use and risky sexual behavior: A review and analysis of findings. *Journal of Adolescent Health,* (19): 331-336.

Hancock, M. and Mains, K.B. (1987). *Child Sexual Abuse: A Hope for Healing.* Wheaton, IL: Harold Shaw Publishers.

Hardiman, Lee. "Traumatic Child Sexual Abuse, Psychological Death, and the Reduction of the Belief in the Power of God." <http://lee_hardiman.tripod.com/trauma-god.html>.

Haugaard, J.J. and Reppucci, N.D. (1988). *Sexual Abuse of Children: A Comprehensive Guide to Current Knowledge and Intervention Strategies.* San Francisco: Jossey-Bass.

Hemfelt, Robert, Minirth, Frank, and Meier, Paul (1989). *Love Is a Choice: Recovery for Codependent Relationships.* Nashville, TN: Thomas Nelson Publishers.

Herman, Judith (1992). *Trauma and Recovery.* New York: Basic Books.

Holmes, M.M., Resnick, H. S., Kilpatrick, D.G., and Best, C.L. (1996). Rape-related pregnancy: Estimates and descriptive characteristics from a national sample of women. *American Journal of Obstetrics and Gynecology,* 175(2): 320-324; discussion 324-325.

Iannotti, R.J. and Bush, P.J. (1992). Perceived versus actual friend's use of alcohol, cigarettes, marijuana, and cocaine: Which has the most influence? *Journal of Youth and Adolescence,* 21: 375-389.

Janessen, Martha (1983). *Silent Scream.* Philadelphia, PA: Fortress Press.

Johnson, J. (1991). *It's Killing Our Kids: The Growing Epidemic of Teenage Alcohol Abuse and Addiction.* Waco, TX: Word.

Johnson, K. (1989). *Trauma in the Lives of Children: Crisis and Stress Management Techniques for Counselors and Other Professionals.* Claremont, CA: Hunter House.

Kasl, Charlotte Davis (1990). *Women, Sex, and Addiction.* New York: Harper and Row Publishers.

Keyes, Ken Jr. (1975). *Handbook to Higher Consciousness.* Coos Bay, Oregon: Living Love Publications.

Knauer, Sandra L. (2000). *No Ordinary Life: Parenting the Sexually Abused Child and Adolescent.* Chicago: Charles C. Thomas Publishers.

Koniak-Griffin, D. and Lesser, J. (1996). The impact of childhood maltreatment on young mothers' violent behavior toward themselves and others. *Journal of Pediatric Nursing,* 11(5): 300-308.

Kruger, Shugar, Cooke (1996). *Co-Morbidity of Binge Eating Disorder, Partial Binge Eating Syndrome, and Bi-polar Disorder.*

Leighty, John M. (1986). *"Smoking: How to Wrap It Up." The Washington Post,* November 19.

LiBenward, J. and Densen-Gerber. J. (1975). Incest as a causative factor in antisocial behavior: An explanatory study. *Contemporary Drug Problems,* 4: 323-346.

Lisak, David (1994). The psychological impact of sexual abuse and content analysis of interviews with male survivors. *Journal of Traumatic Stress,* 7: (4).

Lisak, David (1996). Pain and Perpetuation in Men Abused As Children. *SPSMM Bulletin.* The Society for the Psychological Study of Men and Masculinity, Division 51, The American Psychological Association. <http://www.indstate.edu//spsmm/newslet/Dlisak.html>.

LeSourd, Sandra Simpson (1990). *The Compulsive Woman.* Grand Rapids, MI: Fleming H. Revell, Division of Baker Book House, Co., Spire Addiction.

Lowry, R.D., Holtzman, B.I., Truman, L., Kann, J.L. Collins, and Kolbe, L.J. (1994). "Substance Use and HIV Related Sexual Behaviors Among U.S. High School Students: Are They Related?"

Marano, H.E. (1993a). "Chemistry and craving." *Psychology Today* 26(1).

Marano, H.E. (1993b). Self esteem of adolescent girls as related to weight. *Perceptual and Motor Skills,* 67: 879-884.

McKay, Matthew (1992). *Self Esteem,* Oakland, CA: New Harbinger Publications.

Mason, Avonne and Blankenship, Virginia (1987). Power and affiliation, motivation, stress, and abuse in intimate relationships, *Journal of Personality and Social Psychology,* 1(52): 203-210.

Maynard, R.A. (Ed.) (1996). *Kids Having Kids: A Robin Hood Foundation Special Report on the Costs of Adolescent Childbearing.* New York: Robin Hood Foundation.

McDowell, David (1999). "Evolution of depression in substance abuse (23B)." The American Psychiatric Association 152nd Annual Mtg., Washington, DC.

Meek, C.L. (Ed.) (1990). *Post-Traumatic Stress Disorder: Assessment, Differential Diagnosis And Forensic Evaluation.* Sarasota, FL: Professional Resource Exchange.

Meek, J.E. (1971). *The Fragile Alliance: An Orientation to the Outpatient Psychology of the Adolescent.* Baltimore: Wms. and Wilkins.

Miller, J. Keith (1997). *Compelled to Control.* Deerfield, FL: Heath Communications.

Minnesota Department of Children, Families, and Learning, Office of Community Collaboration (1989, 1992, 1995). *Minnesota Student Survey: Perspectives On Youth.* Minnesota Department of Health.

Minnesota Department of Health, Division of Family Health (1996). *Adolescent Health in Minnesota.* Minnesota Department of Health.

Minnesota Department of Human Services, Performance Measurement/Quality Improvement and Chemical Dependency Divisions (1995). *Minnesota Student Survey: Juvenile Correctional Facilities.* Minnesota Department of Health.

Minnesota Organization on Adolescent Pregnancy, Prevention, and Parenting <moapp@juno.com>. At <www.cyre.umn.edu/MOAPPP/mgnrisk.mtm>.

Moon, Mary Ann (2000). Woman drink and drug to make it through the day, not for sociability. *Clinical Psychiatry News* 28(5): 37. Copyright International Medical NewsGroup, <http://psychiatry.medscape.com>.

Moore, K.A., Driscoll, A.K., and Lindberg, L.D. 1998. *A Statistical Portrait of Adolescent Sex, Contraception, and Childbearing.* Washington, DC: National Campaign to Prevent Teen Pregnancy.

Moore, K.A., Miller, B.C., Glei, D., and Morrison, D.R. (1995). *Adolescent Sex, Contraception, and Childbearing; A Review of Recent Research.* Washington, DC: Child Trends, Inc.

Munson, Carlton E. (in press). *Diagnosis and Treatment of Childhood Trauma.* Binghamton, NY: The Haworth Press, Inc.

Myrors-Wallis, L. et al. (1992). Life events and anorexia nervosa: differences between early and late onset cases. *International Journal of Eating Disorders,* 11(4): 369- 375.

Nakken, Craig (1996). *The Addictive Personality.* Center City, Minnesota: Hazelden.

Nathanson, D.L. (1992). *Shame and Pride: Affect, Sex, and the Birth of the Self.* New York: Norton.

National Center for Health Statistics (1995). *National Survey of Family Growth.*

National Council on Sexual Addiction and Compulsion/The National Office, <www.ncsac.org>.

National Institute On Alcohol Abuse & Alcoholism (1990). No. 9, PH 288, July.

Niehaus, Michael R. *Denial.* "Addictions and More." <webmaster@addic-tions.net>.

Niehaus, Michael R. *Dry Drunk.* "Addictions and More." <webmaster@addic-tions.net>.

One Day At A Time. Al-Anon Family Group Headquarters, Inc.

Oppenheimer, R. et. al. (1985). Adverse sexual experience in childhood and clinical eating disorders: A preliminary description. *Journal of Psychiatry,* 19(2/3): 357-361.

Orpinas, P.K., Baseo-Engquist, K., and Grunbarm, J.A. (1995). The co-morbidity of violence-related behaviors with health-risk behaviors in a population of high school students. *Journal of Adolescent Health,* 16(3): 216-225.

Ozer, E.M., Brindis, C.D., Millstein, S.G., Knopf, D.K., and Irwin, C.E. (1997). *America's Adolescents: Are They Healthy?* San Francisco School of Medicine, University of California.

Parker, B., MacFarlane, J., and Soeken, K. (1994). Abuse during pregnancy: Effects on maternal complications and birth weight in adult and teenage women. *Obstetrics and Gynecology,* 84(3): 323-8.

Parrillo, A.V., Felts, W.M., and Mikow-Porto, V. (1997). Early initiation of sexual intercourse and its co-occurrence with other health-risk behaviors in high school students, the 1993 North Carolina Youth Risk Behavior Survey. *Journal of Health Education,* March/April, 28(2).

Parrott, L. III (1993). *Helping the Struggling Adolescent.* Grand Rapids, MI.

Perry, Bruce. Children's Hospital and Baylor College of Medicine.

Polit, Denise et al. (1990). Child sexual abuse and premarital intercourse among high risk adolescents. *Journal of Adolescent Health Care* 11(3).

Potter-Efron, Ronald and Potter-Efron, Patricia (1989). *Letting Go of Shame.* Hazeldon.

Rohsenow, D.J. et al. (1988). Molested as children: A hidden contribution to substance abuse? *Journal of Substance Abuse Treatment,* 5: 18-18.

Root, M.P. (1989). Treatment failures: The role of sexual victimization in women's addictive behavior. *American Journal of Orthopsychiatry,* 59(4): 542-549.

Rounsaville, B.J. (1999). "Dual Diagnosis, Schizophrenia, and Substance Abuse (23E)." The American Psychiatric Association 152nd Annual Mtg., Washington, DC.

Russell, D.E.H. (1986). *Secret Trauma: Incest in the Lives of Girls and Women.* New York: Basic.

Sgroi, Suzanne M. (1982). *Handbook of Clinical Intervention in Child Sexual Assault.* Lexington, MA: D.C. Heath.

Shostrum, Everett (1968). *Man the Manipulator.* New York: Bantam Books.

Shostrum, Everrett L. and Kavanaugh, James (1972). *Between Man and Woman: The Dynamics of Interpersonal Relationships.* Los Angeles: Nash Publishing.

Shengold, L. (1989). *Soul Murder: The Effects of Childhood Abuse and Deprivation.* New York: Fawcett/Columbine.

Spingarn, R.W. and DuRant, R.H. (1996). Male adolescents involved in pregnancy: Associated health risk and problem behaviors. *Pediatrics,* 98(2pt. 1): 262-268.

Stevens-Simon, C. and Reichert, S. (1994). Sexual abuse, adolescent pregnancy and child abuse: A developmental approach to an intergenerational cycle. *Archives of Pediatric and Adolescent Medicine,* 148(1): 23-27.

Stock, J.L., Bell, M.A., Boyer, D.K., and Connell, F.A. (1997). Adolescent pregnancy and sexual risk taking among sexually abused girls. *Family Planning Perspectives,* 29(5): 200-203, 227.

Strober, M. (1984). Stressful life events associated with bulimia in anorexia nervosa. *International Journal of Eating Disorders,* 3(2): 3-15.

Summit, R. (1983). Child sexual abuse accommodation syndrome. *Child Abuse and Neglect,* 7: 177-193.

Sweeting, Patricia and Gust, Jean (1992). *Recovering from Sexual Abuse and Incest: A Twelve Step Guide.* Bedford: MA: Mills and Sanderson, Publishers.

Symonds, Martin (1978). The psychodynamics of violence-prone marriages. *American Journal of Psychoanalysis*, 38(3): 213-222.

Terr, L.C. (1991). Childhood traumas: An outline and overview. *American Journal of Psychiatry*, 148(1): 10-19.

Terr, L. (1990). *Too Scared to Cry: How Trauma Affects Children . . . and Ultimately Us All.* New York: Basic.

Tice, L. et al. (1989). Sexual abuse in patients with eating disorders. *Psychiatric Meds.*, 7(4): 259-267.

VanPelt, R. (1988). *Intensive Care: Helping Teenagers in Crisis.* Grand Rapids: Zondervan.

Virtue, Doreen (1994). *Losing Your Pounds of Pain.* Carson, CA: Hay House.

Vredevelt, Pamela and Rodriguez, Kathryn (1992). *Surviving the Secret.* Fleming H. Revell.

Waites, E.A. (1993). *Trauma and Survival: Post-Traumatic and Dissociative Disorders in Women.* New York: W.W. Norton and Co.

Wallace, R. (1993). Survey: "Good Grades Don't Give Immunity From Sexual Assaults." *The Orange County Register*, December 1, 6(A).

Washington State Survey On Adolescent Health (1998). *Daily News For 2/26/98.*

Webster's Concise Reference Library, (1996). New York: Smithmark Publishers.

Whitfield, Charles L. (1993). *Boundaries and Relationships: Knowing, Protecting, and Enjoying the Self.* Deerfield Beach, FL: Health Communications.

Ziedonis, Douglas, "Dual Diagnosis, Schizophrenia, and Substance Abuse (23D)." The American Psychiatric Association Annual Mtg., Washington, DC, 1999.

Zierler, Sally et al. (1991). Adult survivors of child sexual abuse and subsequent risk of HIV infection. *American Journal of Public Health* 81(5).

Index

Page numbers followed by the letter "t" indicate tables.

WOMEN SURVIVORS, PSYCHOLOGICAL TRAUMA, AND THE POLITICS OF RESISTANCE by Norma Jean Profitt. (2000). "A compelling argument on the importance of political and collective action as a means of resisting oppression. Should be read by survivors, service providers, and activists in the violence-against-women movement." *Gloria Geller, PhD, Faculty of Social Work, University of Regina, Saskatchewan, Canada*

THE MENTAL HEALTH DIAGNOSTIC DESK REFERENCE: VISUAL GUIDES AND MORE FOR LEARNING TO USE THE DIAGNOSTIC AND STATISTICAL MANUAL (DSM-IV) by Carlton E. Munson. (2000). "A carefully organized and user-friendly book for the beginning student and less-experienced practitioner of social work, clinical psychology, of psychiatric nursing . . . It will be a valuable addition to the literature on clinical assessment of mental disorders." *Jerold R. Brandell, PhD, BCD, Professor, School of Social Work, Wayne State University, Detroit, Michigan and Founding Editor, Psychoanalytic Social Work*

HUMAN SERVICES AND THE AFROCENTRIC PARADIGM by Jerome H. Schiele. (2000). "Represents a milestone in applying the Afrocentric paradigm to human services generally, and social work specifically. . . . A highly valuable resource." *Bogart R. Leashore, PhD, Dean and Professor, Hunter College School of Social Work, New York, New York*

SOCIAL WORK: SEEKING RELEVANCY IN THE TWENTY-FIRST CENTURY by Roland Meinert, John T. Pardeck and Larry Kreuger. (2000). "Highly recommended. A thought-provoking work that asks the difficult questions and challenges the status quo. A great book for graduate students as well as experienced social workers and educators." *Francis K. O. Yuen, DSW, ACSE, Associate Professor, Division of Social Work, California State University, Sacramento*

SOCIAL WORK PRACTICE IN HOME HEALTH CARE by Ruth Ann Goode. (2000). "Dr. Goode presents both a lucid scenario and a formulated protocol to bring health care services into the home setting. . . . this is a must have volume that will be a reference to be consulted many times." *Marcia B. Steinhauer, PhD, Coordinator and Associate Professor, Human Services Administration Program, Rider University, Lawrenceville, New Jersey*

FORSENIC SOCIAL WORK: LEGAL ASPECTS OF PROFESSIONAL PRACTICE, SECOND EDITION by Robert L. Barker and Douglas M. Branson. (2000). "The authors combine their expertise to create this informative guide to address legal practice issues facing social workers." *Newsletter of the National Organization of Forensic Social Work*

SOCIAL WORK IN THE HEALTH FIELD: A CARE PERSPECTIVE by Lois A. Fort Cowles. (1999). "Makes an important contrition to the field by locating the practice of social work in health care within an organizational and social context." *Goldie Kadushin, PhD, Associate Professor, School of Social Welfare, University of Wisconsin, Milwaukee*

SMART BUT STUCK: WHAT EVERY THERAPY NEEDS TO KNOW ABOUT LEARNING DISABILITIES AND IMPRISONED INTELLIGENCE by Myrna Orenstein. (1999). "A trailblazing effort that creates an entirely novel way of talking and thinking about learning disabilities. There is simply nothing like it in the field." *Fred M. Levin, MD, Training Supervising Analyst, Chicago Institute for Psychoanalysis; Assistant Professor of Clinical Psychiatry, Northwestern University, School of Medicine, Chicago, IL*

CLINICAL WORK AND SOCIAL ACTION: AN INTEGRATIVE APPROACH by Jerome Sachs and Fred Newdom. (1999). "Just in time for the new millennium come Sachs and Newdom with a wholly fresh look at social work. . . . A much-needed uniting of social work values, theories, and practice for action." *Josephine Nieves, MSW, PhD, Executive Director, National Association of Social Workers*

SOCIAL WORK PRACTICE IN THE MILITARY by James G. Daley. (1999). "A significant and worthwhile book with provocative and stimulating ideas. It deserves to be read by a wide audience in social work education and practice as well as by decision makers in the military." *H. Wayne Johnson, MSW, Professor, University of Iowa, School of Social Work, Iowa City, Iowa*

GROUP WORK: SKILLS AND STRATEGIES FOR EFFECTIVE INTERVENTIONS, SECOND EDITION by Sondra Brandler and Camille P. Roman. (1999). "A clear, basic description of what group work requires, including what skills and techniques group workers need to be effective." *Hospital and Community Psychiatry (from the first edition)*

TEENAGE RUNAWAYS: BROKEN HEARTS AND "BAD ATTITUDES" by Laurie Schaffner. (1999). "Skillfully combines the authentic voice of the juvenile runaway with the principles of social science research." *Barbara Owen, PhD, Professor, Department of Criminology, California State University, Fresno*

CELEBRATING DIVERSITY: COEXISTING IN A MULTICULTURAL SOCIETY by Benyamin Chetkow-Yanoov. (1999). "Makes a valuable contribution to peace theory and practice." *Ian Harris, EdD, Executive Secretary, Peace Education Committee, International Peace Research Association*

SOCIAL WELFARE POLICY ANALYSIS AND CHOICES by Hobart A. Burch. (1999). "Will become the landmark text in its field for many decades to come." *Sheldon Rahan, DSW, Founding Dean and Emeritus Professor of Social Policy and Social Administration. Faculty of Social Work, Wilfrid Laurier University, Canada*

SOCIAL WORK PRACTICE: A SYSTEMS APPROACH, SECOND EDITION by Benyamin Chetkow-Yannov. (1999). "Highly recommended as a primary text for any and all introductory social work courses." *Ram A. Cnaan, PhD, Associate Professor, School of Social Work, University of Pennsylvania*

CRITICAL SOCIAL WELFARE ISSUES: TOOLS FOR SOCIAL WORK AND HEALTH CARE PROFESSIONALS edited by Arthur J. Katz, Abraham Lurie, and Carlos M. Vida. (1997). "Offers hopeful agendas for change, while navigating the societal challenges facing those in the human services today." *Book News Inc.*

SOCIAL WORK IN HEALTH SETTINGS: PRACTICE IN CONTEXT, SECOND EDITION edited by Tobra Schwaber Kerson. (1997). "A first-class document . . . It will be found among the steadier and lasting works on the social work aspects of American health care." *Hans S. Falck, PhD, Professor Emeritus and Former Chair, Health Specialization in Social Work, Virginia Commonwealth University*

PRINCIPLES OF SOCIAL WORK PRACTICE: A GENERIC PRACTICE APPROACH by Molly R. Hancock. (1997). "Hancock's discussions advocate reflection and self-awareness to create a climate for client change." *Journal of Social Work Education*

NOBODY'S CHILDREN: ORPHANS OF THE HIV EPIDEMIC by Steven F. Dansky. (1997). "Professional sound, moving, and useful for both professionals and interested readers alike." *Ellen G. Friedman, ACSW, Associate Director of Support Services, Beth Israel Medical Center, Methadone Maintenance Treatment Program*

SOCIAL WORK APPROACHES TO CONFLICT RESOLUTION: MAKING FIGHTING OBSOLETE by Benyamin Chetkow-yanoov. (1996). "Presents an examination of the nature and cause of conflict and suggests techniques for coping with conflict." *Journal of Criminal Justice*

FEMINIST THEORIES AND SOCIAL WORK: APPROACHES AND APPLICATIONS by Christine Flynn Salunier. (1996). "An essential reference to be read repeatedly by all educators and practitioners who are eager to learn more about feminist theory and practice" *Nancy R. Hooyman, PhD, Dean and Professor, School of Social Work, University of Washington, Seattle*

THE RELATIONAL SYSTEMS MODEL FOR FAMILY THERAPY: LIVING IN THE FOUR REALITIES by Donald R. Bardill. (1996). "Engages the reader in quiet, thoughtful conversation on the timeless issue of helping families and individuals." *Christian Counseling Resource Review*

SOCIAL WORK INTERVENTION IN AN ECONOMIC CRISIS: THE RIVER COMMUNITIES PROJECT by Martha Baum and Pamela Twiss. (1996). "Sets a standard for universities in terms of the types of meaningful roles they can play in supporting and sustaining communities." *Kenneth J. Jaros, PhD, Director, Public Health Social Work Training Program, University of Pittsburgh*

FUNDAMENTALS OF COGNITIVE-BEHAVIOR THERAPY: FROM BOTH SIDES OF THE DESK by Bill Borcherdt. (1996). "Both beginning and experienced practitioners . . . will find a considerable number of valuable suggestions in Borcherdt's book." *Albert Ellis, PhD, President, Institute for Rational-Emotive Therapy, New York City*

BASIC SOCIAL POLICY AND PLANNING: STRATEGIES AND PRACTICE METHODS by Hobart A. Burch. (1996). "Burch's familiarity with his topic is evident and his book is an easy introduction to the field." *Readings*

THE CROSS-CULTURAL PRACTICE OF CLINICAL CASE MANAGEMENT IN MENTAL HEALTH edited by Peter Manoleas. (1996). "Makes a contribution by bringing together the cross-cultural and clinical case management perspectives in working with those who have serious mental illness." *Disabilities Studies Quarterly*

FAMILY BEYOND FAMILY: THE SURROGATE PARENT IN SCHOOLS AND OTHER COMMUNITY AGENCIES by Sanford Weinstein. (1995). "Highly recomended to anyone concerned about the welfare of our children and the breakdown of the American family." *Jerold S. Greenberg, EdD, director of Community Service, College of Health & Human Performance, University of Maryland*

PEOPLE WITH HIV AND THOSE WHO HELP THEM: CHALLENGES, INTEGRATION, INTERVENTION by R. Dennis Shelby. (1995). "A useful and compassionate contribution to the HIV psychotherapy literature." *Public Health*

THE BLACK ELDERLY: SATISFACTION AND QUALITY OF LATER LIFE by Marguerite Coke and James A. Twaite. (1995). "Presents a model for predicting life satisfaction in this population." *Abstracts in Social Gerontology*

NOW DARE EVERYTHING: TALES OF HIV-RELATED PSYCHOTHERAPY by Steven F. Dansky. (1994). "A highly recommended book for anyone working with persons who are HIV positive. . . . Every library should have a copy of this book." *AIDS Book Review Journal*

INTERVENTION RESEARCH: DESIGN AND DEVELOPMENT FOR HUMAN SERVICE edited by Jack Rothman and Edwin J. Thomas. (1994). "Provides a useful framework for the further examination of methodology for each separate step of such research." *Academic Library Book Review*

CLINICAL SOCIAL WORK SUPERVISION, SECOND EDITION by Carlton E. Munson. (1993). "A useful, thorough, and articulate reference for supervisors and for 'supervisees' who are wanting to understand their supervisor or are looking for effective supervision...." *Transactional Analysis Journal*

IF A PARTNER HAS AIDS: GUIDE TO CLINICAL INTERVENTION FOR RELATIONSHIPS IN CRISIS by R. Dennis Shelby. (1993). "A women addition to existing publications about couples coping with AIDS, it offers intervention ideas and strategies to clinicians." *Contemporary Psychology*

GERONTOLOGICAL SOCIAL WORK SUPERVISION by Ann Burack-Weiss and Frances Coyle Brennan. (1991). "The creative ideas in this book will aid supervisiors working with students and experienced social workers." *Senior News*

THE CREATIVE PRACTITIONER: THEORY AND METHODS FOR THE HELPING SERVICES by Bernard Gelfand. (1988). "[Should] be widely adopted by those in the helping services. It could lead to significant positive advances by countless individuals." *Sidney J. Parnes, Trustee Chairperson for Strategic Program Development, Creative Education Foundation, Buffalo, NY*

MANAGEMENT AND INFORMATION SYSTEMS IN HUMAN SERVICES: IMPLICATIONS FOR THE DISTRIBUTION OF AUTHORITY AND DECISION MAKING by Richard K. Caputo. (1987). "A contribution to social work scholarship in that it provides conceptual frameworks that can be used in the design of management information systems." *Social Work*

Order Your Own Copy of
This Important Book for Your Personal Library!

RECOVERING FROM SEXUAL ABUSE, ADDICTIONS, AND COMPULSIVE BEHAVIORS
"Numb" Survivors

_____in hardbound at $49.95 (ISBN: 0-7890-1457-2)

_____in softbound at $34.95 (ISBN: 0-7890-1458-0)

COST OF BOOKS_____

OUTSIDE USA/CANADA/
MEXICO: ADD 20%_____

POSTAGE & HANDLING_____
*(US: $4.00 for first book & $1.50
for each additional book)
Outside US: $5.00 for first book
& $2.00 for each additional book)*

SUBTOTAL_____

in Canada: add 7% GST_____

STATE TAX_____
*(NY, OH & MIN residents, please
add appropriate local sales tax)*

FINAL TOTAL_____
*(If paying in Canadian funds,
convert using the current
exchange rate, UNESCO
coupons welcome.)*

❑ **BILL ME LATER:** ($5 service charge will be added)
(Bill-me option is good on US/Canada/Mexico orders only;
not good to jobbers, wholesalers, or subscription agencies.)

❑ Check here if billing address is different from
shipping address and attach purchase order and
billing address information.

Signature_____

❑ **PAYMENT ENCLOSED: $**_____

❑ **PLEASE CHARGE TO MY CREDIT CARD.**

❑ Visa ❑ MasterCard ❑ AmEx ❑ Discover
❑ Diner's Club ❑ Eurocard ❑ JCB

Account # _____

Exp. Date_____

Signature_____

Prices in US dollars and subject to change without notice.

NAME_____

INSTITUTION_____

ADDRESS_____

CITY_____

STATE/ZIP_____

COUNTRY_____ COUNTY (NY residents only)_____

TEL_____ FAX_____

E-MAIL_____

May we use your e-mail address for confirmations and other types of information? ❑ Yes ❑ No
We appreciate receiving your e-mail address and fax number. Haworth would like to e-mail or fax special
discount offers to you, as a preferred customer. **We will never share, rent, or exchange your e-mail address
or fax number.** We regard such actions as an invasion of your privacy.

Order From Your Local Bookstore or Directly From
The Haworth Press, Inc.
10 Alice Street, Binghamton, New York 13904-1580 • USA
TELEPHONE: 1-800-HAWORTH (1-800-429-6784) / Outside US/Canada: (607) 722-5857
FAX: 1-800-895-0582 / Outside US/Canada: (607) 722-6362
E-mail: getinfo@haworthpressinc.com
PLEASE PHOTOCOPY THIS FORM FOR YOUR PERSONAL USE.
www.HaworthPress.com

BOF00

FORTHCOMING and NEW BOOKS FROM
HAWORTH SOCIAL WORK PRACTICE IN ACTION

Take 20% Off Each Book! Special Sale

FAMILY HEALTH
SOCIAL WORK PRACTICE

NEW!

A Knowledge and Skills Casebook
**Edited by Francis K. O. Yuen, DSW, ACSW,
Gregory J. Skibinski, PhD, ACSW,
and John T. Pardeck, PhD, LCSW**
This book introduces the theoretical model and skills of
the practice, including a framework for developing a family
health intervention plan, illustrated by case scenarios.
Issues vital to any family health intervention are addressed
in 10 case vignettes that further explain the application of
the practice model.
$39.95 hard. ISBN: 0-7890-0717-7.
$22.95 soft. ISBN: 0-7890-1648-6.
Available Fall 2002. Approx. 212 pp. with Index.

DIAGNOSIS IN SOCIAL WORK

NEW!

New Imperatives
Francis J. Turner, DSW
This book shows how the concept of diagnosis in social
work has been misunderstood and given a negative, narrow
definition in commonly used texts, and how this has had a
detrimental impact on the quality of social work
intervention.
$39.95 hard. ISBN: 0-7890-0871-8.
$24.95 soft. ISBN: 0-7980-1596-X.
Available Spring 2002. Approx. 200 pp. with Index.

HUMAN BEHAVIOR IN THE
SOCIAL ENVIRONMENT

NEW! **Over 600 Pages!**

Interweaving the Inner and Outer Worlds
Esther Urdang, PhD, MSS
Addresses development through the life cycle, discussing
the developmental challenges, tasks, and problems of each
stage. This book examines and integrates systems and
organizational factors, as well as the impact of culture
on clients and treatment programs.
$129.95 hard. ISBN: 0-7890-0716-9.
$59.95 soft. ISBN: 0-7890-1522-6.
Available Winter 2001/2002. Approx. 647 pp. with Index.

THE USE OF PERSONAL NARRATIVES
IN THE HELPING PROFESSIONS

NEW!

A Teaching Casebook
**Edited by Jessica K. Heriot, PhD, LCSW-C,
and Eileen J. Polinger, PhD, LCSW-C**

Over 250 Pages!

No academic description can convey the feelings,
meaning, and effects of mental illness on the individual or
their family. Only narratives and stories based on direct
experience can do so—exactly what you will find in this
book. Each selection is accompanied by questions for
discussion; selected reading lists are provided with
each chapter.
$49.95 hard. ISBN: 0-7890-0918-0.
$29.95 soft. ISBN: 0-7890-0919-6.
Available Winter 2001/2002. Approx. 312 pp. with Index.

VISIT OUR WEB SITE AT:
http://www.HaworthPress.com

RECOVERING FROM
SEXUAL ABUSE, ADDICTIONS,
AND COMPULSIVE BEHAVIORS

Over 300 Pages!

"Numb" Survivors
Sandra Knauer, LCSW

NEW!

This book demonstrates clearly what lengths survivors
of sexual abuse will go to in attempting to avoid dealing
with the pain resulting from their sexual abuse.
$49.95 hard. ISBN: 0-7890-1457-2.
$34.95 soft. ISBN: 0-7890-1458-0.
Available Winter 2001/2002. Approx. 367 pp. with Index.

CHILDREN'S RIGHTS

NEW!

Policy and Practice
John T. Pardeck, PhD
This book addresses the situation of minors at home,
at school, in foster care, and in residential facilities. The
chapter on advocacy offers effective new strategies and
little-known legal precedents that give a much-needed
advantage to parents battling to ensure the educational
rights of children with special needs.
$39.95 hard. ISBN: 0-7890-1060-7.
$22.95 soft. ISBN: 0-7890-1061-5.
2001. 168 pp. with Index

HANDBOOK OF CLINICAL SOCIAL
WORK SUPERVISION, THIRD EDITION

Carlton E. Munson, PhD

NEW EDITION!

This classic textbook has been thoroughly revised and
updated to reflect the changes in the field brought by new
technologies and managed care. Many pages of new
material on every subject—from diagnosis and assessment
to social workers under stress have been added.
$89.95 hard. ISBN: 0-7890-1077-1.
$59.95 soft. ISBN: 0-7890-1078-X.
2001. 720 pp. with Index.

Over 650 Pages!

BUILDING
ON WOMEN'S STRENGTHS

NEW EDITION!

*A Social Work Agenda for the
Twenty-First Century, Second Edition*
**Edited by K. Jean Peterson, DSW,
and Alice A. Lieberman, PhD**

Over 250 Pages!

This second edition discusses the issues of women's lives,
including family violence, welfare reform, mental health,
child welfare, aging, racism, and being silenced.
$49.95 hard. ISBN: 0-7890-0869-0.
$24.95 soft. ISBN: 0-7890-1616-8.
2001. 308 pp. with Index.

ELEMENTS
OF THE HELPING PROCESS

NEW EDITION!

A Guide for Clinicians, Second Edition
Raymond Fox, PhD

Over 250 Pages!

With common sense and minimal professional jargon, this
book will show you how to customize helping strategies
and techniques to the needs of the client, highlighting
components such as writing, developing family trees, and
creating logs and profiles.
$59.95 hard. ISBN: 0-7890-0903-X.
$34.95 soft. ISBN: 0-7890-0904-8.
2001. 320 pp. with Index.

The Haworth Press, Inc.
10 Alice Street
Binghamton, New York 13904–1580 USA